GAMES WITH SHADOWS

RADIUS

GAMES WITH SHADOWS

Neal Ascherson

RADIUS

An imprint of Century Hutchinson Ltd

Radius

An imprint of Century Hutchinson Ltd
62–65 Chandos Place, London WC2N 4NW

Century Hutchinson Australia (Pty) Ltd
89–91 Albion Street, Surry Hills, NSW 2010

Century Hutchinson New Zealand Ltd
PO Box 40–086, Glenfield, Auckland 10, New Zealand

Century Hutchinson South Africa (Pty) Ltd
PO Box 337, Bergvlei 2012, South Africa

First Published by Radius 1988
Reprinted 1988

Designed by John Hawkins

Phototypeset by Input Typesetting Limited, London

Printed and bound by Mackays of Chatham

British Library Cataloguing in Publication Data

Ascherson, Neal
    Games with shadows.
    I. Title
    082   PR6051.S/

ISBN 0–09–173018–X (paper)

Contents

Acknowledgements and Preface

A journalist who, after many years working at home and abroad as a reporter is entrusted with a column of his own suffers – or ought to suffer – a salutary shock. Like most of my reporting colleagues, I assumed that I knew what my own political and social views were; they remained in private store, colouring my reporting of events only in the inevitable, almost involuntary sense that personal views influence one's selection of what seems interesting.

So when, in 1985, Donald Trelford as editor of *The Observer* did me the honour of offering me a weekly column of opinion, I went cheerfully to that private store and began to unpack it. A horrible discovery ensued. Many of the sealed boxes proved to be empty. Others contained disagreeable spiders or mental fragments decayed to illegibility. The fact was that I had largely forgotten what my own views were, or – where I could retrieve them – sometimes could not imagine why I had ever entertained them.

Writing the column (and most of the pieces in this book are *Observer* columns) thus turned into a sustained attempt to find out what I did believe about the world in which I lived, a revaluation of assumptions and prejudices shared by many of my generation who were children during the Second World War and grew up in the Europe which – as Sebastian Haffner has remarked – is Hitler's legacy to us. This enquiry goes on. It may explain, if not excuse, some of the inconsistencies to be found here.

Certain obsessions recur. They can be summed up like this. England – specifically England, as dominant partner in the British State – is a unique nation because it does not understand its own national identity. In this tercentenary year of the so-called 'Glorious Revolution' of 1688, it is plain that the English lack of self-understanding is permitting a rapid increase of uncontrolled State power and a decay of already archaic political institutions. The best years of my life have been passed outside

England, and my instinct is to inspect this strange country through the lens of more sophisticated nations – Poland and Scotland, in particular. England has a 'heritage', but it is not the bundle of nostalgic, Druidic myths currently on sale.

My gratitude for the opportunity to write these short pieces and incorporate them in a book goes above all to *The Observer*, a newspaper of free and inquisitive minds which has sent me to most parts of the world with unfailing generosity. My thanks also go to Bob Silvers, editor of the *New York Review of Books*, and to Karl Miller, editor of the *London Review of Books*, to the *Political Quarterly*, the *New Edinburgh Review* and to the Scottish National Party for allowing me to reprint a lecture to their Party Conference. A special acknowledgement, lastly, to Neil Belton, editor of Radius, for suggesting this collection and for his sensitivity in making the selection.

I

A RUINOUS CITY
Being British

Chords of Identity in a Minor Key

The way that words mutate reminds me of fashions in music. The word – the note – is a constant. But the setting and chord in which it occurs alters with the mood of a nation from major to minor, from the assertive to the mournful and foreboding.

The very word 'change' has changed. When I was young – and not just because I was young – we looked forward with confident impatience to change. Planned, controlled, beneficent change would continue to clear slums, sweep up the remains of empire, raise living and educational standards, tidy away – firmly but kindly – the last aboriginals who still raved about martial glory or the pride of wealth. Now, as it seems to me, change is set almost exclusively in the minor key, change seen overwhelmingly as loss.

I was reminded of this when I read 'The National Question Again,' a book of essays about Welsh identity edited by John Osmond. In one of these essays, there is a quotation from 'the late Professor J. R. Jones.' I know nothing of the Professor, but his words seized me.

He mentions the pain of exile. But then he goes on: 'I know of an experience equally agonising and more irreversible . . . and that is the experience of knowing, not that you are leaving your country, but that your country is leaving you, being sucked away from you, as it were by a consuming, swallowing wind into the hands and the possession of another country and civilisation.'

'Your country is leaving you.' Whose terrible awareness is this? At first, this would appear to be the private pain of minorities, of those who live in declining cultural margins. Professor Jones wrote those words in Welsh. The same thought has been expressed by Sorley Maclean, the greatest Gaelic poet in our century, stoically facing the wind which in 100 years will have carried away those who can read 'Hallaig' without grammars and dictionaries. The Czech poet Nezval wrote of 'a burning leaf of paper on which a poem is disappearing,' and his compatriot Milan Kundera now takes this for an image of Czech culture itself.

But it may be that their country is not only leaving those who live in the lands of 'small languages.' In that same volume about Wales, Raymond Williams discusses 'the visible weakening of England' as the centralised nation-state weakens, as uncertainty sets in about whether there is still a definable 'English way of life' as opposed to a caste-ridden and anachronistic 'way of ruling.' Williams surveys this growing confusion and loss of identity, and remarks: 'Many of the things that happened, over centuries, to the Welsh are now happening, in decades, to the English.'

It was not unexpected to read, in a profile of Douglas Hurd, that the Home Secretary likes the work of the late Philip Larkin. He's a clever, literate man. But I was struck that his favourite poem, known by heart, was the one which ends like this:

> . . . The statues will be standing in the same
> Tree-muffled squares and look nearly the same.
> Our children will not know that it is a different country.
> All we can hope to leave them now is money.

Well, precisely. The children of England stand by their statues, but their country is leaving them. All looks 'nearly the same.' There isn't some public barometer of change announcing the numerical decline of those who speak English or eat Yorkshire pudding or are kind to dogs. (Unless the unemployment totals displayed on Labour town halls fulfil that purpose.) And yet the loss of inner identity and certainty is taking place, as invisible as that 'consuming, swallowing wind.' The worst kind of nightmare is when you seem to enter your home, see again all the furniture that always was there, and do not recognise it.

The outer signs of change are not so important. There are inner-city riots but, as I have argued before, rioting is a recurrent English activity with a long history. There is a large immigrant population, but only idiots panic about cultural and ethnic 'dilution' or 'alienation'; England's blacks become restive in direct proportion to their absorption of English values.

The real loss is in what one might call 'social trust.' The English have always regarded their State, seen as the totality of Ministers, generals, judges, quill-pushing bureaucrats and snoopers, with mild contempt. 'They' sent left-footed boots to the Crimea then, and 'they' screw up the rating system now. What else is new? But in the sense that the State embodies and executes the collective ethics of the English – ensuring fairness in the widest sense, taking away from the unreasonably rich and selfish and giving some of the proceeds to the poor – it has been taken very seriously indeed. The State may have made a poor job of it. But its moral potential, in the hands of democratic masters, has never been much doubted until now.

Today, there is a very real doubt. This Government long ago declared its intention to do away with the 'nanny' State. The results of this intention have included mass unemployment, a glaring increase in inequality and a sense of corrupted moral standards which are most gangrenous at the very top – in the most august City institutions and their connections with the political establishment.

At a deeper level, our present rulers have not merely persuaded the people that the State can no longer be a universal provider. They have – without meaning to go so far – raised the question of whether the power apparatus in London can ever again be relied upon to express in action the collective English values. The English have never bothered to define their national identity. Instead, there are phrases: the tautologous 'we know who we are,' or the comfortable 'we govern ourselves pretty decently.' Now the consuming, swallowing wind is carrying away the second assumption in fragments which are larger year by year. And the first assumption, which leaned against it, begins to sway and tilt. Do the English, after all, really know what they are like, if they cannot 'govern themselves decently'?

Now we are closer to the sources of this sense of 'change as loss,' this failure of social trust, which seems to affect persons of all political faiths. The Home Secretary murmurs Larkin's lament to himself, although a member of a government which seems to believe that money is the only thing worth leaving to our children. Glenys Kinnock, in *Marxism Today*, looks back to the post-war welfare state: 'Ours was a hopeful generation . . . my brother and I were taught to appreciate the orange juice and dinners and milk.' Ken Livingstone belongs to a Left generation which, whatever it says, is post-Marxist in its pessimism; he believes that the human race lost its way when it took up 'selfish, acquisitive' agriculture as a short cut to progress, and is likely to choke itself in filth and radiation.

If England is leaving the English, where will they be? In a limbo. In a condition where, while they see that they have become bad-tempered and unsociable and mistrustful, they also remember older times when they worked together and helped one another in bitter adversity and found a lot to laugh about. That wind which is carrying away 'England' is also removing petrified institutions which in the end discouraged those virtues, although supposed to foster them. It's time, without Scottish or Welsh help, to build a new country.   [*1985*

The Nostalgia Game

'Nostalgia for the Fifties': of all invitations to a party, this is the queerest of all. But we are all invited now. The film of 'Absolute Beginners' opens, Roger Mayne shows his famous photographs of Notting Dale at the Victoria & Albert, 'The Merry Wives of Windsor' has been running in Fifties sets and costumes for a year. The 'certain substance' now found in young mens' flats is Brylcreem. Shall we go, and will it be fun?

It wasn't much fun then. Those poor old Fifties, in which I was very young, didn't even think of themselves as a decade. That decennial game seemed to be over, like most games. The Twenties were said to have been roaring and naughty; the Thirties had been declared unsafe and were fenced off against our curiosity. Anyone suggesting that there had been anything chic about the Forties, years of war and rationing, would have been thought soft in the head. As for our own times, nobody – we knew – would want to remember them.

And yet, in one way, those were infinitely conceited times. When I finished my National Service and went to Cambridge, the voices around and above me were saying something like this: 'History is over. After a million years, the human race has arrived at its destination. We have finally discovered how to run things. There will be no more revolutions, no more slumps and booms, no more inflation, certainly no more unemployment. We have cracked it. All that's left for you to do is to tidy up a few things.'

They went on: 'You may find this dull. You may hanker after romantic periods, and perhaps we will reminisce about the Spanish Civil War for you after dinner. But all that is over. There is Keynes, there is the National Health Service, there is Bretton Woods which has stabilised the world economy for ever. If you want excitement, concentrate on your personal relationships. Stick to the facts, don't generalise, and eschew personal ambition.'

Sobered, we surveyed the cool, grey plateau on which mankind was to spend the rest of time. There were indeed a few unsightly relics. Poverty was not a word in general use any more, but the process of bringing about equality evidently required more work before it was completed. Slum clearance would probably do the trick, combined with plenty of education. A few rich people could be spied, but they were spivvish, marginal figures, soon to die out. The British Empire had to be cleared away too, a matter of leading the natives to the altar for their wedding with self-government and then – happy ever after.

So we resigned ourselves; I joined a debating society, and we talked about personal relationships and the importance of not generalising. Then, one day, a young economist who had been abroad came back to Cambridge, and appalled us. What he said was so shocking, even hateful, that all my efforts to forget it were unsuccessful.

We were doomed, he said. A new period was about to open – he could already recognise the signs – in which attitudes like ours would be useless and even dangerous. Within a year or so, this level crust would begin to break up. A huge increase in earnings and then in purchasing power would take place. There would be a stampede for wealth, great opportunities for ambition, a return of inequality. This period – he was speaking a few years before Harold Macmillan was even imaginable as Prime Minister – would have no use for prim egalitarians, for self-denying intellectual élites. It wanted vigorous, selfish, acquisitive people – and it would find them.

Looking back, I know that this was real prophecy: the rare kind based not on second sight but on intellect used without mercy. At the time, I thought the man was just wicked. In Manchester during the Fifties, where I started work, there was certainly no sign of an end to the grey plateau.

In that city, where one could still use Engels's 'Condition of the Working Class' as a street guide, people were resigned to waiting for what they were entitled to, but assumed that they would get it in the end. It rained softly, ceaselessly; after the cinemas shut, there was nowhere to go but home or to one of the couple of Indian restaurants which had begun to appear. The huge old prostitute who stood under her umbrella by Queen Victoria's statues ('Let me but bear your Love, I'll bear your Cares') would shriek: 'C'meer! C'meer!' as I sloshed towards my bus.

Once I read an article by a man born and brought up in one of the countless brick terraces of south Manchester. He wrote that the supreme moment of his life had come when, as a little boy, he had gone out into the street during an air raid and looked at the sky. Suddenly he realised that somebody, at least, knew that he existed; somebody cared enough to be trying to kill him.

That was the Fifties. Everything dangerous or vivid lay in the past. Long ago, middle-class people had stopped saying, as they used to say in the Forties with a shrug and an experienced smile: 'Well, I expect we'll all be living in some sort of Communism in the future, stands to reason. . . .' Now, speculation was out of fashion. Few people travelled, except as conscripts sent to colonial wars or Korea. Insularity was back; lurid events in Central Europe were studied only by the highly-educated. Everyone hated 'the Germans,' but everyone loved 'our'

German – Bert Trautmann, the prisoner-of-war who became City's goalie.

The years on the grey plateau passed, but somehow those relics of the bad old days did not get tidied away. The stone tenements of Glasgow stood on like outcrops of geology, as they had stood when I was a child. The two cultural nations – those with 'accents' and those even more absurdly styled as 'without accents' – showed no signs of merging. The pound, prices and wages were stable, everyone had a job, and yet many of those who had jobs continued to live like beasts. The British went on waiting patiently for their entitlement, but sometimes the head of the queue seemed to be getting no nearer. And those who ran the Empire were, for unfathomable reasons, still reluctant to give it up.

Was there a 'Fifties culture'? Chairs and tables with spindly legs came in, coffee-bars with glass cups and bowls of brown sugar, and sounds from America which grew louder until they became Bill Haley and then Elvis. The London journals went on with their Francophilia, even while France bulged with the colonial fascism that exploded in 1958. But all this was on the surface. The British remained instinctively obedient, as they always are when governed by caste rather than by money.

For many of us, the Fifties ended in 1956, with Suez. Not for all. In Manchester, there was real shock at the 'Law, Not War' protest. A friend said: 'Dad went in 1914, and I went in 1940, and now the lad has to do his bit. Anything wrong with that?' The real end of the Fifties came with the prosperity and boom at the end of the decade.

Suez didn't reveal Britain's weakness in a flash. That was only seen afterwards. What it revealed was that a British government, even one led by Churchill's heir, could lie, bully and be criminal. And with that discovery, the old faith that history had come to rest, that all our problems were minor ones, dissolved. We were absolute beginners no longer.   [1986

'Tell the Children . . .'

Mr Kenneth Baker, as Secretary of State for Education, is deciding what our children should know. Dozens of worthies are being gathered into 'working parties' to plan 'core curricula': centrally-decided minima of fact which all English schools will be obliged to pack into their pupils' heads. Among these, there will be a working party on history.

Writing in the *Independent* last week, Sir William Rees-Mogg, the celebrated Whig, let his imagination run over what this history core curriculum should be: 'the central understanding of his world that every English child should be given.' (Sir William uses 'England' to denote 'Scotland' as well, although – luckily – Mr Baker's writ doesn't run north of the Border.)

His list of required knowledge falls into two parts. First, there are a lot of dates, marking 'the struggle for democracy at home and the struggle against tyranny abroad': the Reform Bill, the Armada, the Battle of Britain, Waterloo and so forth. Then there is a requirement of culture, scientific and literary, which includes Bacon, Shakespeare, Darwin, Babbage, Gibbon, Handel, Keynes and others. Sir William, who describes English history as a 'golden treasury,' observes: 'As a nation, we have the richest culture in the world and ought to rejoice in it. But we cannot rejoice in it, if we do not know it.'

One is becoming rather tired of these adjurations to stop moaning and rejoice, which have grown more frequent since Mrs Thatcher shouted her order to rejoice over the recapture of South Georgia. Still, Sir William is right: there can be neither moaning nor rejoicing over the past if we do not know it.

Several things about his approach, however, gall me. To start with, it is so Whiggish and priggish. This is the success story which made Britain the most wonderful nation on earth, the unrolling of a manifest destiny. There have been 'follies,' but they were just necessary contradictions in the dialectic of glory ('silly weak tyrants like George III'). Once again, English history is presented as a perfectly-landscaped garden, all the lines of sight converging from trim lawn and ornamental lake to where we stand on the 'now' of a country-house terrace.

This is history only in the sense that the Old Testament is history: the account of a divinely-ordained pilgrimage. But I don't see Canaan when I look out of the window; rather, a kindly and long-suffering nation increasingly puzzled about its identity and in sore trouble. All this deafening propaganda about 'heritage' makes it harder rather than easier to understand the present through the past.

In Anthony Howard's 'Rab', the life of R. A. Butler, there's an account by Butler of the moment in 1941 at which Churchill told him that he was to take on education. ' "I think everyone has to learn to defend themselves. I should not object if you could introduce a note of patriotism into the schools. Tell the children that Wolfe won Quebec." I said I would like to influence the content of education, but this was always difficult. Here he looked very earnest and said: "Of course not by instruction or order but by suggestion." '

Nearly 50 years have passed, and now there will be an instruction or order to tell the children that Wolfe won Quebec. Mrs Thatcher will dictate what schools should teach, while Churchill, even in wartime, felt that he should not. But the notion of a patriotic 'core curriculum' has not changed much.

What is going on here? Under the pressure of New Right intellectuals, education is moving back to a 'subject-centred,' rather than a 'child-centred' emphasis. With this goes a return to élitism, towards the fostering of conventional excellence and away from the search for a schooling which is relevant and liberating for most children in the State system.

Presbyterians were once obliged to study a compilation called 'The Sum of Saving Knowledge'. There is something Calvinist about Mr Baker's plans too. The minority of the 'elect,' those chosen to be saved, will be favoured and assisted. The problem remains of what to teach the reprobate mass of no-hopers. The old ideal of cultivating the best in every child is dismissed. The only thing to teach that dismal majority who will never make it is respect.

It may well be that the standards of historical knowledge are low, and sinking. The French, a few years ago, decided that thematic, internationalist history-teaching had gone too far and introduced a new, more 'national' curriculum reaching from prehistory to the Nazi occupation. But this also means that, just as the world grows smaller and more and more of the citizens of Europe are non-European in origin and culture, history teaching is shrinking back into old-fashioned national myth. The reason is not hard to find. Fear of disaffection and unrest arising in an underemployed and increasingly cosmopolitan mass drives state governments to use education as a propaganda weapon, a machine for manufacturing social unity. This has little to do with either real history or real education.

The underlying idea is distressingly simple. If the proles are taught that the triumphs of kings, generals, inventors and country-house builders are 'their' triumphs, their heritage, then they will be reasonably obedient. But if they learn too much about European peasant risings, when the Black Death created a labour shortage, or about the Irish and Bengal famines, or about the rise of the multinational corporation, or about the struggle against male domination, they may become difficult and even seditious.

And behind all this is the return – it's all a history of restoration – of the idea that the State *can* dictate what its subjects know about history. An absurd ambition, even for the best teachers. The individual's knowledge of history, to be honest, is a rubbish-tip composed of ill-remembered lessons, what father did in the war, television documentaries with half the instalments missed, bodice-ripper historical novels, fragments of local folk-lore, the general idea of what that Frenchman seemed to be saying on the train, a dozen feature movies, what we saw of Edinburgh Castle before the wee boy got sick, several jokes about Henry VIII and that oil painting of the king lying dead on the battlefield with his face all green.

That is the argument for humility on the part of all who try to teach history. The argument for optimism is that, wonderfully enough, most people contrive to make a sort of sense out of that pile of garbage.

And helping them to make sense of it, with humility and humour, is the only sort of history-teaching that is worthwhile. State history, as political manipulation, is false sense-making.

The past, after all, is by definition loss, and Walter Benjamin's angel of history saw 'where we perceive one chain of events ... one single catastrophe which keeps piling wreckage on wreckage.'

George Oppen wrote a poem about a baby in her father's arms. 'Cell by cell the baby made herself, the cells/Made cells ... What will she make of a world/Do you suppose, Max, of which she is made?'

We all make ourselves out of the past, and find our own understanding of how we derive from it. Every child does it in a different way, and can be helped to do it better and more richly. In the teaching of history, it is that – not the curriculum – which is the core.   [*1987*

The Lost World of Small-Town England

The other day, a young woman who works as a television researcher took me to lunch. Over the soup, she told me that her outfit had decided to do one of those 'register-of-change' documentaries by choosing a typical English small town and then getting its people to talk about everything that had happened to them and to their place in the past 40 years. But, she said, somehow they couldn't find the right small town. Everywhere they looked was sort of ... not what they were looking for. They found a town eventually, but it was in South Wales.

I knew what she meant. In the English cultural chromosome, the small-town gene is missing. This lack is only one of the oddities which makes England such a very peculiar, exceptional nation, so unlike its neighbours to north and south. But it is a lack which often strikes me – not least because the English are entirely unaware of it.

In a literal sense, of course there are small towns. They are the places A-roads run through on their way between cities. They have several churches, a market place, a whitewashed old hotel with a musty dining-room, a small industrial estate, a disused railway station which has become a coffee shop. They exist by the thousand, and most of them figure in Domesday Book. But, in another sense, they are ghost towns. In the English reckoning of what is splendid, or significant, or even worthy of nostalgia, the small towns scarcely rate a mention.

The best indicator of significance is fiction. English literature has farm settings, village settings, city settings and – in plenty – country-house settings. Novels which are done against the background of a small town are rare. And many of those are 'just visiting': the cathedral-close novel, in which the characters are boughs or twigs of the landed upper-class tree, or the university-town novel, in which the 'locals' provide an indistinct cast of extras as pub-keepers or cleaning-women.

Contrast the literature of the rest of the world. In American fiction, the small-town novel is the most enduring species of all. Sherwood Anderson's famous 'Winesburg, Ohio' stands for thousands, anatomies of a community built around Main Street which is presented as the essential America. In France, there is the little town where Madame Bovary and so many other characters in so many other novels live, a tiny but self-governing structure of social and political power whose tradesmen and doctors and lawyers reproduce in concentrated, provincial form the ideological arguments of the nation.

Scottish fiction tends to choose the same locus: the small burgh understood as the place where Scottishness is most intense, and often as the arena where cruel, hypocritical repress-iveness (the town fathers) sets out to crush hope and tender sensuality (the town's sensitive sons – this is a literature of patriarchal conflicts in which women are allotted pretty passive roles).

Among many examples, George Douglas's 'The House with the Green Shutters,' or J. MacDougall Hay's 'Gillespie,' come to mind. The softer 'kailyard' novels, sentimental and nostalgic, are also usually set in a small burgh, among the characters of a self-regulating community.

There is any amount of German and Italian fiction of this kind. Since the last war, some of the best Czech novels have also celebrated the sort of small, ancient town which – even more than Prague – is seen as the real carrier of Bohemian history and the national imagination. There is irony and anger about the oppressive power of such places, but an underlying loyalty and love of place as well: Jiři Gruša's 'Questionnaire' is the best of such recent works.

In very different mixtures, and with different emotions, two things are being said in all this small-town literature. First, that any girl or boy of spirit will want to leave Winesburg, but will – in sentiment or in middle-aged reality – eventually return: to cut the place out of oneself is to commit a suicide of identity. Secondly, that a country exists roughly on three levels: the farm or village, the small town, the city. And of the three, it is the small town which shows the nation at its most authentic and least diluted – which is not necessarily its most engaging.

Now back to England. We know where small towns are on the map. But where are they in the consciousness? I went to the library for Raymond Williams's 'The Country and the City,' a book which has formed the ideas of thousands of young people in this country, written by one of the most gifted of socialist historians. But, to my amazement, the small town does not figure at all in this great study of the inter-relation between literature and place. There is the countryside – village, farm or manor house, and there is the city. Nothing significant is noticed in between – no 'Winesburg', no Dorchester or Saffron Walden or Thirsk.

In analysing Lewis Grassic Gibbon's three-volume novel about Scottish life, 'A Scots Quair,' Williams discusses the small farmers who occupy the first book and the urban workers who fill the third. He does not mention the second, 'Cloud Howe,' which is concerned with a Scottish small burgh in the Mearns – the best of the three, in my view. A strange omission for a Marxist critic. 'A Scots Quair' was deliberately composed in the form of the triple dialectic, moving from rural 'substantive' through small-town 'contradiction' to a rather unconvincing urban-proletarian 'synthesis.'

And yet this omission – where England is concerned – isn't just a mistake. Small towns do not 'count'; no critic, angry or nostalgic, sees them as a significant focus of anything. Now, of course, local government reorganisation has removed even their self-managing identity, their mayors and petty aldermen. If there were a town of 'Winesborough' (pop. 5,000) in Essex, it would now be part of a bastard semi-rural authority called 'Ypwinesfleot District Council,' or some such pseudo-Saxon invention.

Why is England held to exist only at two levels – rural and urban – when everywhere else exists at three? As late as 1871, Raymond Williams tells us, over half the population lived in villages or towns with less than 20,000 people, and only a quarter in cities (defined at the very low level of 100,000 people plus). This points clearly to the importance of small towns in English experience in the quite recent past.

I can't explain this. It is plainly to do with the phenomenal way that the landowning interest went on dominating the English economic and political scene through most of the Victorian period. And it is also to do with the failure of the middle class in England to develop a cultural and political perspective of their own, instead of adopting a version of the agrarian, aristo-cratic outlook on life.

There's something here the English don't want to see. Is it snobbishness about 'trade'? Is it fear of confinement in a small community run by a clique of shopkeepers? I don't know, but there is a real mystery about an old European nation which pretends that it consists – always has consisted – only of country folk, gentry and city-dwellers. And even though we are governed today by the daughter of a grocer and alderman from Grantham, a woman defiantly proud of small-town values, I suspect that the pretence will survive her.   [1987

Dead Houses

At Burnmouth the door hangs from a broken hinge
And the fire is out.
The windows of Shore empty sockets
And the hearth coldness

George Mackay Brown

The ruins of a stone house are a powerful image. But the different ways that people respond to it tells us a lot about them – and about the very different historical experiences of being British.

For one part of the British population, the sight of the dead house suggests general desolation. But for another part, for more British citizens than one might imagine, this ruin is not general at all. It is the photograph – the central image – of their own family history and their own past.

The people who lived in houses or cottages like that were their people. Their ancestors lived in these hills, in isolated small farms, in villages or townships. And when the final generation went out of the door for the last time, closing it uselessly behind them, they almost always did so against their will.

When we talk about 'regional policy,' about subsidising remote areas of Britain or areas of industrial decay and unemployment, we are remembering this past of forced migration and asking whether it must also be the future. When this Government effectively brings regional policy to an end, the State is deliberately turning its back on one of its fundamental humane duties.

The question is whether human beings have some sort of right to go on living 'where they come from,' and whether – within its means – a modern State ought to help them to do so.

The British, in their past, directly felt the sting of history in

two main ways. One was fighting in wars. The other was leaving
home, for Britain as it now exists was created by migrations.
The English rural poor flocked to the cities of the Industrial
Revolution. The Gaelic population of Scotland was driven from
its land by eviction and poverty, to settle mostly overseas.
Upland Wales lost its population to the south Welsh industries,
to Liverpool, the Midlands, the Americas.

Beginning with 'Distressed Areas' policy in the Thirties,
there has been a steady effort to transfer prosperity from the
better-off regions – usually in the South and East – to the
poorer – usually in the North and West.

Regional development reached an almost Soviet intensity in
the last war, as both factories and labour were directed into
needy areas and as the War Agricultural Policy poured
resources into marginal farming. After the war, governments
went on steering industry away from the South-East. Politics
was about the redistribution of wealth.

And in some ways, hard to measure, it worked. Scotland,
with only 5 million people, was losing the population equivalent
of one medium-sized town a year in the 1960s; even before the
oil boom of the 1970s, this haemorrhage was beginning to dry
up. But many of the glittering new industries have since
collapsed, after paying wages which put local factories out of
business. And the suspicion grew that lavish grants actually
made little difference to a firm's decision on where to move.

The policy began to wilt in the late 1970s, and Thatcherism
has now almost killed it off. Regional and general industrial
support, costing £914 million in 1982/83, will fall to £360
million in 1987/88. Regional development grants are being cut
from £659 million in 1982/83 to a token £177 million for this
financial year.

The enormous cuts which have castrated local government
have the same effect of making it harder to help those who do
not want to leave home and 'get on their bikes.' The coal
strike's passion showed that this was a battle not only for jobs
but for communities; as pits close in one-industry villages, the
miners face the choice of life on the dole at home or migration.
Earlier this month the Government postponed its plan to lift
rent controls on private housing, but the underlying purpose,

again, was to make it easier for families to migrate in search of work.

The Government, in short, is hacking down one of the tallest and oldest trees in the political forest. And the landscape will change. For years, there has been anxious chatter about the widening gulf between North and South, about 'two nations' and population drift, about the peril to the unity of the United Kingdom which all this is supposed to involve. But Mrs Thatcher is not anxious.

Regional policy, for her, has been largely investment in failure, the breeding of lame ducks. It has been the costly preserving of 'structural rigidities' in regions where there is little private initiative and strong trade unions. Instead, she is letting things rip.

What will happen? Mrs Thatcher is the boldest lady traveller in unknown territories since Freya Stark. She has discovered, for instance, that the British working class will tolerate levels of unemployment two or three times those which were supposed to detonate Red revolution. And, without that discovery, she would not have found the nerve to break down the fence of regional policy and ride into the unexplored lands beyond it.

One result must be that Britain will slither even further into a 'politics of geography.' Labour will be confirmed as the dominant party of the North and West, probably recapturing lost seats in Wales, while the South–East is reserved as the battleground for the Tories and the Alliance.

Economically, the way in which unemployment has spread into the South–East, coupled with the steep fall in the building of council housing which might accommodate migrants, suggests that there won't be an instant southward flood of families looking for work.

One consequence, to be seen already, is that deprived regions will try to organise their own resources for development. Labour's 'Jobs and Industry' pamphlet makes no mention of restoring the old central 'distribution of industry' apparatus. Instead, it proposes a network of regional enterprise boards, and seeks to 'develop regions' *own* capacity for growth.'

Can Strathclyde or Tyneside hold their people and give them work by their own efforts? There is a lot to be said for nursing up what is native and well-rooted, rather than scrabbling for 'branch factories.' But these are regions with some resources. What rural enterprise board can give hope for the future to small hill farmers in Dyfed or Argyll?

And there are other political implications. The economist Graham Hallett has written that 'Great Britain, with no regional tier [he means full regional autonomy] and local authorities predominantly financed through Whitehall, now has the most centralised governmental system in Western Europe.'

But it is not going to be possible to prevent 'regional enterprise boards' which are not dishing out Whitehall funds but finding their own money from seeking greater independence, and organising public opinion to back them up. The ghosts of devolution, regional and national, may soon be walking again.

For, in the end, regional policy is about emotions. They are not just emotions of provincial chauvinism. They are memories of human unhappiness, of the loss of roots and self-respect, asking that beyond the right to work there should be a right to home.

> The poor and the good fires are all quenched.
> Now, cold angel, keep the valley
> From the bedlam and cinders of a Black Pentecost.

[*1985*

Settlers and Natives

Stoke Newington is both a place and an argument. As a location, it is a quite small, mostly residential district of London, within the borough of Hackney and lying a couple of miles north of the City. As an argument, Stoke Newington is about how different social classes treat each other, how they use history and the past, and what Mrs Thatcher's revival of 'Victorian values' really means.

A foreigner – German, Italian, Japanese – would find it hard to see anything worth arguing about there. A very handsome park, a pretty church, narrow and congested shopping streets, rows of jerrybuilt Victorian houses jammed together so tightly that one can almost hear the squeak of an overstrained corset, blocks of featureless council estate flats, black and Asian mothers manoeuvering push-chairs along an inadequate rim of pavement. But along the back streets lie fleets of yellow builders' skips, piles of sand protected from the rain by grimy plastic sheets. Stoke Newington is one of the focuses of London 'gentrification.'

It began as a country village. Then, from Queen Anne's time, some fine houses were built for fine people. Defoe lived here and wrote Robinson Crusoe. A middle-class settlement took place, aided by speculative builders, in the nineteenth century: Edgar Allan Poe went to school in Edwards Lane, and Isaac Watts wrote his hymns here. Much of the Victorian bourgeoisie of London was buried in Abney Park cemetery, off Church Street, now a beautiful jungle.

At the end of Victoria's century, Stoke Newington began to 'decline' as the middle classes moved gradually out and left their villas to working-class families. The place became shabby, then decidedly poor. In the post-war years, West Indians arrived, Turkish and Greek Cypriots, Asians from many countries. And then, perhaps 10 years ago, came the first ripples of the London middle class, soon a tidal inrush of families buying Victorian villas, refurbishing Georgian façades, bringing with them their retinue of health food shops, delicatessens, 'California restaurants,' wine bars and – of course – estate agents' boutiques.

The incomers aren't 'wealthy', by London standards. The rich are a mile behind them, slowly edging north through Islington. The Stoke Newington settlers are teachers, social workers, middle-aged media people starting a second marriage, the highly-educated young who prefer trading to the dole. Many are 'elderly prima-gravidas' – healthspeak for women having babies after establishing a career. There is a disposition to be leftish and 'caring': Hackney in 1983 was declared the poorest borough in Britain.

Around the incomers and their mortgaged Victorian houses, there is decay and poverty. Some of the 'locals' – the West Indian families especially – stand up to these conditions with

vigour. Others, the residue of a population whose most energetic members have managed to move on, are inert and often
sullen about the social change around them.

But what do the incomers themselves say about this place
that they are taking over? Among them, I have met two remarkable men who proclaim powerful views. Though they live only
a few streets apart, they have never met. They dislike one
another's opinions intensely.

One is the writer and journalist Richard North. Influenced
by the thought of Ivan Illich, North is an environmentalist who
once edited the magazine *Vole*. One of the few who have actually
read the work of Samuel Smiles, he sees the local population
as a helpless group robbed of responsibility and initiative by the
Welfare State. In a much-quoted *Times* article, he coined the
scathing term 'The Drabbies' for other incomers who form part
of the social work and local government apparatus: 'people who
tell others what to do and never meet their neighbours.'

North blames 'Drabby' leftist authoritarianism for suffocating
individual initiative and citizenship. He would like to see state
education abolished, and people given money – 'a high and
accessible dole payment' – to form their own independent
schools and run their own neighbourhood services. Rejecting
the categories of social class, he has come close to a Thatcherite
outlook: 'Margaret has headed this society towards enabling
and entrepreneurship, and that is good, and there's no way
back.'

He welcomes the middle-class immigration: what the place
needs is 'busybodies' to reprove litter-louts, to harass cars
parked on pavements, to organise children loitering on the street
because their parents are working or don't care for them, to
cuff 'the burly little goys in Clissold Park . . . when they insult
the pale Hassidic families who go there on Sundays.' For North,
it is the 'locals' who really need the 'hippy skills' of the incomers:
knowing how to brew their own beer or wine, or make
nourishing lentil soup.

The other voice is that of Patrick Wright, a young socialist
intellectual who works for the National Council for Voluntary
Organisations. He is a disciple – if that is the right word – of
Agnes Heller, a Hungarian philosopher who left her country in
1977 to develop her ideas on 'the radicalisation of democracy.'

In his book 'On Living In An Old Country' (Verso, 1985), Wright delivers a biting attack on North's attitude to Stoke Newington and Hackney. 'What he appears to love . . . is the light that he himself becomes in the darkness of this place. . . . He expects to be loved by the people of the abyss, who will surely recognise the voice of their superior redeemer every time he opens his gifted mouth and "talks" to them. These are the narcissistic perspectives of a false Christ . . . .'

Wright is fascinated by the cultural assumptions of the incomers. The 'superior redeemer' angle to the people has its parallel in a fondly conservationist attitude to buildings and history. To justify their colonisation, the new arrivals uncover and declare a local past to their own taste: Robinson Crusoes, indeed, naming the parts of their desert island.

Wheeling his infant son about Stoke Newington, Wright emits comment on every corner. 'Neo-Georgian: the celebration of inequality.' Or, by a prettily done-up Queen Anne house: 'This is not an opening of history to all, but a redefining of history in such a way that it is available only to the few.' The older inhabitants of Victorian villa-terraces are now warned that they live in a 'precious aesthetic unity,' which they would violate if they put louvres in the windows or knocked out the bay windows to have a bigger front room – and, of course, such 'vandalism' wipes thousands off the value of houses which, 30 years ago, were unsaleable.

In this way, the middle-class newcomers can claim to 'possess' Stoke Newington, past and present, to a degree which those who were actually born there cannot hope to match. The natives are even being culturally evicted from the cemetery. Their view is that it's scandalous to let the graves remain hidden under the mass of bramble thicket and saplings. The incomers find Abney Park a romantic green refuge.

My guess is that Richard North's values will prevail – because the settlers will apply them to themselves. The enthusiasm of the first incomers for permissive, racially-various primary schools is waning fast now; soon there will be private fee-paying schools inculcating . . . Victorian values. And the English knack of restoring history into possessive 'heritage' will go on justifying the process. After all, it was the sharp ear of Patrick Wright which, as the Mary Rose was lifted from the sea, heard the television commentator celebrate 'the first time *we* have seen her in 437 years.'   [*1986*

Caring Colonists

'Internal colonisation' sounds rather Sovietic. It suggests train-loads of red-scarved pioneers setting off from Moscow and Leningrad to settle in distant steppes, the planned movement of populations to occupy virgin lands. But in a quiet, slow, unplanned way, it happens within the United Kingdom.

A few days ago, I went to see a very strange settlement indeed. Craobh Haven was the pioneering scheme of an English company, which set about constructing a new holiday town at a remote spot on the coast of mid-Argyll. A marina was built, a street of houses and shops, causeways joining off-shore islands to form a mole (an Iron Age vitrified fort was allegedly dyna-mited because it got in the way). Then the company went bust.

But this is no mere plonking of cement chalets on a beach. A conscientious yet weird effort has been made to 'respect tradition.' Here, like an outdoors exhibition of Scottish architec-ture, is a film-set jumble of styles: pan-tiled cottages from the coast towns of Fife, crow-stepped roofs from old tower houses, tenement blocks with stair-turrets like the urban 'lands' of Scottish cities. All are colour-washed in contrasting pastel shades. Beyond the folly there opens out the azure of the Firth of Lorne, and beyond that again the mountains of Mull glowing silver with snow.

As I stood there, several English people emerged from a 'vernacular' close and approached, thinking I was a liquidator. They weren't giving in, they said. This place had a future. The 21 first settlers were forming an association. They would fight for Craobh Haven (which they pronounced 'Kroove' to rhyme with 'groove').

If their surroundings were unreal, they certainly were not. There was something authentically, splendidly English about their busy, decent determination to get organised, to refuse to be done out of their rights, to 'see something was done.' If the original population of Argyll had possessed a tenth of that assertive self-confidence, I thought, the story of the land would have been very different.

Over all the years that I have known this part of Scotland, there has been population movement and social change which – in the past few decades – became torrential. When I was a child, the people of Lorne and Knapdale were still partly Gaelic-speaking, with a mixture of Lowland small farmers who had settled as sheep farmers in the previous century. The 'big houses' often contained traditional Highland lairds, or their relations. I knew of two English writers (Orwell was briefly one), and an English insurance agent married to a local girl, and a few Polish ex-soldiers.

Gradually, as car ownership spread and as the narrow roads which connected this beautiful land to the world outside were widened, new people appeared. Some were rich farmers from the South, others were well-off couples from England seeking houses for retirement. Then the young began to move in, full of the ideals of the English 1960s: potters, jewellers, neo-peasants, fish-farmers, craftsmen servicing the new yachting boom, or merely hippies.

There was good in this, but bad as well. Small farmers were driven out of business by the wealth of aggressive incomers. The old had to move into town council housing, because the stock of cottages available for single retired people was snapped up for expensive conversion. Jobs promised on 'leisure developments' hardly materialised, as the contractors brought their own labour. There was the odd drug scandal, but above all a sense of alienation: that feeling that 'our country is leaving us.' Unease about the 'white settlers,' as they were called, contributed to the Scottish National Party victory in Argyll in 1974.

Today, half the voices in the hotel where my uncle used to drink a meditative whisky are English voices – behind the bar as well. I would guess that English incomers now form a majority of the population of the Craignish peninsula, around the yacht harbour and holiday centre at Ardfern. The friendly

Englishman who is doing up cottages for summer lets (£140 a week) introduced me to 'the best dry stone mason in the district' – a young man from Matlock, in Derbyshire.

The settlers have brought a new vigour to the place. They are cheerful, enterprising and very hard-working. They even manufacture and sell their own images of Scotland to tourists from the South, from Celtic brooches and 'tablet' fudge to the matchless photographs of Scotland by the English genius Colin Baxter. Small industries like fish-farming line the shore, squeezing out the boat-moorings of the 'natives.'

But somehow the colonisers remain a colony. Incomers with jobs to offer tend to give them to their own kind, and there are now two largely separate economies – and separate social circuits. Expectations are different. The new people want the level of social service they were accustomed to in the suburbs of Manchester or in the Home Counties, and raise outraged clamour if they don't get it. The old way of life, sickness and death in mid-Argyll asked for – and got – very little from the State. Too little, in my view. But to endure without complaint, and without dependence, was the Highland ethic.

Another part of that ethic has always been hospitality. Nobody burns holiday cottages there, as they do in Wales, and incomers are made welcome even when the changes they bring are alarming. A culture is being slowly extinguished, but Gaelic was already much too weak in this part of Scotland to evoke anything like the organised resistance of the Welsh Language Society. And the young English colonists in Argyll belong to the 'caring,' environment-conscious generation. They rebuke one another for scraping the sea-loch floors until there are no scallops left, or for erecting inappropriate houses, or for slighting the prehistoric monuments of the Crinan plain.

There are ironies in all this. Argyll, like most of Scotland, once sent its own colonists all over the world to settle Canada or conquer India, to command black and yellow labourers in tin mines, rubber plantations or tobacco warehouses in Asia and Africa. Of the eight children I played with as a boy, I think none is still in Scotland. Some are in New Zealand, others in Cape Town or Natal. Now the path to their old house is blocked by a Surrey-type 'Private Property' notice. Their own home territory has become, if not precisely foreign, at least no longer theirs.

So a modest, remote place slowly turns into a playground, a 'recreational area' of 'outstanding natural beauty.' Tourism is not new here: relays of Victorian steamers once took visitors along the 'Royal Route' through the Crinan Canal to Oban. What is new is the idea of a place which exists only to 'service' other places, in which inhabitants are redefined as janitors.

The hills remain, and the standing stones, and the grey-lag geese holding their noisy winter parliaments by the sea. But something is lost: a quiet-spoken, reflective, closely related community whose forefathers gave names to every piece of water or stone. In the time of Emperor Severus, a Roman fleet sailed prospecting through the Firth of Lorne. It has taken two thousand years for the Romans to return and settle.

[*1987*

Intelligentsia Wanted

What is it about the English and intellectuals? The poet James Fenton wrote the other day that 'it has often been doubted that we have, in England, such a thing as an intellectual life. Most of our intellectuals are imports.' He went on to list some names, all imported from Central Europe, Ireland, Scotland or Wales. His English candidates were disqualified as 'gentlemen-and-scholars' or as 'writers and men-of-letters.'

This was intended as a gentle lament. But it struck me also as one more version of an old national riddle: an English intellectual is either not English or else, if his papers are invincibly in order, not an intellectual. The facts – the poor old facts – are that as many native intellectuals inhabit the lands between Berwick and the Channel as oriental cockroaches inhabit Charing Cross hospital. From Edward Thompson, fighting the nuclear state from the Left, to Roger Scruton, prince of the authoritarian Right. What is this pretence that they are invisible – or impossible?

H. L. Mencken offered an American version of the riddle when he said that 'the so-called intellectuals of the country are simply weather-vanes blown constantly by foreign winds, usually but not always English.' Here's an admission that England breeds the creatures. But, more interesting, here's this refrain of 'so-called.'

The English behave as if intellectuals were unicorns: if you see one, you know it isn't one. The word is often prefixed by 'pseudo-.' The Oxford English Dictionary offers this definition, dangled with distaste between finger and thumb: 'a person possessing, *or supposed to possess*, superior powers of intellect.' It quotes the *Daily News* (1898) on 'the *so-called* intellectuals of Constantinople who were engaged in discussion while the Turks were taking possession of the city.'

I first heard the word in the summer of 1940, as a small child picking up snatches of grown-up talk. 'Pseudo-intellectuals,' one gathered, supposed that Hitler had won the war and were bolting to the United States, not even waiting to engage in discussion while the Turks took possession. Later information described a round-shouldered, querulous tribe in spectacles, apt to argue with orders and as messy in their laundry as in their personal relationships. As Auden wrote:

> 'To the man-in-the-street, who, I'm sorry to say,
> Is a keen observer of life,
> The word 'Intellectual' suggests straight away
> A man who's untrue to his wife.'

To English distrust of the egghead, the Anglican Prayer Book provides a clue, Queen Elizabeth, sick of divisive theologians, ordered her priests to give Communion with the words: 'The body of our Lord Jesus Christ . . . take and eat this in remembrance that Christ died for thee.' This skewered together two irreconcilables: the Catholic doctrine of a sacramental change of essence from bread to body, and the Zwinglian view of the Eucharist as a mere rite of commemoration.

It was as if, today, a party proclaimed that 'All property will be nationalised within the framework of a free market economy.'

It said to the Reformation intellectuals: 'Shut up, in the name of national unity, or tell your clever ideas to the axe!'

From this was born what we now call 'the English genius for compromise,' the distaste for those who drive ideas to their conclusions without bothering about their usefulness or the mess they may cause. It wasn't born with much dignity. But it survived the intellectual upsurge of the English Revolution in the next century, to become the ideology – rather, the anti-ideology – of the nation as a whole.

Victorian England was crowded with universal minds. But it did not evolve the European intellectual caste of the nineteenth century and our own times: the thinkers and bards as judges and tribunes of the nation, natural spokesmen for its aspirations. Englishness seemed to need no such defence.

English intellectuals in the Thirties who tried, mostly on the Left, to claim for themselves this shamanic authority were treated with derision. The old antagonism between 'aesthetes' and 'hearties' played its part. But so did what I would call 'the London Effect' – the law that any vehement defence of an idea makes the defender irresistibly comic.

London, indeed, is a pretty hostile environment for the 'intellectual life.' Its vast distances and slothful transport impede the gathering of 'circles' to dine together, like the Goncourts and their friends, or to sit chattering in coffee-houses like writers in Central Europe. English writers and painters, let alone thinkers, loathe being lumped into 'movements' with their colleagues. Efforts to construct 'circles' soon fall apart out of sheer self-consciousness, or in the heated arguments over sorting out the restaurant bill for which English literati are famous.

And any fair deal for women also assorts badly with traditional intellectual life. Edinburgh still has a life of this kind; one may go to this pub or that, knowing roughly who may be there and what ideas are being preached or spluttered. But behind each noble male mind, there waits somewhere a woman who is supposed to be ready to get up in her curlers at 1 a.m. and fry egg-and-chips for the excited genius and the pals he picked up at the Abbotsford or the Southsider.

I think it was the Countess of Eglintoun who, in Edinburgh's verminous Old Town, grew tired of the men of wit and spirit whom she used regularly to feed at her table. She eventually threw them out and took to entertaining rats instead. She found them more grateful, and with better manners.

Ingratitude, all the same, is a necessary trait in the intellectual. The fight against tyranny and stupidity, whether it is the struggle of Russia's 'superfluous men' in the time of Nicholas I or of the Polish intellectuals against the occupier and the autocrat, instils mistrust of every government, every ideology which puts 'national unity' first – as, in its mild way, the English ideology does.

But regretting the weakness of English intellectuals, as a group, might then come close to an absurdity: to regretting that England has never known occupation or state terror. A country which has never feared the extinction of its language and culture, which sees no need for a lay priesthood of men and women to keep the candle of truth burning through dark times, is simply a happy country. There are few of them left. Why spoil this one by importing the poisonous self-doubts, the savage mockery and the polemics of total rejection, which are proper to unhappy nations?

There is no full answer, except to say that the conditions for that happiness are coming to an end. English institutions no longer guarantee freedom and justice as they once did; worn out, they offer only a pretence that all is still well. State power grows, while recourse against it shrinks. There is a retreat from kindness and tolerance, a new sense of public unfairness.

The English, in short, are no longer sure that they know what they are like. Those who lead are no longer sure of why they act, or of what will happen in this unfamiliar society when they do – witness the babble of confusion emitted last week by the hierarchy of the BBC, supposed to be custodians of a few simple old principles.

It's time that England raised a mirror to itself, and tried seriously to recognise this changed, present face which the past has been fashioning. Journalists can give only glimpses. It takes intellectuals to make a mirror.   [*1985*

The English Bourgeoisie

Think of a great, sere countryside. Scattered over its surface, there lives a peasantry divided into two races. There are those – the mass of them – who inhabit ordinary cottages and bothies, managing adequately in good seasons but at the mercy of the drought. There are, however, others who stay in stone houses passed on from generation to generation, living sometimes austerely but after good rains with a mysterious ease and opulence.

This is on its surface a dry country. The mass live on land irrigated only by rainfall. Here and there, the air traveller sees the twinkle of dams, some built by the State in recent years and many more by private people, which mitigate times of drought and pass on stored-up rainwater – often at a price – to the ordinary peasants. But deep under that surface there lies a subterranean lake, a buried water-table.

And the stone-housed people have wells. This is their secret. In the yards of their farms stand old Victorian headworks of iron, covering the shaft which reaches down through the beds of light soil and clay to the geological depth where the water lies. It is not the most modern equipment; only a trickle of water reaches the surface, enough to keep a few beasts alive and to irrigate the vegetable garden but still more than anything which can reach the rain-dependent majority. When times improve, though, and long rains or heavy winter snow have raised the water-table closer to the surface, the crops around the house grow with a richness and variety which the rain people cannot achieve.

This is a simile for traditional English middle-class wealth. The rain people are the wage-earners, directly subject to the fluctuations of employment, inflation, pay-packets. The dams are the accumulations of wealth which are immediately visible on the surface of society: the fortunes of the speculators and the resources of the Welfare State. And the stone-house dwellers are those, whether they are themselves active capitalists or in the salariat or merely rentiers and maiden aunts or even well-spoken tinkers flogging cheesecloth blouses down the Portobello Road, who have access to the accumulated wealth of the ancient English middle-class.

'Access' is the important word. It isn't so much a matter of outright possession. We know that England is still a country of spectacular inequality in the matter of actual ownership of money and property, so far as this heavily private matter can be discovered and measured. While 90 per cent of the land in England and Wales was still tenanted (i.e. in estates) in 1880, no less than 50 per cent was still tenanted in 1975. Estimates of total wealth held by percentages of the population swing about a good deal (the '7:84' formula is one of many), with J. R. Revell calculating that the top 5 per cent in Britain as a whole owned 75 per cent of wealth in 1960, and the Open University's 'Patterns of Equality' course suggesting that the top 25 per cent own 70 per cent of wealth. But beyond this lies the question of who – beyond the titular possessor – has a standard of living or way of life which is dependent upon that money.

How does the old British élite so serenely survive? How – to put it another way – is it possible for a married couple aged about 35 and earning, say, £5,000 a year to own a house in Islington or Chelsea worth £35,000 and send two children to private schools charging at least £1,000 a year? In some ways, it is better to go back a few years, before the explosion in London house prices, and to ask how in 1960 a young married man earning £1500 could set about buying a house which then cost £7–8000?*

To call upon Charles and Melissa Heigho wouldn't have told you much. Rush matting, a few nice rugs, one or two small but very good bits of antique furniture, a 'daily woman', quite likely no car 'because we can't afford one.' Television by Radio Rentals, underpants by Marks and Sparks. 'Wealthy' is obviously the wrong word. Inspecting Charles's bank account would probably show a small but painful overdraft, no more than a hundred quid or so but the subject of much remonstration at

* This was written in 1976: these quoted prices have only an archaeological interest.

home, and possibly a few hundred in a deposit account or building society.

Yet this is where the English ruling class is reproducing itself, discreetly ensuring another generation of security and privilege within the Secret Garden whose key no fumbling socialist Chancellor has yet discovered. The bulge under Melissa's gingham smock is another little Public Schoolboy, destined for the administrative grade of the Civil Service, a place in a merchant bank or a Headship of Chancery in some embassy. And he too will grow up without much cash but with things which only substantial money can buy: more of them if capitalism is thriving and fewer if there is a season of social-democratic austerity.

We all know that the age of the mighty private entrepreneur is gone. Charles's grandfather built railways in South America, beating down Indian insurrections with a golf club. His great-uncle patented a new chemical bleach and poured sulphurous torrents of waste into Yorkshire rivers. Melissa's great-grand-father was a Cornish tin-miner who rose to marshal diamond-mining Kaffirs in Griqualand West. All that is over. Nobody in either family, it's probable, is creating wealth in that way now. The male descendants earn salaries, good or less good, with a larger farmer here or there and perhaps the odd owner of an advertising agency. What we are dealing with is the most discreet, sophisticated and effective system of wealth *transmission* the world has ever seen.

The fortunes of the *Gründerzeit* have gone into family trusts. Capital is invested in stocks and shares. Often a part of this investment remains in the shares of private companies, that secret and unquantified sector of British capitalism whose shares have only a nominal value in public but which represent infinitely higher sums if they should ever be realised.

As far as possible, this capital must remain intact and undistributed. Primogeniture helps here. When Charles's father dies, he will leave his share of old 'Venezuela' Heigho's money in a will-trust, the income of the investments to support his widow while she lives, and his children will receive only token sums at his death. When Charles's mother dies, the capital may be subdivided among the children but most of it will probably stay with the eldest son who may decide to spend some of it – against the frantic advice of family lawyers and the bitter opposition of his relations – but is expected to transmit the main capital once more through his own will-trust. He does not have to do so: English law permits him to leave his money to a cat's home, especially if he has no children, or to the Symbionese Liberation Front. But convention usually wins.

Three peculiar features of English middle-class *mores* arise from this. The first is the common spectacle of relative austerity in the midst of unrealised wealth. The income from shares in such a trust may often be quite small, and in the case of private family companies, exiguous. Outside conditions matter too. In the post-war period, very little water was reaching the surface: income from shares was slight, the trappings of wealth were scarce and exceptionally costly, and the possibilities of actually making money through buying and selling – the sale of houses or land, for instance – were bleak. In these circumstances, with the water-table intact but exceptionally difficult to bring up to ground-level where it could be used, the English upper classes presented a picture of impressive dilapidation. 'Poor as church mice', they used to say, 'the Brondesburys are eating cold rice pud off gold plates . . .'

Matters had become very different by the mid-Sixties. Americans who had sent the Brondesburys CARE Parcels and Hershey bars in return for a look at the Muniments Room now scratched their heads: how could the church mice be driving two new cars, paying Eton fees and flying to Rhodesia for Christmas? The answer lay of course in the revival of share income and the lavish possibility of capital gains. To borrow from a family trust against prospects, a request once rejected with outrage by trustees and solicitors, was now frequently tolerated.

The young must still, in general, do without 'their' money. But even in the worst times, the spirit of the trust is respected: a certain standard of living is essential. Somehow the odd few thousand to put down on a house is almost always forthcoming, the trust offering large sums at very low rates of interest on security of the house itself – no bad deal for posterity, as it turned out. A third of the price of Charles's first house will have been provided in this way, possibly more, although he must raise a mortgage to provide for the balance.

The second feature is the arrant sexism of the system. This

isn't merely the habit of primogeniture in favour of sons. It is the moral pressure laid upon widows, whose survival – often on an income stingy in proportion to the capital involved – denies 'my money' to impatient children and beneficiaries. Alienated money becomes a monstrous fetish impossible to propitiate: the woman who persuades the trustees to disgorge in favour of her children is betraying the Mosaic law of English class maintenance, while by refusing to permit a distribution she may make her children wish her dead. Literature has spread the notion that old women 'enjoy' power of this kind, one of the crueller sexist myths.

And thirdly, there is the importance of death, the Spring Festival of rentier capitalism. Birth is an event of slight importance, save for the clan's responsibility to take out insurance policies guaranteeing the boy's fees at a public school. Marriage matters little more, especially now that the 'marriage settlement' (that tribal arrangement which created a new trust whose income was to supply the young couple, but which would be broken up if the marriage were dissolved) has become so rare. Death, however, brings about the creation of new trusts, the distribution of money, the casting-off of old investment patterns and older family advisers. In the office of the Heighos' solicitors, one more black tin box stuffed with papers is added to the stack, the name of the corpse painted carefully in white on the side. Another will drags towards probate: another baby trust is born.

Abstinence, fear of women, the celebration of death. No wonder the English middle class took over the Druid legends as their myth of origin. The transmission of wealth, so beautifully articulated to the maintenance of domination in the professional and State élites, remains proof against almost any disaster save social revolution or a sustained hyperinflation. But the kindness and tolerance of the English middle-class (rather less impressive than the kindness and tolerance they have contrived to mediate to the English masses who put up with them still) is born of the confidence of an Order, a melancholy Druidic caste, and not from a sense of individual vigour. Just as their huge reservoir of wealth is used largely to maintain social identity rather than to generate production, so well-born English businessmen will convey that they make money out of reluctant duty rather than because they want to be rich.

The great eighteenth-century antiquary William Stukeley got it right in his poem 'The Druid':–

> 'From grinding care and thrift secure,
> Arrived at years of life mature,
> Unenvy'd for a Fortune great;
> Above contempt for low estate,
> Let the remainder of my days
> In private life serenely pass.
> Unnotic'd I would chuse to dwell,
> Yet in a house, and not a Cell . . .'

[1976

The Spreading Slime

Last week, the *Sunday Times* delivered one of those onslaughts on whingeing left-wing intellectuals (it called them 'intelligentsia,' using the Russian word incorrectly as usual) which have become a regular feature of Conservative journa'ism. The phrase 'moaning Minnies' was not employed. Instead we got 'erudite moaning,' 'left-wing laager,' 'sniping from the sidelines,' and 'ideals out of kilter with the aspirations of plain folk.'

This kind of English stupidity is an organism so primitive that it is apparently impossible to kill off. It reminds me of *Physarum Polycephalum*, the gigantic slime mould recently bred by scientists at Bonn. Bright yellow and about two millimetres thick, this monocellular creature – neither plant nor animal – grew to a size of 10 square yards before the scientists took fright and froze it. It can smell its favourite food, and move towards it at a speed of up to two centimetres an hour. This favourite food is porridge.

Stultitia Polycephala, or populist imbecility, is the English slime mould. Large tracts of the landscape have already been covered by it. Nourished on the porridge of resentful prejudice, it smothers thought under a jelly of servile national unity.

The mould exuded by the *Sunday Times* is a highly instructive specimen. It is at first sight surprising that this emanation of highly-paid Murdoch journalism smells so strongly of social envy. We read that this disaffected 'intelligentsia' moves aimlessly between Islington and the Groucho Club, that it surrounds 'the country's more fashionable dinner tables,' that it consumes Montrachet at 'favourite watering-holes.'

Only yesterday, the intellectual enemy was held to be grubby products of the polytechnics, inhabiting the social work departments of provincial cities, typing out their hatred in grotty little houses crowded with snotty, neglected children, and in general constituting a threat to the 'civilised heritage.' But now the Right has adopted the envy-fantasies of the old Left. This is the language of – say – a Labour militant during the first Wilson government, imagining disloyal capitalists trotting to their clubs, swooshing about in Bentleys and drinking champagne without taking their top-hats off.

It takes some mental adjustment to find the hated eggheads in this new location: identified as well-off, 'fashionable' and exclusively London-based. They are somehow on top, while underneath – or 'out of kilter' with them – are the aspirations of 'plain folk.' I had thought that 'plain folk' had finally died out of journalese, or had been laughed out, but here it comes again: England's equivalent to the Nazi *gesundes Volksempfinden* – healthy folk-instinct.

The suggestion that the most powerful critics of Mrs Thatcher's Britain are a clique of Armani-clad pinkoes based in London's club-land is too silly to contradict in itself. But what is happening here supplements Mrs Thatcher's larger project to abolish socialism as a significant element in Britain politics.

The intention is to 'denationalise' the intellectual Left, by contrasting its discontent with the happy, dynamic Golden Age which the mass of the nation is alleged to be entering. Those critics are presented as an irrelevant élite, self-excluded from participation in glorious times as religious reactionaries or those with bourgeois hankerings excluded themselves from the French or Chinese revolutions.

The truth is that those who have the most cogent things to say against the way we are governed are – as they always were – scattered across the country, addicted to anoraks and bicycles, on the whole ill-rewarded, and stimulated by Bulgarian wine and the odd whisky. But that makes them hard to marginalise in propaganda terms, so they are replaced by a fictional metropolitan coterie of 'internal *émigrés*' which is a more suitable target for envy and contempt.

We read that the intellectuals are 'increasingly divorced from the land (they) live in,' and that 'the nation is not listening to them.' Much of the thinking and artistic community takes 'a low view of Britain,' refusing to rejoice in the spread of house-ownership, the distribution of shop-floor shares, the 'job-creating 4 per cent growth of the economy' or the 'steady decline of unemployment.' Instead, this elegant but alienated fringe 'is content to be smugly negative,' because 'devising constructive alternatives is too much like hard work.'

It's worth adding up this language for a moment. The target group is being described as deficient in patriotism, rejected by national opinion, unjustifiably rich and hedonistic in lifestyle, workshy and . . . negative. Anyone who has ever sampled the language of the Soviet media towards dissidents and the recalcitrant young, especially in the Brezhnev period, will recognise this stuff at once. It's the old call to get your hair cut, stop listening to foreign broadcasts, and start writing positively about life in new towns or the personal conflicts of factory managers. It's the voice of the populist boor through the ages.

What, though, of the charge that the carping intellectuals have nothing to offer – no alternative to Mrs Thatcher's programmes? One retort is that – so far – the issue of carping licences does not require a pledge to positive ideas. Why should it? But is it true that the disarray of the Left, inside and outside the Labour movement, is so total that no coherent alternative exists, no appeal beyond the call to unite against That Woman?

I think that remains true. The initiative is still with Mrs Thatcher's 'modernisation' drive, rushing forward in this third administration with renewed energy into yet another programme of sweeping legislative change. Labour rolls about in the slip-stream, its counter-suggestions still more of an incoherent wish to restore fragments of the past than a competing vision of the future.

But it will not always be true. In two respects, both of course unintentional, 'modernisation' is slowly creating a new landscape in which it will be easier for Labour – or its ruling coalition behind Neil Kinnock – to operate. The changes in housing, nationalised industry and the trade unions reduce Labour's crippling obligations to blocks of organised power on the Left, leaving the party's hands freer and its mind more open. Secondly, the breakneck centralisation of Britain and the increase in police and State power since 1979 invites a public backlash, in which democracy at every level is seen to be in danger.

And the alternatives are beginning to appear. Professor Eric Hobsbawm, bestriding *Marxism Today* as usual, calls for a 'social coalition' crossing class divisions which would accept a more privatised economy but would invest in a genuine reconstruction of industry and infrastructure. Hilary Wainwright, a leftist wary of social coalitions, writes in her book 'Labour, a Tale of Two Parties' that the correct programme now is 'democratic reforms aimed at the main centres of power,' including devolution, electoral reform, control of the secret services and the City, a Bill of Rights . . . in short, the sort of programme long associated with the Alliance and derided by conventional socialists.

Interesting ideas, fertile seedlings of a convincing competitor to Thatcherism. Best of all, they do not flee from new realities but proceed from them. These intellectuals fear and detest much about this régime, not least its spreading slime mould of national-unity rhetoric. But they are building within its walls, not 'sniping from outside.' In a few years, even plain folk may take them seriously.

Dracula in Britain

The Romanians are growing fed up with the Dracula cult. Gone are the days when – as Dan Ionescu remembered the other day on Radio Free Europe – 'an off-duty cook from a hotel in the Carpathians used to pop up out of a coffin to thrill foreign tourist parties.' That was profitable but demeaning. And it got in the way of Romania's fiercely possessive attitude to its own history.

As most people know, Bram Stoker's novel 'Dracula' was a cheerful Victorian fantasy. The trouble is that he took a real person's name in vain. I quote the late Constantin Giurescu: 'There ruled in Wallachia Vlad the Impaler (1456–1462), also called Dracula, son of Vlad the Devil . . . He distinguished himself as a dreaded enemy of the Ottomans . . .' Vlad the Impaler is now being built up as a mighty patriot who 'favoured economic progress and the establishment of order,' a predecessor of President Nicolae Ceausescu. This makes it rather urgent to establish that he did not flap around biting women in the neck.

A recent article in *Contemporanul* by Adrian Paunescu stated that the Dracula myth was 'one page in a vast output of political pornography directed against us by our enemies.' Paunescu was replying to a letter from Mrs Hoggett, a Romanian living in Britain, objecting to a programme about Dracula with Vincent Price which she had seen on television. Mrs Hoggett complained that it made all Romanians look like vampires.

For Paunescu, this was part of a concerted campaign by 'reactionaries of every colour' to slander 'the very idea of being a Romanian, as well as the eternal idea of Romania.' In subsequent issues of the magazine, some suggested that Paunescu had gone over the top, while others implied that it was a dirty Hungarian plot to tarnish the glory of the Impaler.

Vampires, incidentally, do exist, even if Vlad was not one of them. I well remember the Hamburg Vampire in the middle 1960s. He climbed into a flat and drank the blood of a young woman, who asserted that before he came through the window she had felt a deadly chill and become unable to move. The sceptical police took her off to hospital, where the Vampire was actually caught halfway up the creepers on the wall, on his way to have one more for the road. He ended up in a mental clinic. The victim and the police officer in the case ended up telling their story in convincing detail on German television.

In Britain, many will chide the Romanians for not having a sense of humour, for spoiling a piece of harmless nonsense. But I think that they are basically in the right. Paunescu may be an ass; Romanian official history is itself burdened with a thick fringe of chauvinist garbage about 'the glorious civilisation of the Thracian-Dacians' and their King Decebal (sic). But the Dracula cult does raise real questions about stereotypes of other countries, and about the stereotype a country wants to present to itself.

We need Dracula, because it means we don't have to take Romania seriously or see the reality of Transylvania – one of the loveliest places in Europe, but also the site of Europe's worst minority conflicts. We needed Idi Amin and the Emperor Bokassa, because they obscured the boring fact that not all black African States are grotesque tyrannies.

We also need all the stories we can get about cretinous and brutal Russians. This explains the venomous attacks by the *Spectator* on Martin Walker, the *Guardian* correspondent in Moscow – 'the authentic sound of tongue licking boot.' Walker's crime is to write about nice Russians who are neither Communists nor dissidents, and to observe that the KGB is often more open-minded than the Party (an elementary truth about most Communist régimes). But such talk makes it harder to kill Russians, when the moment comes. For imbeciles, this is spiritual treachery.

But what about Britain's own Draculas? Could it be that we, too, maintain displays of nonsense about ourselves and our past which draw flocks of foreigners, leaving them with an impression which includes both affection and derision? Yes, we do.

Scotland's Dracula appears annually in the Edinburgh Festi-

val's Military Tattoo, kilted and twirling a huge silver poker as
he struts in front of the massed pipe bands playing 'Scotland
The Brave.' To the coal miner from Midlothian, the unemployed youth from Easterhouse, this is about as remote from
normal experience as a New Orleans funeral jazz band, but
both know that this is the show that is expected from them.

England has its pageantry, but its true Transylvania lies
increasingly in its 'stately homes.' In November last year, the
Prince and Princess of Wales opened in Washington the
'Treasure Houses of Britain' exhibition, a selection of the
contents of these houses. Writing in this paper last week, Dr
David Clark, Labour's environmental spokesman, pointed out
that the National Trust now owns 188 houses open to the
public, with 'scores more that the public never see.' He
protested that the Trust had become so preoccupied with
acquiring and preserving historic houses that it had lost sight
of its original purpose of preserving the countryside.

Stone and brick last: wood and mud do not. This is a problem
first of all for archaeologists. The first settlers in Britain are
classified by their flint tools, although almost everything they
used must have been wooden. Soon this becomes a social divide.
The Romano-British establishment leaves brilliant mosaic pavements and huge foundations behind: the common people leave
only postholes, almost imperceptible shadows in the soil where
once a wooden pile rotted away.

The contrast grows worse in more modern times. The
English 'heritage' which is thought worthy of preservation
becomes largely the palaces and manors of the rich. It is not
just that visible history is one-sided. It is that the national effort
of 'preservation' accentuates this one-sidedness. As Patrick
Wright wrote the other day in *New Socialist*, 'if we define history
only in terms of its grandest remains, an acutely impoverished
image will emerge.'

He quotes the example of Castle Drogo in Devon, 'the last
castle in England.' This gloomy place, built to the design of
Edwin Lutyens, was completed in 1930. Its owner was Julius
Drewe, magnate of Home & Colonial Stores, who was advised
that the Norman–French version of 'Drewe' was 'Drogo.' The
original name of the place, I believe, was Piddledown Common.

If the National Trust had taken over Castle Drogo to make

an example of how the English commercial classes yearned for the rural life-style of the old aristocracy, one might sympathise. But the result is merely to reinforce the impression that English history is the history of the wealthy and powerful.

So an absurd process begins. The more England moves away from the world of the 'stately homes,' disabling their owners by taxation, the more these houses are flung on the mercies of the National Trust and distort the image of the 'English heritage.' In the end, the National Trust is driven to display the precise antithesis of modern times, implying that everything which is now built or done is a betrayal of tradition.

This is a sick outcome. It would hardly be more unreal if the Duke and Duchess of Transylvania welcomed National Trust coach parties by emerging from coffins and advancing on them with protruding fangs. But, given that society through the Trust now keeps and maintains them in their old homes, they scarcely need more blood to suck.   [*1986*

Greater Privilege Hath No Man . . .

The sense of privilege has aspects of virginity. Its loss, a surrender to experience, is irreversible. I'm talking here not about privilege as the hustings debated it during the election. The politicians meant advantage bought by wealth and defended by organised selfishness. I mean something else: the feeling of awe and gratitude over inherited superiority.

When I was a child, I used to ponder the miracle which had located me in the fortunate classes of the strongest and most virtuous nation upon earth. The groan of the odd German raiding plane scarcely disturbed our nights at school; the trembling of earth and heaven as the American bomber streams passed overhead did not disturb our happy, wondering complacency. We munched our macaroni cheese and paid attention to an atlas that still seemed mostly red. The privilege of Britishness appeared absolute, though we sometimes asked each other if the grace of being born here and now was luck or destiny.

I remember the first dent in that certainty. The headmaster used to gather senior boys, a docile little group in brown dressing-gowns, to sit on his study floor and listen to Mr Churchill on the wireless. But one day, he unexpectedly called the whole school together and said this: 'You ought to know that the United States Navy is now larger than the Royal Navy. That is all.'

So we were not, after all, the strongest. Gradually we resorted to a more evasive, snobbish definition of British privilege. The Americans had more ships, but ours were stronger. Their fighters were faster, but ours more agile, German armaments had technical perfection – *Vorsprung durch Technik* – but would always be outdone by British soldiers with wonky tanks and a sense of humour (how comic, this month, to see the same defensive contempt for German thoroughness in London reviews of the Berlin Philharmonic's concert at the Festival Hall!).

In this, if we had known it, we were at the end of a long British tradition of what might be called 'jingoism with a human face': the habit of teaching war as a game in which the display of character was at least as important as its outcome in victory or defeat. The National Army Museum has opened an exhibition of the work of Lady Butler, the nineteenth-century 'battle painter' whose work was so much admired by Queen Victoria. Lady Butler was not, with exceptions, interested in painting martial triumph, or even sabre-flashing courage. 'The Roll-Call' shows guardsmen after a battle in the Crimea, wounded, shattered with exhaustion, scarcely able to drag themselves to attention, and yet – except for one who has just fallen dead – still upright and answering to their names.

Courage in endurance, suffering rather than victory, were her favourite themes. Nobody at the time thought her work defeatist, or 'anti-war.' She was displaying war as an examination in selflessness and character, patriotism as an expression of moral virtue. It was held that the British would always pass that examination well. So they often do. But, in the real world, so do others – even the enemy.

'Greater love hath no man than this, that a man lay down his life for his friends.' In the war years, these words were endlessly repeated to us, mostly by people who were neither soldiers nor priests. It was not until long afterwards – no doubt through inattention at Bible classes – that I realised that this was part of the leave-taking of Jesus from his disciples. I had vaguely supposed that some past Prime Minister or Poet Laureate had made the pronouncement. It did not occur to me that this was not a British adage for the British.

And then, one day, I saw a man do that. I was a National Service officer engaged in the so-called 'Malayan Emergency,' the guerrilla war launched by the Malayan Communist Party against continued colonial rule by Britain. We hunted them; they hunted us. We seldom collided. But the morning came when, as we lay in ambush among the rotting logs of a clearing, six Chinese guerrillas emerged from the jungle wall and came towards us.

When the storm burst at them, the first three staggered and fell at once. The others bolted for the trees. Two made it; the third folded to his knees a few yards from sanctuary. I saw, and still see, his clothes tattering under the bullets. And then a man ran back from the jungle and, taking his comrade under the armpits, began to drag him towards safety.

Within a few seconds, he too was dead. Afterwards, all was confusion: the sight of what we had done, the truck bumping up for the bodies, the rubber planter's wife squealing with delight and wishing she'd brought her camera. This was, it seemed, success. But inside my head, imprisoned by the whistling deafness of gunfire, a voice repeated the old words about greater love. Now I had seen a man give his life for his friends. But I had helped to take that life, and he was not British but a Hokkienese boy, the son – as it turned out – of a village bicycle dealer somewhere in Pahang.

After that, I found that my sense of privilege had come to pieces. It did not vanish entirely. I had a better education than most; I have seldom been badly hungry; I have never been out of a job or behind barbed wire. But my sense of awe at the

Providence which had mysteriously allotted me Britishness – that had gone.

The other day, I heard a BBC reporter talking about the Malaysian Communists. Some 600 of them have finally emerged from the jungle in southern Thailand and accepted the Government's offer of a patch of land, a hut and a small grant of cash in return for living a peaceful life. They – or rather their fathers and grandfathers – first went into the jungle to begin their struggle, then against the Japanese, in 1941. There was a brief pause in 1945. Their leader, Chin Peng, was given the Order of the British Empire and marched in the Victory Parade through London. But in 1948, as Britain declined to grant what was then Malaya independence, they returned to the jungle.

Nobody seems to know where old Chin Peng is. Some say he is dead. Others say that still, in some bamboo brake in the mountains, an ancient figure in canvas Badminton boots sits under a roof of plaited leaves and pens the ideographs of his military orders. After 46 years, he is the echo of a gunshot in the forest which makes the gibbons fall silent, a movement of the fronds when there is no wind, a footprint on the sandbanks of a deserted river.

He failed. The great military effort of the 1950s did not liberate his country, which eventually gained independence as the bourgeois, multi-racial State of Malaysia. In 1960, a sort of peace was declared, and his bases withdrew to the remote Thai border regions. Some 6,000 of his men and women died in the decades of struggle.

And yet, as Józef Piłsudski said, 'to be defeated and not to give in, is victory.' Chin Peng and his soldiers, cruel as they sometimes were, have won whatever it was that Lady Butler's weary guardsmen won. It was a man of his who took away my own sense of collective moral superiority, something with which younger generations in this country are no longer concerned. The Chinese, however – and most of the Malayan Communists were Chinese – still have it. One may call that 'Great-Han Chauvinism,' racial arrogance or whatever one likes. It remains, in my sense of the word, their privilege.   [*1987*

The English Riot

After a great riot, there is much to be cleared away: the rubble, the burned-out cars, the broken glass. But then, for weeks afterwards, there is work to do clearing away the thick layer of nonsense which sifts down like ash from the stratosphere upon us all.

It is familiar nonsense. We hear that the fearful events at Brixton and Broadwater Farm were 'mere criminality,' that they were instigated by professional agitators (the old 'stormy petrel' theory which has attended every disturbance for centuries). We hear that it was all the fault of the police or, conversely, the natural consequence of harbouring an alien, 'ungovernable' race in British cities. We hear the tragic, understandable cry of a policeman: 'This isn't England!'.

But it is. Rioting is at least as English as thatched cottages and honey still for tea. It is right to be appalled when young men – black and white together – burn, loot and rape and fight the police with petrol bombs, knives and guns. But it is badly wrong to conclude that we are entering unknown territory, that a violent break has been made with some 'law-abiding,' gentle past of plebeian Britain to which intellectuals like Orwell, Leavis, even T. S. Eliot, used to appeal.

Before the organisation of a proper police, there were countless popular explosions, from the Gordon riots of 1780 which left over 200 dead in London to upheavals like the Reform riots in Bristol in 1831. People spoke then about 'the dangerous classes,' about 'human vermin' and 'moral sewage.' The London police were first issued with firearms in 1883, when 821 officers received training in their use. There was Luddism, the 'Captain Swing' movement in the countryside, the Rebecca riots in rural Wales.

But in 'modern times,' within living memory, the tradition has persisted. This country was torn by violence in 1919, for example. First came the race riots against black seamen, which flared around all the major sea-ports. Then came the outbreak in Luton, when crowds burned the town hall with petrol; there were over 100 casualties and troops had to be brought in. The next month, the police went on strike in Liverpool, and there followed days and nights of fighting and looting, put down by troops who had to charge with the bayonet while tanks moved into the Scotland Road area. All through that summer, crowds of young people challenged and fought the police in London – in Brixton, Tottenham and Wood Green, among other places.

There were unemployed riots in 1921, and much bigger outbreaks in 1931. In Manchester, the Army was called out in support of the civil power, and the police used high-pressure hoses against the mobs. In Glasgow, the police attacked a demonstration of 50,000 people on Glasgow Green, precipitating a huge riot in which there was widespread looting and the storming of defended tenement blocks.

Behind these full-scale riots, potential violence simmered permanently in the poorest quarters of the cities. This was thought deplorable, but not a cause for panic. Sir Robert Mark, in his memoirs, remembers violent street battles in Manchester as he – then a plain copper on the beat – went in for an arrest. But to him there was something 'cheerful' about it. In such tumults, accompanied by drunkenness and looting at times, 'a good time was had by all.'

Rioting, in short, is one of the instruments of British political behaviour. It is a terrifying instrument, not often used, but it is the traditional resort of those who feel excluded and oppressed by the social and political structure under which – rather than in which – they live.

Home Secretaries, by the nature of their job, are almost bound to overlook this. Douglas Hurd predictably said that all the riots were 'the result of criminal action,' but – as he observed in a striking interview the other day – he is emphatically not a Minister of the Interior. He does not 'command' law and order or tell the police what to do; his job is not much more than mediating between the needs of the police and prison services and the wishes of the Government.

The nation turns to him for the first comment after a riot, but in fact he is only able to mention the problems it sets the police. Unless the Prime Minister chooses to utter, everything about a riot except its 'criminality' aspect will be ignored.

I remember, a dozen years ago, meeting Sir Robert Mark in an Oxford college. Just as I joined the group around him, he was completing a thought. I caught only the last sentence which has, none the less, always stayed in my mind. He said: 'You will see in the next few years that the police will be recognised as the most important social service.'

An indefinable chill settled on me. On the face of it, this was a liberal thing to say: a promise of a new, caring gendarmerie whose task would be not only to repress the villain but to organise youth clubs, tend the single parent, suggest beneficial hobbies to the unemployed. For the Home Office, read the Ministry of Love. And, indeed, Sir Robert's thought has now issued in the ideal of 'community policing' and other hopeful projects.

I don't want to insult all this effort when I say that the Old Bill remains the Old Bill, and the policeman's lot is happier when he accepts that. The police is for enforcing law and order. It is not for alleviating the conditions which give rise to crime, a job for politicians. One of the nastiest features of Mrs Thatcher's Government has been to abandon whole regions of social responsibility and dump the consequences on the police. The miners' strike was one example, and the White Paper on Public Order (offering police commanders essentially political powers over demonstrations) was another.

The 'police as social service' is interventionist. You go into bad areas, you poke about with good intentions, you come on naughty activities and then you have to do something about them. Much trouble has been avoided in the past by leaving 'the dangerous classes' alone in their burrows as far as possible; one thinks of 'Campbell Bunk,' that lawless antheap of old north London, which the police only raided when disorder approached the civil war level. Ferreting about for suspects, let alone frightening ladies into heart attacks or shooting them, would have detonated Campbell Bunk like an ammunition dump.

Much has been written about the history of British rioting. It tends to show that rioters are not all 'scum' or 'criminals,' and that they often have quite a clear idea about why they did what they did. After the fearsome disorders in Watts, California, in 1965, the blacks described their action as a 'revolt' and believed that good would come of it. The mood in Broadwater Farm, even after the atrocious killing of PC Blakelock, is one of defiant pride. They see the police (wrongly) as their enemy: now at last they have fought the enemy, and nothing will ever be the same.

The last word can stay with Jerry White, a contributor to *New Society* just after the inner-city outbreaks of 1981. He wrote: 'Riot has classically been a collective weapon of the politically powerless – to get those with power and wealth to share a little more and to take notice; to effect revenge; and to preserve traditions and rights from attack.' [*1985*

Enforcing 'Culture'

The opera at Glyndebourne, in the Sussex Downs, is a very 'civilised' affair. Londoners who can afford the tickets go down by train to Lewes, wearing dinner jackets and evening dresses, and are taken on to the theatre by coach. In the interval, they picnic on the lawn out of wicker hampers.

Invited to Glyndebourne the other day, I was among the last to climb into the already full coach. In our party was a young woman some eight months pregnant. She stood there in the aisle, and four dozen penguins sat there in their seats goggling up at her. I have to say that, in the end, somebody did get up and give her his seat, after prompting. But during that long, reluctant interval a thought came into my head: 'You are uncultured!'

I remembered this a few days ago at the Edinburgh Festival, where I took part in public debates with Soviet writers and journalists about *glasnost*, free speech and the idea of culture in general. The word *Kultur* set off from Germany in the last century in several directions, and – as it colonised eastern and western Europe – acquired different meanings. 'Culture' is about being well-read and going to operas and exhibitions. *Kultura*, in the Slav sense, is about all that but also about how it is assumed to make you behave.

In the buffets of Polish railway stations, you often find a notice saying that 'we do not serve those who are drunk or uncultured.' To be uncultured – *nekulturny* in Russian – does not just imply that you have not read Shakespeare or Pushkin, or listened to the music of Penderecki or Borodin. It means that you vomit on the pavement or walk around in public with your flies open.

The other day in Warsaw, I listened to a row in a taxi queue between a journalist saturated in vodka and a woman with a bag of shopping. The journalist was shouting about all the books he had written and the brutish ignorance of Poles who did not appreciate them. The woman told him to put a sock in it. The man replied at length that she was pretentious and a whore. The woman, at even greater length, soused him with Poland's incomparable vocabulary of invective and, as she climbed into a taxi, remarked that all the journalist's education had left him with a culture quotient of zilch.

That woman would have agreed with me that the busload of Glyndebourne penguins with their beaks open for Mozart were uncultured. On the surface, there is something very attractive about the notion of culture which permeates all aspects of life, and something depressing about the idea that a man can close a great novel or take Bach off the turntable and be just as foul to his wife or ruthless to his clients as before. High culture which does not overflow into daily life is about as vital as a dollop of aftershave.

But there are problems here. In the very first of these colums, I suggested that the word 'civilisation' was dead. The Third Reich killed it. 'The idea that there was some necessary connection between Beethoven and benevolence, between Mantegna and mercy, collapsed as totally as the Frauenkirche in Dresden . . . It was supposed that something (of high culture) rubbed off. Auschwitz corrected that.'

No general law exists which connects cultural diffusion – the level of literacy, the number of theatres per head of population, the total membership of poetry clubs – to noble and humane behaviour. I am not saying that nothing ever rubs off. Plainly it does. Now that few in England go to church, the reading of novels is probably the most effective training for emotional life – and for distinguishing between right and wrong. The electrician from Gdańsk, Lech Wałęsa, used to say warily that he had never finished a book in his life, but in 1980 it was obvious that characters and ideas from Polish literature were constantly prompting him and his colleagues in the Solidarity leadership. On the other hand, the Russians – who regard themselves firmly as *kulturny* people – behaved like wild beasts to German women in 1945.

The hard-pressed faith of teachers in their job is usually based on the hope that the more boys and girls know and read the less likely they are to become vandals, thieves and muggers. It's an assumption which can never be proved. Children from better-off families show better academic performance, have better job chances and more resources for blameless amusements. Pupils who do well and stay longer have less time to behave badly in the outside world. These are truisms, which don't test that decent assumption which makes teaching bearable.

But how would it be if the proposition were pushed a stage further – if schools were judged not only by their teaching but by the behaviour of their pupils? Just that is suggested by a document circulating in the Department of Education, which has come into the hands of the *Observer*.

This is a 'discussion document' offering a quite new way of assessing the performance of secondary schools – or, as the paper puts it in Thatcherese, their 'value for money'. It is time, the author says, to do away with 'inert performance indicators' like mere achievement in education. 'It is acknowledged that a major deficiency is that the outcome measures [sic.] currently available are limited to those based on examination achievements.' Social behaviour must be taken into account too.

The document suggests that police files on the pupils should be used as an 'indicator' of a school's fitness for investment. Figures for truancy, lateness and absenteeism will also be fed into the computer. So will the proportion of pupils taking part in extra-curricular activities, and even the number of school-leavers from the previous year who 'have an active interest outside work.' Local opinion on how the pupils look and behave on their way to and from school will be another statistical 'indicator' of what value for money the State is earning.

Some people who have seen this fat-headed proposal think it smells of Fascism. That is overdone. To me, it is a perfect example of the ambiguity of Thatcherism: on one side, all the rhetoric about free choice and small government, but on the other side a rapid and highly authoritarian increase of State power.

We hear a lot about how parents should run the schools and also be responsible for the behaviour of their children, in the Victorian way. Here, however, we have a plan to penalise schools, not parents, for what pupils do outside them. Schools would have to enforce not only Mr Kenneth Baker's State-defined 'core curriculum,' but a police definition of good behaviour as well.

The practical impacts of such a policy are easy to foresee. Schools in poor areas would become poorer. The concept of a 'good school in a bad neighbourhood' would be lost. Worse, though, are the political implications.

A wider view of 'culture' which reaches from music and literature to street manners is alluring. But that is the business of society, not government. States which use party members to enforce low-level *kultura* are called totalitarian. States which propose to use school teachers as auxiliary gendarmes patrolling private lives are merely stupid and uncultured. [*1987*

'Don't Be Afraid – and Don't Steal!'

Thomas Masaryk, the father of Czechoslovak independence, once gave his people some advice, as in 1918 they faced the alarming prospect of taking over responsibility for themselves. And it was alarming. Czech nationalism, even on the eve of independence as the defeated Austro-Hungarian Empire began to fall apart, was not the incandescent, totally confident variety. With many Czechs, it was what Dr Conor Cruise O'Brien has called a 'low-intensity wish'; they wanted independence, but were not certain how much they wished to pay for it. Certainly, they did not wish to get shot to pieces for it, as they had at the Battle of the White Mountain in 1621, when Bohemia lost its liberty, or in 1848 when the Prague revolutionaries were bombarded into surrender by the guns of Windischgraetz.

They were not badly off – the Czech level of industrialisation and the standard of living were much higher than those of the Hungarian or Polish subjects of the Austrian Empire, and in some ways higher than those of the German Austrians. The Czechs felt that they had a lot to lose if it all went wrong. All round them in 1918, Europeans were killing one another with relish, waving this flag or that. It was all dangerous. Czech nationalism had been pretty moderate, concentrating on culture and the language but not pressing for much more than devolution. In Vienna, the Czech deputies in the Reichsrat shouted and filibustered, succeeding only in making government more difficult. In Prague, Czechs broke German windows when it seemed safe to do so, or punched Germans at football games. It wasn't noble, but it was, in its sulky manner, a way of life.

But now the Austrian Empire was clearly going to collapse. The Czechs would have to take full State independence, willy-nilly. It had all been decided for them somewhere else, in committees of allied statesmen sitting with Czech *émigré* politicians far away in Paris, London or Washington. Later, Masaryk was to say: 'The future must know how difficult it was to live in a nation which had been liberated but not yet educated for liberty'. But it's all the more remarkable that they did catch up with that education so fast, making out of the new Czechoslovakia the most democratic, prosperous and stable republic of all the nation-states created after the First World War.

Anyway, it was on the eve of independence – or on the brink of the precipice, as it must have seemed to some Czechs – that Thomas Masaryk gave his piece of advice. As a professor and a liberal humanist, he could be long-winded and obscure. This time, however, he was very brief indeed. He said to the Czechs: 'Don't be afraid – and don't steal!'

What did he mean by that? Why should independence suddenly turn the Czechs into a race of thieves, and even if there were to be an outbreak of burglary in Prague after Masaryk had become the first President of the Republic, why should it matter so much? But the Czechs understood him very well. Like the Scots, they had acquired over the years their own double nature, their own Bohemian antisyzygy.

There was the sentimental, emotional side of being Czech: the love of their own history, the telling of tales, the joining in the lovely, melancholy songs everyone knew by heart. But there was also the furtive, sly, materialistic side – the Czechness of the Good Soldier Švejk – with its tendency to malice, envy and selfish greed. When Masaryk said: 'Don't steal', he was telling the Czechs that they would have to rise to their future. If independence was not a moral achievement, it was nothing.

Is there a morality about nationalism? Here at Dunoon, you have been talking about the 'how' questions of a free Scotland – how to convince the Scottish people of your capacity for leadership, how to relate to other parties and movements, how to reconstruct the social and material base of this damaged nation. But there are of course also lists of 'why' questions. Why do you want Scotland to be independent? Why do you demand that this nation – which continues so doggedly but invincibly to exist – should also have its own state? Why should any nation be independent?

I know that every man and woman here has a personal answer to these 'why' questions. Answers like these:- Because if Scotland does not achieve self-government, this society will erode until it loses its identity altogether – 'Scotland free or a desert'. Because independence is the only position from which the Scottish economy can be rescued. Because independence will release pent-up Scottish initiatives and encourage them to breed. Because the St Andrew's House anomaly – an executive without a legislature, government without a democratic component – is a political atrocity, all the more in times when Scotland is repeatedly governed by the appointees of a party which has no national mandate.

All of these are cogent and sufficient answers to that 'why?' They are at the practical, operational end of the range of possible answers. What about the other end? Here we can find statements like 'Independence is the destiny of a nation', or 'every nation has an inviolable right to govern itself'. As far as I am concerned, these remain no more than statements, beyond anyone's power to verify. Bring me a destiny, so that I can dissect it and see if it contains a hunched-up, embryonic nation-state. Bring an inviolable right down to the yard, so that we can run a violate-to-destruction test on it.

It's one of the characters of the Scottish national movement that it has swung between extremes: a humane pragmatism which is not much concerned with general principles, on the one hand, and the outer fringe of metaphysical dogmatism on the other. I mean here the *heraldic-dogmatic*, the nineteenth-century beginnings of the modern movement which almost seemed to argue that if the coat of arms was correct, the free nation would materialise behind it, and the *juristic-dogmatic*, the argument that the nation had automatically regained its freedom of action because the Greenshields Case of 1709 had violated the terms of the Treaty of Union, or by various opimistic constructions put on the United Nations' Charter.

But what about the thought, neither pragmatic nor dogmatic, that the attainment of national independence has a moral end: a condition in which people are not afraid and do not steal? This is not a dimension much discussed in Scotland. Statements that 'it is time to end the begging-bowl mentality', or 'let us get away from the cult of failure', or even 'it is better to die on one's feet than to live on one's knees', while often valid in themselves, do not really fill this gap.

I want to say a few things today about the moral content of nationalism in central and eastern Europe: specifically, in the histories of Poland and Czechoslovakia. Both nations – when I say Czechoslovakia, by the way, I am really talking about the Czechs rather than the Slovaks – assumed that the struggle for self-government and independence had a significance which was not merely political or material. But they identified this moral meaning in strikingly different ways: the Poles seeing in their fight a universal and almost mystical purpose, defined in terms of religion or in terms of the historical designs of providence, the Czechs striving to embody in the independence of their nation a number of more conventional moral values, of which the most important was Truth.

It should not be hard, especially in this nation, to see whereabouts in history the linking of morality with national struggle began. It begins in the Bible, in the story of the Children of Israel. This people considered their search for a land, their sufferings, their exiles as chapters in their long obedience to God, who had prepared a special – sometimes terrible – destiny for them. The Jews were also the first to understand the significance of memory for a nation; the Commandments had to be remembered in order to be obeyed and nothing, not even the worst punishments along Israel's journey, must be forgotten. To remember was their Eleventh Commandment. The Polish poet Czesław Miłosz, in his Nobel Prize speech in 1980, said: 'It is possible that there is no other memory than the memory of wounds. At least we are so taught by the Bible, a book of the tribulations of Israel. That book for a long time enabled European nations to preserve a sense of continuity – a word not to be mistaken for the fashionable term, historicity'.

This recognition of the importance of the story of Israel has always come easily to Poles. Let me quote from another writer, Kazimierz Brandys. In his 'Warsaw Diary' for 1981, he wrote: 'Precisely 24 years ago ... a Soviet writer by the name of Alexander Chakovsky asked me what the Poles' real concern was in October 1956. He used the term "petty bourgeois revolt". I answered that the concern was for moral law. "Well, that's a provincial point of view" the literary representative of a great metropolis said, laughing indulgently. "Judaea was a province too" I said, "a little province that gave the world the Old and New Testaments". Chakovsky grimaced.'

The plight of Poland which bred modern Polish nationalism was unique. Up to the end of the eighteenth century, Poland had existed as a state for some eight hundred years. For 400 of them, it had been the Polish-Lithuanian Commonwealth, formed out of a union between the Polish kingdom and the Lithuanian Grand Duchy which had some resemblance to the Anglo-Scottish Union. It was a large, fairly stable state with a monarch limited by parliament and, in the later period, elected by the noble estate. Compared to the narrow despotisms of Prussia and Russia which arose on either side, Poland was remarkably tolerant and democratic.

But at the end of the eighteenth century, Poland fell into weakness and was partitioned between Prussia, Russia and Austria, finally vanishing from the map in 1795. It did not reappear until 1918. During that century and a quarter, the Germans and Russians, especially, used every kind of terror to eradicate the Polish language, the culture and the Catholic religion, as well as to crush with terrible bloodshed a series of vain national uprisings.

From the very beginning of the partitions, Poles saw their fate not merely as unjust but as a great act of international wickedness. Greed, lies and violence had prevailed over truth and virtue. Just before Poland completely disappeared, the Polish ambassador in St Petersburg wrote to warn his king that the Russian Empress Catherine II intended to destroy Poland by moral subversion as well as bayonets. 'For Your Majesty ought to know that Her Imperial Majesty has conceived a secret stratagem not to allow into positions of power in Poland people who are at the same time wise and honest.'

As the years passed, Polish feelings about their cause began to be expressed in language which was mystical as well as political. The strongest and most gripping of these Romantic metaphors was the idea of Poland as the collective Christ. Especially after the failure of the November Rising in 1831, religious Poles asked themselves – much as the Jews asked themselves in the Old Testament – why God was inflicting this punishment on his own flock. Listen to the answer of Poland's most loved poet, Adam Mickiewicz, writing in 1832: 'Poland said: whosoever will come to me shall be free and equal, for I am freedom. But the Kings when they heard it were frightened in their hearts, and they crucified the Polish nation and laid it in its grave . . . But . . . the Polish nation did not die. Its body lieth in the grave but its spirit has descended into the abyss, that is, into the inner lives of all people who suffer slavery in their own countries. On the Third Day, the soul shall again return to the body, and the nation shall arise, and free all the peoples of Europe from slavery'.

Poland as the Messiah: crucified for the nations of the world, then to rise from the tomb to redeem them by its sacrifice. These ideas did not stay with a coterie of intellectual exiles. They spread throughout Poland, and became one of the most significant ways in which ordinary people understood their own nation.

The historian Joachim Lelewel was an agnostic and a liberal. Yet he invented a theory of Polish history in which he presented Poland as liberty's 'ambassador to humanity'; the darkess of the Polish partitions was only the prelude to the dawn of universal liberty for the whole human race. This was, if you like, Mickiewicz without God.

A great deal has remained from this clump of ideas known as 'Messianism'. The most striking, because it is an approach of the Catholic Church in Poland which is very obviously shared by Pope John Paul II, is the notion that God created Man in three concentric but equally sacred circles: the individual, the family and the nation. The earthly tyrant who raises his hand to destroy an ancient nation is violating God's law as surely as if he were destroying the rights and the moral independence of a single man or woman. In this way the nation also becomes divine, an integral part of God's creation of Man. This is why the present Pope bends down to kiss the soil whenever he arrives in a foreign country.

No idea ever lifted the national cause as high as Polish Messianism did. But, on the other hand, not all Poles were mystics and Romantics. Life had to go on. After another failed rising in 1863, a mood of resignation set in. People asked whether the insurrectionary tradition had not been more destructive than sustaining.

Instead, the case was made for sober hard work to build up the economy, improve agricultural methods, spread basic and technical education. This stream of thought, known as Positivism or as Organic Work, ought to be very familiar to us, for this has been the dominant attitude of many intelligent Scots, including those retiring people in St Andrew's House, for generations. In that spirit, the Polish thinker Smolenski at the end of the last century told the Poles to stop thinking about the loss of State independence as the main event in Poland's experience. The State had gone, but the nation survived. Smolenski wrote: 'The organism we call the State is not the centre of all aspects of life, and its history is not the quintessence of the past. In addition to creating their own State, the Polish nation left a legacy to civilisation which survived the Fall, and this is the main theme of history'.

In the end, these two currents, Romantic and practical, came together, without losing their moral charge along the way. They were both present in the ideals of Solidarity, which was at once a worker's revolution, a national movement to restore the reality of independence to Poland's internal life, and a crusade against corrupted values. This is a paragraph from the Solidarity programme, agreed at the union's first and last congress in 1981: 'What we had in mind (in establishing the union) was not only bread, butter and sausage but also justice, democracy, truth, legality, human dignity, freedom of convictions and the repair of the Republic. All elementary values had been too mistreated to believe that anything could improve without their rebirth. Thus the economic protest had to be simultaneously a social protest, and the social protest had to be simultaneously a moral protest'.

The Czech case was very different. The Poles were utterly confident of their nationhood, of their right to statehood, and that Heaven was on their side. The Czechs were not certain of any of these things by the late nineteenth century. They had lost their independence in 1621, nearly a century before the Scots and 174 years before the Poles. Their ruling class had been slaughtered and replaced by Germans; their proud Hussite Protestantism, not unlike the faith of the Covenanters, with its motto 'Truth Will Prevail', had been crushed by the Catholic Counter-Reformation. When their national revival began in the nineteenth century, the Czechs never imagined they could win by force of arms. As their historian Palacky said then, it would have to be by the force of the spirit. But they did not think of this spirit as if they were the children of Israel; there was nothing inevitable about their victory. In fact the Czechs have always lived with the fear that 'Czechness' – the language and even the national identity – is really quite fragile, something which could actually vanish from Europe altogether. Today, the novelist Milan Kundera, who fears that the whole Czech experiment in nationality may be doomed – *Finis Bohemiae* – can be compared to a prophetic Gaelic writer and thinker like Sorley MacLean. As they work, they have always with them the thought that in a hundred years time, nobody will be able to read their writing without a dictionary.

So, to reassure themselves about the strength of their spirit, the Czech nationalists took some short cuts. In the early nineteenth century it was thought that an authentic nation must be able to show an epic, Homeric remote past.

Vaclav Hanka, the librarian of the new National Museum in Prague, announced in 1817 that he had found an eleventh-century manuscript, a great poem about ancient Czech civilisation in the time of the Princess Libuše. Then came another, the 'Song of Vyšehrad', and then 'The Love Song of King Wenceslas'. They showed that the Czechs had lived in a highly organised and cultured state while the Germans were still rolling about in the mud and eating acorns. Unfortunately, they were all fakes. Hanka had written them himself. The man who finally declared their falsity was Thomas Masaryk. He drew on himself a torrent of patriotic abuse. But he stuck to his guns: the Truth must Prevail, and a national pride founded on lies was worthless to him.

Today, we should be more tolerant than Masaryk. We talk easily about the forging of a nation, but forgery has played a very real part in the foundation or revival of many nations. In Scotland, we should know that better than most. Ossian was a forgery, but the emotions about nation and history roused by James Macpherson's pastiche of genuine Gaelic myth cycles was real enough. Finland's national epic, the 'Kalevala', emerged rather later, but doesn't bear close inspection either.

Welsh heroic poems of antiquity which inspired a generation

of Welsh patriots and Jacobin revolutionaries in the early nineteenth century were written by Iolo Morganwg in the back room
of the King Lud pub, off Fleet Street in London. And don't
imagine this is dead. In the late 1970s, the Soviet press
announced the discovery of the *Vlesova Kniga*, an ancient chronicle of Russian civilisation spanning the era from the ninth
century BC to the ninth century AD, describing how the ancient
historical motherland of the Russians stretched across the Eura-
sian steppes as far as the Amur river. All as phoney as a
Guinness word of honour – cooked up by an *émigré* Russian in
the 1950s – but it wasn't safe in the Soviet Union to demolish
its authenticity until this year.

I am sure that all of us here would agree with Masaryk that
national pride grown in a pot of fraud is just a weed. But these
forgeries have another meaning. In this hall, you have been
working to create a new nation-state, not to revive what is gone,
and the new Scotland will not be the ancient Scotland. The
Irish Declaration of Independence begins: 'In the Name of God
and of the dead generations . . .' Do not let the dead bind the
living, for all the love and respect you have for them. That has
been an Irish problem, and it remains the sickness of the
English, so lost in contemplation of 'heritage' and pageant spectacle that they have no sight of their own national condition.

To use the word 'we' in Scotland is to refer to 'us now': to
we who exist now and not then. Nationalism is innovation, using
selected fragments of the past to build a new house. That is
only forgery if we pretend that the new house is the old one.

Thomas Masaryk thought that nationalism was a way to a
greater, wider humanity, because justice for one's own nation
could not be built on injustice to another. Morality abroad: and
at home. It was the truth that must prevail, as Jan Hus had
said, and prevail without the help of the sword. Masaryk said:
'Unless we have some internal argument for equality springing
from our souls, then only Marx will be able to oppose capitalist
violence with communist violence'.

Some now feel that Masaryk did not know the facts of international life. His Czechoslovakia worked hard, sang well, practised fairness but in the end – at Munich – was betrayed and
destroyed by bigger states caring nothing for morality. But in
another sense he did not fail. Masaryk made a two-way link

between decency and the nation. He argued that nationalism could never become unscrupulous without losing its creative nature, while those who sought to restore decency and honesty could only do so by increasing the independence of their own communities.

'Truth Will Prevail' – 'Don't be afraid – and don't steal'.

You cannot guarantee that a nation-state that applies these principles will never be crushed. But you can be certain that such a nation will rise again.   [*1986*

Lecture to the annual conference of the Scottish National Party.

Scottish Contradictions

'There is a storm coming that shall try your foundation. Scotland must be rid of Scotland before the delivery come'.
James Renwick, on the scaffold in 1668.

I would argue that there remains one, and only one contradiction in Scottish society which is fundamental. This is the old contradiction between self-assertion, and self-distrust.

It would of course be easy to propose many other contradictions. We live in a rich country and yet are poor; we appear to have the means for self-sufficiency, in terms of resources and land, and yet are economically dependent. We consider the further diffusion of political authority, within Scotland as within Britain, as an almost unquestionable good, however we interpret the content of the word 'devolution', and yet Scotland is a country regionalised, fragmented and divided by geography and tradition to a degree which I find frightening enough already.

But I believe that many Scottish contradictions can be discussed within the broad self-assertion/self-distrust paradox. Take for example the mystery of a people almost extravagantly devoted to the events of its own past, and at the same time so amazingly indifferent to preserving the monuments of that past. When Glasgow destroys a mediaeval university to build a goods yard, or when Edinburgh University blows its monstrous and still expanding crater of devastation in the midst of the seventeenth- and eighteenth-century buildings of the South Side, we would appear to be confronting a society which prefers its past good and dead and even dematerialised into myth. The antiquarianism of Walter Scott, who would certainly have fought against both acts of official vandalism, was none the less of this nature. Scottish history was only safe for the historian or novelist to approach and touch when it was certain that the beast's limbs, the Cameronian tradition for example, had finally lost the power of movement. Only then could an Old Mortality be written, even-handedly sanctifying the brave men on either side at Bothwell Brig. Live Scottish history was to be feared. People might act upon it, imperilling the stable order of the present. The battlefield must be tastefully landscaped, a place for peaceful self-congratulation without partisanship except that of the most harmless and sentimental kind. Self-assertion, and self-distrust.

Scotland still suffers from cultural pessimism in an acute, though declining degree. This is an expression with German origins, used to denote an apocalyptic belief in the decline and decay of a national substance and a national morality in the face of industrialisation. The Russians adopted it, as they adopted so many nineteenth-century German ideas, but slightly altered its content: the Russian version of cultural pessimism is the notion that various forces – it could be Tsarist oppression, or the decline of religious belief, or even the experience of the Mongol invasions – had decisively demoralised the masses of the people to the point at which they were 'dark', a force which if unleashed could produce only chaos and anarchy. The corollary, of course, is that democracy has become impossible, and that such a country can be ruled only by an autocracy or by some limited élite composed of the enlightened. (It is interesting to see such ideas forcefully expressed in the political writings of Amalrik and Solzhenitsyn, the Communist régime playing the part of the demoralising force.)

We do not have our Solzhenitsyn, but we have our cultural pessimists. Take the case of Mr Norman Buchan MP. No man knows better, or loves more the popular culture of the Scottish people. Few have done more to defend and encourage it. And yet the very extent of his knowledge dismays him, understanding how much has been irrevocably lost and destroyed by Scots themselves. More than most people, he is aware of the erosion of Scottish self-confidence, and in consequence he cannot believe that Scottish self-government can be other than the handing-over of society to these destructive forces: petty, philistine, and repressive. Only internationalism, in his case socialist internationalism and brotherhood, can make Scotland progress and save it from itself. Such is the sense which Mr Buchan might give to 'Scotland must be rid of Scotland before the delivery come'.

Before going back to this question of internationalism, I would like to raise another symptom of the contradiction which may be called 'Dochertyism'. Docherty, an Ayrshire coal miner in the early years of this century, is the central character in William McIlvanney's novel of that name. He is a powerful, loyal, indomitable figure. And yet his own son grows up to call him a coward. When it comes down to it, Docherty's response to his own situation is a moral rather than a political one. 'They' can take everything away from a working man, he believes, but a fight can be put up to stay human, to behave decently, to prevent 'Them' turning a man and his family into animals. When another son gets a girl into trouble, he throws him out of the house. His politically-minded son, however, dismisses this moral form of last-ditch resistance as worthless, the comforting delusions of the wage-slave.

'Docherty' tells us something about the depoliticising, socially disabling effects of hard times. In Scotland, these times are still upon us in reality and in tradition and living memory. Tam Docherty was free with his fists, where honour was concerned, but never found – in his own times – a way to change the system. Self-assertion and self-distrust appear as consequences of the Industrial Revolution and of economic exploitation. The Euro-Scot report stands as evidence that Scottish generations still continue to grow up feeling degraded, resentful and hopeless, prisoners of our primal contradiction.

Empty Scottish rhetoric of self-assertion would fill a small, sad dictionary. 'Tartanry' is familiar enough, and the private touchiness of the wee mon is familiar too. Modern Scottish society is notoriously marked by the lack of a large, confident and politically influential middle class, a lack which made scarce the bourgeois value of tolerance. But did not Labour, which more or less inherited Scotland this century from the Liberals and the Church of Scotland, develop its own rhetoric of self-assertion which became empty too? Socialist internationalism, which once meant something in the days of John Maclean and Willie Gallacher, seems to me often to serve a deliberate avoidance of the issues. Those who resist devolution on the grounds that they are 'internationalists' usually turn out to be 'British patriots', the most insular and isolationist of all creeds. Politicians who say they want Scottish self-government in order to end a separation from the outside world rather than to commence one, seem to be on harder ground.

I would like to speculate a little more about the extent to which Labour has succeeded, if not replaced, the presbyterian churches as the pervasive authority in Scottish life. The Church of Scotland, based on the small community, was not easily adaptable to the sudden emergence of huge urban proletariats and has often lost touch with the industrial worker. In such areas, the control of preferment and social assistance and even the provision of a world-view has generally passed to the Labour Party and to some extent to the trade unions themselves.

Without minimising the secular scale of this change, the Party none the less inherited much from the Kirk. In particular, the self-assertion/self-distrust contradiction has been carried on.

Both were organisations whose legitimacy was traced back to an original rebellion. Labour arose from the revolt against nineteenth-century *laissez-faire* capitalism, the presbyterian churches from the revolt against the Papacy and the established ruling groups of those times. Both institutions maintained this rebellious, levelling stance long after they had gained effective control of the societies they arose to emancipate. Inevitably, a degree of false consciousness arose as the original enemy diminished into history. The self-assertion which strikes defiant postures against a departed enemy becomes an empty self-assertion, whether it is Davie Deans ranting against the persecutors of the savoury remnant or a Labour politician blaming the defects of municipal housing on the machinations of fat cats in the City who want to restore total free enterprise. The problems of eighteenth-century small tenants were not encompassed in the threat of a Stuart restoration, any more than the problems of a miner at Newcraighall are summarised in the possibility that the Earl of Dalkeith wants his pits back. The real enemy was, or is, different.

Twice in Scotland, then, the party of rebellion has become the party of authority. Self-distrust, doubt about the individual's entitlement to realise his own potential through social action, has often been enhanced by both powers. Take, for instance, the sections of the Longer Catechism dealing with the commandment to honour thy father and mother. It is explained that 'father and mother' signify authority in general. The catechism details the duties of inferior to superior – and vice versa, because this is not an autocratic social creed: the superior has his obligations too. But social bonds are described exclusively in terms of duties, never in terms of rights.

Much the same attitude has been discerned by Labour's critics in the party's approach to local government. The party member or council tenant is expected to fulfil his duties of turning out at election time or paying his rent, but he is not very effectively encouraged to participate between times in the running of his own party or community. He has rights (we should remember, by the way, that the Longer Catechism was composed over a century before the formulation of the concept of the rights of man), but the exercise of those rights is largely performed by elected authority on his behalf.

Scotland never had a great laicising movement, even though it was one of those countries – unlike England – in which the church exercised an influence which sometimes reached theocracy and often approached it. This is unusual in Western Europe, with the Irish exception. Such a laicising, liberal movement in politics has been a condition of the modernisation of such a society in terms of social attitudes. Its absence, as a great source of national and personal confidence, as an educative force, leads famously to queer misperceptions. Poland never had such a movement either (like Scotland, never having experienced the rule of a confident and prosperous native middle class). Just as Polish workers will riot in the belief that the Communist government means to abolish Christmas or exterminate its own people by free contraception, so a Scottish worker will – in some parts of our country – do violence for the contorted superstitions of Orangism.

Our country is very individualist, but not very democratic. Self-distrust has focused on the possibility of self-government, as if national feeling and pride were – in a contradictory manner – private emotions which had no place in the public domain. The Scottish version of history seem to oscillate between extolling the virtues of passive suffering and glorifying moments of volcanic, almost involuntary violence. Where are the episodes in which the Scottish people, by holding together and labouring patiently and wisely, achieved something?

We are beginning to escape from the great contradiction now. But self-government, even independence, cannot normalise Scotland by themselves. They must lead on to a cultural revolution, a society in which the people rebel, easily and goodhumouredly, every day of their lives. Then, and not when we are rid of ourselves, will the delivery come.   [*1976*

Paper for the Church of Scotland Colloquy on Devolution.

Stonehenge and its Power Struggles

It's startling to meet a revolution in a museum – especially in the National Museum of Antiquities in Edinburgh. But the new exhibition there, 'Symbols of Power at the Time of Stonehenge,' is a revolutionary act. It breaks with the old traditions of British archaeology. It nails up a recklessly bold manifesto about the nature of the past. It challenges us to reason about both past and present in a new way.

What is shown is astonishing enough. It is a blaze of ancient gold, of arrogant treasure in metal, stone and pottery gathered not only from Scotland but from all over Britain, from France and Holland and both Germanies. It is rich for the imagination; you sit within the replica of a stone circle from Aberdeenshire, watching dawn and dusk pass over the hills it has guarded for 4,000 years while the crows chatter in the trees, and the spine creeps. You see the building of Stonehenge in computer graphics, or the almost Japanese lightness of a wooden shrine from Bargeroosterveld in Holland. You are on the threshold of sensing how lost peoples connected reverence with power.

But the theory being put forward is more exciting still. David V. Clarke and his colleagues who made the exhibition think they know how inequality began, in the centuries between about 2500 and 1200 B.C. The leaps and assumptions they make have appalled some archaeologists. This is as momentous a rebellion for prehistory as the 1874 *Salon des Refusés* was for painting.

The theory runs like this. In about 2500 BC, people lived in small farming settlements in a state of primitive equality, worshipping their ancestors in communal tombs containing the bones of generations. Gradually communities linked together into regions. A new sacred leadership could call on enormous reserves of labour to build communal monuments, like Stonehenge itself. This new power élite claimed that it could communicate directly with the gods, no longer through the mediation of the dead ancestors in the tombs.

As time passed, new élites arose to challenge the power of those who controlled the monuments. (Clarke and Co. have no time for old theories about successive invasions to explain cultural changes: they see change as the product of internal social power struggles.) These new groups possessed the secret of metalworking, a hereditary craft which soon transformed the families who possessed it into a dominating class.

The old sacred leaders fought back, heightening their prestige with even richer regalia like jadeite axes and ceremonial stone maces, and huge crescents of beaten Irish gold which they hung round their necks. But they were doomed. By about 1700 BC, the metal workers' power was triumphant. They took over and adapted some communal monuments, like Stonehenge; others fell into disuse. The new rulers expressed their power and ideology by gorgeous individual burials. The age of collectivism was over; the age of individualism and of class power had begun.

The force of the Edinburgh show is double. First, there is this new account of history, a flag bravely run up which may well be shot full of holes. But the second impact is deeper. Archaeologists are daring to speculate at last, to go beyond mere accounts of what is found to guess about what sort of people and communities produced the finds.

For generations, prehistorians have played safe by sticking to 'fact,' to recording and comparing pottery fragments, postholes, arrowheads. Fantasy and generalising were disreputable. Museums became the dull places they mostly remain. No wonder the late Sir Mortimer Wheeler barked: 'We have been preparing timetables: let us now have some trains!'

Then, some 15 years ago, the 'New Archaeology' began to hit this country. It sent trains rattling off in all directions. It demanded that scholars and diggers should have ideas and prejudices. It said that it was nonsense to expect 'facts' to 'speak for themselves': the archaeologist was merely listening to his own preconceived ideas without admitting it. The American J. R. Platt wrote scathingly: 'We speak piously of taking measurements and making small studies that will "add another brick to the temple of science". Most such bricks just lie around the brickyard.'

This approach, born of the new philosophy of structuralism and the older doctrines of Marxism, turned 'the scientific method' on its head. A digger no longer opened a burial mound to 'see what the evidence says.' He made his hypothesis about its meaning first, then excavated to see if the contents proved him right or wrong.

Archaeology had blown up. And in the confusion, archaeologists darted about looting other disciplines: anthropology, cybernetics, sociology, aesthetics. A frightful jargon rose and mercifully fell again ('a single multistage cultural assemblage system trajectory!' exclaimed one zealot over something or other). But the profession was liberated. In the past, archaeologists felt that their science was immature, even inferior to other, older sciences; they feared that if they pushed out their frontiers beyond their trays of bits and pieces, some academic

Jupiter would crush them for presumption. Now, as Edinburgh shows, they have come of age.

'Symbols of Power' teaches us that nothing is static, that communities 4,000 years ago lived in a condition of social change and political competition as communities do today. This is the importance of junking the 'invasion' idea, which implied that ancient people lived in an unchanging eternity until alien immigrants rushed in to inaugurate a new period of changelessness with different equipment. On the contrary, it seems that around Stonehenge there lived conservatives laden with gold and divine knowledge, scheming to defend their influence against local rebels and sceptics – who, in turn, chafed to get rid of the old frauds and run things in a modern way with Beaker pottery and metal tools.

But the exhibition – and the New Archaeology that lies behind it – are also about ways of looking at Britain now. They are a call to look at a city street with its own symbols of power – the BMW, the police uniform, even the girl's vermilion hair – and to see them as signs of displayed wealth, of state authority, of aspiration, rather than just as 'facts.' They suggest that when we buy a newspaper we should examine how it fits in with our ideas about its owner and his ambitions; about its selection of news to suit his interests; we should not let its contents 'speak' for themselves.'

When the rulers who controlled the communal monuments ordered those gold crescents, they decorated them with precisely the patterns used on the Beaker pots preferred by their adversaries. This was very 'English,' in our own terms. They were trying to stop the rot, to stop history, by disguising the old order with the superficial fashions of the new.

England teems with this sort of thing. The cathedral has a disco in the crypt, the prince affects the language of 'street credibility.' Or – a favourite of mine – we have adopted the idiotic term 'stately home' for huge buildings which have been centres of power affecting the lives of hundreds or thousands of people, whose function as a 'home' has been in comparison trivial.

'Symbols of Power' (open till mid-October) lets its visitors stumble into the street resolved to hold opinions, to be critical, to refuse to accept objects and sights and pageantry for 'what they are.' Charles Darwin said: 'How odd it is that anyone should not see that all observation must be for or against some view, if it is to be of any service.'   [*1985*

The Means of Grace, the Hope of Glory

Work is a dull way to get rich. In spite of all Mrs Thatcher's coaching, the people of these islands – the English in particular – remain attractively lazy. Even those who are still in work fantasise about a miraculous windfall of wealth allowing them to knock off for keeps. Although it's a fact the middle classes prefer not to know, most people in this country have reached their earnings peak in terms of real wages well before they are 30. The rest is drudgery.

There are daydreams about winning the pools, about legacies from unknown Australian aunts, about (this affects mostly professionals) being monstrously and unjustly libelled by a newspaper. But the sweetest and oldest of these daydreams is summed up in two words which still accelerate any heart: Buried Treasure.

The imagined moment of discovery has a force equal to any fantasy about sex or glory. Yesterday, it was the ploughman who stirred with his boot the muddy discs in the furrow and suddenly – with suffocating excitement – saw the flash of gold. Today, it is the bulldozer driver who climbs down to inspect the heap of what seem to be old tin plates and basins, who sees through the oxidised crust the outlines of gods and nymphs playing their pipes and swinging their robes, and knows that he has become a rich man.

This is a venerable country, which has been hiding its treasures in the earth for some 4,000 years. Much has been found, and nobody can tell how much has corroded away to nothing. But under the turf and heather and even under the pavements of Britain, in undiscovered graves and hoards, in stone cists or clay pots or simply loose in the moist earth and peat, there is silver and bronze, jewels and gold in quantities beyond imagination.

Putting it in such a coarse, greedy, even lascivious way will have unsettled every reader who cares for genuine archaeology. But we live in the age of the metal-detector. Thousands of people all over Britain belong to 'treasure-hunter' clubs. Equipped with electronic detectors, they spend their free time sweeping the ground-surface until the detector's murmur rises to a screech. Then they dig.

For over 10 years now, archaeologists and 'treasure-hunters' have been fighting a guerilla war. Professionals will tell stories of savage fist-fights in darkness, of shotguns discharged, of night ambushes over precious sites which end in wrestling in the clay and chases over the fields.

Some progress has been made towards an armistice. There are now clubs which have learned to work with archaeologists as a team. There are decent farmers like Simon Drake, of Dorset, who used a detector to collect a medieval coin hoard from his field and reported it to the coroner. But there are still cultural atrocities. Last August, gangs of treasure-hunters got away with over 2,000 Celtic coins from the site of a temple at Wansborough in Surrey, working by torchlight and leaving 'a Passchendaele landscape' behind them.

The law is on the side of the professionals. 'Treasure Trove' was defined 350 years ago like this: 'When any gold or silver, in coin, plate or bullion hath been of ancient time hidden . . . whereof no person can prove any property, it doth belong to the King.' However, if the Crown decides to keep the treasure, the finder is rewarded with its full market value – which, as far as I can see, is the only streak of truly reckless generosity in the entire practice of the British State. (But the generosity has limits. The family of the treasure-seeker who found the Thetford hoard of Roman jewellery in 1981 got only a third of its value, because the find was not reported for over six months.)

On the face of it, this is a straight moral issue between the 'guardian of the national heritage' and selfish, plundering vandals. And yet the row over treasure-hunting and detectors goes back deep into the historical consciousness of the nation. Professor E. P. Thompson's idea of the 'free-born Englishman' and his unwritten rights is in play here.

It is striking that the treasure-hunting movement is very much a working-class affair. When the Council for British Archaeology began seriously to take fright at the damage being done, the clubs attacked the CBA with a revealing line of abuse. They alleged that archaeologists referred to them as 'scum'. They asked by what right a so-called intellectual élite claimed to own Britain's past, or used state authority to block the harmless pastime of ordinary folk out to make a few bob in the open air.

There were elements of an ugly, 'know-nothing' populism in this. And it felt like a populism of the Right. One hunter referred to 'the smear campaign being conducted against us by the KGB – sorry, CBA . . . more fitted to publication in Peking or Moscow than in London.'

But behind this bluster there is the memory of a genuine tradition, of a poor peoples' dream handed down from one generation to the next. For the man who finds a treasure is a free man. The ploughman who comes across a crock of gold can cock a snook at the lord of the manor, buy his wife a silk gown and depart. The stonemason who finds a Roman proconsul's ransom of silver under the wall has escaped his foreman, his debts, his appointed station in life, for ever.

And in a static, class-bound rural society, in the centuries before football pools or labour mobility, what other escapes were there? One might run away, hoping to become more than a 'sturdy vagabond'. One might join an army, with the thought of being made a captain for valour or sharing the plunder of a sacked city. None of these compared with the dream of buried treasure, the golden miracle. Tales of those who had found wealth at the end of their spade or between the roots of an oak tree circulated endlessly. This, perhaps, was what Mr Micawber meant when he insisted that something would 'turn up'.

And it always has turned up. Our first chronicles show an almost obsessive interest in the discovery of buried treasure and the sensational 'breaks' in normal life which follow. The marvellous Lady Chapel at Ely Cathedral is the result of a fourteenth-century marvel; the cathedral tower had fallen and money to build the new chapel had run out, when the holy Brother in charge of the works turned up a pot of treasure. A rain-shower came on; he prudently sent the other workers indoors to shelter while he dug the urn out of the soil and took it to safety. Its riches paid for the completion of the chapel.

The hope of treasure was also the idea of a right – if only the right to luck. But it also held a queer attitude towards the past. Nobody knew why riches had been hidden in the earth, although there was an assumption that there had been a distant age of gold. The past was something which – like grace – might suddenly and almost terrifyingly open itself to a humble person. And that grace should be accepted. When the ancestors gave, who would dare to refuse?

The hill under Richmond Castle opened to a potter named Thompson. In a cavern lay treasure, a sword and a horn. He fled in panic, and a voice called after him: 'If thou hadst either drawn the sword, or blown the horn, thou'dst been the happiest man that ever yet was born.'

I am on the side of the archaeologists, and against the treasure-hunters – fewer, now – who rob us all of our history to fill their pockets. But the professional should not be priggish. He should remember that the man with the metal-detector is a member of the past he is defacing, and that his sense of a right to it can only be modified, never dismissed.   [1985

Secret Passions of the British

'Except possibly for a few last shots, the Battle of London is over.' (Duncan Sandys at a press conference, 7 September, 1944.)

'On the evening of Friday, 8 September, 1944 . . . at 6.34, totally without warning, a huge hole appeared in the middle

of the roadway opposite number 5, Staveley Road, Chiswick.'
('Hitler's Rockets,' by Norman Longmate.)

The first V-2 rocket had landed on London, to be followed by
something like a thousand others. They killed nearly 3,000
people, destroyed about 20,000 houses and damaged 600,000
more. The V-1 flying bombs had caused over 6,000 deaths;
ordinary Londoners were near the end of their tether already.
Now this.

Or rather – now what? The luckless Duncan Sandys,
appointed 18 months before to deal with the rocket threat,
heard the unmistakable double crash of the missile from his
office and knew at once what had happened. But the Londoners
were not allowed to know. For two months, as chunks of
London suddenly disintegrated, the Cockney bush telegraph
tried to make sense of it; here it was a 'gas main,' there, 'some
secret war work' had blown up. But the existence of German
rocket missiles had already been published, and by the time the
Government came clean in November, most people had guessed
what was going on.

One of the queer effects of the V-2s was the amount of dirt
they dislodged. Soot jumped out of chimney-pots, like a row
of black exclamation marks in the sky. Leafing through Mr
Longmate's new book, I was left not only with images of devastation and misery but with a fine, gritty coating of questions hard
to brush off the mind. This apparently transformed London of
1985, this plantation of glass and concrete towers – how far
have we really come from that grimy, class-conscious old city
under fire, and how far from those times when government's
idea of the citizen's first duty was that he should not ask
questions?

The London I saw in glimpses as a wartime child was black,
tremendous and above all silent. Standing outside Euston at
dawn, I once heard the crack and rumble of a distant V-2, a
sound made vast by the utter quiet of streets without traffic.
From a train on a viaduct, I looked down on human beings:
drab swarms among broken buildings. Yet they struck me as a
collective creature with an awareness of its own identity, not a
mass but a people. Where is that people now, or has it dissolved

away into atoms of owner-occupying bliss, tower-block isolation, aimless pilgrimages down the aisles of Safeways?

At this point in reflections, many Socialists grow soggy and maudlin. Then there was a natural radicalism abroad; now, in contrast, the millions passively lap up their opinions from 'the Tory media.' The passivity and the indifference to politics as an instrument of change are real enough. But the opinions? If governments continue to keep secrets from the people, as they did in 1944, then the people have learned in retaliation to keep secrets from their governments.

And these are mostly secrets about their own emotions. When Eisenhower visited London around 1960, an ailing, uninspiring President at the end of his run, nobody expected that Londoners in their hundreds of thousands would quietly leave work and come to line the streets for him as he drove in from the airport. When John Kennedy succeeded him and was proclaimed as the young Augustus of a new Golden Age, I was sent out to sample the 'vox pop.' and found to my amazement that working men and women regarded his election with disgust: bad enough that he was a Papist, but worse – far worse – that he was the son of Ambassador Joe Kennedy, 'that Yank who said we'd surrender to Hitler.'

In a north London shop, the other day, somebody barged a queue for cakes. 'No gentleman!' said the girl behind the counter loudly. 'Never happen in Russia!' added a customer, and suddenly I was surrounded by old ladies telling one another how Russian men stood up for pregnant women on the Moscow Tube, how the Russians knew what to do with muggers, how a Russian mum would never raise a hand to her kids.

So much for 40 years of Cold War. There is an obstinate dream here, the British insistence on feeling a deep, frustrated affection for the Russian people which is now almost unpolitical. And if it has lasted this long, in the teeth of so much, it is obviously here to stay.

And all of these buried emotions, transmitted across a change of generations, find their source back in the experience of war. After so long, they have weathered into disjointed prejudices; like a religion which has decayed into a cult of icons, the coherent view of the world which once gave rise to these passions has fallen apart.

But back then, as the rockets plunged down on London, people felt that they understood something, not just a sense of common cause against the enemy, but a recognition that victory was not enough. And that the enemy was not just abroad. It was an omen that the V-2s, by pure accident, avoided the West End and the districts of privilege more completely than the manned bombers or the flying bombs before them.

Even when Werner von Braun stopped his rockets and was served his first American breakfast of fried eggs, bacon, toast with real butter and proper coffee, the Londoners keeping the rain out with bits of sack and plastic sheeting continued to brood on what his ballistic missiles had taught them. The world was unsafe; it was unsafe because it was unjust; let's make a new one.

Ferdinand Mount writes in the *Spectator* that 'if the experience of the war had done anything, it was only to consolidate the belief . . . in co-ordination, nationalisation and the ability of civil servants to run anything.'

As a report from the bowler-hat zone of London, that remark might stand. As an account of the mood of 1945 at large – and it was very large – it is a joke. People did believe in 'co-ordination,' national and international, because the free play of bankers' economics and extreme nationalism had produced poverty and war. But by 1945, the population had learned to put its trust in firemen and soldiers rather than in civil servants. Nationalisation? Public ownership was seen only as a step towards social ownership, in which industry would be controlled by its own workers.

What the British got, of course, was indeed bureaucratic. The statutes of the Attlee Government achieved a huge stride towards equality and justice which stopped short of any real change in British institutions, and which gave away no real power to the citizens. But Mass Observation in 1947, among other polls, showed Labour voters ready for even greater changes and impatient at the Government's caution. The nationalised industries seethed with discontent and unofficial strikes. The new boards proved as remote from ordinary workers as the old managements.

The mood of vigour ebbed. Gaps in the railings which keep us away from the State and its secret garden of knowledge were repaired. Those who ask too many questions are still considered unpatriotic – or, as we say now, 'divisive.' But somewhere underground there still flows a stream of mingled scepticism and visionary hope, its source far back in a ruinous city whose people discovered that their system of government was even more exhausted than they were.

Old V-2 combustion chambers still lurk in toolsheds, or serve as flowerpots. They helped to give Londoners dreams which are not all nightmares. [*1985*

II

DRUIDS
The Politics of
Unreformed Britain

A Spectator Sport

'The Spectacle has effectively suppressed all genuine play. The desire to play . . . is returned to us as sport, toys, gambling and competition.'

So runs the argument of a pamphlet called 'The Bad Days Will End,' which I borrowed from a young woman the other day. For 'play' one can roughly read 'free and spontaneous behaviour.' The authors are Situationists, members of a perky old sect which, nearly 20 years ago, supplied a lot of the intellectual ammunition for the 1968 students' revolt. They believe – roughly, again – that States maintain their power by mesmerising the people with an endless parade of changing 'Spectacle.' Politics become a variety of entertainment, which offers the individual a completely false picture of what is really afoot. 'The Spectacle' tells him what to think and – above all – trains him to loll back and watch the show rather than to take part in it.

But the tract is disappointingly vague about the remedy. The Situationists deplore technological toys, which you simply watch performing as 'passive spectator.' They recommend instead 'play' which is 'bond-forming and imaginative,' as long as it's not too competitive. That doesn't get us very far. The friend who lent this work to me recently went on a march which invited the City of London to come and play, but she wound up spending the night in a very overcrowded cell.

All the same, the 'politics of spectacle' idea remains alluring. Washington provided a fine example last week, when Jane Fonda, Sissy Spacek and Jessica Lange gave evidence on Capitol Hill on the plight of the American farmer – as actresses who had starred in the latest wave of movies about the decline of family farming. The farmers themselves and their wives sat applauding in the audience. We are told the actresses had learned a lot on location. But this is the start of a road which ends with a peerage for Peter O'Toole for leading the Arab revolt, with Martin Shaw addressing the Royal Geographical Society on Scott's Antarctica, and – of course – with a gibbet out in the sagebrush for the well-known cattle rustler Ronald Reagan.

Mrs Thatcher's Britain uses the politics of spectacle in a very obvious way. Her public doctrine is an exhilarating call to the individual to 'play': get out there, grab the ball, ignore the restraints of team and rule and just start scoring. The reality, however, belongs to the unemployment figures. Every month, there are fewer players and more spectators.

You can see exactly this contrast in the industrial cities of northern England and Scotland. If they were totally derelict, they would be less interesting. But in their once-devastated centres, new and busy little cultures have sprung up as a fortunate few supply one another's needs and tastes with boutiques, word processors and wine bars. And all around this lively nucleus stand the silent housing schemes, inhabited by thousands of human beings with little or no work, and with no apparent relevance to this 'recovery' in their midst.

They have television, which informs them that their rulers regard their plight with grave concern. But the game they watch, when it isn't football or snooker, comes increasingly to resemble musical chairs at a late stage in the round. A few people are still dashing around, ears cocked to the music. But most of the players are out. Being British is becoming a spectator sport.

Neil Kinnock gave us bad history when he said that Mrs Thatcher was creating the conditions 'in which Fascism flourished.' It wasn't political apathy born of unemployment that brought Hitler to power, but the frantic politicisation of a ruined middle class, obsessed with 'national treachery' and 'the Bolshevist menace.'

Our condition is bad, but quite different. The problem in Britain is not a Weimarish glut of politics, but a growing lack of faith in politics of any kind. As Alexander Herzen noticed in nineteenth-century Russia, a sense of irrelevance drives people into quietism rather than revolt; the 'Superfluous Men' in the autocratic years of Nicholas I offered no threat to the Tsar. In Britain today, the awful hang-over after the miners' strike has intensified the feeling that combining and acting to bring about change is a barren form of activity.

When did it begin, this process of turning players into mere spectators? I first noticed it during the 1979 campaign over the devolution referendum in Scotland. The 'No' camp concentrated on one argument which was not so much basic as just base. They didn't bother to denounce the policies a Scottish Assembly might follow. They said squarely that a parliamentary system in Scotland was wrong because the elected members and officials would have to be paid salaries, and money spent on representative government was – don't we all agree? – money down the tube. It was a campaign against politics itself. And, though the 'Yes' voices were more numerous, it won a very substantial vote.

Many years ago, in British Columbia, I remember coming across a born-again Social Credit Premier named Bennett. Vancouver was a pretty innocent place then, and when the Bennett Government started throwing its weight about to the tune of slogans like 'Progress, Not Politics!,' and 'We Prefer Criticism To Come From Within Our Own Ranks,' there were only a few people who thought they had heard something like that before somewhere. Bennett's was a businessmen's government, banging on about free enterprise and every citizen's right to hack down the forests. At the time, it just struck me as eccentric. But now I realise that I heard something like Mrs Thatcher before somewhere.

Anyway, 'Progress, Not Politics.' How much progress there has been in the past six years, and for whom, is debatable. But the retreat from politics is all too marked. One cause of it has been the teaching of successive Labour governments that politics meant only the redistribution of public and private wealth. It followed that when Mrs Thatcher and the monetarists locked away the wealth and closed down the apparatus for redistributing it, there seemed nothing much left to be political about. Especially in local government, most of our politicians have passed their careers arguing about how to divide up the cake. Suddenly, no cake.

Those who have enough originality to conjure up cakes without flour – like Ken Livingstone, that master of 'imaginative play' – are rare.

With the retreat from politics has come a new school of 'spectator studies.' First there was a fad for writing the histories of newspapers. Then there came the vogue for writing history *through* newspapers, the story not of what happened but of what we were told was happening. Northcliffe's press version of the 1916 Cabinet crisis matters more than the evidence of state archives; the miners' strike has already produced far more dissertations about media distortion than about what really went on at the pitheads or in Mr Scargill's executive. 'Manipulation is the message.'

Games with shadows and changing reflections threaten the citizen's most elementary weapon of self-defence: memory. As episodes are presented, then dexterously whipped away and replaced with others, the sense of continuity is lost. It's like settling to a whole evening of television: Brazil was good, but now it's time for Bitburg and then we forget all that for the Scottish rates drama, up to the arrival of the Chinese Prime Minister. Suddenly, you discover that you have been asleep and the screen has gone blank. You go to bed with a splitting spectator's headache. [*1985*

Policing the Market-Place

The trouble about a free market economy is that it requires so many policemen to make it work. Six years into the reign of liberty inaugurated by Mrs Thatcher in 1979, there comes the Home Secretary's new White Paper on Public Order. Another thick salami slice of traditional methods of protest is criminalised. Another instalment of unwieldy weapons is unloaded on the police, who will now be expected to ban or control the route, size, duration or location of demonstrations.

Mr Leon Brittan calls the White Paper 'a libertarian safeguard.' Alexander Herzen called that sort of talk 'coherent rubbish.' Laws which extend the State's power to stop people doing what they want are sometimes necessary. But libertarianism is about letting people do as they please, on the cheerful assumption that what they please will please everyone else as well. A 'libertarian safeguard,' in fact, is a contradiction in terms.

And yet it's a contradiction right at the heart of what is going on in this country. Try the experiment of contemplating those pretty words 'free market.' Probably you visualise a colourful street jammed with stalls; jolly vendors are crying the virtues of rock-hard tomatoes and lovely haddock, with an ear cocked to the offers next door, in case they are being undercut. How nicely it all works, as those who sell cheaply prosper, and those who sell over-priced goods that no-one wants are obliged to wheel their barrows away in shame!

But 'free'? The truth about big markets is that they require big policing. There are people selling stolen goods, and people selling new potatoes which are old potatoes. There are pickpockets. And there are racketeers who take bribes and protection money, with the sanction of a nasty duffing-up, from those who want a stall in a good position.

Another point about markets is that they consist not only of buyers and sellers, consumers and producers, but of tomatoes and haddock. When we talk of a 'free market economy,' we should remember that while all of us are consumers, most of us are tomatoes and haddock and potatoes as well. How free in the labour market is a 45-year-old welder living in a council flat at Gateshead who has been made redundant at Swan Hunter? How free is a smoked haddock?

So it begins to seem a little less odd that a government which has so spectacularly withdrawn from economic intervention in the market-place should also be a government under which the State's coercive power has made its most spectacular increase since the war. There were nearly seven times as many police bans on marches between 1981 and 1984 as in the preceding 10 years.

The miserable whitewash of last week's parliamentary report on the Special Branch hardly conceals the ground-ivy spread of political surveillance in recent years. The slightly thicker whitewash of the post-Bettaney report on the Security Service tried to cover the fact, now familiar to anyone with a TV set, that a right-wing group within M15 had managed to switch the Service's priorities from foreign subversion to the 'inner enemy.' The proliferation of phone-tapping and bugging has defeated Parliament's attempt to discover its extent, let alone to reduce it.

And all this is not because mainland Britain is becoming more rebellious. In the post-war years, when the Communist Party reached its peak of popular support and when – for instance – the old Revolutionary Communist Party (Trot.) was laying down dumps of automatic weapons acquired from returning soldiers, the police manpower allotted to them was only a fraction of the forces now arrayed to snoop on the far Left. The militancy of the trade union movement achieved its high-point in the early Seventies, from which – the miners excepted – it has sagged away. The universities, fizzing 20 years ago, are now, to borrow from Sir Walter Scott, 'as quiet as the grave, or even as Peebles.'

So this arming-up of the State is about something else. To say that the freer the market-place, the more police it needs, is only half the story. It is also true that if one kind of control is scrapped, another must be introduced; new liberty offered by one hand is promptly pocketed by the other.

If the Government withdraws from industrial disputes, that merely means that some other limb of the State will be appointed to cope with conflicts left to boil over. The flat refusal of Mrs Thatcher and the NCB to talk to the miners was a sham gesture, for the job of preventing trouble was delegated to the police. And when they were ordered to force entry to the pits for strike-breakers, all police commanders in coal-mining areas knew what would happen. They and the mining communities paid a bloody price for that fake 'non-intervention.'

So 'small government' really implies 'big police.' A police magazine took the point during the miners' strike, when it asked: 'Are we here enforcing law and order, or enforcing the Government's policies?' The same question returns with this White Paper. The 'senior police officer on the spot' is now to decide where demonstrations may take place (and *if* they may take place, if they are marches), how long they may last and – most absurd of all – how many people may attend them.

It's not just that these are fussy and fatheaded restrictions on liberty, worthy of the Habsburg dynasty in its senile years. It's not even that they won't work in practice. It is that these decisions are political decisions, absolutely party-political decisions, on which Labour supporters would hold one view and Conservative another. Police officers have no business to regulate political life in this way, and they know it. They face a wretched choice: to ignore these new duties, or to behave like a party gendarmerie.

Foreigners might be forgiven if they thought that 'English bobbies' were being transformed into a ZOMO or a *Volkspolizei*. But what is emerging is not so much a police state *à la polonaise* or *allemande* as a disastrous and increasingly dangerous weakness in British institutions.

The English have never come to terms with the existence and nature of the State (I say 'English,' because the Scottish constitutional tradition is a Continental one and more realistic about these matters). There is no constitution, no doctrine of popular sovereignty; merely the archaic notion that Parliament is absolute and tells its state servants what to do in the name of us all.

But the other day a shaft of light burst into this attic of seventeenth-century junk which passes for British constitutional thought. There was a great kerfuffle during the Ponting trial, when the judge and the Attorney-General suggested that the interests of the State were whatever the Government said they were. Unfortunately, those gentlemen were dead right. The British State is not impartial but is the instrument of whatever group happens to hold power in society.

So let us follow this discovery to its conclusions. Let us be French and have politically appointed prefects to replace what's left of elected local government. Let them, as delegates of Whitehall and the Cabinet, take political decisions about demonstrations and marches, instead of pretending that these are just pavement-clearing measures suitable for police discretion. And then, when we have admitted to ourselves how powerful and political the State has become, we will be in a better position to build modern and effective defences against that power.   [*1985*

Druids

I seem to have upset a number of readers, most of them Welsh, by pointing out the importance of forgery in the forging of a nation. Let me try to sort this out. I was not saying that nations have to pass an authentication test, like Hitler Diaries, before admission to the UN. Their validity doesn't stand or fall by the element of fakery or fantasy which goes into creative nationalism.

Painters of portraits depart, sometimes amazingly, from the precision of a photograph. Novelists are by definition liars. In fact, as Muriel Spark once remarked, they are also theological criminals of the worst kind, for they create human beings without the power to redeem themselves. None of this matters when it comes to judging the soundness of a portrait, a novel or a nation.

What does matter is that historical nonsense can get in the way of progress. A people which clings to a quite fraudulent vision of its own nature and the origin of its institutions is revealing that it is in bad trouble, that it is refusing to adapt to new conditions in case its whole social structure falls apart in a cloud of rust. Britain seems to me to be suffering from trouble of this kind. Accordingly, as this was the week of the Summer Solstice in which the Druids were forbidden to appear at Stonehenge, I have decided to write about Druids.

The first point, which still dismays some people in spite of the popularisation of archaeology in recent years, is that Stonehenge and the Druids have nothing whatever to do with one another. Stonehenge is a megalithic monument erected some 4,000 years ago by people whose language and beliefs remain unknown. The Druids, as far as we can make out, were a priestly caste common to the Celtic peoples who inhabited northern Gaul and the British islands in the centuries before and after the Roman conquest.

But the question of who the Druids really were and what they did is less interesting than the revival of the 'Druid idea' in recent centuries. Welsh, Irish and, to a lesser extent, Scottish cultural nationalism disinterred this pagan Celtic priesthood and invented suitable myths about it. Much more extraordinary, the English did so as well, although the Druids had no more connection to the Saxon-Norman tradition than they had to Stonehenge. The Druids and the 'Ancient Britons' were co-opted by the English as ancestors of the modern British State.

Virtues which were – and are – thought of as English were given pedigrees, back to the 'dark groves' in which priests, clad in white, sacrificed bulls with golden sickles. When Milton wrote to Parliament in 1643 to argue for a divorce law, he claimed that 'it would not be the first, or second, time since our ancient Druides, by whom this Island was the Cathedrall of Philosophy to France, left off their pagan rites, that England hath had this honour vouchsaft from Heav'n, to give out reformation to the World . . . Let not England forget her precedence of teaching nations how to live.'

There was some argument about whether heathens supposed to have burned people alive in huge wicker containers could properly be seen as precursors of the Church of England. But by the eighteenth century, the Druids were generally seen as pre-Christian Christians with a gentlemanly taste for the countryside and a passion for patriotic liberty. William Blake came to believe that 'the patriarchal religion,' including that of Jesus, began in England: 'All things Begin and End in Albion's Ancient Druid Rocky Shore.'

When Labour MPs dedicated to pulling Britain out of the Common Market sing 'Jerusalem,' they are actually singing about the Druidic origins of Christianity. Blake's mystical Anglo-centric nationalism suits them well.

Have we got the Druids finally out of our system? Certainly, with the exception of Wales, self-declared Druids are thinning out. Since 1919, five different Druid bodies have lodged requests to celebrate Midsummer Sunrise at Stonehenge, but only one – the British Circle of the Universal Bond – seems to survive. The Ancient Order of Druids, a secret society established in 1781, enrolled the young Winston Churchill at a ceremony in 1908, and is still going. Apart from that, English

Druidism seems to have faded into the woolly paganism of the Peace Convoy.

But in another sense, we are still living in Druid country. Everything in England, in order to be good, has to be ancient. This attitude has two results. One is the unfortunate assumption that what is ancient is therefore good. The other is the habit of pretending that institutions and rituals invented rather recently are part of the Ancient British fabric. In the dim, hallowed places where Britain worships itself, many of the bones in the reliquaries are made of celluloid or even polyester resin.

The 'age-old pageantry' is often newer than living memory. Many royal rituals, including much of the coronation service, are concoctions, and the uncritical reverence for royalty is not very old either. With a few exceptions, the orders of chivalry are Victorian. The English rural landscape, so 'immemorial,' would make Milton suppose himself in a foreign country. Parliament meets in the replica of a Victorian chamber, but the nature of party, Cabinet and State have little to do even with the nineteenth century.

This modern Druidism (this habit of assimilating the new into the old) can be seen as a wonderful capacity to adapt without pain. But Britain pays – increasingly – a penalty. The mania for continuity is obscuring the difference between what is new and what is not merely antique but thoroughly worn-out.

Curiously enough, the only British institution not considered to have venerability is the economy. This leads to what, in my view, is the fundamental misjudgment about this country: 'Britain has the finest institutions in the world, but they find it hard to function properly just at the moment, because our economy doesn't work.'

The truth is the exact opposite. The reason that Britain's economy doesn't work is that British institutions are in terminal decay.

The decay is at its most advanced in the proudest institution of all: in Parliament. At a time when state power is stronger and more pervasive than it has ever been in years of peace, the citizen has less power to examine and to fight against official decisions than in any other democracy.

England in the seventeenth century experienced the first

modern revolution. Parliament destroyed the absolute right of kings, but took the doctrine over itself. This doctrine of the unlimited sovereignty of Parliament reached its full, absurd stature in the Victorian age. It has become as much of a Leviathan as the divine right of kings, preventing the emergence of any doctrine of popular sovereignty, of any constitution which puts the people and their charter of rights above Westminster.

A Parliament which claims it has total power cannot, rather naturally, face up to the fact that the state machine has now escaped its control. It cannot supervise an economy. It cannot share power with its subjects, or imagine anything except the House of Commons which could represent them or defend their rights *against* power. It cannot imagine being overruled by a Constitutional Court. Like an animal, it cannot think about itself.

And yet there are still those who believe that this archaic doctrine must not be touched, that this is still the same Ark that 'free-born Englishmen' built three centuries ago, that it is the rabbit's foot which keeps nasty things away. Now, that is what I mean by Druidism. [*1985*

Mr Gladstone the Land Raider

The small houses stand far apart from one another, and yet are related. On the low-lying ground of the west coast of Lewis, or South Uist, the houses seem to float on the land like separate ships in a convoy. This isn't a group of individual farmhouses, neither is it a village. It is the rarest of British communities: a crofting township.

There is no more ancient form of community in all Europe. It is the nearest thing to a peasantry that Britain can show. It is a community which treats land as a joint possession; the township has common grazing land for its members and, in a very few places, still ballots each year for who will till the patches of 'inbye' arable land. Most of Europe, it would seem, lived in this way in the Iron Age. Much of Africa still does.

Just a hundred years ago, Gladstone's Government passed the Crofters' Act of 1886. It was one of the most extraordinary, 'un-British' and imaginative laws a London government ever put through. Its importance was not merely that, without the 1886 Act, there would now be no townships, almost no people in the Isles and 'crofting counties' and – pretty certainly – no living Gaelic language. It was that the Act broke totally with the dogma of *laissez-faire* and market forces, and with the British tradition – still in force now – of an uncontrolled free market in land.

The Crofters' Act did not 'give the land to the people.' The landlords still remain. But their rights were broken. The Act gave crofters security of tenure: they could no longer be evicted at will. It established an independent body to set 'fair rents.' It allowed the crofter to leave his tenancy to his children. Many newspapers of the day, backing the enraged landowners, called it pure communism, and screamed even louder when later Acts set about the purchase of land to redistribute to the crofters.

So ended the miserable tale of the Highland Clearances, the century during which the landowners – often the old clan chiefs – coaxed or violently drove their tenants off the land and into emigration. In non-Gaelic Shetland, the 1886 Act was an even greater day of liberation. It broke overnight the debt-slavery through which merchant lairds forced tenants to pay rents in fish and buy goods with truck-tokens at the merchants' stores, on pain of eviction.

The Act and its successors recognise something which is anathema to our present rulers: the State's duty to help a people's wish to stay in a land and a way of life that they love. In their long struggle, conducted by land raids, occupation and fights against bailiffs, police and troops facing men and women armed only with sticks and stones, the people of the Highlands and the Islands challenged the very principle of private property. A Tiree crofter imprisoned for a land raid said: 'The earth belongs to the people, and not to the Duke of Argyll or any landlord.'

The crofters did not ask to own their fields as individuals.

They used the Bible to show that land should belong to the people as a whole, as the soil was apportioned among the Children of Israel in the time of Moses. The Highland 'land leaguers' formed a close alliance in the nineteenth century with those who fought the land war in Ireland; Parnell spoke for them too, when he preached 'the eternal truth that the land of a country, the air of a country, belong to no man. They were not made by any man and they belong to all the human race.'

One might have expected that this centenary of the Act would be widely celebrated. There have been commemorative exhibitions in Stornoway and Edinburgh, and a fine historical picture-book, 'As an Fhearann' (From the Land) published in English and Gaelic by Mainstream, of Edinburgh. But contentious Scotland is still divided about the crofting question.

Professor Gordon Donaldson, the Historiographer-Royal, advised the Post Office not to issue a special stamp, on the grounds that the Act had been a disaster which only led to more emigration. Professor T. C. Smout makes the same point and calls the Act 'an economic irrelevance.'

It is true that the Highland population dropped even more rapidly after 1886, falling by nearly 30 per cent between 1881 and 1931. This was mostly due to the decline of the fishing industry and to better communications with the Scottish cities. Land hunger remains, and the need of the crofting communities to regain huge tracts of pasture taken from them before 1886 to be used as private sheep farms and deer forests. But the biggest truth is that, without the protection laws, the Gaelic community would by now have entirely vanished.

Problems remain. Soldiers returning from the Flanders trenches seized acres which they considered they had redeemed with their blood. The last wave of land raids took place in 1948, in Knoydart. Even today, 0.01 per cent of the Highland population own two-thirds of the area, 38 people own 84 per cent of Sutherland, and 76 people own 84 per cent of Rossshire. Almost all crofters supplement their incomes by fishing, weaving or commuting to light industry, and – especially on the mainland – the need to regain estate land for township common grazings remains desperate.

Crofters do not regard themselves as romantic earth-nurture people. In the right conditions, crofting could be a highly efficient form of land use. As a Crofting Commission report put it back in 1937, '(the crofter) has long since rejected the role of the noble son of Nature who rejoices in homely fare . . . he prizes his Gaelic culture, but not to the extent of being treated as a museum piece.'

But this is a story important not only for a part of Scotland. Meditating on the 1886 Act, one can draw lessons for the past and present of Britain. The first is that the Act would never have happened without the background of the tremendous unrest in Ireland, leading to the land reforms which broke up estates and redistrubted them to the peasantry. In turn, this huge break with British reverence for landed property was possible only after the experience of land reform in India. Lord Napier, whose commission preceded the 1886 Act, had been the administrator of Madras.

And to look back on the superb figure of Gladstone himself is to understand what we have lost; a gigantic confidence. This year is also the centenary of his fall, betrayed and defeated in his attempt to carry the Irish Home Rule Bill of 1886. Gladstone had the power to challenge all orthodoxies, from the sovereignty of Parliament and the idea of a unitary State to the sacredness of private property and the free market in land. For him, the British Constitution and tradition was not an untouchable Druidic Ark of the Covenant, but something made by men for men, elastic enough to be changed radically in order to fit new needs.

But today, everything has fossilised. Debates on economic policy, civil rights, devolution, show a small-minded terror of making exceptions lest the whole antique British structure collapses. The Crofters' Act would be unthinkable now, and so would be laws to protect the small farmer throughout Britain on the lines of modern French or German practice. This is the year to honour Gladstone, but also to mourn the finest of all Victorian virtues: flexibility.   [1986

Gladstone's Defeat and Our Loss

The anniversary of the 'Anglo-Irish Agreement' is not a very happy first birthday. We have no sturdy infant, but a poor little creature guarded still in its ward by brawny, apprehensive nurses. A friend of mine involved in its conception told me that the Agreement was intended to acquire 'incremental assent' from the Ulster Unionists. Marching, oathing and covenanting, they have so far offered it only excremental dissent.

A hundred years ago, in 1886, another such plan fell dead at birth with a crash that shook British politics for a generation. This was Mr Gladstone's first Home Rule Bill, offering all Ireland a simple, sweeping version of what we would now call devolution.

The 1886 Bill arose from a hung Parliament, in which the Irish Home Rulers led by Charles Stewart Parnell held the balance between Salisbury's Tory Government and Gladstone's Liberals. Late in 1885, Gladstone changed his mind and announced his conversion to Home Rule. The Parnellites joined him, Salisbury fell and Gladstone became Prime Minister at the head of a large majority in the House. A few insects dared to suggest that The Grand Old Man had changed his opinions merely to get back into office. But this, as usual with Gladstone, was a Saul-Paul conversion of fearsome sincerity.

It all went wrong. The Scottish Liberals, for all their Presbyterian revulsion from the 'Papist' Irish, stood firm by Gladstone; so did the Nonconformist Welsh. It was English Liberals – Chamberlain, Hartington, Bright and the rest – who deserted, defeating the Bill and the land reform that was to go with it.

Just before the defeat, at the Bill's second reading, the 77-year-old Gladstone made his last, unforgettable appeal. 'Ireland stands at your bar expectant, hopeful, almost suppliant. Her words are the words of truth and soberness. She asks a blessed oblivion of the past, and in that oblivion our interest is deeper than even hers. . . . Think, I beseech you; think well, think wisely, think, not for the moment but for the years that are to come, before you reject this Bill.'

All the same, they rejected it. But here one has to get a grip on oneself. It's all too easy to surge off on the current of Gladstonian rhetoric – a sensation rather like surfing down a tidal wave of Guinness – and declare that this is the centenary of Britain's last chance with Ireland, that all the bloodshed of the succeeding 100 years stems from England's failure to pass the First Home Rule Bill. That, however, is bad history.

Even if the Bill had been passed, would it have worked? While Gladstone did not ignore the feelings of Ulster Protestants, he grossly underestimated them. It is easy to blame the Tory Unionists for fanning those flames in later years. But Lord Randolph Churchill, a Tory populist, had already taken his opposition to Home Rule to the Belfast crowds, provoking wild riots, and they had been told that 'Ulster will fight, and Ulster will be right.' The writ of a devolved Dublin Parliament would simply not have been obeyed in the Protestant North.

And it was not the débâcle of 1886 which turned Irish nationalism away from the parliamentary track and back towards the Fenian tradition of violence. Gladstone's defeat left the Home Rulers quite sanguine, confident that they would get what they wanted from Westminster in the end. The root of evil lies in Parnell's fall in 1891, after his naming in Kitty O'Shea's divorce. English moral humbug (not Irish Catholic feelings) made Gladstone declare he would no longer co-operate with the adulterer Parnell.

Knowing that Gladstone was the only statesman who could deliver Home Rule, the Irish MPs had to choose between the cause they loved and the leader they revered. Most chose the cause; the party split. A young Irish generation saw Ireland's hero broken because their men at Westminster had bowed to English pressure, and the turn away from the ballot-box and back towards conspiracy and revolution began.

Most politicans invent their own Ireland for themselves. I remember Andy Tyrie, chief of the Ulster Defence Association, telling me that most Northern Catholics were not Republicans at all but secret Unionists. Parnell's people imagined a large number of Northern Protestants eager for Home Rule from Dublin. And Gladstone, too, with his respectable and respectful, 'almost suppliant' Ireland – how much easier to imagine the Irish as the poor cousins of his own Midlothian electors!

And yet there is a great deal worth remembering from the 1886 Bill and the debates it generated. It may not have been a turning-point in Anglo-Irish relations. But it makes amazing reading in Britain today. We live in a State whose constitutional arrangements are stiff with age, hopelessly unsuitable for a modern society but treated – in a superstitious, dogmatic way – as untouchable. A hundred years ago, those arrangements still had some spring left in their timber, and statesmen were not afraid to strain them.

Think of the Devolution Bills of the 1970s, fat catalogues of fiddling little provisions for every detail of the Scottish and Welsh Assemblies. Gladstone's 'Government of Ireland' Bill was just 17 pages long, with a mere 41 clauses. It did not spell out what an Irish Parliament could do. It did the opposite: listed what an Irish Parliament was *not* allowed to do. For the rest, Dublin could pass what laws it pleased.

The financial side of the Bill was marvellously simple and confident. There was almost nothing of the suffocating web of Treasury regulations which now insist that scarcely a penny drops without Whitehall permission, nothing of the dogma of 'unitary demand areas' enforcing fiscal uniformity. In 1886, London proposed to keep coinage issue and Customs and Excise duties. The Irish Parliament could invent and levy any tax it liked, or none. But Dublin had to pay London fixed annual sums for the armed forces, the national debt and the Imperial Civil Service. How it raised the cash was Ireland's affair.

Gladstone's first plan was that the the Irish should leave Westminster. Otherwise they might in theory vote on English and Scottish matters, although English and Scottish MPs could no longer vote on Irish affairs. In the 1970s, this non-problem returned as Tam Dalyell's 'West Lothian Question' and utterly baffled the imagination of the House of Commons, although the proper answer to the 'West Lothian Question' was brief: 'So what?' Gladstone was later forced to climb down on this point, though the Irish were as happy to depart as most English MPs would have been to see them go.

It's true that Gladstone accepted the central lunacy of the British Constitution: the dogma of the total and inalienable sovereignty of Parliament. But his Bill would, in practice, have made it almost impossible for Parliament to revoke Irish devolution. Nobody would dare to try and fence in the almighty House of Commons like that in our time.

After reading the chronicles of 1886, and in spite of all the illusions of that grand debate, I feel a sense of loss. Not so much about an answer to Ireland's misery, perhaps only to be overcome when both sides in the North are induced to hate us more than they hate each other. The loss is a loss of vision, imagination, confidence to change the State's architecture to make room for new times and needs. Gladstone was ready to knock down walls. But the ancestors of our modern preservationists, who are too awed to change a coal-scuttle of the Ancient British system, knocked him down instead.   [*1986*

Telling Sid

'Sid! Sid . .?' But he's gone at last, and none too soon. The British Gas shares have been sold to the public, a national asset has been privatised, and Sid is off the hoardings just as the graffiti artists were getting his measure. Whatever he meant – Shareholders' Immune Deficiency? – he has melted away into the mists of hyperbole and gold-rush psychosis which gave him birth.

Mrs Thatcher calls the process 'popular capitalism.' Britain is now offering crash privatisation courses to governments from Paris to Singapore. One nationalised industry after another is 'floated' and its shares are sold on the market, a process which is to culminate with the auction of British Coal and British Rail.

The Government itself is astounded at the stampede for profit it has unleashed.

But 'popular capitalism'? Contemplating the manifold imbecility of this slogan, the first people I am sorry for are those who really do believe in untrammelled capitalism, the apostles of the free market who dwell in the Adam Smith or David Hume Institutes. Because privatisation, as performed by this Conservative Government, amounts to a custard pie flung in their faces.

Where is the free market in all this? 'Privatisation' simply means the reconstitution of monopolies: public enterprise without competition, but rather better protected against government regulation in the name of the consumer.

Mrs Thatcher went to Hungary and admired the new entrepreneurs there. But what can she say to Tibor Liska, darling of Hungarian and British free marketeers and the most terrifying economic visionary alive, who preaches the endless, shark-pool struggle of entrepreneurs to offer a public service at lower cost? Capitalism is about Mr Jones driving the appalling British Telecom out of business with a better telephone network, or Mr Smith bankrupting Sid with his own gas rigs and pipelines. Not much sign of that.

Secondly, the fact that something like an average of 15,000 people per constituency will have bought shares in these pseudo-private monopolies by the time of the next general election does not create 'popular capitalism,' whatever that may mean. Here we are dealing with a set of elderly, quackish and absurd prescriptions for overcoming 'social divisions,' which have drifted around the Conservative and Liberal parties for generations.

It is alleged that to spread share ownership throughout society gives ordinary people 'a direct stake in the means of production and distribution.' It is suggested that by putting money into British Gas or whatever it may be, classes hitherto outside the capitalist system finally give that system their historic assent.

This is pure nonsense, and in several ways. What has happened is extremely simple. In order to raise cash for tax-cutting, the Government has offered an astute but astonished nation outsider prices for odds-on favourite horses: 'a ten-pound note for a fiver.' In their millions, the British have accepted the invitation to have a flutter. This is nothing to do with normal private investment in shares, as practised by the old middle classes. It is a rapid gamble on a hot tip – something the working class has always been good at.

There is not the slightest evidence that spreading share-ownership affects political or class behaviour. The West Germans have been pursuing a 'property formation' strategy for 30 years, without visible effect; if there are fewer strikes and higher productivity there or in Sweden, it is for quite different reasons to do with better management, better collective bargaining structures and so forth. Even Communist Hungary now sells shares to its population, but at least the Hungarians don't pretend that they are transforming society by doing so.

There is confusion, too, with the rather different idea that private businesses can improve their stability and morale by selling shares to their own employees. In their flotations, TSB, British Telecom and British Gas have all given preference to their own staff. This sort of scheme is puffed as 'co-ownership,' the paternalist way to take the sting out of genuinely radical ideas for workers' control of industry. The figures, however, show that although employees share schemes have risen from about 30 to over 1,000 since 1979, the concept of 'co-owner-ship' is usually hot air.

British Aerospace, for example, sold three million shares to its workers. This sounds good, until you discover that this is just 1.3 per cent of the total shareholding. As Michael Smith remarked in the *Guardian*, if all these worker-shareholders decided to sell their stock on the same day, 'it is doubtful whether it would even register on the Stock Exchange.'

This brings me to a more general point. A lot of sancti-monious guff is still customary at board meetings about 'our duty to our shareholders.' In fact, the individual shareholder is the lowest form of life, as far as the City of London is concerned. Those who keep long-term investments, as opposed to rapidly cashing-in on a good speculation, are mostly passive, infinitely manipulable creatures who seldom turn up to meetings and are quite irritated to be consulted about anything.

They are the earthworms in the garden of private enterprise. They are useful, they appear to consume whatever lowly diet they prefer, but the cabbages and roses go to the gardeners.

And if, by chance, a worm turns (as some did when TSB went public, or when Guinness took over Distillers the other day), they are crushed by the overwhelming power of the great institutional shareholders, the big finance houses, banks and pension schemes which own over 70 per cent of traded shares and almost invariably vote with the board of any company. So much for the myth that the 'little shareholder' – and 99.7 per cent of Britoil's shareholders are individuals – control the enterprises in which they invest.

'Privatisation' of this kind, in short, changes little in the structure of the economy, in the real distribution of wealth and power, or in the tensions between social classes. The one real fact here is that a huge number of surprised but grateful people have been invited to make a quick killing. The result is much as it would have been if Mrs Thatcher and her Ministers had ridden through the land scattering golden guineas to the mob. A gratitude is felt, which fades as the guineas are spent – or are found to be made of zinc under the gilt.

That's all. And yet everyone raves on as if a new age had dawned. People who point out – rightly – that Labour's nationalisations did not transfer power to the people, or even to their employees, seem to think that they can effect that transfer by dishing out share certificates. The SDP, for instance, wants to 'privatise' State industries by handing out free shares in them to the populace. This is a dream world.

As usual in Britain, there is Druidic nostalgia around. Bring back the Age of Gold, in which every yeoman was a merchant venturer. Let me end with a caution. Not long ago, we privatised the British State – through the franchise flotations which began with the Reform Act of 1832. Now we all have our share certificate, allowing us to vote. And do we, even now, really own or control that State?   [1986

The Case for a Bill of Rights

This Friday, Sir Edward Gardner will try to persuade the House of Commons to pass a Bill of Rights. The title is awesome and evocative. It is supposed to recall the 1689 Bill of Rights which – in turn – is supposed to have set the seal on the Glorious Revolution of 1688. What is this project, and does it matter, and do we need it?

It isn't really like the old 1689 Bill at all. The English like to think of the first Bill of Rights as a noble manifesto laying down the principles of constitutional government and individual liberty. This is because the English prefer not to incur the bother of reading it. Actually, that document is a down-to-earth political paper, saying nothing much about inherent and indefeasible this or that but a great deal about the rotten things that Kings have been doing which they must now stop doing.

Sir Edward's Bill, in contrast, does specify general human rights: freedom of association and expression, the right to privacy and a fair trial, and so forth. It consists of the European Convention of Human Rights, which – if the Bill passes – will become a British statute. The Convention is the text on which the European Court of Human Rights bases its judgments, the court at Strasbourg which in recent years has declared so many decisions of the British State to be violations of the rights of man.

There ought not to be any doubt now that liberties in Britain need protection. This particular Government has practised an odious combination of *laissez-faire* in the economy and society with a rapid increase in state and police power over the individual. Few democratic countries with a written constitution would have got away with the Public Order Act, the tilting of court rules against the accused or the string of laws reducing trade union rights – to name a few recent offences.

But we have no constitution and therefore, no defined rights.

The State is happy to be prosecutor and judge in its own cause. Take recent events. The police smash down a journalist's door. They occupy the offices of the *New Statesman* to search them. They also launch cavalry charges against demonstrators at Wapping, in the course of which a number of identifiable journalists doing their job are battered by clubs and trampled by horses. The Home Secretary is responsible politically for the police. But which authority in the land carries supreme responsibility for the defence of press and broadcasting freedom? Stap me, if it isn't the Home Secretary again!

By itself, a Bill of Rights cannot halt a drift towards authoritarianism and towards conflicts born of injustice. But it offers a ledge of legal ground on which the injured subject may stand and fight. By incorporating the European Convention into British law, the Bill – if passed – would save us the slow and fearfully costly business of taking an appeal abroad to Strasbourg. The 'importing' of the Convention raises, however, some ugly doubts in my mind.

The hope of Sir Edward Gardner is that the Bill would 'ensure that the rights of British people are protected by British judges in British courts.' Yes, well ... British judges? With their track record? My own first impulse is to reply: 'Thanks, but no thanks!' If I wanted my rights upheld against Government, I would not feel safe until I found myself up before a German, French, Dutch or Greek judge – somebody who was at least trained to think in adult political terms.

Here we have the Ponting case judge who said that the interests of the State were the same as the policy of the Government of the day. We have Lord Denning observing that justice could not have miscarried in the case of the Birmingham pub bombers because that would imply that the police had engaged in perjury. We have their lordships' judgment in the thalidomide case, when they refused to permit the *Sunday Times* to publish facts of desperate public interest, a decision, which Strasbourg reversed. Thanks, again, but no thanks.

Lord McCluskey, in his Reith lectures, presented this argument against a Bill of Rights as a question: 'Why it should be supposed that elderly lawyers with cautious and backward-looking habits of thought are qualified to overrule the judgments of democratically-elected legislators . . . I do not profess to understand.'

That is all right as far as it goes. But it doesn't go far enough. The Strasbourg judges have, as a matter of fact, delivered some quite reactionary and authoritarian opinions recently. They are not a panel of radicals or liberals. But neither are they 'elderly lawyers with . . . backward-looking habits of thought.'

Many Continental judges are young, energetic, modern-minded and intelligent, and they most certainly are qualified to overrule the judgments of legislators. The real implication of Lord McCluskey's words, which he in no way intended, is that to make a Bill of Rights work, we may need a new breed of judges.

Here, at last, the underlying point of a Bill of Rights begins to appear. The thin end of a gigantic wedge is being inserted. I don't know how much the Bill would do for bullied British subjects. But one thing is certain: it is absolutely alien to the practices and theory of the British State and, if it survived, would begin to subvert, split and topple them one after another. And that is why – on balance – I am for it.

In a leading article last year, *The Times* said that 'at first blush' (I like that) the Bill would seem just another law which Parliament could amend or scrap as it pleased. But it was supposed to be a fundamental statute guiding all other laws, so that couldn't be right. And yet if it were entrenched against parliamentary meddling, that would shatter the whole traditional doctrine of the sovereignty of Parliament . . .

The last blush is the one that counts. The doctrine of parliamentary supremacy is the curse of British politics, the Druidic dogma which makes effective reform of our institutions almost impossible. A Bill of Rights challenges that dogma. It suggests that there should be some authority to which even Parliament – or the Crown-in-Parliament – should be subordinate. In most modern countries, this is a written constitution, which is not just a sacred piece of parchment but a statement that the people are the ultimate source of power, that the State and its legislature and its civil servants and laws are the servants of the people.

It's argued that constitutional reform is of no interest to British citizens, a fad for lawyers and academics. But that has suddenly and rapidly ceased to be true. A poll in 1985 showed that only 55 per cent of the sample thought our democratic institutions still worked well. Nearly a third felt their rights were not sufficiently protected, and 46 per cent wanted a Bill of Rights.

A few weeks ago, another poll showed that the desire for a Bill of Rights had risen to 71 per cent – and three-quarters of the sample knew about the European Court and what it did. This, it seems to me, marks the dawn of a real popular understanding about what is wrong in British life. My fear is only this: that British judges and parliamentarians, by rendering a Bill of Rights ineffective, will create a disillusion so powerful that it will halt this enlightenment in its tracks. [1987

The No-Go Area

Many years ago, when I was even more gullible than I am now, two kind gentlemen took me to a City chop house. They were tweedy, they were fatherly, they had ginger hair growing out of their ears. They were in charge of some money entrusted to them by my family. As later transpired, they were about as honest as night is day.

It was a murky, downstairs place, where men were drinking port from what looked like half-pint tumblers. Suddenly one of those figures rose, and advanced towards me. I recognised a school friend, a merry frivolous lad from a Jewish theatrical dynasty. 'Get out!' he said to me in a terrible voice. 'You here? Of all people? Get out of this place, before they lay hold of you and make you into what they have made of me!'

It was a scene from Victorian melodrama, the speech of the emaciated boozer or gambler who rises from his bed of rags to shriek that warning which always goes unheeded. My friend, however, wore the three-piece chalk-stripe suit of a merchant banker. I tried to laugh. Perhaps he was drunk, or mad. He peered at me, then turned and shambled back to his table. I don't know what became of him. But his irruption, something like that of a Purgatory soul surging out of the dark to seize Dante's elbow, was something I have never forgotten.

This sense of the City as a subterranean place apart, a sort of West Beirut into which fresh-faced lads will be ill-advised to tread, isn't mine alone. It's only spread by events in recent months and weeks: here are streets ruled by Deadly Ernest Saunders; by Halpern of the Topless Fiona with the million-pound salary; by Tony 'The Animal' Parnes, by the Lloyd's militias and the public-school Druzes of Morgan Grenfell. Hundreds of others, their sins as yet unaudited, only sit and sweat. Beirut, too, is a self-regulating city.

Outside those precincts, there is a public inclination to have a good laugh. The City is less stuffy than it was, but its godfathers are still apt to tell the rest of us how we should behave. It's the familiar message about pulling together, working harder, acquiring a new sense of the common weal and not asking for more wages. A thousand Guildhall speeches by nervous politicians still suck up to the City as the mighty cornu-copia of national prosperity, model of financial responsibility and all that.

This is now modified by mention of the odd rotten apple in the barrel. Why this is thought reassuring, I don't know. What if one were to call the City a fine can of corned beef with only the odd maggot?

This thought of preachers whose own state of grace is dubious allows me to recall the mighty Caradoc Evans, once the terror of Godly Wales, whose books were banned from Welsh public libraries. Caradoc Evans, who published some of his cruellest anti-clerical outbursts in the *Western Mail*, was eventually driven to exile in Fleet Street, whence he was rescued by the love of a good, rich woman. Some of his works have just been reissued in Wales, an event as astonishing as if Mr Gorbachov were to order publication of 'The Gulag Archi-pelago' in Moscow. Anyway he would have appreciated all this.

The preachers, wrote Evans, lived off the fat of the land, while the peasants were 'labouring all the light hours to keep them in comfort ... they say to the congregations: "People, bach, we are the Big Man's photographs".' He went on: 'They close the doors of the public houses and open the gates of Sion at a late hour for prayer meetings, and I know of dreadful things that have befallen servant girls at the hands of praying men on the road home from chapel.'

And, indeed, before the Big Bang and the deregulation of the City, grave and smooth faces appeared in the prints and on the screens assuring the 'people bach' that they were the Big Man's spitting images. Now this! And yet our City of the Plain has been spared brimstone. Instead, its vacant thrones are now being occupied by an invasion force of poker-faced old Scotsmen, sent for because the English suppose the Scots to have standards.

When I laugh at all this, I do so uneasily. There is something about the way that the rest of the nation looks at the City which is horrifyingly antique. Here is a place apart yet in the midst of us, which is held to do something useful and even on balance necessary, but which – on the other hand – can only do so by following standards of morality quite alien to most ordinary people. It suits us to harbour this colony of sin, but it is somehow comforting to reflect that its creed is so foreign to our own. . . .

And with that a vision from the past begins to assemble itself. Here is the Christian baron in his castle, with his loyal feudal subjects huddled around the keep, and there – in their own quarter outside the walls – are the fur-hatted merchants who speak strange languages and worship curious gods, who enforce their own private justice and practice wickednesses like usury. They are Jews or Lombards, Scottish pedlars or German craftsmen, but heretics all. Sometimes the baron's men chase them and beat them. But to punish them by death or expulsion would be unwise. Without their money and their learning, how could the baron make war?

And this, roughly, is where we have stuck. Other countries seem to have dissolved the finance industry into their general awareness of what makes up a national economy. The Frankfurt bankers are not loved by most West Germans, but they are certainly not regarded as mysterious. Britain, however, remains medieval in its ignorance of the Square Mile. I suppose that 99 people out of 100 assume that they could never understand what goes on there, and that they would be morally revolted if they did. The grove of glass towers by the Thames is treated still as if it were a foreign enclave, the Kitaygorod of old Moscow.

This, of course, is preposterous. The City has certainly enjoyed and encouraged its protective mystique, inducing the average 'politician bach' to fear that if he brought the Big Man to account, he would come out in boils and every factory in his constituency would close. But the popular combination of dislike and awe in the face of City finance is only another aspect of Britain's inability to come to terms with the elementary facts of trading life – the prejudice of landed aristocracy mediated to the masses.

The City of London is a tough old institution. And the business of providing investment, credit and a money market is not inherently complicated. These abuses of take-overs, share-puffing, naked speculation and fraud which do so much harm to industry are only a monstrous street-riot of looting and greed which has developed because British political society still thinks of the City as a no-go area.

The trouble is that there is a deep sense of complicity between a no-go City and a no-go State, which is now engaged in protecting its own secrecy by hounding journalists and broadcasters all over the landscape. A good government would go into the City with drums beating and clean it out, destroying nothing the economy really needs in the process. A good government – which we do not have.   [1987

A Dumb-Bell World

I don't know what the Westland affair is really about. Reading, viewing, listening – at times collapsing into wild laughter – I have become convinced that I am missing some point. It's not about helicopters, not about the free market, not entirely or even mostly about personal ambitions.

It obviously proceeds from Mrs Thatcher's way of running her Cabinet in the manner of Stalin running his evening parties at the dacha. She winds the gramophone; her Ministers dance together; outside in the snow, the van for Siberia waits with engine running. Hysteria mounts. One Minister treads painfully on another's toe, and suddenly there are screams, flailing fists, blood and vodka everywhere and people running for the door. OK, but what is the Westland quarrel *about*?

One striking aspect of the business is its language. The matter of who shall own Westland and who shall be blamed is to a great extent conducted in the language of 'I am more pro-American than thou.' Again, I am pretty sure that this is deceptive; for all his current rhetoric, Mr Michael Heseltine's past record makes it unlikely that he went berserk for the sake of European military industries. But for some reason, he and other politicians have translated their rage into a loyalty competition over the American connection.

There are younger fogies who defend the unimpeded play of market forces on Westland (so long as they can impede the forces they don't want in the market). They proclaim that to oppose the Sikorsky bid is an ungrateful, xenophobic insult to our mighty American partner. Then there are those older and more cunning fogies who tell us that the true loyalty to the United States is quite the opposite. In Washington (they say), people are yearning for Western Europe to end its tiresome dependence on America by building a separate capacity to defend itself – even if that means a touch of protectionism which might incommode the odd American corporation.

The second argument is an endearing, disingenuous old whore. It has been around for years. It is, beneath the pious nonsense, the ancient British hankering to manoeuvre the United States out of direct influence on British political and economic affairs while retaining – even increasing – America's obligation to defend these islands if they are under threat. It is something out of 'Upstairs, Downstairs' – the Americans should stay in the pantry until they are rung for, when they must present themselves fully equipped and at the double.

And one understands this very well. Who doesn't remember Dubček saying that a democratic Czechoslovakia would be a better partner for the Soviet Union, or Jacek Kuroń arguing that a 'Finlandised' Poland would offer Moscow a stable friend and a prosperous neighbour? (No, I know that Republicans don't put Democrats in labour camps.)

Sincere or not, the way British governments talk in public to the United States has grown increasingly servile. Assent to 'Star Wars,' assent by silence to American policy towards Nicaragua which Britain might have softened. In private, the language is quite different. Certainly, our policy imposes a basic dependence, especially since Britain's deterrent ceased to be 'independent.' But do the Americans require all this fawning? Or can it be that the chorus of loyalty is really meant to drown voices of dissent at home, to impose a loyalty test by which patriotism is defined by ritual homage to the 'special relationship'?

A queer article by Roger Scruton appeared in *The Times* last week. He complained that criticism of the United States as an 'imperial power' was now spreading to sections of the Right. Wicked voices suggested that Britain was a 'dependency' or 'client state' of America. The truth was that 'the British Empire lives on in America, just as the Roman Empire lived on in Byzantium, although in a form more vital, more industrious and more generous.'

So we are really they, a dependency of our more generous selves. This reminded me of the old Welsh assertion that America was really British because the Indians spoke Welsh, proving that they were descendants of Welsh colonists brought there by Prince Madoc three centuries before Columbus.

Before Americophilia as mad as that, reason falls silent. Scruton adds, incautiously, that Harvard University is 'a bastion of European culture.' Yes, but against what? Against the Iroquois? Or against an 'actually existing America' which is not British and not even very European any more, but setting off down tracks which no longer look like paths broken for Europeans to follow?

> Cerebrotonic Cato may
> Extol the Ancient Disciplines,
> But the muscle-bound Marines
> Mutiny for food and pay.

I see cerebrotonic Scruton in this poem of Auden's, extolling an Anglo-America which would never have existed even if no Italian, Irishman, Slovak, Pole or Jew had reached Staten Island.

In a less fantastic form, though, this way of looking at the relationship is quite common. Up to about 40 years ago, those who governed the British and told them what to think inhabited a blob-shaped mental world. It comprised the Home Counties, London south of the Park, Westminster and the Inns of Court. Now, after decades of Fulbright grants and academic exchanges, their descendants inhabit a world shaped like a dumb-bell. At one end, the Home Counties, etc., then a long, thin bit, then another blob consisting of Washington DC and some habitable bits of Manhattan and New England.

The rest of the world, outside this 'civilised' dumb-bell, is dark and potty. It speaks foreign languages; it suffers rather disgustingly; nobody can spell its statesmen. Dumb-bell people feel as uneasy in Prague as in Glasgow. When they say 'Europe' they mean Dorset, Tuscany and Vermont.

I find as many dumb-bell people among journalists as among politicians. The number of news editors who take their opinions from American magazines, if not from the copious bulletins of the US Embassy, seems to grow rather than to decrease. If Britain were ever to change course, even into a mild version of non-alignment, these 'cadres' would feel that their country was leaving them.

To criticise this Atlantic provincialism is to be accused, most comically, of 'xenophobia.' Philip Norman wrote a raging article the other day against visitors who still found the United States a place of 'excitement and energy,' and overlooked the 'bureaucracy, the snobbishness, the obscene medical system and the beggars' that impress him there. My point is not about the way the Americans manage themselves, but about the way the British manage their dependence upon the United States.

For we do live under an *imperium*, if not an empire. Few great powers have imposed a lighter tax in obedience than the Americans levy on us, and most people here still accept the general bargain of dependence in return for protection. But a client state we are.

This is a relationship which can be lucidly managed, but only if we keep a clear head. It is an arrangement of self-interest, not – as the Westland language implies – a mystical marriage to be kept holy by flattery and insincere obeisance. After all, the British might one day decide to go a different way. And it would be a pity if the dumb-bells jumped off into the Atlantic.

[*1986*

Thatcher's Dream

I had not quite realised, until I saw Mrs Thatcher on television last Wednesday, that she intended to remove what she calls 'socialism' from Britain altogether and for good. This was my mistake. She has said this on several occasions since the 1983 election although never, I think, with the pertness she displayed last week.

Out will go the carpets and curtains, whose faded red 'does not go with the British character,' to be replaced by pastel shades which match rather than contrast. Mrs Thatcher means to do the place up in the American manner, with two co-ordinate parties both committed to 'freedom under the law' and to 'the free enterprise system.'

One may laugh, scream or gape. But that is what she says.

Let's avoid the argument about whether the Labour movement in this country is properly to be termed socialist or not. When Mrs T. says 'socialist,' she means 'Labour.' She does not wish simply to defeat the Labour Party. She means to demolish it, and to throw its structure, institutions and ideology into the skip.

What country does she think she is living in? Scotland, to start with, is plainly not part of that *pays imaginaire*; it returns a majority of Labour MPs which grows at each election and will be larger still next time. Is it that nameless country which is England south of the M62 motorway between Hull and Liverpool, containing about 90 per cent of the British Tory vote? But in that land too there are great enclaves – presumably foreign and un-British – who do not find Labour policies alien to their traditions.

But the 'what country' question isn't about geography. It is really addressed to Mrs Thatcher's assumptions about what sort of society we live in now and what its real inheritance from history is – social, economic or moral.

Stalin used to talk about 'non-antagonistic contradictions,' meaning roughly that if workers in the Soviet state rebelled against their bosses, their revolt could not be a genuine class struggle. Mrs Thatcher, similarly, assumes that our real 'contra-dictions' have been ironed out; that the weak no longer have any inherent need to combine against the strong.

She does, at least, admit the need for some form of parlia-mentary opposition. But who will be the 'Democrats' to her 'Republicans'? Shrewd commentators – Anthony Bevins on the *Independent*, Adam Raphael on this paper – draw out her logic to imply that there should be two parties: her own Tories and the Tory 'Wets.'

These fantasies are released on 'actually-existing' Britain: scarcely a society equal enough, prosperous enough, fair enough or free enough to divide its needs between a Tory Tweedledee and a Tory Tweedledum. This is not just a matter of the North–South divide, or of appalling unemployment. For those lucky enough to retain a job, Britain is a low-wage economy in which most manual workers reach their earning peak in their early twenties. Outside the middle-class professions and the bureaucracy, there is no ascending escalator of rewards which slows down only as retirement approaches.

It is my belief that a historic explosion of middle-class wealth and purchasing power is very close, especially in London. Almost nothing suggests that this will flow into productive investment, spreading jobs or raising real wages. Instead, it will take place just as British governments are presented with the famous 'poisoned chalice': the burden of power at the moment when oil revenue fades away and leaves us with the shrunken, neglected remains of traditional manufacturing industry.

Wherever the proper ground for a pleasant partnership of free-enterprise parties, it will not be found in the 1990s. Britain is still a place of painful inequality which will grow worse, not better, just as we enter the economic rapids.

The first tugs and shocks of those rapids can already be felt. Mrs Thatcher complains – indeed, Mr Kinnock complains – of the fanatical, stupid excesses of some Labour local authorities. These are no more than the mirror image of her own 'conviction' politics. They emerge at a time when, for all her talk of 'freedom under the law,' the coercive power of the State against the citizen is being expanded – by new police powers, by authoritarian changes to the law – on a scale never seen in Britain outside war-time ... or since the Peterloo years. Impoverishment, repression and dogmatism do indeed invite a political 'realignment,' but hardly towards the *laissez-faire* consensus dreamed of by the Prime Minister.

Then there is the proposition that 'socialism' is in some way un-British. This reminds me of Solzhenitsyn's almost pathetic insistence that Soviet communism is not an adaptation of Tsarist patterns of rule and obedience but their opposite: a non-Russian imposition devised in the alien minds of Germans and Jews.

If Mrs Thatcher were saying that Muscovite communism is alien to Britain, few would disagree. If she were saying that the ideology of the Labour movement is un-British, on the other hand, then a moment's glance at two centuries of working-class struggle would render her remark too silly to discuss.

But what she means, I think, is that collectivism with a levelling ethic, encouraged by State action, does not fit with her idea of the sturdy British individual. This thought is not so much nonsense as a fragment of widespread mythology.

The only particle of truth here is that the English (to be specific) have never developed more than an ambiguous relation to the idea of the 'State' – which they still confuse verbally with terms like 'nation' and 'government.' Socially, however, the British in recent history have shown a preference and talent for collective behaviour which is without parallel in Europe.

This has ranged from 'macro' to 'micro.' At one end is the phenomenal capacity for patriotic mobilisation, shown most recently over the Falklands war. At the other is – or rather was – the cohesion of families and groups of families asserting some control over their living conditions. In between lay the infinite web of associations for collective action: combinations, craft unions, church-based organisations, leagues for this or that, societies for every conceivable serious or frivolous purpose, sport groups, boozing clubs, informal savings and benefit circles, silver bands and pigeon fanciers.

Out of this universe of collective experience – acquired in what is still casually called an 'age of individual enterprise' – came two very simple ideas. One was that unity is strength. The other was that, whatever the nobs say, one man is as good as another but usually needs help to make that manifest.

The atomisation of British society is producing apathy rather than enterprise. Reviving that old collectivism is what Labour is really about. One could wish that that party were less blindly patriotic, and more imaginative about ways to harness that social cohesion, but Labour is undeniably attached to the roots of British attitudes. Meanwhile, Mrs Thatcher really must stop behaving like the late Walter Ulbricht of East Germany who – in Brecht's taunt – wanted to dismiss his population and appoint another.   [1986

Last Leader

After crossing the river, the little band of Palaeolithic hunters huddled together shivering on the far bank. They were cold and wet, but they still had their flint-tipped spears. Men and women together, side by side collected dry brushwood at the top of the sandy shore and tried to start a fire. Here at least the ground was firm, unlike the flat swamps of the south bank, and in the distance ahead they could see a line of northern heights, shaggy with forest. There should be deer there, perhaps a mammoth. The fire took hold and warmed them. Soon the group was spreading out and – without regard to colour, sexual preference, age, size or creed – beginning to gather the nuts, berries and tubers and to share them democratically, once more in balance with the environment and with one another. And as the evening shadows lengthened, the first members of the species Homo Erectus to arrive in London fell to their normal diversions, or 'what we would consider a life of idle luxury – music, dancing, relating to each other, the constant flow of conversation'.

So Ken Livingstone might imagine the first inhabitants of the GLC area. They call him a Trot, but there is much more in him of a far older generation of palaeo-socialists. For Livingstone believes in a social version of the Fall, in a State of Nature and – almost – a Garden in which human beings lived with one another, innocently, equally, without private property or surplus, without stress, in balance with nature. In a long conversation with John Carvel, far the most astonishing and winning part of this book, he lays out his own Livingstonian anthropology. These wandering bands did not know war, as the inhabitants of the nuclear-free zone of Lewisham shall not know war. They were 'a very together, well-organised and sophisticated proto-culture'. Everything that we are today has emerged from the hunter-gatherer tradition. 'All of our ability, the development

of our intellect, all of our early culture grows out of those
kinship groups operating overwhelmingly in a co-operative
way . . . The hunter-gatherer is what humanity is.'

So far, so Fourier, or Rousseau or St-Simon. The most
interesting question about state-of-nature utopian thinkers is
where they insert the Fall and what they consider to have
played the serpent. Ken Livingstone has no doubts. It was
the introduction of agriculture, the Neolithic revolution 'twenty
thousand years ago', which ruined everything. For a start, it
accelerated the growth of population until the ecological balance
collapsed. 'Hunter-gatherers have a basic diet which means you
can't wean children easily. It's all hard, scrunchy stuff. There's
no animals' milk or mushy foods.' And with the junk food of
planted crops came the creation of wealth, surpluses, hier-
archies, technology.

> 'If you look at the way the City of London works, it is operating
> in exactly the same way as the most primitive of those societies
> based on agriculture. . . . The basic motive force is greed and
> exploitation, which is there from the start once you move away
> from that co-operative group. We haven't learned to cope with
> surpluses and distribute them without greed becoming the major
> motive factor and the desire for power over others. I do not think
> that is a natural state for humankind to be in.'

This is all fearful heresy to those – like myself – reared on
the work of V. Gordon Childe, whose Marxist version of the
natural state was located precisely in the world of Neolithic
agriculture, perceived as a non-competitive, co-operative and
equal society bonded together by kinship and by the need to
give and receive food surpluses to relieve crop failure. For
Gordon Childe, the 'origins of inequality' were to be found in
the invention of metallurgy, creating, out of the families who
possessed the secret, hereditary castes which would eventually
develop into a primitive bourgeoisie with all its attendant vices
of greed, privilege and war.

But then Gordon Childe, as a Communist, took a basically
optimistic view of history. His metallurgical Fall might have
wrecked the 'undifferentiated substantive' of primitive farmers.
It was, however, the first 'contradiction' in a dialectic which
would in the end create equality and co-operation at a higher

synthesis – the victory of the industrial world proletariat. What is fascinating about 'Red Ken', so much a child of the Seventies, is his pessimism. A man who does not see history as in at least some sense a progress will never make a recognisable Communist, whether Stalinist or Trot. Talking, or rambling on, to Carvel, Livingstone derides the whole idea of progressive evolution, biological or social. 'It's there in the thinking of a lot of people around Stalin – the idea that man is getting better, that we are part of this inevitable upward progress. We're not really . . . We're still trying to adjust to changes that came over us twenty thousand years ago.' Well, it was there in the thinking of a lot of people around Karl Marx as well. But Ken Livingstone, a man for compassionate issues rather than ideologies who was brought up in south London suburbs rather than among proletarian terraces, simply points to the city around him as evidence of negative evolution. People now live on their own, surrounded by other isolated people. They do not gather tubers with their comrades, neither do they enjoy that 'music, dancing, relating to each other, the constant flow of conversation' which is proper to the species. 'The isolation you get in society, particularly urban society, where people are frightened and embarrassed to turn to other people for support, means that we are living in a way which is completely at odds with the best part of fifteen million years of evolution which turned us into what we are.'

And at this point Citizen Ken brings on the reptiles. Everyone who can read a paper knows that he keeps lizards and salamanders; given the sort of press he gets, millions probably think he uses them to enrich the cauldrons of lesbian separatist covens dancing on Peckham Rye. In fact, he uses them not for food but for thought. Some lizards, he explained to Carvel in the second part of this immortal conversation, reproduce by parthenogenesis – females reproducing themselves without male involvement. (First the Russians discovered such a lizard. The Americans denounced it as a fraud until they discovered one of their own. 'So it's now established that the superpower blocs have parthenogenic lizard parity,' says Livingstone.)

He sees an analogy here with his view of human development. The lizards who developed parthenogenesis at once collected an enormous short-term advantage: by avoiding all the dangers and uncertainties of sexual reproduction, they solved the problem of keeping the species going. But in the long term, the solution must lead to extinction. The gene pool is not mixed, healthy mutation and adaptation cease, and a population of identical, mindless little creatures without an original idea or physical variation among them will be easily wiped out by some catastrophe.

It is not difficult to see what the chairman of the GLC is getting at. On that cursed day when hunters first broke the soil and threw seed into it, the human race began a parthenogenic leap forward: all the variations and mutations of social relationships were abandoned for the gigantic increase of security and population that agriculture guaranteed. Society lost the capacity to adapt, locking itself into one mould of greed and competition. 'We may be just trundling along on a dead end which suddenly cuts off the whole of the human race very violently and rapidly.' Unrestricted population growth, or pollution, are as likely to bring humanity to that dead end as nuclear war.

And is there no way back? John Carvel inquires. No way back to the state of nature and the pursuit of berries and tubers, the chairman implacably returns. But by establishing little islets of non-competitive association, rafts of co-operative production on the capitalist sea, a start can be made on restoring society's capacity to mutate and adapt. With the help and subsidy of GLEB (Greater London Enterprise Board), humanity can begin retracing the wrong turning taken by the Neolithic revolution.

All this will reduce many archaeologists, many professors of anthropology, probably many GLC ratepayers, to speechless fury. Hunter-gatherers? Lizards? Thoughts like these, even the affectionate John Carvel concedes, 'in the atmosphere of work-aday politics ... sound positively loopy'. So much the worse for workaday politics. Ken Livingstone is a utopian socialist, a man who does not fit most of the categories crammed round his neck by the media. He is anything but a Trotskyist, although he will gladly use small Trot groups for support when it suits his tactics. He is not a working-class politician formed by poverty, but neither – as Carvel points out – is he a 'paperback Marxist' from a 'lumpen polytechnic'. He had no real higher education, and his grasp of theory, as the hunter-gatherer-parthenogenesis hypothesis shows, is wonderfully sketchy and personal. In most ways, he is more of a classical anarchist than a Marxist. His style is to work through a constantly changing series of caucuses, cabals and temporary alliances; one of the reasons why the Parliamentary Labour Party hates him so fervently is that Livingstone dislikes the discipline of permanent political structures, even though he still seems anxious to enter the House of Commons. If there is anyone in European politics whom he resembles, it is Erhard Eppler, the veteran Social Democrat in West Germany, an infinitely graver and more consistent thinker who nonetheless commands a similar coalition of leftists, life-stylers, Green-minded socialists and nuclear disarmers, whose outlook is also pessimistic and who was the first in his party to welcome the 'end of growth' and put forward a sweeping reform programme which did not amount to the mere redistribution of capitalist surplus in years of expansion.

Ken Livingstone complains that the society he lives in has almost killed off the capacity for social 'mutation'. But, as a matter of fact, he himself is a mutation. Citizen Ken is one of the first known examples of a new strain of politician entirely resistant to all known forms of media poison. The last ten years have brought campaigns against the personal and public lives of selected left-wing politicians of a viciousness scarcely seen in Britain since the Victorian period, but none of these campaigns – not even that against Arthur Scargill – acquired the intensity of the hounding of Livingstone. Scargill and Benn, of an older generation, have developed signs of paranoia under this treatment; Tatchell was nearly destroyed by it. But Livingstone actually feeds on pesticide. The more hysterical the abuse, the more provocative he becomes. The quotes about the IRA, the Royal Wedding, gay rights and black pride continue to flow; his wretched Labour group on the GLC have often paid the price, pockmarked by the shower of missiles aimed at their leader and obliged to watch many of their most 'popular' measures obliterated from view by the latest scandal over 'Red Ken' and his big mouth. Meanwhile, Livingstone himself was turning the publicity steadily to his own advantage, emerging as a skilled, unflappable and charming radio and television panellist and interviewee. Increasingly, his case has been heard, and Londoners have developed for him both affection and some respect. Carvel observes that 'Livingstone's crucifixion in the media formed the basis of his subsequent political strength and popularity.'

Most of this book, naturally enough, is about local government and London politics. Livingstone was welcomed to power with the headline 'Red Ken Crowned King of London'. John Carvel shows what a mockery those words were and are. Britain is the most over-centralised state in the Western world, in which local authorities have always been tightly hobbled, and today the Government – through 'rate-capping', through the abolition of the Metropolitan Counties – is engaged on reducing that slight room for manoeuvre even further. Political prejudice against Labour-dominated authorities plays its part, but the real situation is little short of a creeping nationalisation of local government by Whitehall – by the Treasury in particular. The *Daily Express* last year published a cartoon showing 'Red Ken' digging the grave of democracy, but the whole bizarre, impudent, exhilarating history of his administration at County Hall shows that he and his colleagues have been trying to give local democracy the kiss of life on what appears to be its deathbed. The sullen, morose sea of overcrowded humanity that is London has never been encouraged to develop a sense of active community. Who, after all, is remembered as a leader of London? Dick Whittington, perhaps Herbert Morrison. Ken Livingstone has dealt mostly in symbolic politics – there was little else left to deal in – but he will be remembered as the man who gave Londoners their only revelation of common identity since Marshal Goering abandoned the Blitz. He could not be a giant-killer, but he made fools of the giants. Michael Heseltine, as Secretary for the Environment, bungled the legislation to cut the GLC's revenue. The judiciary made imbeciles of themselves in their eagerness to crush the cheap fares policy by pronouncing, in effect, that all forms of subsidy were a misuse of ratepayers' money. The onslaught by the gutter press made Citizen Ken into a folk-hero. Mrs Thatcher, in her eagerness to suppress him and to destroy what remains of local authority freedom, has deeply offended the Conservative conscience in a way which may well contribute to her fall.

Ken Livingstone has also been lucky. Like many obsessive manipulators, he has almost come unstuck on many occasions, saved usually by the blunders of his enemies. He was rescued from taking the consequences of the appalling financial muddle which had developed at the GLC after his first six months as leader only by the surge of sympathy after the judges condemned the fare cuts. The Labour group might well have unloaded him for his 'they are not criminals or lunatics' remark about the IRA bombers, and for his invitation to Sinn Fein to visit County Hall, if the Home Secretary had not changed the focus of the uproar by 'excluding' the two Sinn Fein MPs from the British mainland. He declared that Labour would stay in office and simply refuse to raise transport fares after the law lords' judgment, and was saved from a terminal collision with the law by the mess the Tory GLC opposition made of the crucial debate. And luck has repeatedly frustrated his deplorable hankering to get into Parliament: he was only narrowly defeated at Hampstead, and although he was winning the murderous guerrilla faction war for the nomination at Brent East in 1983, Mrs Thatcher called the election before the sitting MP, Reg Freeson, was finally 'deselected'. Why Ken Livingstone wants to enter the House remains a mystery. The place is full of ageing gadflies who achieve nothing beyond turning the Speaker's face purple, and who lack the delicious power to do things like cover London with nuclear-free zone notices and witty posters at the ratepayers' expense.

He is no administrator and, really, no hero. He has a cheerful super-rat gift for dodging upwards through chinks in situations. He is a shameless carpet-bagger and opportunist with a gift for bringing together coalitions of people who all slightly suspect him for different reasons but find his flair irresistible (in this, he has something in common with Lech Wałęsa, whom he probably regards as a clerical fascist). As a schoolboy, taught at Tulse Hill Comprehensive by the expansive Philip Hobsbaum, he became, in his own words, what he was to remain: 'an argumentative, cheeky little brat.' John Carvel, who obviously admires him, often seems in this book to shake his head with exasperation over the chances Ken takes with his reputation. And yet, if the GLC is to die, Ken Livingstone has ensured as the last leader of Greater London that it will perish in a display of vigour, ideas, experiments and sheer entertainment that dims any Lord Mayor's fireworks on the Thames. It may be because he has such a passion for the Irish – seeing them perhaps as hunter-gatherers in arms – that he has turned a sober funeral of democracy into a spectacular wake. [*1984*

A review of 'Citizen Ken' by John Carvel (Chatto, London, 1984).

The Great Cash-In

Under the surface of London, there are strange tremors. Something is rising to the surface, and when it bursts through it will – so I begin to believe – create a new and almost unrecognisable type of urban society. It will shatter our expectations about social progress, and eventually threaten the whole management of the British economy. That something is middle-class money.

A few months ago, I wrote about the way that London was ceasing to be a city with a large, organised factory proletariat and reverting towards a capital in which a huge, underemployed plebs or 'people' works to service a wealthy minority. Since then, it has become clear that the coming changes may be far more dramatic and frightening. What I didn't see was quite how wealthy the minority would be.

This theory starts with something now familiar: the price of private housing in central London. Ever since about 1970, the value of this housing stock – above all old, 'gentrified' and renovated houses – has been rising steeply. So far this year alone, the prices of second-hand houses in the central area have gone up by around 20 per cent, although in other parts of Britain the value of all private housing has scarcely kept pace with inflation or even dropped below it. One colleague lives in a one-bedroom, third-floor flat in Paddington which cost him £60,000 some 18 months ago and can now be sold for £80,000.

Until now, there has been a habit of regarding these colossal values as 'fairy money.' If you have to pay as much or more to buy another when you sell a flat or house (unless you move to the provinces), then its effect on your bank account is slight. But this may be about to change – a thought I owe to Michael Elliott of the *Economist*, who is writing a book about it.

For cashing-in time is coming. It's a matter of time and generations. James and Lavinia Yupsley, journalists in their late twenties, are living in a mortgaged house in Islington worth £120,000. His father Daniel Yupsley, a successful solicitor, and his wife Vanessa are living in a paid-off flat worth much more. Just possibly, old Bill Yupsley, James's grandfather, is living in yet another inflated-value house, having decided not to retire to the country after his career as a smart dentist. All this may also be true of Lavinia's family.

Now the older occupiers of 'fairy money' houses and flats are beginning to die. Their heirs do not need the property left to them, and will sell it. What this means is that in the next decade or so the upward-mobile middle and professional classes of London will acquire staggering reserves of liquid cash. Even after current mortgages and tax are paid off, the possession of £500,000 spending money will become common. On television's 'London Programme' this month, an estate agent boasted: 'You can't get very much for a million pounds in central London these days ... a fairly ordinary four or five bedroom family house is about £850,000.'

The inward migration of professional talent and ambition to London will go on, so that – unless the economy suddenly collapses – the private housing demand will be maintained. At the same time, the outward migration of working-class Londoners will continue, keeping up the supply of housing to be 'privatised' or improved.

This is very big money. How will it be spent? For spent it will be: savings and investments will absorb only a fraction of it. Country houses, villas on the Mediterranean, yachts will take up some of the new wealth. But the social profile of London will be transformed, as there arises a minority equipped with a purchasing power comparable only to that of the Kensington Arabs, whose standard of living will be out of all imaginable proportion to that of the majority of the city's population. This will mean a return to degrees of inequality unknown in Britain for a hundred years.

A segregation as blatant as that of apartheid is approaching, founded on inequality of wealth but built up into an entirely separate way of life in separate institutions. This segregation is already beginning, growing out of the traditional division of London classes by urban areas.

Take education, for example. Twenty years ago, the liberal middle class of London sent children through the whole state system. By the late 1970s, there was an embarrassed consensus that comprehensives 'weren't good enough *yet*,' but state primary schools remained acceptable. Today, the same group not only assumes that comprehensive schools are unthinkable, but is beginning to pay hundreds of pounds a term for *private* primary education at new day schools in central London.

With the new wealth, this simply means that a large hereditary caste with its own culture will regain the monopoly of power once enjoyed by the products of the public schools. The period when class barriers seemed to be crumbling and growing permeable will appear as a brief reversal of the normal trend, a 20-year blip in the history of class in England.

But this development converges with the other process I mentioned at the outset: the transformation of the London working class. As Ken Livingstone saw, Labour's vision of London is out of date. The big-factory epoch of the city is almost over (it lasted for only 40 or 50 years), and the great union-organised workforces of the past have disintegrated. Londoners are reverting to older patterns of employment: trading, small crafts, a multitude of transient jobs that add up to servicing the main possessors and generators of wealth themselves. In this way, too, London is travelling backwards through time towards a relationship between wealth and labour that is almost pre-capitalist.

Stripped of big words, what does this mean? Among other things, the return of servants. Not living in, like 'Upstairs, Downstairs': there isn't room for that. But commuter servants, as in Johannesburg, who catch a 5 a.m. train in a distant suburb to wear maid's uniform or even butler's livery all day. On another page today, Michael Dineen quotes a brochure for a Bayswater apartment block illustrated with the picture of a pretty Victorian tweeny, all white lace and black bombazine.'

It means a huge service and craft population, making clothes and cutlery, furniture and designer rugs for the rich, mending their electronics and guarding their homes. It means a capital city not unlike the pattern of eighteenth-century Paris, where almost all employment depended on the needs of the Court and the thousands of privileged royal functionaries around it.

Once again, outrageous wealth will be justified because it 'keeps people in work.' It will also keep them in a squalid new servitude, as the public transport, health and education of the capital rot away – not least, for lack of rented accommodation for those who should run them.

This New Class of the capital would tower over the rest of Britain, distorting its whole development. In the end, its power would not be tolerable. Perhaps the provinces would challenge it. Perhaps the Londoners themselves. Cabinet-makers, coachmen, lawyers' clerks make the bloodiest revolutions, not orderly factory workers.

There are bad dreams here. Let the new money flood London: for a time, it would be Ben Jonson's 'Fleshfly, summer is with thee now!' But then a very hard wind would rise.

[*1986*

Capital

Coming back from anywhere to London depresses me. Coming back from the contented provincial splendour of Lyons makes for specially gloomy reflections. Etymologically, they are the same place: Lugdunum and Londinium both denote the 'dun' (stronghold) of the Celtic god Lugh – who is dimly remembered here as King Lud, as in Ludgate Hill.* Lyons in 1987, however, is on the way up, whereas London is all too squalidly on its way down.

In the Roman centuries, temples and imperial palaces covered the slopes and summits of the Fourvière hill. The villas of the

---

* It has been pointed out to me that linguists now reject this. The etymology of 'London' remains unknown.

rich and powerful can be located, but where the common people lived, the potters and bakers and those who cleaned the marble plazas with mop and bucket, is not at all clear. Models of ancient Lyons, showing the stone but not the clay and thatch, strike me as an extreme, mad projection of how the capital city of the British state may end up.

In the politics of returning inequality, which is the theme of Mrs Thatcher's eight years in power, London plays a spectacular part. Argument persists about the concept of 'two nations,' divided by wealth and political allegiance, and there are sensible warnings that it is misleading to see this division in geographical terms alone. It is not just in the North that an 'underclass' is expanding so rapidly. But it is in and around London, above all, that the new 'overclass' is appearing.

Recently there appeared John Rentoul's book 'The Rich Get Richer'. Rentoul observes that there are really three 'nations:' the poor, the rich – and the super-rich, or, as he puts it, 'the haves, the have-nots and the have-lots.' His conclusion, rather unexpected, is that while there has been a sharp increase in differences of *income* in the Thatcher period, the differences of *wealth* have merely stopped decreasing.

Before Mrs Thatcher's victory in 1979, Britain had less income differences than most industrialised countries: the share of the top 1 per cent had halved since 1945. Now the income share of the top 10 per cent has returned to its 1960s level, rising from 6½ times that of the bottom 10 per cent to 7½ times between 1979 and 1983. The figures of those living at or below the Supplementary Benefit level were around 6.1 million in 1979, and are now almost 12 million. The size of Britain's 'underclass' has nearly doubled, amounting today to almost a fifth of the entire population.

Wealth, on the limited figures available, has not changed much in distribution. It is a basic but still astounding fact of British life that the richer half of the population owns *all* the wealth that is worth talking about. The average 'marketable assets' of the lower half were worth only £2,140 in 1984; the property of the upper half averaged £33,580. What has stopped, in other words, is the trend towards more equal distribution of wealth in the richer 50 per cent.

But the scale of new 'overclass' wealth remains awe-inspiring. The top 1 per cent owns 177 times the average of the bottom half. Some wealth remains 'in the ground,' like the £22 billion held in family and discretionary trusts. Much of it, though – and this is the important change – is becoming more liquid and disposable, turning into straight purchasing power. The gigantic potential value of private housing in London and the South-East, accelerating at up to 100 per cent a year in some parts of central London, is now about to be realised in cash through inheritance. There are some 20,000 millionaires now, and – so Rentoul reports – about 280,000 people who can live off unearned income without working.

It was a bishop who announced the other day that British society had evolved from the shape of a pyramid to the much more satisfactory shape of a diamond: large in the middle, but tiny at the top and bottom. That diamond, though it may be the Prime Minister's best friend, is paste. A better image would be an Eiffel Tower, with the view and the big lights at the tip of the spire.

Back to London. I have written before about the middle-class wealth explosion which lies ahead, based on housing values even more than on astronomical new salaries and perks, leading towards a city whose main employment is serving and servicing the rich. But what happens to those in between?

How can services – including the central Civil Service – carry on in London faced with such inflation? How can their workers be recruited, and how can their employers, private or public, afford to subsidise them to live in London? Even the rich who wish to move into London have problems. The Reward Research Surveys consultancy estimates that a family living in a five-bedroom house will increase their annual outgoings by nearly £22,000 if they decide to work and live in Greater London.

The wind is blowing already. Primary schools in the Inner London area have 400 vacant teaching posts which – even in times of unemployment – they cannot fill, and the ILEA is desperately recruiting as far away as Australia. A Yorkshire teacher earns £9,318 after five years to buy a semi costing £29,000, while a London teacher earns £10,428 towards the same house costing about £80,000. Many London boroughs and health authorities report the same shrinking of staff. One can predict 'a catastrophic fall in education, health care and social service provision' in the capital. Another way of putting it is this: Londoners who can't pay will become ignorant, neglected, disease-ridden proles.

In its informal, British way, London is becoming a 'closed' city as Moscow is 'closed' to all but a few immigrants from the rest of the Soviet Union. And this affects not only the social services but the Civil Service itself. Strategies of 'London weighting' subsidies or 'excess rent allowances' like those just increased by the Treasury are not going to be enough to keep the door open. Staff cuts, which reduced Civil Service numbers by some 100,000 in recent years, will not be enough either. The flow of new recruits into the central State bureaucracy from outside London is already diminishing. How can they afford to live there?

But, of course, they do not really need to. Teaching and healing have to happen where people live. Administering, under the sign of the computer, can be done anywhere.

The proper answer is Canberra, or Islamabad. It is transferring the capital of the State to a normal environment where its rulers can live at a normal cost. The English, however, will never agree to take Parliament out of Westminster; the permanent under-secretaries would rather die than lose their clubs. All the same, the whole of Whitehall could shift to Milton Keynes or Telford, leaving only the most senior, 'political' civil servants in London. Even the Foreign Office could go, taking the embassies with it.

Labour governments have 'dispersed' fragments of the Civil Service around the country, but in the interests of developing the regions. Mrs Thatcher cut that programme down almost to nothing. But now, one hears, there is renewed discussion of such ideas in the Civil Service: this time, because London is growing unaffordable.

The end of 'London rule' would be a moment of real progress. It would begin the break-up of centralised power. It would change the way the English understand their nation. It would slow the enrichment of the 'have-lots.' Best of all, though, it would start a long-overdue divorce between those who have State power and those who have private wealth.   [*1987*

The Land and the People

Grow less food! A gramophone record which has been playing the same old tune in the background of my entire conscious life has suddenly been taken off. It was Dig for Victory and All Power to the War Ag. It was Step Up Milk Production, it was Clear Bracken for more cattle to graze. It was We Have the Most Efficient Farmers in the World, and eventually it was Build the Grain Mountain – and grow filthy rich.

In the uncanny silence which has fallen, distant sounds and voices echo more clearly. The sounds are the slamming of doors, as bank managers refuse loans to ten thousand small farmers going bankrupt and as City fund managers climb into their Porsches to drive away from their agribusiness grain prairies for ever. The voices preach new gospels. Farmers must become countryside wardens. Their job is not to grow food but to keep the land looking pretty. Fields are not for crops but for golf courses, riding schools, 'broad-leaf coppices,' or even Barratt villages.

The great farming crash is upon us, and the word 'fallow' is no longer pejorative. D. H. Lawrence once imagined a fresh planet without people, just 'grass, with a hare sitting up.' But this is not what fallow Britain will look like.

Left to themselves, the fields would fur over with weeds, waist-high and then head-high. Bushes would be followed by small trees, and eventually – in most of lowland Britain – by dense and scrubby secondary forest. Much of this land would revert to waterlogged swamp, as field drainage broke down. It would be good for birds, but also good for rats, mosquitoes and accumulations of weed pollen to make the nation sneeze and to smother its gardens. In the dimness of the tangled under-brush there would lurk, like the débris of a forgotten battle, millions of abandoned cars, refrigerators and – especially – agricultural machines.

This prospect terrifies the Government, the planners and the environmentalists. This is why, as the subsidies wind down at last, they have invented this new idea of the farmer as museum custodian, whose duty is to preserve the look of the rural 'heritage.' The ancient motto of the Polish peasantry, using their scythes sometimes on the wheat, sometimes (attached to a pike) on Imperial Russian soldiery, was 'Nourish and Defend!' The motto of British farmers will from now on be 'Prune and Pretend!'

Writing in the *Independent*, Richard North points out what nonsense it is, anyway, to treat this countryside as visually unchanging: 'it is in fact both man-made and a relatively recent invention.' The hedge-pattern is not older – usually – than the Enclosures: the bare uplands were bared by a combination of ruthless forest-felling, the eviction of human beings and the ecological murder inflicted by sheep.

And, incidentally, this new turn in farming offers sheep more damage to do. In John McGrath's new show, 'There is a Happy Land,' which began its three-part run on Channel 4 last week, a Gaelic song proclaims 'My curse upon the Great Sheep: where are the children of kindly folk who left me in my youth, before the country of Mackay became a desert?'

This refers to the Highland Clearances, families driven out to make way for sheep. But the surviving crofters are now dependent on income from sheep themselves. As sheepmeat is about the only EEC rural product not in surplus, its support will for the moment remain. But that – for sure – means that British farmers will now bolt into sheep-raising as a last resort.

The result is all too predictable. In a few years there will be a mutton mountain. Then sheep subsidies will be slashed in turn, and the crofters, in company with most small upland farmers in Britain, will face catastrophe.

This is not what either the Government or the environmentalists want to happen. Their hope, in this entirely new period, is that smallholdings would increase and prosper as the big farms ceased to be 'viable.' To keep the countryside fit for townees to enjoy, the land would have to retain its population. A vision begins to take shape of happy cottage families, tending a few acres of organically-grown buckwheat or rye, serving cream teas to spectators as they milk goats in a demonstration byre, supplementing their income by letting the grown children commute to the nearest Japanese car plant.

I don't want only to jeer at this change of heart. A break with the traditional belief that agricultural progress means letting big farms grow bigger by driving the small farmers off the land is very welcome. But such a new policy would need a complete change in British attitudes towards the rural economy.

In this country, with the exception of the Scottish counties subject to the Crofting Acts, the small farmer is unprotected. He faces the full blast of competition for land from big land-owners, from incomers backed by City fortunes, from multi-national agribusiness concerns, from state corporations like the Forestry Commission. Even if the price of land goes on falling, the strong will continue – a little more slowly – to consume the weak.

A century ago, when the first Crofting Act was passed, Aberdeenshire had more crofters – tenant smallholders – than any of the Highland counties which came under the Act's protection. Now there are almost none. The slaughter of the Great War, the agonising rural slump which followed and then the growth of uncontrolled capitalist farming in the past 30 years did for them. How may this process be halted?

It requires a completely new deal, a decision that the small farmer must be assisted to stay on the land – as he is in so many European countries – by legislation. The tax system must be revised to encourage the transmission of smaller farms to the heir. The sale of such farms must be controlled, giving first option to other farmers in the same category and only exceptionally allowing large landowners or rich incomers to acquire it. A special land bank should be founded, offering cheap loans. Central heavy-equipment parks should be established, capable of carrying out the essential jobs like drain-digging and track repair which the small farmer can ill afford for himself (this was done during the last war). Above all, large farms and estates which don't meet stiff criteria of good land use should be purchased and broken up for re-sale.

Some years ago, the banker Iain Noble was driving through the Highlands and picked up an Israeli hitch-hiker. He pointed out various landmarks, observing that this belonged to Lord X and that was the property of Sir James Y. Finally the hitch-hiker turned to him in bewilderment. What did he mean? How could a loch or a mountain 'belong' to anyone?

This question, strange and then all at once not strange at all, worked its way into Noble's mind. Not much later, he left banking to become the founder of a college of Gaelic culture and language in Skye. But if Britain is to be 'fallowed,' then we all have to understand that story.

To halt agricultural growth is to call into question the sacredness of private property in land. Even when we now say that, suddenly, we seem to have a glut of land instead of too little, it's the 'we' that matters. This is a rare chance to recognise that, in the end, the use of the land is a decision for the community.   [*1987*

A Scottish Temple

Overlooking Edinburgh, near the summit of the Calton Hill, there stands a Greek temple. It was built in 1829 to house the Royal High School. In the 1970s, it prepared to be the home of a Scottish Parliament. But in 1979, Westminster rejected the result of a referendum on devolution, and since then it simply stands and waits for a final decision on its future.

In the way that one places fiction and myth in real landscapes, I realise that for me this has always been the temple of Artemis in Tauris, where the exiled princess Iphigenia served as priestess. Below is the surge and smoke of a city, rather than the desolate waves of the Black Sea breaking on the foot of cliffs. But something is waiting to be rescued there, as Iphigenia waited until Orestes and Pylades came.

The place isn't always empty. Every so often, the Scottish Grand Committee – the Scottish members of the House of Commons – come and hold their sessions there; a Tory gesture to national feelings, and a queer, deformed shadow of what might have been. Although Labour has a solid majority, 41 out of the 72 seats, the Conservatives govern Scotland through Malcolm Rifkind, Secretary of State, and his team of Tory junior Ministers. The Grand Committee may talk, but may not vote or decide. Its chairman is a Tory; its debates are cut off promptly at 1 p.m. Many MPs do not bother to attend, or leave early to catch the London plane.

Last Monday was different. The public galleries were packed, and demonstrators waited outside. Debating time was extended to 3.30, and a record number of some 45 Scottish MPs arrived. Not all arrived on time. In true 'Scotrail' tradition, the train from Glasgow left half an hour late and then was blocked by another broken-down train at Linlithgow. Nine MPs on board, including Donald Dewar, due to make Labour's opening speech, contemplated holding their own debate on the railway Tannoy.

This time, the Grand Committee was discussing 'the administration of Scotland': in other words, devolution. The Conservatives, the only party which remains steadfastly opposed to a Scottish Assembly, saw no point in this, but Labour – now more united than ever before in its demand for an Assembly with strong economic powers – got its way.

The debate began in a predictable, depressing way: the politicians settled down to regurgitating the devolution arguments of the 1970s and blaming one another for saying 'A' on one occasion and 'B' on another. Finally a voice from the gallery bellowed: 'Get on with the future!' He was shushed and reproved, but after that the discussion picked up some quality. A piece of ceiling about nine inches square, apparently dislodged by the eloquence of Anna McCurley (Con., Renfrew West & Inverclyde), fell and narrowly missed a civil servant. This, too, was a reminder – that time for repairing Scotland's structure is not unlimited.

Labour made much of its 1984 'Green Paper' on devolution, offering an elected Scottish Assembly powers over most internal affairs with the right to raise money through its own income tax; Donald Dewar spoke of 'an exciting, important constitutional reform' which would restore confidence to Scottish politics. The Tories said an Assembly would be expensive and useless, and pointed out waspishly that only 27 Labour MPs out of 41 had shown enough interest in devolution to turn up. The SNP said Labour's Assembly would be too weak, a Westminster puppet; the Liberals complained that it would not be elected by proportional representation.

Nothing could be decided; no conclusion could be voted. The five-hour debate on Monday was in many respects lame; those who came hoping to see visions of Scotland's future got little more than the familiar sight of politicians justifying their previous utterances. But interest in self-government is rising again. Seven years after the fiasco of the Scotland Act, which was passed by the Callaghan Government but withdrawn when the Scottish referendum produced a majority in favour which did not amount to 40 per cent of the electorate (the infamous, 'Cunningham Amendment'), the idea of a Scottish Parliament is popular once more.

A poll last February disclosed that four out of five adults wanted some form of Assembly. More striking still, a third favoured total independence. These are very startling figures, a higher self-government vote than any recorded in the 1970s. But they have to be qualified. First, they do not reveal the urgency of the wish, which may be of low intensity. Secondly, party loyalty in Scotland is still much stronger than loyalty to a constitutional idea. One of the strangest facts in the land is that most of those who say they would like Scotland to break the 1707 Union with England and become once more an independent nation are Labour voters – supporters of a party doggedly loyal to the Union.

Thirdly, there is no real sign of a powerful revival in the Nationalist vote. In the regional elections of May, the SNP achieved some recovery but certainly did not collect anything like that 30 per cent who say that they agree with the SNP's central policy: independence. The only real change on the party scene is the catastrophic defection from the Scottish Tories as the Government hits its own class constituency with one blunder after another, from freezing improvement grants to mishandling education to enormous rate increases. They have 21 seats out of 72, and – if nothing changes – would be lucky to keep 15 at the next election.

If Labour win the election and govern by themselves or with the Alliance, there will, I suppose, be an Assembly in Edinburgh. I suppose . . . but at Westminster there is a wily, Druidic attachment to archaic shrines like the omnipotence of Parliament which may have ways to frustrate it. If the Tories win, then we just have one more note in the crescendo of recent years – the Scots voting with increasing desperation and solidity against Conservatism and being rewarded with another set of Tory Ministers applying London Tory policies from the Scottish Office.

Another country which had reached this point would be about to boil over. Government by a Scottish Whitehall with no Scottish Westminster to hold democratic control; administration by a party with no popular mandate whose policies are detested; one elector in three prepared to say, even casually, that Scotland should secede from the United Kingdom . . . but where is the passion that should by now be making the pot bubble?

The absence of that passion is explained by the most terrible of all the results of Mrs Thatcher's seven years: the loss of confidence in politics itself. The power of the State grows, and its coercive might; at the same time, government gives up its task of redistributing wealth. We have sunk so far that few believe that elected governments, this party or that, can do much about the curse of mass unemployment or change the face of a decaying city.

Ten years ago, the nerve of the self-government movement in Scotland was the hope for change: our Parliament, our policies. Now, I believe these poll results with their queer lack of resonance express something different: formless bitterness, despair, the pity and fear of Scottish people for their own country. Iphigenia still makes her lonely sacrifices by the sea, but the warriors with whom she can escape have not yet come to Tauris.   [1986

Coals in the Bath, Sun on the Brain

'The more national newspapers there are, the more difficult it is to tell them apart,' wrote Paul Foot in a recent *New Statesman*. He concluded that, so far, more seemed to mean worse – 'an apparently irresistible spiral of declining standards.' And after displaying some lumps of trivial muck dredged from our free popular press, he noted: 'As soon as you think the depths have been plumbed, the newspapers – feeding off each other's garbage – go lower.'

There is an economic mystery and a cultural mystery here. Ten or 15 years ago, I belonged to a group of journalists peering into the future of journalism. We supposed then that an historic collapse was approaching in Fleet Street, that 'variety' would be fatally reduced to perhaps four or five national dailies and Sunday newspapers. We also supposed – wrong again – that the day of the monomaniac newspaper tycoon had passed, and that the Press would come under the control of enormous faceless conglomerates interested mainly in cement or cat-food.

Somehow, we have ended up with more 'popular' national dailies – six, counting the imminent *'Daily Eddie Shah'* – but even less variety. And the romantic appeal of owning a newspaper still persuades ambitious men to buy one, or several, and to invest millions which would certainly be more profitably dug into cat-food or cement.

Leaving the economic puzzle unsolved, there remains the cultural mystery. Why, in the late twentieth century, do millions of British people go on reading tabloids whose mental level would not strain the intellect of an over-sexed gnat? Foreigners, presented by British Airways with the *Sun* or the *Star*, think of protesting until they see smartly-suited young British businessmen in the next seat immersed in the same papers. Visiting trade unionists, asking their British colleagues for 'please, the journal of the Left,' turn over the pages of the *Mirror* in growing bewilderment.

The usual explanation is terse: 'We give them what they want. People buy our papers, don't they?' This sinks towards the level of 'Fifty million flies can't be wrong – eat dung!' But it is an explanation which, in this class-ridden society, cuts deep into pious middle-class opinion.

Part of the awful lack of self-confidence on the intellectual Left arises from the fear that those who read the *Sun* really are '*Sun*-readers,' that the space between the ears of millions of British proletarians consists of a tabloid-shaped slot. When the moan goes up, at party or union conferences, about 'the Tory gutter Press,' all too many of the moaners think that workers would automatically switch from blue to red, if the slot were filled with a socialist tabloid.

Seventy years ago, Lady Lilias Margaret Bathurst, proprietor of the *Morning Post*, told her editor that 'the public are marvellously ignorant and will believe anything.' It's odd to find sections of the modern Left agreeing with her, sharing, indeed, a venerable form of class prejudice: for coals in the bath, read *Sun* in the brain. It's even racialist. It implies that there's a hereditary mental defect in the British people, which prevents them from reading intelligent regional daily papers (as many West German workers do, taking them home to enjoy at night) or absorbing serious news and argument (like the numerous Italian workers who read *L' Unità*).

But, of course, there is no hereditary defect. The British absorb hours of news and analysis through television, sometimes of demanding quality. They are not much worse educated than, say, the French. What we have here is a public which is capable of reading infinitely better newspapers than it usually does. And this has been true for generations. Orwell observed during the war that popular papers not only soared in circulation but 'print articles which would have been considered hopelessly above their readers' heads a couple of years ago.'

What, then, is the secret appeal of these papers which treat their readers, in every sense, as boobies? For some reason, I suddenly remembered a scene from many years ago in Argyll. Every so often, an ancient vagrant known as 'Old Tobermory' used to appear and knock on the door. When a few people had collected, he would perform a sort of staggery dance and then launch into a whining, tuneless chant whose syllables had once been Gaelic. The custom was to hear him out and then reward him, but this was not mere charity. People got something from Old Tobermory. They got – and I don't want to suggest a meanness here – the curious but very intense satisfaction of knowing how much better they could have danced and sung those numbers themselves.

On the whole, the British don't believe what they read in their tabloids. They trust the sports pages; the rest is assumed to be saucy nonsense lightly seasoned with ground-up fact. It is, in short, a performance to be appreciated precisely because one can see through it and recognise it for a performance. And this recognition, this small daily feat of seeing through the cheeky buggers, is a daily source of satisfaction. The reader of the *Star*, whose life may otherwise feel like the bottom of a heap, folds away the paper with a sense of having outwitted somebody.

And the outwitted somebody – that's a journalist. Those who write these papers, college-educated technicians of 'writing down,' often take themselves quite seriously. They worry that they are blunting their talents by processing news to attract the hairy, grunting readers they imagine out there. 'Laddie, just remember you're writing for Mrs McGinty of Maryhill Road,' says the news editor, smashing some faintly challenging story onto his rejection spike. But down in Maryhill Road, it is Mrs McGinty – who has a bust television set and running damp and numerous opinions based on long experience of the world – who is laughing at him. She thinks his paper is daft. That's why she reads it. Who are the boobies now?

Reading papers you despise is an addictive habit. Somebody suggested putting up a plaque in the coffee-house frequented by the Viennese man of letters Karl Kraus, worded: 'Here Karl Kraus sat every day, reading the newspapers he detested.' But it's a bad habit, not only because it wastes time and money that could be better used. It is also bad for liberty.

Where freedom is left unused, there is no freedom, and a Press which does not use its freedom to inform is not a free press. Informing is what counts; columns of opinion (like this one) matter a lot less. In Poland, one may read some bold and witty opinion pieces in papers stripped leafless of real information by the censors. A paper which could keep its readers informed, but chooses not to, is hard to describe convincingly to a Pole. So are its readers.

Habits are hard to break. But that big joke about the tabloid Press – that the contempt of writer for reader is only surpassed by the contempt of reader for writer – is growing less funny. Readers, I hear, have begun to bombard those papers with articles or ideas for serious stories as they never did before. Some journalists, impressed by this, want to print more hard reporting and less garbage. A 'quality popular paper' is not a contradiction in terms, and might do well, if the mad economics of publishing allowed it to survive low circulation at the outset. For how much longer will the working people of Britain – just like middle-class commuters on a train – hide their real face behind their newspapers?

[*1985*

Journalists Behind the Wire

Like most people, I saw on television the journalists going to work for Mr Murdoch in his new plant at Wapping. Blurred figures filing down between the barbed-wire – I couldn't make out a face to recognise – they all shared an attitude: hunched-up, heads down between shoulders, collars up in the drizzle.

'The Caudine Forks' said a memory from Latin lessons. After that battle, the victorious Samnites made their Roman prisoners walk under a yoke. Yes, they must have walked like that.

So I went along to see for myself. Mr Murdoch, it seems, assumed that his printworks would be assaulted by waves of typesetters with fixed bayonets, supported by light armour and by suicide car-bombs driven by Shiite machine-minders. Roll after roll of razor bladed wire form a defence in depth. Ten-foot steel gates, electronically controlled, are covered by swivelling television cameras. Police, supported by private security men, guard the entrance. There are ramps to block vehicles, search-lights, half-visible men photographing visitors from an empty factory next door.

A German correspondent, amazed, writes that it is like the East German border, a film set which just can't be for real in a Western country. He isn't quite right, for it is even more like a police station in South Armagh. The old East End of London, for those who built this grotesque and horrible place, is bandit country where the natives are hostile.

The natives? A handful of pickets stand near the entrance, from the night shift who would have been producing the *Sun* if they had not been sacked. A taxi arrives. A young woman reporter, in a fur coat, digs frantically into her handbag to find her pass, trying not to see the picket who approaches the taxi window. 'Can I have a word with you? Judas did it for only 30 pieces of silver. Going to sleep well tonight, are you?'

Her shoulders go into that pathetic hunch; she crouches as the taxi moves on into the defence zone. Presently, two buses come out very fast, lights out, curtains drawn. The picket says his three sentences again, but nobody stops. There are a few boos and groans, and the buses tear away down East Smithfield.

Those buses contain my colleagues, the journalists of News International who have been defeated. Mr Murdoch did not mess around with them. He ignored all his house agreements with journalists, and told them to choose: go to Wapping and be rewarded with a £2,000 rise and private health insurance, or be sacked instantly and without compensation. Most of them went to Wapping, some cynically, some wretchedly. A few still refuse.

There is defeat and defeat. It's nearly a year ago now that the coal miners of Maerdy stepped back to work behind the colliery band, knowing that not one of them had crossed the picket line. This defeat is more complex than the failure of the miners' strike, but also more devastating in its consequences.

The TUC's weakness is manifest. The electricians ignore its commands, indifferent to the threat of suspension. The attempt to block newspaper distribution is failing, because the courts have ruled that it is illegal, but also because union members in the TGWU are indifferent to orders. The printers, so obstinate at the negotiating table, seem impotent and without militancy when turned out on the street. The journalists ignore their own union's instructions, cross picket lines and take over the jobs which belonged to production unions.

This is a historic collapse of organised labour, of its old discipline and solidarity. For so long, the print unions blocked the introduction of computer technology which made their crafts unnecessary. In the end, Rupert Murdoch – like a general who loses patience with chatterbox democracy – planned and carried out his lightning act of force, a *putsch* which in the event met almost no resistance. And it isn't only newspaper proprietors who will learn from this. All British employers can now contemplate the 'American way' of solving labour disputes: mass dismissals, production in a fortified site, the use of foreign technicians on contract to get the new machinery rolling and train a new, far smaller and more docile work-force.

But I want to come back to the journalists. They should be happy. They always resented the print workers. Now the printers have been liquidated and the journalists are learning to operate thrilling new direct-input keyboards for more pay on newspapers with a brighter economic future. And yet they aren't very happy. For in spite of all their hostility to the printers and their interest in new technology, Mr Murdoch – when D-Day came – treated his 'journos' as just one more enemy.

He stuck a gun in their back. Sign here, he said, or it's the bullet. You aren't worth negotiation, and I'm in a hurry. Get into these buses, disobey your union, cross the picket lines and start work behind the razor-wire of Fort Murdoch – now. Some readers, I know, will say that those who write for the *Sun* and the *News of the World* have no self-respect to lose. All the same, there is a stink of loss at Wapping.

Who do these journalists think they are? There was a time when journalists thought they were gentlemen and professionals – a claim treated satirically by other gentlemen and professionals. Then they concluded that they were white-collar proletarians, although of a superior kind, and joined the TUC. More recently, they have – we have – fancied the title of 'communicators,' educated specialists with a particular social responsibility for opening the reluctant official oyster to inspection.

All these dreams ended harshly at News International last week. Mr Murdoch's 'journos' are as interchangeable as microchips; the chip which doesn't fit is a reject. And there's another old-fashioned idea: that – as C. P. Scott of the *Manchester Guardian* put it – manager and editor walk together, but the manager walks a step behind. The editor is independent, bound first to the journalists he leads. But when Andrew Neil, editor of the *Sunday Times*, broke the Murdoch conditions to his staff, they heard him speak as an enthusiastic representative of management. He was not 'us' but 'them,' something alien and new in serious British journalism. And they split down the middle, accepting the move to Wapping by a majority so thin as to be almost meaningless.

The new way of production will change British newspapers more radically than anything since the abolition of stamp duty in 1855. The fall in production costs may break the financial dependence on advertising. It may soon be possible to launch and profitably maintain a first-class 'quality' daily paper with a circulation of 100,000 or perhaps far less – until now, the vain dream of those who long to see a politically varied and responsible Press in Britain.

All fine hopes. But then I see again those figures hunched in shame, the wire and the guards, the violence done to the independence of journalists and the integrity of editors. It is easy to sneer at 'the hacks who caved in to save their mortgages'; they have little chance of finding another job when they join the 5,000 dismissed printers and the four million unemployed. And yet that new free Press of the possible future will need men and women with guts and high spirits to write it. The self-respect and confidence of this journalistic generation are hanging on the old barbed wire down at Wapping – and bleeding to death.   [1986

Ancient Britons and the
Republican Dream

'The country is filled with anxiety and ill-feeling, and with the sense of a dishonoured public life'.

So writes Karl Miller, in the introduction to the latest anthology from the *London Review of Books* which he edits.[1] It is a moral statement, placing in a moral category all that is now amiss with the economy, the political style and the distribution of power in the United Kingdom. As such, I take it to be fully in the tradition of John Mackintosh. One of his gifts, often disconcerting to his party colleagues, was his capacity to judge and speak as a citizen and not only as a politician. This implies a language which is not that of U-turns or of so-called 'presentation', but of right and wrong, health and sickness. The United Kingdom, and Scotland within that kingdom, is in a poor way, which is liable to grow in both senses poorer; but there is a strange paralysis of the political ingenuity which might alleviate the situation. As they said in Warsaw in 1981, 'the Polish crisis is that nobody knows how to find a way out of it'. John Mackintosh was an Enlightenment man, certain that the power of rebellious reason could overcome. I know that he would have found our present-day fog of resignation the real dishonour of public life.

By using the phrase Ancient Britons in my title, I am suggesting that we live in an archaic political society. Its myth of origin is in many ways as fraudulent as the myth of an Ancient Britain served by all-wise Druids. It is the painful contradiction between this unreformed political structure and the rapid transformation of our social environment which is responsible for much of that 'anxiety and ill-feeling', and which lies at the root of economic dysfunction, mass unemployment and the growing antagonisms between society and the repressive power of the State. Perhaps it seems strange to write of the present Government as archaic, or an instrument of archaism. Mrs Thatcher is a moderniser, in her own terms, and her Government is anti-historical in at least two ways. She has severely cut State support for culture in all its aspects, from education as a whole through the British Council to the maintenance and development of the past through archaeology or conservation. Moreover, she has declared war on a number of institutions which she accuses of wishing to turn Britain into a museum, most prominently traditional trade unionism.

But in fact this leader's call to modernity rests heavily upon appeals – often spurious – to the values of the past. Patrick Wright, in his book 'On Living in an Old Country',[2] remarks: 'The Falklands adventure made a new combination possible: this small war enabled Thatcher to draw up the legitimising traditions of the 'nation' around a completely unameliorated 'modernising' monetarist programme. This new and charismatic style of legitimisation fused a valorisation of national tradition and identity with a policy and programme which is fundamentally destructive of the customary ways and values to which it appeals'.

Critical of some aspects of the past, Mrs Thatcher is all the more uncritical about the political heritage – above all, about the nature of the British State. Note the November 1985 Queen's Speech, with its emphasis on the enforcement of public order and even more reduction of those few liberties still left to local government. There is a queer dialectic between the relaxation of economic controls and the dismantling of the Welfare State on one hand, and a striking increase in the repressive and centralising power of the State on the other, a dialectic which this Conservative Government has dramatised rather than initiated, for it was also beginning to operate under the 1970s Labour governments. It was this Prime Minister who articulated the pseudo-historical slogan of 'Victorian values'. But harping on the theme of 'national unity' (supposed to be an essential Victorian feature) is a nervous twanging practised in our times by all the main political parties. I would oppose to this a remark made recently in *Le Monde* by the sociologist Alain Touraine, who asked: 'Should we not recognise the inevitable and even desirable existence of conflicts between the strategy of the State and the demands of public opinion? Instead of subjugating society to the State or the State to society, let us admit that it's the nature of the western world to experience an ever growing separation between the State and civil society'. He goes on to deplore the absence in France of a demanding public opinion willing or capable to argue for this separation in the face of the State. We are not much better off in Britain.

I believe that the British State is to be categorised as an *ancien régime*. It is closer in spirit to the monarchy overthrown in 1789 than to the republican constitutions which followed in France and elsewhere in Europe. It is true that French Jacobin republicanism introduced – or perhaps reinforced – a rigid centralisaton of State power which has some parallels in the extreme overcentralism of modern Britain. But it also established the doctrine of popular sovereignty, based on the notion of the rights of man, expressed in a constitution of supreme authority to which the citizen could – in theory – appeal over the heads even of the National Assembly. I am arguing here for a British version of republicanism, and it is my view that while Jacobin centralism is exceptional among republican projects, the principle of popular sovereignty and a written constitution is an almost universal element of definition.

We all know about the penalty Britain has paid for its economic priority – for being the first nation to experience an industrial revolution. We understand much less well the penalties incurred by Britain's – more properly, England's – priority in *political* development, by the fact that England underwent in the seventeenth century the first modern revolution. The English Revolution, to put it crudely, simply transferred absolutism from the king to Parliament. One may talk about the doctrine of the Crown-in-Parliament: the reality is that the House of Commons still possesses an absolute, undivided sovereignty which no Republic, *unie et indivisible*, can match. In effect, no higher institution can overrule what the Commons may decide by the majority of one vote. There is no doctrine of popular sovereignty – the half-formed Scottish version of that doctrine vanished with the Union of Parliaments in 1707. There is no written constitution, as the supreme authority to which the subject can appeal. There is no way in which Parliament can share its absolute power, except by lending it as a loan revocable at any moment – a lesson we in Scotland learned during the devolution debates. Federation is unthinkable. It would entrench rights in a part of the United Kingdom which Parliament alone could not overrule. For the Druids of Westminster, charged with weeding the sacred grove, such an impious violation of the sovereignty of Parliament would bring the oak trees crashing to the ground – no doubt leading to crop failure, plague and Roman invasion as well.

Under this Ancient British regime, the subject is almost helpless before the huge extension of State power that has taken place since 1945 and which is still taking place. The idea that the subject has an effective recourse against the executive through his MP has long been a joke, which the introduction of various ombudsmen has only made richer. A proliferation of isolated tribunals only makes the absence of a coherent code of administrative law more glaring (another institution which would require a written constitution and falls under the Druid ban). The principle of official secrecy still renders the defence of civil rights (which strictly we do not enjoy, as they are not embodied in positive law) about as easy as the work of a jeweller under a 15-watt bulb.

How often these complaints have been lodged – by John Mackintosh, in particular! And yet the *ancien régime* persists, the weight of its inefficiency more crushing every year, almost untouched by Republican principle. In what sense is it 'ours'? In Poland, Lech Wałęsa is one of many who have referred to the nation as a 'house'. The image suggests a tenement, overcrowded and dilapidated no doubt, whose inhabitants none the less recognise a duty to hold together; not to quarrel irrevocably, but to co-operate in repairing the fabric. That is a usable metaphor for the value of national unity. But Britain as 'nation' seems to me to present itself less as a house than as a temple – that sacred grove, indeed. We do not live inside this grove, but outside it; we approach it, perhaps tiptoe across its turf on suitably escorted occasions; we pay it reverence but we do not own it, we, the living. For this nation-grove belongs to the nation of myth which includes the dead ancestors. 'They' are the major component of 'we'.

We are dealing here with a concept of almost biological continuity which blatantly derives from the central principle of sanctified monarchy – the principle of hereditary succession. Applied to a whole society, it is a collectivism which submits the appeal of the individual in the present to a constitutional court of ghosts and skeletons – to the judgment of the past. It is no bad definition of the republican spirit to say that a Republic keeps the dead firmly in their place – not necessarily a dishonourable one, but certainly not a place of authority.

It is an irony that a government so dedicated to *laissez-faire* and to private enterprise presides over a State regime whose ethos is so collectivist. Its creed of economic individualism has, in this sense, no effective institutional foundations. The historian Larry Siedentop has observed[3] that 'the liberalism of the British constitution has been an essentially pre-individualist liberalism'. Britain was scarcely touched by the great social-political conflicts of continental Europe, between monarch and people, between empire and nation, between the lay State and the universal Church, out of which emerged republics based on the codified rights of the individual.

And yet we often describe Britain as a middle-class democracy, and is not militant individualism the defining characteristic of a middle class? Well, often and in most places – and I would include Scotland among most places, here as in so many other areas closer to the model of a small, normal European nation. But in England this generalisation runs into severe difficulties. In the 1960s the group around the *New Left Review* drew attention to the limited social and political results of the seventeenth-century upheaval and suggested that England had not experienced a bourgeois revolution. This absence would go a long way to explain, within the Marxist schema, the inner weakness of the British Left and the peculiar difficulties of approaching the threshold of a proletarian revolution. Another way of attacking the problem is to note the extent to which the English middle class, especially the later industrial bourgeoisie, adopted aristocratic values which hindered the development of that confidence and dynamism thought proper to their class.

In a remarkable article published eight years ago in the *Spectator*,[4] Siedentop asked why the British middle classes had ceased to be the carriers of an individual concept of society. Tocqueville had warned of the plight of a society which had lost the advantages of the aristocratic condition without gaining the advantages of the democratic condition. Siedentop wrote: 'The very openness of British society in the eighteenth and early nineteenth centuries led ... to the middle classes assuming quasi-aristocratic attitudes and accepting a more corporate conception of society ... There followed a partial collapse or failure of middle-class values and ideology which is basic to an understanding of the condition of Britain today. It is the chief reason why the individualist movement here has been contained, if not reversed'.

He remarked that 'the weakness of the individualist drive – what Marxists would call bourgeois ideology – is costing Britain dear. For that is the reason why Britain has not developed the impulse which might be expected from the wider spread of education, income and opportunity'.

It is another of those contradictions in which Thatcherism seems so rich that the individualist drive is being frantically signalled forward with whistles and green lights precisely at the moment when that 'wider spread' of education, opportunity and income has been stopped dead in its tracks and even induced to move some way backwards. So far, I do not see much response to green lights in the manufacturing sector, although the City of London is very appreciative. Travelling as a journalist, I frequently meet British salesmen and businessmen abroad. Their appetite for commerce and competition is still curiously weak. I look for contrast to – for example – West German businessmen I know, who show every sign of actually *enjoying* buying and selling. The activity which brings them profit also brings them pleasure. They admit this quite shamelessly. But captains of British industry suggest that they carry out their thankless duty of manufacture and commerce for the sake of the nation, a sort of defensive self-identification as public servants in private clothing! The corporate spirit of aristocracy again. The capitalist tiger prefers to register himself as the regimental mascot-sheep.

The point is this. The historic weakness of the English middle class proceeds from exactly that seventeenth-century compromise from which the British constitution proceeds. The middle class identifies with the *ancien régime* and is unable to see the advantages of overthrowing it and advancing to a condition of politically-guaranteed individualism. In return, however, the archaic nature of our State arrangements and the corporate ethic which they encourage repress bourgeois initiative at every turn. A recent poll in the *Mail on Sunday* reported that 48 per cent of the sample considered themselves not to be ambitious. I would not go as far as an American psychology textbook I picked up many years ago, which stated in its first chapter: 'Absence of the competitive instinct must be considered the primary neurosis.' All the same, such a degree of resignation in a western capitalist society in the 1980s is very startling indeed.

Let me sum this topic up with a statement which is already becoming worn by use – or perhaps by my own over-use of it in the past few years. It is commonly and comfortingly said that there is nothing basically wrong with British institutions – 'the finest in the world' – but that they are not working well at present because the economy is in such a bad state. The reverse is true. The reason that the British economy does not work is that British institutions are in terminal decay.

The Druids are determined that we shall not perceive this. I have spoken of the cult of the Ancient British grove, in which the dead are not 'they' but part of 'we'. What has come down to the present is defined as 'heritage', imposing duties as well as conferring privileges, an essential component of national and personal identity. It was the sharp ear of Patrick Wright which picked up the television commentator at the raising of the *Mary Rose* as he celebrated 'the first time *we* have seen her in 437 years'.

Here is the notion of a historical continuum. Now, I do not deny that a cult of history, a sense of continuum, can be invigorating. I know Poland too well to deny it. Polish nationalism and radicalism have always been restorative. In 1863, the Russian exile Alexander Herzen tried in vain to bring into a common front the Russian and the Polish enemies of the Tsar. He concluded: 'The ideal of the Poles was behind them; they strove towards their past from which they had been cut off by violence and which was the only starting-point from which they could advance again. They had masses of holy relics, while we had empty cradles'.

Within the sealed time-capsule of Polish experience, mere linear time becomes distorted. The poetic dramas of the early nineteenth century have a utility and relevance as direct as that of a telephone directory, for Poland's plight has not changed its essential shape since then, and the cast of characters spawned by that plight change only in the way that the names of actors change as they succeed to a part. Events which are important appear to have happened more recently than less significant ones. Some events which ruptured the sealed continuum are agreed not to have taken place at all. For over forty years after the Nazis destroyed it, the Royal Castle at Warsaw remained a hole in the ground. Now, however, the guide who takes you round the minutely-reproduced Castle will point across a court-yard and draw your attention to 'the only Renaissance window which survived the Baroque reconstruction'. The window has been there all the time, the Castle has been there all the time, but some malign disturbance of the ether made it for a while impossible to perceive.

Conservatism, in the literal sense, can go no further than this. This is not to say that Polish political aims are reactionary, but that – as with Solidarity – they wish to restore relics that are familiar: independence, social justice, civil liberty, the limiting of State power. The Russian cradle, filled in 1917, is empty again. But if another child is ever laid there, its face will be entirely new.

English manipulation of history is quite different. Here, time is linear to a perfectly oppressive degree. We are gazing from the terrace of a country house down carefully-landscaped perspectives of barbered lawns and positioned trees. The eye is masterfully led down a vista of elements (this battle, that cabinet) chosen to combine with one another into a single artistic experience. You could say: 'Prune back that Reform bush and make the Tolpuddlia bed twice as big'. But you would feel a bit of a vandal.

I'm exaggerating, of course. There is vigorous argument among English gardeners, and items of history are being repos-itioned all the time. But there is still an assumption that 'our' (in quotes) history can only have one focal point, one perspective. In France, by contrast, it is thought evident that French history as perceived by a Communist, by a middle-of-the-road Republican and by a Catholic monarchist will be a matter of three quite different gardens. This is emphatically not Druidic thinking.

But there is another contrast to English historical landscaping, and that is the Scottish awareness of Scottish history. It isn't an insult to the enormous pioneering work of historians here in the last 40 years to suggest that the public perception of history in Scotland remains chaotic. Time is not generally used to enforce perspective, and instead there is a scrapbook of highly coloured, often bloody scenes or tableaux whose sequence or relation to one another is obscure. But there is a source of energy in this dislocation. As in Poland, what is more intense appears to be in some way nearer: its impact is not diminished by informed distancing. I take for example the tableau of the murder of Archbishop Sharp on Magus Muir which has so powerfully seized the imagination of Scottish writers. Innocent of context, stripped of explanation, this murder takes place always now, in our Scotland. The contorted face of Hackston who has bungled the killing and is now urging his horse to stamp on Sharp's head is your face and my face; when the screaming is over and they open Sharp's little snuffbox to find his familiar, we all hear distinctly in the silence the sound of the bumble-bee escaping from the box and spiralling away across the heather. Walter Scott tried to play the Druid, to organise scenes like these into a mere heritage and say that they were over. But he did not really succeed, and the ferocity latent – occasionally patent – in Scottish society shows they are not over.

I have tried to outline some of the ways in which a particularly English historiography and concept of the continuous nation has been used to legitimise the *ancien régime* – the unreformed British State – and to discourage republican ideas. But of course the question is not just how to describe this but how to change it, and here we come up against a great curiosity. Why is it that the idea of radical constitutional reform appeals only to the centre of British politics? (It's no mystery why it appeals to nationalist movements in Scotland or Wales.) The Social Democrats have proposed sweeping changes; the Liberals have for many years supported proportional representation and constutional reform, including federalism. Both parties in the Alliance have published versions of that formula which attribute economic failure to the decay of institutions. The curiosity is that the Labour Party remain, in their overwhelming majority, hostile to this approach. We ought to remember, once again, John Mackintosh's lonely struggle to persuade his Party to think, in the wider sense, politically. But the orthodoxy of Labour, transmitted down the Tribunite line from Bevan to Foot, has remained a sort of debased economic Jacobinism. One day, the unreformed electoral system will deliver another huge Labour majority in Parliament, which will use centralised State power to redistribute wealth. This remains the dream. It would be unfair not to mention some recent, if marginal changes of emphasis, like Labour's new regional policy which would transfer some responsibility for economic growth to local initiative. But Labour are not a republican party. Labour still believe that they can achieve their ends through the existing State, through existing institutions.

Labour's outlook remains corporatist rather than individu-alist. Siedentop, to quote his *Spectator* article again, blames the absence of a powerful middle-class ethic. He writes: 'Just as the French bourgeoisie acquiesced during the seventeenth and eighteenth centuries in the growth of centralised royal power, in order to destroy their local aristocratic oppressors, so the British working class has acquiesced in the centralisation of power during the twentieth century in order to destroy what it sees as social privilege – the middle class masquerading as an aristocracy'.

One could stop to argue about the wisdom of a policy of class defence, in a period when working people are so intensely concerned with their individual rather than their collective destinies. But I am more interested in the consequences of Labour's fatal fascination with the instruments of actually-existing Britain. The consequences can be implied by stating this proposition, which is fundamental: it is not possible to build democratic socialism by using the institutions of the Ancient British State. Under that I include the present doctrine of sovereignty, Parliament, the electoral system, the Civil Service – the whole gaudy old heritage. It is not possible, in the way that it is not possible to induce a vulture to give milk. The British regime is designed to preserve privilege, to prevent the effective distribution of power and to smother the individual who counterposes his own interests to the collective interest of the mythic nation. It is democratic in the sense that the Powderhall Sprint is democratic; it is socialist in the sense that the National Coal Board is socialist.

The Jacobins themselves knew that the Revolution required new institutions. Marxism's warnings about the problems of a socialist movement confronted with the state apparatus of the previous régime have stood up well – tragically well – to experience. But Labour appear still to believe that the British Parliament under George III could have composed the American Constitution and applied it to the Thirteen Colonies.

So it appears that in fact it is precisely Labour, out of all the British parties, which stands to gain most from constitutional change, but which is most stoutly opposed to is – dismissing it, indeed, as a middle-class irrelevance. Instead, Labourism makes an effort to claim the heritage for itself, and compete with the Tories as the party of 'the nation'. This is not only absolutely unhistorical, in a multinational state like the United Kingdom. It is doomed to failure even as a tactic, for this is a game which the Tories and the régime itself will always win. Patrick Wright[5] suggests that Labour's failure to appropriate the 'nation' is inevitable 'not least because the nation to which Thatcher appeals so successfully is articulated . . . against post-war statist reform. While actually increasing the powers of the centralised State, this Conservatism is also thriving on widespread disillusion with the bureaucratic corporatism of the welfare state'. The nation or national interest to which Labour appeals. Wright goes on, is perceived as grey, inhuman and undignified. 'Starkly opposed to this, "the nation" to which Thatcher has learned to appeal is full of adventure, grandeur, ideas of freedom, ceremony and conscripted memories (of childhood or war, for example) . . . There are indeed "two nations" in the symbolism of Thatcher's Britain, but these are not the two nations of habitual definition: the division is not so much between rich and poor or North and South, but rather between the grand . . . symbolism of Empire and War on one hand and the bureaucratic imagery of the welfare state on the other'.

In whose name, then, should a mass party of the Left speak in Britain of the 1980s? Not in the name of the nation, but not in the name of one class either. How about in the name of the people? It is not a nation or a class which demands Liberty,

Equality, Fraternity, but the living – all the living – inhabitants of a definite country at a definite moment: now.

It is for the Left, above all, to develop this notion of a 'people', free of British national mythology but also free of a false, defensive collectivism which threatens to become part of that mythology. Democratic socialism is about co-operation and community. But that can now only be reached by an indirect route. Labour cannot get there by syndical and class struggle alone; it must become the party of individual liberty as well, fighting for the rights of the citizen, for his power to challenge the bureaucracy, for institutions which enfranchise him – whether these are administrative courts or local pressure groups or community co-operatives. A war against the State is waiting to be fought by a mass 'freedom party' of the Left. Its battles should be for a written constitution, for the doctrine of popular sovereignty, for a just electoral law based on proportional representation, for a code of administrative law and a constitutional court, for a sweeping reform of Parliament and its proceedings, for the option of federal status for those parts of the United Kingdom that wish it, for an entrenched grant of far greater competences to local authorities including the power to levy variable rates of taxation, for the demolition of the English legal professions and their replacement by a judicial system in which justice is affordable and judges come from all classes and age groups . . . For the abolition of the monarchy? I hold this to be – in Reformation language – 'a thing indifferent'. If the cult of the archaic nation is demolished, the monarchy – no longer called upon to sanctify it – will reduce to the scale of a harmless focus of affection and newspaper scuttlebutt. It is not the last king or queen who should be beheaded. It is the last Druid whose brains should be knocked out with the last volume of Walter Bagehot.

We are living in an increasingly airless room. Hope has been pumped out of it, and replaced by a scent of decay, by Karl Miller's 'anxiety and ill-feeling and . . . sense of a dishonoured public life'. If unreformed State power goes on expanding, and popular misery deepens, convulsions and unconsciousness will ensue. We must escape, or at least kick open the windows. We must transfer power to the people, but that will remain a dead political cliché until Labour, especially, understand that this transfer cannot now be achieved by the old, direct methods of syndical and class struggle, still less by a Labour government acting through the British State. This society requires drastic and immediate constitutional change. And the simplest way of justifying that change is to say that it would allow people, at last, to fight for themselves. [*1986*

The John P. Mackintosh Memorial Lecture, University of Edinburgh 1986.

---

[1] 'London Reviews' (Chatto and Windus, London, 1985).
[2] P. Wright, 'On Living in an Old Country' (Verso, London, 1985).
[3] L. Siedentop, 'The Strange Life of a Liberal England', *The Times Literary Supplement*, September 1985.
[4] L. Siedentop, 'The Impotence of the British Middle Classes', *The Spectator*, 30 December, 1978.
[5] 'On Living in an Old Country', op. cit.

III

EUROPE
A Barbaric Continent

Tiring the Romans

'Europe is dead!' This, one hears, was the opinion expressed by a flight of Reaganite hawks who visited London the other day.

One's first retort, from beyond the tomb, is that if there is no life in Europe, President Reagan's men should have been more discriminating about death when they prepared his visit this week to our silent continent. It seems that there are good bones and bad bones. We lie dead at Bitburg, and dead at Bergen-Belsen, but some Europeans are evidently more dead than others. The President's first itinerary assumed that the Wehrmacht and the Waffen-SS would be more responsive to him than the victims of the concentration camps.

This distinction has been hastily abolished. But there are still many armies of bones who are not reckoned worth talking to at all. When Chancellor Kohl went to Belsen last week, there was a separate ceremony – which he did not attend – for the 50,000 Soviet prisoners-of-war who perished there in numbers equal to those of the Jewish dead. President Reagan might reserve a word of respect for them without buckling the supports of the Western Alliance. But he probably won't.

Still, this is not the sort of deadness the President's disciples in London were complaining about. They find the leaders of Western Europe suffering from a lack of ardour which could be fatal if left untreated. When offered new missile systems, or visions of defence by an array of fireworks in space, they merely whine. When warned that the Soviet Union is hunched over a giant console controlling urban terrorists, coal miners and peace marchers in a minutely planned campaign for their undoing, they titter. They are flaccid, they are effete. European civilisation lives, with all its museums and palaces, its restaurants and pessimistic movies, but this is just the luminescence on the belly of an old mackerel if the raw instinct for self-preservation is extinct.

This is a grand old point of view. As clichés go, it has enjoyed a long life. It therefore deserves to be promptly stood on its head.

The 'over-civilised' point, first. On 3 September 1939 delirious crowds stood outside the British and French embassies in Warsaw to celebrate their declaration of war on behalf of Poland. Most people shouted 'Long Live France,' or 'Long Live England' (the Polish for Great Britain being too much to expect on a hot autumn day). This was pathetic enough, as neither Britain nor France fired a shot to save Poland from destruction. But one anonymous man, clambering on the shoulders of his friends, went further. He cried: 'Long Live European Civilisation-

It has always seemed to me that the events which followed his cry demolished the term 'European civilisation' for ever. Certainly, many of the palaces and paintings survived (though not in Poland), and Europeans today read and write more than ever. But the idea that there was some necessary connection between Beethoven and benevolence, between Mantegna and mercy, collapsed as totally as the *Frauenkirche* in Dresden. As late as 1939, Europeans who were already living in the period of total politics and mass populism still accepted the propaganda of the previous epoch, when kings and dukes – however cruel and stupid in their persons – were also the patrons of high culture. It was supposed that something rubbed off. Auschwitz corrected that.

For Europe is not a civilised place, a region which is polished but rather lifeless. It is a barbaric continent, heaving with a crude vigour which is now beginning to crack apart the marble slabs of imperial order laid across it by the post-war settlement 40 years ago. There is a lot wrong with that order, but it has at least restrained the Europeans from slaughtering one another for an unprecedented span of time.

Squashed under the enormous weight of Soviet domination, the Eastern nations of Europe have had no opportunity to display savagery. But in the West, conflicts waged outside Europe have shown what ferocity lies only lightly buried. France fought devastating wars in Indochina and Algeria, and came close to civil war in the Algerian aftermath. Portugal soaked Africa in blood. Britain remains one of the most pugnacious and military nations in the world, whose forces have been almost constantly in action somewhere in the world since 1945.

But barbarism is not just a readiness to fight. More often, the barbarian expresses his vigour through duplicity. France under the Fourth Republic and then de Gaulle was as maddening a partner for the Americans as President Ceausescu of Romania has been for the Soviet Union. Mr Mikhail Gorbachov now studies with distaste a row of Communist régimes which require Soviet support and Soviet fuel to stay in power, but which will always wriggle away from the path of virtue if they can. The European NATO allies have shown truly barbarous inconsistency by alternately squealing for more solid tokens of American military support and then grousing about the tokens when they arrive in the shape of cruise and Pershing missiles. Star Wars will be the same story. As the Romans knew, the real trouble with barbarian allies is not so much that they rebel as that they are inconsequent.

As the Romans knew . . . could it be that there is a 'civilised' Roman quality which the United States and even the Soviet Union possess and Europe does not? Perhaps a muscle-bound innocence, an enduring surprise that others may not recognise their good intentions. Perhaps it is just patience, the ability to stay put in distant places. A Roman legion might spend generations on Hadrian's Wall. There are US barracks in Bavaria and Soviet barracks in Mecklenburg where young American and Russian soldiers drill on the same squares where their fathers, and their fathers' fathers, drilled before them.

Books pile up, devoted to what the superpowers have done to Europe. There are volumes on the Sovietisation of the East, on the Americanisation of the West. But nobody, I notice, has asked what Europe has done to the superpowers.

Let's remember, first of all, that it was the Europeans who brought them into Europe and pitched them into confrontation. Adolf Hitler's lost gamble in 1941 brought Soviet power up to the Elbe. Ernie Bevin, as much as anyone else, persuaded President Truman to leave American forces on the Continent.

Bogged down in the European swamp, the Romans have

spent unthinkable totals of money and manpower. The Americans financed the post-war economic recovery of the West. The Soviet Union runs its own side of Europe at a net loss.

And neither has bought peace of mind. Across his western fence, Mr Gorbachov sees the gibbering mess of Poland, all crucifixes, generals and nationalism. The Americans have had to watch Western Europe acquire their technology and then impudently sell its fruits to the Soviet bloc. The swamp is alive, but mostly with leeches.

What have we done to them? After 40 years in Europe, the New Soviet Man has lost his clean jaw-line and become squat, liverish. That American boy who, so long ago, rode the jeep with the white star of liberation has grown grey and paranoid, and moodily kicks the Nicaraguan cat.

It is the Romans who have aged so terribly, and Europe which has grown barbarously young again. E. P. Thompson says that 'Europe is meditating now a declaration of independence.' But who is really dependent on whom, 40 years on? My friend Francis Hope used to say: 'When the child is grown-up, it's time the parents learned to stand on their own feet.'

[1985

Axel's Castles

Axel Caesar Springer, the West German newspaper tycoon, died a week ago. When I heard the news, I saw again the streets of Berlin brimming with red flags and heard – from nearly 20 years ago – the voices of tens of thousands of marchers roaring his name. 'Dispossess Springer!' they shouted, and 'Springer, we are coming for you!' But the second thought which came to me was a question. Why, after all, was he so frantically hated by so many?

He was a tremendous Anglophile. British officers licensed

and encouraged him to start his first newspapers, back in ruined Hamburg in 1948, and Springer always fancied a décor of leather armchairs and brown panelling which he thought 'typically English.' And his life's achievement – the establishment of an empire of raucous, nation-wide popular papers which relied for their appeal on sex, schmaltz and the bullying of left-wing scapegoats – was the introduction to West Germany of a very British institution.

Any Springer editor had to subscribe to four principles, which do not sound shocking when written down. These were the peaceful reunification of Germany 'in liberty,' reconciliation between Germans and Jews and firm support for the state of Israel, rejection of all forms of totalitarianism, and defence of the 'social market economy.'

Some called Springer 'fascistoid.' That was idiotic. The British military authorities gave him a licence to open newspapers because they thought that his brand of anti-communist, liberal entrepreneurship was what the Germans needed. He started the radio programme magazine *Hör Zu* and then the *Hamburger Abendblatt*, his first daily evening paper. Its slogan was 'Be Nice to Each Other.' He wrote before he launched it that he wanted 'to make a paper whose motor is today's heartbeat, which obeys only its own laws.' This was a recipe for a populist press which would break with the stale old German tradition of papers tied to political parties.

The empire grew. He started the serious conservative daily *Die Welt*, the cheap and rabid *Bild-Zeitung* which now has a circulation of over five million, and two popular Sunday papers. He acquired the remains of the pre-war Ullstein publishing giant in Berlin, and owned a virtual Press monopoly in Hamburg and West Berlin. When people complained that he had no mandate to force his own politics on the nation, he would refer to 'the daily, overwhelming vote of the readers for my papers.'

One of the anti-Springer buttons of 1968 warned: 'It will end badly for Springer.' As the years passed, he became a sad man, preoccupied by a mystical version of Protestant faith. His son killed himself in 1980, leaving the empire without an heir. Most of his causes became irrelevant or unpopular, and his political campaigns became rarer. At the end, his chief mourners were the leaders of Israel, whose nation he had supported with faithful and spectacular generosity from his own fortune.

Why, then, did so many Germans – not just the young Marxist Left of the 1960s but Social Democrats and liberals too – come to see Axel Springer as their arch-enemy? This hatred reached its peak in the late 1960s, the time of the student revolt, of the first entry of the Social Democrats into government, of the *Ostpolitik* which began to dismantle West Germany's threat to redraw the frontiers established in 1945. There was the 'Dispossess Springer' campaign, the call for a 'Lex Springer' against newspaper concentration, the fiery 1968 riots which tried to stop the distribution of his papers, the decision by German writers to refuse contributions to the Springer press.

The wrong way to look at Springer is to judge him by British standards. Set against the ethics of the *Sun*, the economics of *The Times* or the political ambitions of the late Lord Beaverbrook, Axel Springer and his papers seem – if not innocuous – almost restrained, almost 'wet.' But this was West Germany. This was a fragile state traumatised by the Nazi past, seeking to restore the good name of the nation and to escape a conservative tradition which had helped to put Hitler in the saddle, in which a gulf of silence and horror separated parents from children.

The Springer Press was burdened with the legacy of Chancellor Adenauer. It preached reunification within the 1937 frontiers and within NATO – which made reunification impossible – and to this day uses quotation marks to refer to the 'German Democratic Republic,' after years of calling it 'the Soviet Zone.' Those who questioned the Adenauer blind-alley approach were often dismissed as Communist dupes.

Bild-Zeitung, in a land of thin skins, adopted a line of demagogic, often mendacious abuse. Willy Brandt was reminded at election times that he was illegitimate, and had returned to Germany in Allied uniform. Student leaders were traduced as agents of East German Communism; when *Bild* advised its readers to take the law into their own hands and one of them shot Rudi Dutschke, many Germans felt that Axel Springer might as well have pulled the trigger himself.

When I was living in Bonn, a *Bild* readers' campaign against an article by my wife brought a deluge of hysterical hate mail, and I was physically threatened by a Springer reporter. For me, this was just a gutter Press in action. But this sort of thing rang a quite different bell with idealistic young Germans. Venomous personal bullying had been a speciality of the Nazi Press. They said, wrongly but understandably: 'Here we go again. . . .'

But now, looking back on it all, it seems to me that the deepest wound inflicted by the Springer Press was cultural. It wasn't just the political slant or the methods of those papers which roused such fury. It was an underlying assumption. *Bild* challenged head-on the traditional right of the German intellectuals to act as the nation's conscience, to prod and stimulate the masses with new ideas. *Bild*, in its 'Americanised' way, said something like this: 'Ordinary people care only for cars, sport, sex and the box, and why not? What you eggheads call their prejudices are the will of the majority – and we are its voice, not you.'

The right to consume, to be passive and not to think – this was unheard of as a German manifesto. The Left wore badges saying '*Bild Macht Dumm*' – *Bild* makes you stupid. Novelists like Grass and Böll lacerated the Springer Press with their wit and eloquence. But there was enough truth in Springer's claim to hurt them. Ulrike Meinhof, who was a good columnist before she took to the gun, wrote: 'His newspapers have more influence on German workers than their trade unions.'

Out of this grew a whole theory. The student Left of the 1960s concluded not just that the German workers didn't want revolution but that the working class as such had been castrated as a political force. If there was to be revolution, it could begin only in the universities themselves. It was a theory which owed as much to Axel Springer as to the books of Herbert Marcuse. It was a theory whose collapse left West Germany with some democratic reforms, but also with the disillusion of Ulrike Meinhof and her friends, who escaped down the sterile path of terrorism.

Konrad Adenauer, near his death, told Springer to remember three things: never trust the Communist, atheist East; be a good friend to Israel and the Jews; always be careful with the precarious balance of the German people. It was the third commandment that Axel Springer broke.   [*1985*

The Cost of Bitburg

Take your seats for this week's meditation: the fortieth anniversary of the surrender of Nazi Germany. When I lived in Berlin, I had my own special seat for such May commemorations. It was a view undisturbed by parades or statesmen, seen from under a tree growing in the roofless palace which had once been the Museum of Prehistory.

It was a most peaceful place. The Berlin Wall blocked off its main entrance, and the Saxon voices of East German border guards occasionally broke the silence. There were no neighbours; the site of the Gestapo prison on Prinz-Albrecht-Strasse, next door, had become a dirty field. Only lovers and American intelligence patrols ever visited the great ruin. Underfoot, fragments of pottery from Schliemann's Troy crunched – the archaeology of a museum – and formed an accidental rock-garden for minor plants.

Tucked under a broken tile, I once found a heap of old newspapers. There was a copy of the upmarket weekly *Das Reich*, with a leader by Reichsminister Dr Goebbels entitled 'War as the Measure of Human Worth.' And a tatter from a 1945 *Morgenpost*, referring to '*unser geniale Feldherr, Adolf Hitler*' – our genius of a warlord. . . .

The tree rustled its spring leaves where the cupola had once been. Germany did not merely lose that war, one tall tree ago, but lost it with a cataclysmic finality that has no precedent.

Today, as President Reagan gets through his bad moments at the Bitburg war cemetery, many Germans will be wondering whether 'reconciliation' and 'atonement' have turned out to be just one more lost effort. 'They are going to squash Bitburg into 18 seconds,' blabbered a Presidential aide. Bigger mistakes have been made in even less time.

Afterwards, I suspect, it will be put around in Washington that the President really displayed courage – 'showed balls' –

by going through with this and standing up to the Jewish lobby in the United States. But it is imagination, not courage, that he lacks.

There are, in fact, words which can be spoken in a cemetery which includes the graves of the Waffen-SS, and they are words about the elemental savagery latent in all nations and the temptation for all governments to harness it. But heads of government avoid this sort of talk at war memorials. I can think of only one statesman who would have known what to say at Bitburg – Willy Brandt.

The human damage – never mind the political damage – from this uproar is double. Enough has been written about the desolation and anger of those whose kin suffered under the SS, the Jews above all. But a deep and unkind hurt is done to German men and women, now old, whose young men lie in the war cemeteries and who now see them all slandered as murdering Nazis by foreign television teams scuttling among the graves. And the parents of the Waffen-SS dead: they did not deserve this. If Princess Michael did not recruit her father into Himmler's Black Order, no more did they pin the death's-head badge on their sons.

Lack of imagination again. In America, and in this country too, there is an enormous defect of imagination about the Third Reich and about its relevance to modern Germany. It's a defect with some honourable, decent roots in societies which have never known occupation, dictatorship or modern revolution. The French, in contrast, did not feel that their entire under-standing of the human race was collapsing when they entered Nazi concentration camps in 1945. Their historical experience, like that of Russians, Poles, even Italians, to some extent protected them. But the Americans and the British, for all the wartime propaganda about Nazi atrocities, went morally naked into Buchenwald and Belsen.

There is a distinct generation of young British officers for whom the shock of witnessing Belsen was a crippling event. Their world simply had not allowed for this. Some became bitterly anti-German. Some (and I have known a few) became mentally unstable. In a new book about the German collapse ('In the Ruins of the Reich,' Allen & Unwin £9.95) Douglas Botting quotes a British captain who entered the place shortly after its liberation. 'I was very near a nervous breakdown. I was paralysed by the whole thing. To me it was completely beyond tears – unless you feel you can cry when humanity dies. To my way of thinking it was humanity itself which had died this inglorious death of degradation and filth. . . .'

Those who have assumed the world was round and find that it is square can either work to make sense of their discovery or – feeling it too great a threat – explode it into fantasy. Our whole gigantic Nazi fiction industry (and I have even seen a comic about Treblinka) is really a violent effort of collective repression.

The British captain told Mr Botting that 'I'm sure it could even have happened here, in England.' And this, precisely, is the perception which is being repressed. Nobody, seeing the garish garbage that is the average war movie, could imagine such things taking place in Cambridge, Eng., or Cambridge, Mass. When they did take place at My Lai, Vietnam, most Americans were at first incredulous.

Repression, all the same, has its function in the lands of the Protestant ethic. By inflating the Nazi past into unrecognisable nonsense, the Americans especially have managed to preserve their optimism and construct a close working relationship with West Germany which will survive, not entirely unspattered, the Bitburg stupidity.

To ask the dismayed Germans to understand the uses of 'repressive fiction' would be to over-tax them. Their defect of imagination is elsewhere. All nations are self-admiration societies, and cannot be expected to see themselves as collectively criminal – let alone for 40 years. The East Germans and Austrians have adopted easy psychological escapes: the Nazi horrors happened in another country, in capitalist Germany or in Austria forcibly annexed to the Reich . . . not here.

The West Germans, whose society has actually changed far more profoundly than theirs, can't play these convenient games. Instead, their cartoon self-image is the 'German Michel,' a trembling shrimp of humanity who wears a nightcap and feels outwitted by everyone. Michel expects foreigners to find him ugly or stupid. But the idea that somebody might fear him or see him as a threat is utterly beyond his grasp.

In the end, Bitburg does not matter that much. Reconciliation is a fact, achieved mostly by sheer forgetfulness but also – to a small and precious degree – by combining memory and imagination.

Herbert Sulzbach is 91. He has given most of his life to helping the British and the Germans towards friendship, but in 1914 he was an artillery lieutenant in the Kaiser's army. A few months ago, the five survivors of the Ipswich branch of the Old Contemptibles – those who fought in 1914 – held what they knew must be their last parade. They decided to ask a German, Herbert Sulzbach, as their final guest of honour, and they found that he had been in action against their own battalion just 70 years before.

What do we celebrate on Wednesday, VE Day? Hitler's defeat, and Europe's liberation, and things like Ipswich. But if we are really trying to remember honestly, this day is about something more basic and marvellous than any of those, about the simple fact which the Russian and American soldiers yelled out as they spun drunkenly to balalaika music at Torgau on the Elbe. '*Voyna kaput*! – The goddam war is over!'   [*1985*

The 'Bildung' of Barbie

Certainly he remembered Klaus Barbie, said the old baron when I telephoned him. He had robbed the family of its jewels back in 1946, assisted by two other SS officers on the run. But the baron's sister knew more. Just you wait in your hotel room, he continued jovially, and I will fix a meeting with her and call you right back. What was the number of your room? *Na schön* . . . be patient and wait there for my call.

So I sat and waited. Half an hour later, there was a knock on the door. I opened it, and suddenly the small room was overcrowded with two bulky men, one in a fawn trenchcoat, the other in a black leather jerkin. Badges flicked out: *Kriminalpo-*

lizei. Who was I? What was my interest in Klaus Barbie and the jewel robbery? How long had I been in the city? I began to laugh; the man in the leather jacket allowed himself a smile, with a twinkle of gold tooth. A room search was briefly debated, then thought not necessary. The man in the raincoat looked frustrated. I was, it seemed, no more than what I claimed to be: a British writer researching for a book about Klaus Barbie, the SS and *Sicherheitsdienst* officer who had been the most famous torturer in the Lyons Gestapo and then an agent of American intelligence in post-war Germany.

Why had the baron called them, I asked. More interesting, why had they instantly responded to his call? To this, they offered no clear answer. They prepared to leave. The man with the gold tooth murmured pleasantly something about old men, about difficult times, about people of a certain generation who had strange things in their memory or on their conscience. . . .

Brooding on this, I went to the public prosecutor's office. A polite lawyer apologized: there were no files left about a robbery committed so long ago; everything had been destroyed; it was routine. But the police would probably have at least an entry confirming that a trial had taken place. Not at the main police headquarters, but at a little office in the Goethestrasse. I could mention his name. A short ride by streetcar took me there. The electric locks on the door seemed elaborate, but after a few moments, there was a buzz and the door yielded inward.

The man who let me in smiled broadly; this time I could see the whole of his gold tooth. He had exchanged the jerkin, for a handsome three-piece suit in Prince-of-Wales check. He and his chief had made some preparations for me; the nonexistent Barbie file was on his desk. I was not allowed to read it – 'the new laws protecting the privacy, of the individual, you understand' – but my hosts riffled about its pages and fed me suggestive bits. There was a sense of compensation for a little misunderstanding. I left, comprehending even less of what was going on in this town. 'Oh, *those* two!' said a surprised German friend at lunch afterward. 'What on earth did they want with you? They are Department K14, what we used to call the political police.'

To research the past of a particular Nazi in West Germany is constantly to encounter the sense that you are missing some point. Plenty of German students and journalists undertake such research, but always instrumentally: to topple some political opponent with a revelation about his past, to prove that today's capitalist is yesterday's fascist, to use the testimony of the repressors to discover more about the resistance of those who were repressed. The simple question: 'What shaped this person so that he could do these things?' is not held to be interesting. This can easily be misunderstood; a suspicious foreigner can read evidence of pro-Nazi machinations into what are no more than the curiosities produced by German bureaucracy and history.

Officer Gold-Tooth covers political subversion, and when that job started under the Allied occupation over thirty years ago, it dealt primarily with fugitive Nazis supposed to be plotting against the British and American forces. The prosecutors in another town, I discovered, had known for twenty years exactly where Klaus Barbie was living in South America and under what name; they never bothered to pass the information on simply because their instructions were to deal with Barbie's movements on German territory. In the late Forties, prominent ex-Nazis and SS veterans with evil records often banded together secretly with all the apparatus of code-words and forged papers, but their object was less to revive the Hitlerian Reich than to keep out of jail and acquire enough cartons of Camels on the black market to trade for the cans of Spam and bags of coal they required to stay alive.

I did most of my work in Trier, the city on Germany's western border where Barbie was brought up. As I grew to know the place a little, so the enterprise came to seem like some Asian shadow-play: it was quite easy to get local historians to recount the drama of the town's history under the Third Reich, but a severe breach of the convention to demand that the surviving actors appear in person. One early Sunday morning, walking in the market square and listening to the rumbling and groaning of Catholic church bells, I thought of three old men, none of whom I was able to meet, now awake and shuffling in slippers to prepare their coffee: Albert Urmes, who was once the Nazi propaganda director in Trier; Willy Torgau the Communist, who spent most of the Hitler years in prisons and headed the denazification tribunal when the French army arrived in 1945; and Erich Süsskind. After years of bullying and discrimination, Süsskind and his wife and their small son were deported to Auschwitz in the winter of 1943. At the selection on the ramp, he asked his son if he wanted to stay with him or his mother. The boy went with his mother, which proved to be the way to the gas chamber.

Erich Süsskind survived. When he was liberated in 1945, he weighed some seventy pounds. Not only his wife and son, he found, but his parents, his four brothers and sisters with their families, and almost the entire family of his wife had been exterminated. But Erich Süsskind, unassuming and alone, and as if it were the most natural thing in the world, went home to Trier and reopened the little cobbler's shop that had been taken from him eight years before. There were almost 800 Jews in Trier when Hitler came to power. Today, there are perhaps thirty. Süsskind does not talk much about the past. But he is loved in the city for one laconic sentence uttered on his return: *'Die Trierer waren es doch nicht*! – It wasn't the people of Trier who did it.'

Trier is a polite, conservative city. The fact that its two most famous sons appear to be Karl Marx and Klaus Barbie is accepted with distaste but without protest. Neither fascism nor communism has gained much authentic support in this ancient Roman capital on the upper Mosel river, close to the frontiers of Luxembourg and France, regularly wrecked and plundered by foreign armies on their way to the Rhine valley down one of Europe's most inviting invasion routes. Trier is a frontier city, sharply patriotic by tradition, whose dominant politics have always been Catholic and conservative. This year's official celebrations of the centenary of Marx's birth, in the pretty little mansion on the Brückenstrasse, which once housed a French governor in Napoleon's time and then, after 1933, the editorial offices of the *Nationalblatt*, were a pallid affair. At another ceremony held in the high school where both Marx and Barbie were taught, the dignitary invited to unveil a plaque observed comfortingly that the school could not be held responsible for having educated the author of *Das Kapital* ('Why did you bother to come?' shouted irritated boys at the back of the hall).

The spirit of the school, the Friedrich-Wilhelm Gymnasium, has in fact always been an enlightened, almost liberal Catholicism, hostile to political extremes and carefully independent of the bishop. If young Dr Krapp, the headmaster, felt depressed when I asked him for essays by the pupil Barbie, he was too courteous to show it: files were hunted out, photocopies made, and the mystery of Barbie's development discussed. How did this sensitive, pious small boy, so withdrawn that few of his school contemporaries even remember him clearly, metamorphose into a torturer?

Even today, and whatever their views, pupils at a German high school navigate cautiously when writing answers about religious belief. Liberal the Friedrich-Wilhelm Gymnasium may have been, but it was never prudent simply to dismiss religious faith as nonsense when taking the main state examination to matriculate. Barbie tried to dodge the issue by suggesting that matters of faith 'affect the inner man' and were therefore not proper topics for logical discussion. Exactly ninety-nine years before, the boy Marx – a Jew baptized a Lutheran – dared to sail a bit closer to the wind: 'Before we examine the basis, nature and effects of the union of Christ with the faithful, we should see ... whether Man cannot by himself reach the End for which God called him forth out of nothingness.' Both, of course, were prevaricating. Barbie was already a member of the Hitler Youth when he wrote, committed to anticlerical neopaganism; Karl Marx was high on Hegelian revolutionary liberalism. Both passed the examination, Marx with far greater distinction than Barbie.

Among Barbie's examiners was Dr Michel, one of his form teachers, who was later to provide a rather disconcerting example of civil courage and its penalties. In 1937, with Hitler in his fifth year of power, Dr Michel ordered his pupils to turn all the desks around so that they faced the door rather than the blackboard. Until now, there had been a crucifix on the end wall of every classroom, above the teacher's head. A new decree had ordained that the cross must be removed and hung over the door, to be replaced in the position of honour by a portrait of Adolf Hitler. Dr Michel's class were thus obliged to turn their backs on their *Führer*. He was instantly reported by one of his colleagues. But all that happened to him was a transfer to another school.

The Nazis in Trier were always outnumbered by the Catholics, and scored miserably in free elections during the Weimar Republic. Even after Hitler assumed full power in 1933, Catholic dissidents – as the case of Dr Michel showed – enjoyed some immunity. But there was no attempt to use this strength. Instead, Bishop Bornewasser (who much later attacked the Nazis over the euthanasia programme) tried to conciliate the new regime by declaring a pilgrimage to the Holy Robe, Trier's most famous relic. Nazis in uniform shepherded the foreign pilgrims about the town and lined the streets; party dignitaries stood beside the bishop at the cathedral door to welcome important visitors. A film of this episode, one of Hitler's easiest propaganda victories, is kept locked in the diocesan archives at Trier. There also exists a photograph of Bornewasser standing with Goebbels and giving the Nazi salute. It remains unpublished. 'To explain it would be too complicated in a caption,' the owner told me. At the time that the photograph was taken, the new Nazi mayor of Trier was banning Jews from public swimming pools on the grounds that their cheeky and tactless behaviour was upsetting normal citizens.

The creaking and gasping of the lovers in a room along the hotel corridor has died down. Then the silence is broken again by a hoarse voice from the direction of the river outside: '*Hilfe, Hilfe!*' The voice grows faint, then returns with new desperation. I open the windows, letting in a swarm of river flies, and peer out over the Mosel at the arches of the Roman bridge, at the indifferent headlights of late cars. The source of the voice is invisible. The river is black, with trembling silver flowers of reflected light from the lamps on the bridge. Now the voice from the dark water is screaming and sobbing: 'Help – O Gott! – help me. . . .' Windows begin to open along the hotel; guests peer out.

The police van drives straight down the bank to the water's edge: a floodlight goes on, and suddenly there is another silver flower in the black water, this time with a struggling fly caught in it. '*Bleibt doch ruhig* – stay calm!' repeats a loudspeaker. Men wade into the Mosel and vanish; there is the sound of wet commotions, more sobbing. Flashlights dance up and down as a man is pulled up the bank. An ambulance drives slowly away, bouncing over the uneven turf. I look along the front of the hotel, where a head protrudes out of each window. Only the window of the two lovers remains shut.

The Polish writer Artur Miedzyrzecki writes: 'Misery is close by, right outside your window. But it doesn't affect you directly. Sleep. So a person hears and does not hear the cry for help. A person does not realise that violence is occuring. He realises it when everything is over. Too late to do anything. . . . Heroism is first and foremost the courage to see in time.'

In the morning, the Trier newspaper does not mention anything about a man in the river.

Klaus Barbie once cared about the misery outside his window. It was a phase, in his late teens. He joined several Catholic young men's groups, who went about the city feeding derelicts and visiting the prisons. It was a way of relieving the guilt and confusion of his life at home, where his father, a village schoolmaster, was drinking himself to death. Some of his acquaintances thought this quiet boy was a natural recruit for the priesthood. Barbie himself once considered studying theology. Then, in his twenty-first year, everything changed. His father and his handicapped younger brother died, the pension on which the family hoped to finance Klaus through university was cut off, Hitler came to power, and Klaus became a Nazi.

He never explained this sudden change, and nobody in Trier can account for it. Such conversions were common enough in 1933. He looked into the glaucous, pale blue eyes of the *Führer*, was dazzled, and fell. All his previous life, his loyalties and beliefs and sufferings, became irrelevant. 'I have become a serving member in the mighty retinue of the *Führer*,' he wrote later that year. And he remained true. Forty years later, an acquaintance in Peru remembers, a joke about Hitler made Barbie, who was then using the name 'Altmann,' leap to his feet, turkey red, shrieking that he would tolerate no insult to the leader in his presence. Year by year, he observed Hitler's birthday. 'He lacked only patience,' he wrote recently to another SS veteran. 'If we "young ones" had been allowed to take charge in time, he would be alive to celebrate his birthday now. . . .'

It is easier to explain why he made such a brilliant party career so young: adjutant to the Trier-Central Nazi chairman at twenty-one, at twenty-two admitted to full membership of Reinhard Heydrich's *Sicherheitsdienst* (SD), the SS intelligence service. Barbie, it seems, was the Nazi stool pigeon in the Gymnasium. The party in Trier saw its main enemy in the Catholic youth groups, especially strong in the high school; Klaus Barbie was a member of one of these groups and was a priceless source of information about his own schoolmates.

In the underpass leading to the Friedrich-Wilhelm Gymnasium, Dr Krapp's pupils have written with a spray can: 'Better to be a Universal Dilettante than a Specialized Idiot.'

Trier is a beautiful city again, rebuilt carefully after bombing and American artillery tore out its old heart. Rococo churches and Renaissance palaces collapsed; only monuments of dictatorship – the gigantic Roman gateway, the Porta Nigra, and the concrete flak bunker – survived unshaken. Its politics today, dominated by the Christian Democrats, are tranquil, and the arguments that generate ideological heat are mostly about symbols. Lieutenant-Colonel K., an earnest and intelligent soldier, combines the roles of a Bundeswehr officer, a historian of the working-class movement in Trier, and an elected member of the Social Democrat opposition in the city council. When he proposed changing the name of the street still dedicated to Hindenburg, the Christian Democrat city fathers said that such shocking demagogy reminded them of Goebbels. When he suggested that the council formally revoke the grant of honorary citizenship made to Adolf Hitler more than forty years before, they said that they had never heard anything so outrageous since the speeches of Julius Streicher. Nothing is proved by all this except how deeply and effectively the Trier establishment has buried the past.

And it is not only the Nazi past that has been buried. On a back wall in the municipal art gallery, I found a small, untitled painting by Peter Krisam, showing French Moroccan cavalry charging a civilian crowd in the marketplace. It was a spirited, angry little canvas, marked only with the date, 1923, hung in an obscure corner. But with that date, a corner of the historical coffin lid began to creak upward. This painting was about the Trier which for hundreds of years understood itself as Germany's western bastion against French imperialism, the city where the word 'France' did not stand for red wine and berets but for bayonets, for *spahis* riding down demonstrators, for attempt after attempt to lever the whole border region away from its German allegiance. This is an aspect of Trier which is scarcely mentioned in public in these days of Franco–German reconciliation (besides, there are still 20,000 French troops quartered in and around the city). But it was the aspect that dictated the political climate in which Klaus Barbie grew up. That date of 1923 referred to the climax of Franco–German conflict in the aftermath of the First World War, as French occupation troops tried to impose on the population a chain of puppet 'separatist republics' intended to bring about the secession of the whole Rhineland from the Reich. Louis XIV had blown up many of Trier's medieval churches, Napoleon annexed the whole region to France, and after 1945 France refused to permit the return of Trier's hinterland in the Saar to Germany and ruled the town with a harshly effective network of *Sûreté* agents and informers.

Here at last was a key to the '*Bildung* of Barbie.' The folklore of his childhood was composed of fresh memories of resistance to the French and their tame 'separatists.' His own father came from the Saar, cut away from Germany after the defeat of 1918, and after fighting the whole war on the western front, he had taken part in the patriotic, anti-French resistance. When Klaus Barbie entered the Friedrich-Wilhelm Gymnasium, there were still older boys who could boast of their experiences dodging the scimitars of the *spahis* in the market square in 1923.

And here, too, lay a clue to one of the sickest manifestations of Barbie's character: his hero-worship of Jean Moulin. Barbie, with the Lyons *Einsatzkommando*, captured the French resistance leader in 1943, who had been betrayed by one of his own countrymen to the foreign occupiers. Moulin died soon afterward of injuries which Barbie still claims were self-inflicted but which most witnesses say were the result of Barbie's interrogation methods. Everything that Barbie has said since, however, suggests that he identified in Moulin the German patriots, some of them partisans and saboteurs, who paid for their guerrilla war against the French occupants of 1923 with their lives, and who had become the mythical figures of his own youth.

When he faced this calm, resolute prisoner in Gestapo headquarters at Lyons, Barbie saw only a mirror image from recent Rhineland history. He did not grasp the difference between a nationalist fanatic and a democratic politician like Moulin. Instead, he thought he recognised – this squat, trivial, warped little policeman – the special human quality and stature which, as a Nazi, he had been trained to worship and blindly to obey. But this superman, this 'member of history,' was at his mercy. And, if the evidence can be believed, Barbie fell upon him, battering and clubbing him until Moulin was a bleeding wreck beyond recovery. In an interview, Barbie once gave away a horrible fragment of the truth: 'As I interrogated Jean Moulin, I felt that he was myself.'

Many years after the war, 'Altmann' made a business trip from Bolivia to Europe. He had been twice condemned to death in France *in absentia*, and there was a warrant out for his arrest. But he took a risk. He went to Paris, to the Pantheon where Moulin's remains now rest. In that empty place, the man who had begun life as a Christian idealist, who had passed through the careers of a Nazi torturer and an American secret agent, and who was now a corrupt businessman in South America, paid his indecipherable respects.   [*1983*

The Death Doctors

On a winter morning in Frankfurt, when it was still dark, the journalists were taken into a small, well-guarded room to show them the defendants at the forthcoming Auschwitz trial. That was in 1963. I remember staring at those faces, as the photographers scrambled among them, as if physiognomy would begin to unlock the mystery of how human beings – what sort of human beings? – had done those things.

Here and there were the faces of wild beasts, grinning uncomprehendingly: terrible Boger with his yellow eyes, the great skull of Kaduk. There was no mystery about them. When Etty Hillesum saw faces like those guarding the trains as they drew into the camp at Westerbork to begin the deportations to Auschwitz, she thought of the line in Scripture which says that God made man in His own image and, for the first and last time, her religious faith was shaken to its roots. But then there were the others. Mulka, the camp adjutant, looking like a bad-tempered old shopkeeper, or Perry Broad, who had been one of the youngest SS guards, still a sleek and youthful man in an immaculate three-piece suit with the expression of somebody accused of parking his Jaguar in a pedestrian zone. Their appearance told me nothing.

And there were the doctors. These men, trained in famous academies and some with high research qualifications, bound by the Hippocratic oath, had carried out selections on the ramp – dividing the incoming torrent from the trains into those who were sent straight to the gas chambers and those who were to be worked to death. Some had killed thousands by injections, or carried out experiments on helpless men, women, and children. Most had taken part in internal selections within the medical blocks, consigning to death those with infectious diseases, those too weak to be worth keeping, and those whose bodies had fulfilled their purposes in research.

If the sight of the doctors answered no fundamental questions, neither did the evidence as the long trial got into its stride. It became clear that the doctors above all had subscribed to an 'Auschwitz code of values' which could not be reconciled in their own minds with the charge that they had betrayed all medical or human standards. It was not even as simple as 'evil, be thou my good.' Early in the trial, one witness described how a group of Polish children had been brought to Auschwitz after being caught stealing coal. Since there was at the time no separate block for children, they were distributed among different huts. However, a medical decision was taken that 'it was morally dangerous for children to sleep among adult men.' So the children were taken to the medical block and given lethal injections. 'In this way,' said the witness quietly, 'the morals of the camp were preserved.'

More than twenty years have passed since that trial, and it is only now, after reading Professor Lifton's book, that I have begun to understand the fundamental question 'How could they?' – the subjective process in the minds of these doctors which allowed them to assimilate killing to the commandment of healing. But the importance and stature of 'The Nazi Doctors' is much greater than that remark suggests. This is not only one of the most important works on medical ethics yet written. It also breaks through the frontiers of historiography to provide a convincing psychological interpretation of the Third Reich and the crimes of National Socialism. No one will be able, in my view, to write perceptively about those times in the future without referring to this interpretation, without bringing into the centre of the analysis the dynamic which Lifton calls 'the biomedical imperative.'

Rudolf Hess said in 1934 that 'National Socialism is nothing but applied biology.' It was an appeal to which a large part of the German medical profession responded with a sense of dazzled, revolutionary liberation. Medicine was no longer just one profession among others, or one of many branches of applied science and research. It had become *the* profession, the central intellectual resource of the New Order. Doctors acquired a status that engineers, nuclear physicists, even generals could not approach. Doctors were 'biological soldiers.' Medicine was breaking away from mere 'Christian' or 'Judaic' compassion for the individual, and from the passive, remedial job of healing the sick. From now on, medical science would address itself to the 'positive' task of actively shaping the future of the human race, to cultivating and pruning genetic stock for the future, to using 'biological laws' in the service of a new understanding of the wholeness and interdependence of all life.

Lifton establishes the chronology, the steps that led eventually to doctors – not professional SS officers, but doctors of medicine – performing the supreme sacral rite of National Socialism: the selections on the ramp at Auschwitz. There were five such steps. The first was coercive sterilisation. The second was the killing of impaired babies and children. The third was the so-called 'euthanasia' programme, the killing of impaired adults – cripples and the mentally handicapped – in the gas chambers of special institutes and adapted hospitals. Then came the extension of 'euthanasia' to impaired or racially undesirable inmates brought from the concentration camps. Finally came the mass extermination of entire racial groups in the *Einsatzkommando* operations and then in the death camps.

The ideas of 'racial hygiene' or coercive eugenics were circulating widely in the early years of this century, and not only in Germany. By 1920, for example, some twenty states in the United States had laws for the compulsory sterilisation of the 'feeble minded' and criminally insane. But in Germany, such thoughts were fatally to converge with new concepts about euthanasia. In Anglo-Saxon societies, as Lifton remarks, euthanasia implied on the whole the right of a person to choose death. In Germany, however, it had been argued since the late nineteenth century that the State as the supreme social organism retained the right to impose death on some of its subjects in the interest of the collectivity, the sacrifice of lives in war being only the most obvious precedent. An influential book published in 1920 by Karl Binding and Alfred Hoche, *Die Freigabe der Vernichtung lebensunwerten Lebens*, put forward the concept of 'life unworthy of life,' which was to become central to Nazi thinking and practice. The authors, a professor of law and a professor of psychiatry, declared that the destruction of 'unworthy life' was in itself a healing process – a treatment for the social organism; they discussed the 'ballast existence' of human beings reduced to empty shells and prophesied 'a new age . . . [There has been] an overestimation of the value of life as such.'

Hitler and the other Nazi leaders seized upon such literature, adding it to their mental brew of racialist dogma, collectivist theory, and paranoia about '*Volkstod*' (the dying out of the Germanic race). In 1933, the first year of Nazi power, a compulsory sterilisation law was applied to a list of mental and supposedly hereditary afflictions, including schizophrenia, hereditary blindness and deafness, and even inherited alcoholism. The programme was intended to sterilise nearly half a million people in its first phase, though Lifton believes that it was applied only to 350,000 at most. A national index of persons with hereditary taints was established, and the infamous Racial Institutes for Hereditary Biology and Racial Hygiene were set up.

'Euthanasia' – Professor Lifton rightly uses quotation marks, for this was State killing, and the word is one of the earliest and ugliest of Nazi euphemisms – began in 1939. It was preceded by the Knauer case, the birth in Leipzig of a gravely malformed child whose parents appealed to Hitler for the right to end its life. Hitler's accord, with an assurance that any possible legal proceedings against the doctors concerned would be quashed by the *Führer*, led to the establishment of a commission under Hitler's personal physicians to register 'life-unworthy' children and organise their killing.

Here for the first time doctors were dealing with the reality of 'biological soldiering': killing as healing. The deceptions were for the benefit not only of parents but of the medical staff as well. Although parents who refused to surrender their children to these institutions were coerced and threatened, there was much talk of 'latest methods for healing'; children were perfunctorily 'treated' for some time before being given lethal sedative overdoses, and doctors laid much emphasis on the research value of autopsies.

Already gratuitous cruelty was appearing. The extremes were represented by the abominable Dr Pfannmüller at one such institution in Bavaria, who introduced 'the natural method': death by starvation. A member of a party of visitors describes how he pulled a dying child from its bed; and exhibited it 'like a dead rabbit,' explaining that only a few more days were needed. 'The picture of this fat, grinning man, in his fleshy hand the whimpering skeleton . . . is still vivid in my mind.' Pfannmüller exemplified a syndrome on which Lifton lays much emphasis: the association of sadism with omnipotence fantasies which came to affect many Nazi doctors.

The killing of adults 'unworthy of life' began with an order from Hitler in October 1939, after the outbreak of war. 'Patients considered incurable' were to be medically killed. But Lifton, in a memorable passage, warns against the temptation of interpreting this as only an aspect of war preparations and emergency measures:

> Rather than medical killing being subsumed to war, the war itself was subsumed to the vast biomedical vision of which 'euthanasia' was a part. Or, to put the matter another way, the deepest impulses behind the war had to do with the sequence of sterilisation, direct medical killing, and genocide.

The programme to kill 'unworthy' adults, known as T4, after

the Berlin address of its headquarters at Tiergarten 4, was a huge affair. Directed by a large medical and ancillary bureaucracy, it was conducted at six main centres in Germany and Austria. Gas chambers were introduced for the first time, as the mental hospitals of the Reich disgorged their 'incurables,' and there was a complex cover-up system of reassuring letters to relatives and of falsified death certificates. Jewish children had already been killed in the earlier programme, and a number of Jewish adults were now sent to T4 centres from the camps – Jews alone required no medical paperwork or phony diagnosis to be murdered.

It is well known that T4 was halted in 1941, as a result of the only serious civilian protest in the history of the Third Reich. The facts leaked out: public demonstrations took place and Count von Galen, the Catholic bishop of Münster, delivered the famous sermon in which he declared the entire programme to be a blasphemy against God: 'poor unproductive people if you wish, but does this mean that they have lost their right to live?' Less familiar abroad is the resistance, religious and professional, put up by a few physicians. Professors like Karl Bonhoeffer and Gottfried Ewald, both psychiatrists, resisted and so did several Protestant pastors involved in running mental hospitals. Paul-Gerhard Braune, the only objector who was arrested, wrote directly to Hitler condemning the very concept of 'life unworthy of life' and warning that unless the 'intolerable' programme was halted, the moral foundations of the nation would be undermined.

In fact, T4 only paused, to continue for the rest of the war on an 'informal' basis in which the central bureaucracy was dissolved and the medical staff of the killing institutions were left to carry on the work at their own discretion. The next step had already been taken. Early in 1941, the T4 leaders had agreed to allow Himmler to use their facilities for an operation to rid the concentration camps of 'excess' population: 'asocial' and invalid inmates.

This was the penultimate step to the death camps. The operation, known in office jargon as '14f13,' for the first time merged the SS empire of the camps with the biomedical purging of society. The doctors were now working closely with the SS; gas chambers were in use; the victims were being selected on grounds that no longer had much to do with any objective health criteria but a great deal to do with racial origin and political attitude. It was for 14f13 that the euphemism 'special treatment' (*Sonderbehandlung*) was first introduced to denote killing. Doctors in white coats appeared in the camps. Collective diagnosis was applied to Jews, and Lifton quotes some of the labels used. 'Inflammatory Jew hostile to Germans,' or 'Anti-German disposition. Symptoms: well-known functionary of the KPD [German Communist Party],' or 'Diagnosis: fanatical German-hater and asocial psychopath. Principal symptoms: inveterate Communist.'

It was not long, however, before camp commandants were dispatching indiscriminate parties of victims chosen by their own guards for 'special treatment' in the T4 gas chambers, simply to reduce overcrowding. By now, T4 staff were extracting gold teeth and fillings from corpses and forwarding them to headquarters in Berlin. It is no wonder that Lifton calls 14f13 the 'medical bridge to genocide.' (Lifton here adds a detail which, to the best of my knowledge, has never been followed up in Germany. In 1942 a T4 'mission' went to Minsk on the eastern front. Its assignment is not known, but there are strong indications that its task was the killing of wounded German soldiers suffering from severe cerebral or psychological damage. Both Bishop von Galen and Braune had earlier expressed the fear that this would be one of the logical consequences of the programme).

The basis of Lifton's method in this book is an extensive series of interviews. He spoke to twenty-nine men 'significantly involved' in Nazi medical programmes, including doctors implicated in T4 and employed at Auschwitz. He also interviewed a dozen old Nazis described as 'nonmedical professionals,' and eighty Auschwitz survivors from the medical blocks, many of whom were in the tragic category of 'prisoner-doctors' working under the supervision of masters like Eduard Wirths, the chief physician, or Josef Mengele. Lifton, who is himself Jewish, conducted these meetings as he felt a scholar should, restraining although not actually denying his own intense emotions, dissembling to a pardonable extent with some of the Nazi doctors by concealing from them the real extent and aim of his book.

This enterprise has already proved too much for some critics, for whom the idea of a Jewish academic tactfully, even at moments tenderly, addressing questions about their psychological stresses to men who did ramp duty at Auschwitz is – simply – unbearable. Such objections seem to me quite wrong. There is an overriding need to know the process by which highly educated and intelligent people contrived to justify to themselves their participation in acts like those. The alternative is to leave – for instance – Mengele protected behind generalisations about 'the best in all of us' or even 'the banality of evil,' observations which hide him and his colleagues from examination as surely as the bulletproof screen shielded Eichmann at his trial.

The second part of Lifton's book is a study of individual behaviour at Auschwitz, primarily of the Nazis doctors but also of the prisoner-doctors. Lifton introduces this section by remarking that the place might well have been named the 'Auschwitz Centre for Therapeutic Racial Killing,' and emphasising that Nazi ideologists indeed regarded it as a rather special and secret kind of public health venture. The doctors there referred in jest to 'Therapia Magna Auschwitzensis'; shortened to 'TM,' the abbreviation came to be their unofficial euphemism for the gas chambers. That was the approach that rendered it necessary that doctors, not other camp officials, should supervise the selection process.

Their responsibilities were arduous. They included not only selection on the ramp and supervision of the killing process, but selections within the camp, direct killing by injections (mostly by phenol), certifying death at individual executions, signing false death certificates, overseeing tooth extraction from corpses, controlling epidemics, performing abortions, observing floggings, offering advice on cremation and other means of corpse disposal, and – very important – general advice on controlling the influx of prisoners into the camp itself, which of course affected the proportion of arrivals sent straight to their deaths.

Here, as Lifton says, the healing-killing paradox was at its most acute. Hard as it is to understand, the medical staff took seriously their obligations to maintain 'standards of health' at Auschwitz. However, the price of protecting the inmates' health (if that is the right expression: their average life expectancy was about three months) was to keep up a high killing rate among new arrivals at the ramp, and often to recommend the gassing of whole blocks of the camp which had become infected with typhus or other diseases, or were otherwise unmanageable.

There also remained the other, broader aspect of healing-killing: the necessities of the biomedical vision which required the curing of the Nordic race by ridding it of Jews and other 'poisonous' elements. The doctors, in short, were invited to see their task as a supreme expression of medical responsibility, its value only emphasised by the fact that most doctors initially found it difficult to carry out – and some found it impossible. However, once these physicians had convinced themselves that they were still acting as doctors and not as slaughterhouse foremen, their sense of omnipotent rectitude could become extreme. The tale of the Polish children gassed to protect camp morals is one example. Another is the fact, cited by Lifton, that suicide by prisoners was regarded as a most serious offence and was followed by a careful official inquiry.

By contrast, the prisoner-doctors, most of whom were Jewish, faced their own dilemmas with open eyes. Essentially, they were all dead men and women on furlough; for any reason or none, at any moment, a prisoner-doctor could be dropped back into camp or gas chamber. Nonetheless, they did what they could to save lives, to help the sick in the medical blocks, and to restrain or mitigate the 'hobby' programmes of research which individual Nazi doctors were carrying out on prisoners. In order to do these things, they were obliged also to enter the awful paradoxes of Auschwitz. They provided lists for selections to the medical block doctors, knowing that the more reliable they were in assisting the death process, the more effectively they could persuade their masters to let them help others. In matters like the distribution of medicine – ten aspirins a day for a block containing thousands – they were again choosing candidates for survival by rejecting other claims to live. As Lifton says, in Auschwitz a rare syringe was worth more than a human life.

Curious, conditional bonds sometimes arose between these prisoner-doctors and the SS physicians; born of expediency, these bonds – as between terrorists and their hostages – could acquire some depth. The ties could be confessional, professional (doctors talking to doctors), sexual, or even scientific, for some of the prisoner-doctors, although appalled at the brutality of the experiments on prisoners, became almost in spite of themselves emotionally committed to their success. A few SS doctors, like the man named here as Ernst B., not only took pains to keep their prisoner-helpers alive and well-fed but even arranged forbidden meetings with their relatives in the main camp.

The extraordinary prisoner-doctor Hermann Langbein, who was in touch with a resistance group in the camp, managed to establish a sort of ascendancy over Eduard Wirths, the chief Auschwitz doctor. As his secretary, Langbein was able to extract concessions from Wirths, to encourage him in his power struggle against the SS political office, and even to dissuade him from resigning in a moment of despair. In three categories, however, the prisoner-doctors killed voluntarily. They killed vicious *kapos*, as indicated by resistance cells; they killed dangerous maniacs on the medical blocks whose behaviour threatened to get the whole ward 'selected'; most reluctantly, they also aborted babies or killed them at birth, in order to save their mothers from the gas chamber. As Dr Olga Lengyel, one of the prisoner-doctors, said: 'I marvel to what depths those Germans made us descend.'

Two psychological terms are advanced by Professor Lifton to interpret the adaptation of the Nazi doctors. These are 'numbing' and 'doubling,' and they have, of course, a validity which can extend far beyond the crimes of the Third Reich into any situation where human beings consent to behave in ways that contradict a previously internalised moral code – including war itself.

'Numbing,' a term Professor Lifton has formulated in earlier work, is fairly self-explanatory. Selection duty on the ramp was accompanied at Auschwitz by an almost literal numbing: the doctors drank heavily in what became a carefully observed group ritual, and encouraged shaken or reluctant newcomers to get drunk with them. More generally, the doctors protected themselves against impulses of pity or horror by a battery of mental devices. Racial ideology was the most important. Lifton suggests that the doctors tended to regard Jews not simply as 'subhumans' beyond normal human consideration but as people who were in practice already dead by virtue of their presence in the camp. Experiments on living prisoners could thus be experienced by the doctors as a form of autopsy, and some of the contradictions that so horrified outsiders – for instance, careful antiseptically performed surgery on patients, who were then at once killed off – were evaded.

Josef Mengele provided numerous examples of such 'extreme numbing,' but so did the doctors of the T4 programme, including leading figures like Karl Brandt, an admirer of Albert Schweitzer and a man whom many contemporaries remembered as noble and upright: many decent Germans were bewildered by the revelations at his trial after the war. At the lowest level, 'numbing' was only an extension of self-protective attitudes: the hardening to horror required in any casualty ward, or the 'sawbones' humour common among surgeons. At the 'euthanasia' centre of Hadamar, a drunken party with music and mock sermons was held in the cremation room to 'celebrate' the ten thousandth victim.

'Doubling' is a more complex idea. Lifton is defining the construction of a second 'Nazi' or 'Auschwitz' self. He is not, he insists, talking about the lasting dissociation of 'dual personality,' but about a temporary dissolving of psychic glue as 'a means of adaptation to extremity.' The second self accepted an entirely different set of criteria within the extreme circumstances. 'Conscience' at Auschwitz meant performance of duty, loyalty to the doctors' and SS groups, the 'improvement' of camp conditions (i.e., making Auschwitz function more efficiently). At the same time, the prior self continued to exist, to be entered on leave when a doctor returned to his family: or when Rudolf Höss, the commandant, went home at night to his luxurious house and played lovingly with his children.

'Doubling' was a difficult feat, nonetheless. The strains were evident in Eduard Wirths, the chief camp doctor, a man formally responsible for all deaths in the medical blocks and co-responsible for the regular decisions on how many from the incoming trains were to be gassed and how many to be admitted for slave labour to the camp. Wirths was opposed to random brutality; he improved conditions in the medical blocks and reduced the rate of killing by injection because it was deterring prisoners from reporting sick. Yet this 'aura of moral scrupulousness' did not prevent him from carrying out his own revolting experiments on typhus infection or cervical cancer. His letters home show a tormented personality who surrounded his wife and children with – as Lifton puts it – 'a quality of absolute purity and goodness.' He wrote that his duties must be performed for the sake of 'my children, my angel,' a German mission on behalf of that absolute purity of his other life. When Wirths was arrested in 1945, a British officer observed that he had shaken hands with a man who had caused the deaths of four million people. At that moment, Wirths understood that his 'doubling' had collapsed, that the consequences of what the 'Auschwitz self' had done were about to flood his prior self and his family with disgrace. That night, he managed to hang himself.

Lifton conducted a long and fascinating series of interviews with 'Ernst B.,' an Auschwitz doctor who had refused – successfully – to conduct selections and who was remembered with gratitude by many surviving prisoners and prisoner-doctors as a man who had worked consistently to save lives, improve conditions, and obstruct some of the worst medical experiments of his colleagues. Here Lifton found himself in the midst of confusing debris left over from both 'selves.' For much of the time, 'Ernst B.' was candid and open about Auschwitz, admitting to shame and guilt. At other moments, however, he would veer into a harder, 'Nazi' line. The Third Reich had used 'primitive methods, but there was something that was right.' He consistently defended his doctor colleagues, refusing to take the easy and partly justifiable course of dissociating himself entirely from them. Most curiously, he stood up strongly for Mengele, and tried to persuade Lifton that Mengele had been a man of high integrity, that he was never cruel, and that his experiments on prisoners constituted 'real scientific work.'

Mengele is the subject of a section of Lifton's work, and also of a book by Gerald Posner and John Ware. While Posner and Ware present a chronicle of Mengele's entire life, from youth in Günzburg to his pseudonymous grave in Brazil, Lifton is concerned only with the Auschwitz period and its implications. He observed: 'While he is obscured by his demonic mythology, he has in many ways earned it. . . . My task is to try to understand how his individual psychological traits fed, and fed upon, the Nazi biomedical vision.'

It is, indeed, a very great pity that Josef Mengele was never caught and tried. Retribution apart, the survivors needed to understand just who, and what, it was that they so much feared. One of the twins from Mengele's camp kindergarten said:

> I would wish to have a good front-row seat. . . . To me he is the key to my sense of fear from everything that is German. . . . I would be very interested to hear the details and to see him pass [through] this metamorphosis of turning back into a person instead of God Almighty.

Mengele was the most adept 'doubler' of them all. The visual sense of him survives very clearly: neat and handsome, his black uniform immaculate, smiling pleasantly or whistling Puccini as he distributed death or life on the ramp, sometimes dashing into the oncoming torrent of human beings with a shout of 'Get those twins over here!' In the medical blocks, Mengele's absolute unpredictability terrified the inmates. His kindness toward some of 'his' children, gypsies or twins or children with eyes of contrasting pigment, seemed quite genuine. This in no way impeded his ability to have them killed without any apparent feeling, or indeed to kill them himself for dissection. There was no chink in this armour, no way to 'get around' Mengele or to take precautions against his changes of mood. And playing his 'Auschwitz self' plainly gave him enjoyment, the pleasure of acting out the fantasy syndrome of sadism-omnipotence which affected so many of the Nazi doctors. Was this a man who loved his work, or who was in love with his own actor's reflection in the black mirror of Auschwitz?

The Mengele myth afterwards became so potent that the world now believes that he alone performed all the Auschwitz experiments, that he commanded the entire medical department or even the camp itself, that he committed atrocities that in fact never happened, and that he performed all the selections on the ramp – a fantasy that even some survivors share. However, Mengele was not the only experimenter, and – in terms of the deaths and agony inflicted – not the bloodiest. One should remember also Professor Clauberg, the only Auschwitz doctor with a real international reputation – for his infertility research – who carried out injections of caustic substances into the Fallopian tubes of hundreds, perhaps up to a thousand, Jewish women, or Horst Schumann's irradiation of male and female genitals, or the programme sponsored by Bayer (makers of aspirin) which involved the wholesale slaughter for dissection of patients given an experimental drug against typhus.

Mengele did research on dwarfs, on noma sufferers, and on heterochromia (contrasting eye colour) – in the latter work, gypsy children were killed and their eyes dispatched in boxes to the Friedrich-Wilhelm Institute in Berlin. But his obsession was with twins. By 1944, he had collected some 250 individual twin children; he did most of the measurement and examination himself, and provided the children – who looked on him as an 'uncle' – with above-average care and nourishment. The twin unit was provided with a special laboratory and dissection suite, complete with a large library. Mengele killed some 15 per cent of his twin subjects, which meant that many of them survived Auschwitz.

What was he after? He was plainly driven by a furious ambition to achieve academic fame, and the twins research was intended to form the basis of his *Habilitation* – qualification as lecturer and then professor. But opinions still differ both about the quality of his work and its purpose. Lifton tends to the view that he made exaggerated scientific claims for erratic and unsystematic work. He has also concluded, after initial scepticism, that Mengele was – as many prisoners have suggested – working not on genetic determinism but on learning 'the secret of multiple births,' a discovery that would have had enormous implications for Nazi ideology and the accelerated breeding of 'outstanding' racial types.

For the Nazi doctors, Auschwitz was the great temptation. It was not just that commitment to 'research' was a handy catalyst for the numbing and doubling processes of self-deception. It was the blinding opportunity offered to ambition by a place in which live human beings were easier to come by than laboratory rats – to quote one particularly foul example, human flesh was used for blood experiments because it was far more plentiful than scarce animal meat. Some of the doctors said openly that it would be morally unforgivable to pass up this unique chance of research on living human beings: another instance of the healing-killing paradox. History has no more terrible example of the Faustian bargain: for the chance of renown, for their own diseased vision of the higher good of the race, these doctors sold their souls.

Some paid their debts on earth. Many of the doctors were executed after the war, and many committed suicide. A number of them got off lightly. Professor Verschuer, who had supervised Mengele's research and who was the recipient of those boxes of human eyes, was reinstated in a chair at the University of Münster after the war. A committee of fellow professors considered his case, and pronounced that 'it would be pharisaical for us to regard in hindsight isolated incidents in the life of an otherwise brave and honourable man, who has had a difficult life and frequently displayed his nobility of character, as an unpardonable moral stain.' Similarly, the German Chamber of Physicians, sitting in 1955, refused to withdraw the title of doctor of medicine from their colleague Professor Clauberg.

Josef Mengele got clean away. Doggedly shielded and financed by the Mengele clan, using the wealth of the family agricultural machinery factory at Günzburg, he survived for 35 years until – a miserable, sick, frightened old man – he had a heart attack and died while swimming in Brazil in February 1979. When his bones were finally identified in 1985 I had the chance to look at his diaries, a stack of notebooks piled on the desk of a magazine office in Munich. They seemed no more than the ramblings of a sour exile engaged in lying to himself about the past, and offered little to grow excited about. To my surprise, however, Gerald Posner and John Ware have written a book on Mengele – well researched and wonderfully free of all the customary fantasy and exaggeration – that makes fascinating reading.

They dredge up for rueful examination all the nonsense about Mengele as the *Führer* of heavily guarded Nazi enclaves in the jungle, all the phony announcements that he had been found or had escaped arrest by hours. It is – alas – all too clear why Mengele evaded capture and retribution for so long. The reason is that nobody tried hard enough or long enough to find him. His cover was not difficult to penetrate. In fact, in his Argentina years, he abandoned concealment altogether and frequently used his own name. Even after his move to Paraguay in 1959, a typist at the West German embassy in Asunción was able to remark casually that her broken ankle had been set by a German doctor named Mengele. His nineteen years in Brazil, from

October 1960 to his death in 1979, took him from one fairly amateurish concealment and pseudonym to another, much of the time within reach of the city of São Paulo or, finally, in its suburbs.

Any dedicated team of investigative journalists, given time, patience, money, and a modest element of luck, would have tracked him down. No such team appeared. Posner and Ware, a New York lawyer and a British television producer, were the right kind of investigators, but they only began their hunt when Mengele was already dead.

Before 1960, the year of Eichmann's kidnapping from Argentina by a Mossad unit, few people were much interested in Mengele. In that year, however, the West German press began to give copious publicity to his crimes, and rewards were offered. The West German authorities, in contrast, did little until they went into a final burst of activity long after his death. In spite of the pressure of the late Fritz Bauer, public prosecutor in Frankfurt and the real architect of the 1963 Auschwitz trial, the police failed to intercept the steady flow of letters between Mengele and his family in Günzburg, or the busy correspondence of Hans Sedlmeier, the family lawyer, who supplied Mengele with money, visited him on several occasions, arranged his trip to Switzerland to meet his son Rolf, and dealt with the various families who sheltered him in Brazil. One raid on Sedlmeier's house was frustrated by a police source in Günzburg who tipped off the intended target. It was not until May 1985 that a more securely planned raid hit Sedlmeier again, and found reams of Mengele correspondence and data in his wife's cupboard. As for the West German embassy in Paraguay, its efforts to lay hold of Mengele in 1959 and 1960, when he was living under its nose, were puny.

The Paraguayans themselves, President Stroessner in person and some of his henchmen, were responsible for the obsessive conviction in Europe and North America that Mengele was hidden in that country, although – as Stroessner and Co. knew very well – he had remained there for only a year. Why did they not say openly that he had gone? In fact they did so, but only after they had told so many lies and behaved so evasively that nobody believed a word they said. Their motive seems not to have been any political sympathy for old Nazis, but something much more Latin American: furious patriotic resentment at the way that Nazi-hunters and foreign governments seemed to be pushing them around. They were damned if they would help foreigners who insulted Paraguayan sovereignty and made disparaging remarks about the regime. The result of their refusal to cooperate was, of course, to make things far worse. The world concluded not only that Mengele was still in Paraguay but also that Stroessner was an old German fascist who was deliberately protecting his own.

Every con man and hack who could raise money from a credulous newspaper was soon reporting sure-fire sightings or near-miss meetings, almost all in Paraguay. A more serious question is why the Israelis missed him. Posner and Ware have taken much trouble to seek the answer, and have talked to many of the Mossad men involved. The explanation turns out to be prosaic: bad luck, and lack of resources. In 1960, Isser Harel, then head of Mossad, made some efforts to find and seize Mengele while he was in Argentina on the successful operation to kidnap Eichmann. In spite of a few good leads, Isser Harel had neither the time nor the men to do the job thoroughly. Two years later, however, the small Mossad team under Zvi Aharoni made a breakthrough. An ex-SS officer named Willem Sassen agreed to help, and soon established that Mengele was living in Brazil under the protection of a certain Wolfgang Gerhard. Aharoni and his men trailed Gerhard to a farm near São Paulo. And there, while they were eating sandwiches and contemplating the next move, three men rounded the corner of the track and passed within feet of them. Two were Brazilians, but the third was an elderly European with a moustache. It is almost certain that this was Josef Mengele.

Near certainty was not good enough for Aharoni, who flew to Paris to meet Harel and plan the kidnapping. Here the witnesses contradict one another. Aharoni says that Harel ordered him to drop the Mengele inquiry and concentrate on the case of Yoselle Schumacher, a child abducted by his Orthodox grandfather to prevent his parents from taking him back to Russia. Harel claims that he carried on the Mengele operation, but failed to confirm the identity of the man on Gerhard's farm. What is certain is that, when Harel was replaced shortly afterward, his successor, Meir Amit, insisted on the concentration of Mossad's efforts upon tasks directly connected with the state security of Israel. Mossad, simply, was too small to pursue effectively both the hunt for old Nazis and more urgent problems like Nasser's attempt to develop ballistic missiles.

Nobody else came anything like as near to Mengele as the Israelis. But the Mengele-hunting industry boomed on for more than 25 years, fuelled by sensational nonsense about vast Mossad raiding projects. Many of the most amazing tales emanated from the offices of Simon Wiesenthal in Vienna.

Posner and Ware make a judgment on Wiesenthal that seems to me fair. There is no doubt that many of the Mengele sightings or Mengele hide-out reports that Wiesenthal spooned into the jaws of credulous newsmen were quite baseless, and that a man as tough and shrewd as he was should have known that they were baseless. He encouraged the idea that he was a spider sitting at the centre of a world-wide web of agents and informants, which was unfortunately not the case. However, Wiesenthal was not by nature a boastful fantasist out for headlines. His problem was that the Jewish Documentation Centre was a hopelessly under-financed one-man operation. If anybody had given Wiesenthal the money and agents he really needed, I have no doubt that he would have found his man. As it was, he took the only sensible course open to him: using every means to raise publicity and keep the world excited about the search for Mengele, in the hope that – eventually – a reliable informant would be persuaded to come forward. But in spite of all the rewards and feature movies and pseudo-trials staged *in absentia*, none did so. One detail however, continues to nag. What happened to Willem Sassen, who found the way to Mengele in 1962? Or, more properly, what happened to his information, and why did Aharoni and his colleagues apparently sit on it, instead of passing it on to others who might have made good use of it? This is a hole in the story which Posner and Ware do not fill.

On the subject of Mengele, both books have drawn on the testimony of Dr Miklos Nyiszli, a Hungarian Jew whom Mengele appointed as his personal research pathologist. His memoir was first published in an English translation in 1960, and Seaver Books have done well to issue it again now in a cheap paperback. Nyiszli saw more than any other survivor whose writings are known to me. Mengele's dissection laboratory was set up in one of the crematory blocks, and Nyiszli's job was not only to assist his research but to care for the health of the *Sonderkommando* – the special work squad of Jewish prisoners whose appalling task was to assist in the process of gassing and cremation. Each *Sonderkommando* was put to death after about four months, and Nyiszli was a witness both to the ultimate secret of mass murder and to the heroic revolt of a *Sonderkommando* on the night of 6 October 1944 (all were killed, but only after they had blown up one of the crematories and killed dozens of SS men with weapons smuggled in by the Polish resistance).

Nyiszli was not, it seems, very popular with other prisoner-doctors, who resented his remarkable privileges and felt that he put altogether too much professional zeal into his work for Mengele. But we do not have to like him in order to recognise that this is the best brief account of the Auschwitz experience available to a reader, even though – like both Lifton's book and that by Posner and Ware – it would have been greatly helped by a plan of the camp itself. The book also reprints the famous essay by Bruno Bettelheim which served as its foreword in 1960, and which added so much fuel to the agonising controversy over Jewish behaviour in Nazi Europe. I do not agree with it, but its eloquence and outrage must guarantee it a permanent place in Jewish historiography.

'The Jews of Europe,' Bettelheim wrote, 'could have marched as free men against the SS, rather than to first grovel, then wait to be rounded up for their own extermination, and finally walk themselves to the gas chambers.' The essay also includes Bettelheim's attack on the Anne Frank legend, in which he claims that the Franks should have obtained guns and gone down fighting, and – here I sympathise – he criticises the stage version of the *Diary* for the way it ends with Anne proclaiming her belief that there is good in all men. For Bettelheim this speech 'denies implicitly that Auschwitz ever existed.'

The opposite point of view is put by Etty Hillesum, the young Dutch Jew who voluntarily entered the Westerbork transit camp to help her friends and her people as they awaited the trains to Auschwitz. Her own train left in October 1943, and she did not return. The new volume of her letters is a supplement to the wonderful 'An Interrupted Life' which was based on her diaries.* But even a person as brave and original as Etty Hillesum could write, a few months before the death she foresaw quite clearly, that 'this is something people refuse to admit to themselves: at a given point you can no longer *do*, but can only *be* and accept.'   [*1987*

---

* Pantheon, 1983.

A review of 'The Nazi Doctors: Medical Killing and the Psychology of Genocide' by Robert Jay Lifton (Basic Books), 'Mengele: The Complete Story' by Gerald L. Posner and John Ware (McGraw-Hill), 'Auschwitz: An Eyewitness Account of Mengele's Infamous Death Camp' by Dr Miklos Nyiszli, translated by Tibere Kremer and Richard Seaver (Seaver Books), and 'Letters from Westerbork' by Etty Hillesum, introduction and notes by Jan G. Gaarlandt, translation by Arnold J. Pomerans (Pantheon).

The Shadows Over France's Feast

With less than four years to go, France is already preparing a gigantic festival of self-congratulation. In July 1989, it will be 200 years since the French Revolution began.

Robespierre organised the Festival of the Supreme Being. In 1989, Europe will be treated to a Feast of the Supreme Nation. What modern French people now think about the Revolution is another matter, which I will come back to. But official France admits to no doubts. The republican nation of today will be ritually confirmed as the mighty and worthy descendant of the First Republic, 'united and indivisible,' which emerged from the flames and blood of 1789.

France under President Mitterrand displays a queer contradiction. At home, there has never been a time when so many
of the founding myths of the Republic have been so widely
challenged, whether it is the Gaullist-Communist legend of the
immaculate Resistance or the value of the Great Revolution
itself. But abroad, French nationalism has never seemed so
uncritically smug.

The sociologist Alain Touraine asked the other day why the
Rainbow Warrior fiasco had moved the French so little.
Everyone had enjoyed the political scandal. Almost nobody had
protested against the deed itself. 'The Greenpeace affair – or
rather the absence until now of a Greenpeace "affair" in the
line of great affairs of the past – should alert us to the profound
degradation of our political life.'

Where, asked Touraine, was that generation of left-wing
intellectuals who had protested so valiantly against French policies in the past, and where was the spirit of 1968 or of the
anti-nuclear and 'green' movements of the 1970s? 'The State
imposes its own discourse, while social actors disintegrate or
even seek to incorporate themselves in a State which is more
and more corporatist. . . .'

I remembered Touraine's lament last week, when I read in
Le Monde an ineffably complacent article about the Saar. It is
just 30 years since the people of the Saar, a small coal-and-
iron territory between France and Germany, voted overwhelmingly to reject 'European status' and to become a constituent
part of the German Federal Republic. The message of the
article is that if Paris had been a little more tactful, a little less
greedy, these benighted people would not have listened to
horrid German nationalists and deprived themselves of the
chance of permanent membership of the French family.

But it wasn't like that – not at all. A thick coat of pious
whitewash covers the true story of France's behaviour towards
the western provinces of Germany, much of it sloshed on by
Germans anxious for reconciliation. It can be retorted that
Germany's behaviour towards the eastern provinces of France
– in 1871, 1914 and 1940 – was far worse. No doubt. So what?

The French ambition to annex Germany west of the Rhine,
including the Saar, goes back to Louis XIV. French troops took
the Saar in 1684 and again after the Revolution, in 1792. In

1918, the Saar's mines were awarded to France and the territory was administered by the League of Nations. In 1935, with Hitler already ruling Germany, the mostly Catholic and working-class Saarlanders voted by 90 per cent in a plebiscite to return to the Reich. But in 1945, the French were back again. The Saar was forced into a customs union with France, and General Grandval became its viceroy.

Back in 1935, Shiela Grant Duff was the *Observer's* correspondent in the Saar. She passionately supported the group of democrats who campaigned against incorporation into the Reich, but wrote that the Saarlanders 'were wholly German by nationality.' How, then, was it possible for the Saar to become a French protectorate for 10 years after 1945 and even – in 1952 – to give 60 per cent of its vote to the puppet government run by the Catholic politician Johannes Hoffmann?

The people of the Saar today have no doubts about the answer. French thuggery, they reply. The Saar, like other border regions of Germany under French occupation, was effectively dominated by the *Sûreté*, which in turn had been swollen by untrained and vengeful veterans of the Communist sections of the Resistance. Anyone turning up to work with a black eye was greeted with the joke: 'Been with the *Sûreté* again?' The Communist Party, like Hoffmann's own Christian People's Party, was licensed. All parties supporting union with West Germany were banned.

France exploited the wealth of the Saar, and French carpetbaggers took over the management of mines and steel mills. Hoffmann, known contemptuously as 'Yo-Ho', had fought the Nazis in 1935, but was now hopelessly pliant and resorted to expelling his political critics from the territory. When he let the French get the Warndt coal district, the Saarlanders sang: 'Yo-Ho the phoney miner's son/Sold the Warndt for Judas's sum.'

It all ended happily. Adenauer and Mendés–France cobbled up a shaky arrangement making the Saar a 'European territory' with French currency. Asked to vote on it, the Saarlanders flung out the 'European statute' by a huge majority and at last joined the Federal Republic. Yo-Ho's power evaporated, and the Saar is now ruled by the Social Democrats.

With the Saar referendum of 1955, three centuries of French imperialist expansion to the east came to an end. The Germans of the Saar and the Moselle valley retain their memories; the French military presence in a city like Trier still has a conqueror's obtrusiveness, as the American and British presences in – say – Frankfurt or Düsseldorf do not. But the episode is over. Why, then, bring it up again?

Because a nation which cannot confront its own past honestly is a nation with problems. The Saar is a tiny place; most people in France have scarcely heard of it. But in the Saar, the French State was twice insulted, once in 1935 (when just 0.4 per cent voted to join France), and once in 1955, 20 years later. And that, it seems, is still not acceptable.

The Revolution of 1789 produced the Jacobin ideology of the centralised State as the engine of social progress. This ideology has transformed the world, mediated through statesmen as different as Hitler and Roosevelt, Lenin and Attlee. As French leftism decays, those who once protested, signed declarations and marched in the streets have lost every ideal save State-worship itself.

And yet the approach to 1989, bicentenary of the Revolution, is raising all kinds of doubts beneath the confident' official surface. A hundred years ago, the Third Republic proudly proclaimed its middle-class radicalism as the true heir of 1789. Mitterrand's socialism carries less conviction. From left to right, historians and thinkers raise their doubts.

Some point to the Terror as the source of modern totalitarianism and genocide. Some, in direct challenge to the Jacobin tradition, say that the real revolution was the counter-revolution, when the Vendée peasantry rose in 1793 against government from Paris. The republican consensus which made the France we know is beginning to crack up.

But the State survives, increasingly respected for its mere power rather than for its older function as the provider of liberty and equality. Will 1989 simply celebrate the birthday of the first bureaucracy? Or will the critics manage to promote a real debate about the nature of French State power and the way it has been used in the world – from the Saar to Auckland and Mururoa?   [1985

Greek Civil War – Rambo-Style

The other day, I saw the film 'Eleni,' based on the book of the same title by Nicholas Gage. It is a very bad film indeed, gurgling with sentimentality, burdened with the sort of dialogue which makes you twist your ankles together like a schoolchild wanting 'to be excused.' But it has a negative importance. It pricks once again Britain's neurotic conscience about Greece.

The story can be briefly told. Nicholas Gage, born Gatzoyiannis, was a child in a Greek village during the civil war. Communist forces occupied the village and began to organise the removal of children to Communist countries in Eastern Europe. His mother, Eleni Gatzoyiannis, managed to smuggle Nicholas through the lines. For this and other 'offences,' she was shot by firing squad on 28 August, 1948.

Years later, as an American journalist, Gage returned to Greece and tracked down the man who had ordered his mother's murder. He took a gun with him. But in the end, he could not pull the trigger. Instead, he wrote a tormented, intense book, a mixture of fact and fictional reconstruction. As a Greek story of war, exile and revenge, it has much power. As an account of what happened during the civil war, it is understandably but painfully one-sided.

The film was made in Spain, not in Greece. Gage has explained that his village – Lia, in the mountains near Albania – wasn't suitable, because it had been modernised. Greeks give another version: that the Greek cinema technicians union refused to work on the film because they considered the original book a distortion of history. Whatever the truth of that, the film vulgarises the story until the Communist soldiers become sadistic thugs, the peasants all resentful victims, and the children sent across the border are all forcibly abducted from weeping parents.

Unlike the Spanish, the Greeks are only beginning to assess

their Civil War objectively. Over half a million people died between 1946 and 1949 as a result of the conflict, and Greece became a genuinely open democracy only five years ago. But enough is available to suggest that the film's subtitle – 'An Unforgettable True Story' – is absurd.

In 1948, the Communist-led 'Democratic Army' numbered 26,000, by American estimates. This scarcely suggests that it had no popular support. The atrocity of Eleni's death took place during years of ruthless mass killing by both sides: the unpunished murderers are by no means only on the Left. The federation of village councils around Lia has issued a statement attacking the 'civil war atmosphere' portrayed in the film. 'It is an insult to the memory of those who suffered and sacrificed themselves on the altar of the liberation struggle to bring back those historical memories which form the cross of martyrdom of the Greek people . . .' This is hardly the tone of people supposed to have regarded the Communists as alien oppressors.

Greece touched me only twice – and indirectly – in the post-war years. The first time was when a gentleman from the Greek embassy came down to my school and gave us sheets of smudged, staring little faces – the 'abducted children,' still missing. The second was when I was a boy reservist in the Royal Marines. My squad was trained by a group of Commandos who had fought alongside the Communist partisans in Greece. Several had Greek wives, and several were Communists. They taught us their sort of war, not square-bashing; they treated us as human beings with minds, not as rookies to be screamed at. And they would sometimes talk to us about the hopes of a people's army in a country poorer than we could imagine.

These were two irreconcilable sorts of information. Making sense of both is not just a Greek duty, but a British one, given that Churchill's 1944 intervention to keep the left-wing resistance out of power was the genesis of the civil war. As A. J. P. Taylor wrote, 'only the British followed the German example and took armed action against a popular national movement while the war was actually on.'

What about the children? Some 28,000 were taken away, most to Yugoslavia but others to Albania, Czechoslovakia, Hungary, even Poland. The guerrillas asserted that their parents had willingly sent them out of the war zone to be properly fed and educated. It's clear that many families – like Eleni's – were not willing at all. But others, possibly most, seemed to have assented, and many went to join their children when the rebellion collapsed. The Red Cross reported in 1950 that in Yugoslavia 7,812 Greek children out of 9,106 were living with their relations. In spite of the outcry over their fate, the Greek Government later proved remarkably unwilling to have them back.

England's Civil War lies over three centuries away. Few people in this country can now conceive of the nature of such wars, their combination of fanatical, messianic certainty with a lust for kindred blood that feeds on itself. It is easier here to understand the Spanish Civil War as a conflict between fascism and democracy – an international struggle – than as a gigantic Spanish fratricide which took on the colouring of rival ideologies in Europe.

Perhaps this is why the British are much less willing to see the Greek Civil War as a social conflict than the Greeks are. Early this year, the Channel 4 film 'The Hidden War' – an attempt to tilt the balance of historical knowledge by presenting the Civil War through the eyes of the defeated – met a perfect barrage of protest from a certain British élite in retirement: the generals, diplomats and intelligence officers responsible for British policy in Greece during the 1940s. Without British intervention, they claimed, Greece would have become one more Soviet satellite.

There is little to back that up. In October 1944, Churchill and Stalin drew up their grisly little scrap of paper dividing Europe by percentages. Churchill scribbled: 'Greece': 90 per cent British.' Stalin ticked it with a blue pencil. For once, he kept a promise. He didn't want a Communist Greece, and cynically betrayed the Greek Communists in their struggle a few years later. The British earned plenty of Soviet abuse for their support of the Right in the Civil War, but in practice Stalin stood back and let the British – later, the Americans – do what they liked in Greece.

If the British had not piled into Greece in 1944 and afterwards, there would pretty certainly have been a Communist republic, following a Yugoslav course. It would have begun with popular support, but – like the early Tito regime – would probably have committed atrocious crimes and mad idealistic blunders. Then, given Stalin's attitude, my guess is that it would also have broken with the Soviet Union and taken an independent path.

Here, somebody can shout: 'Objection!' Because – it can be argued – all the savagery of civil war and all the repressions of the 30 years of right-wing rule that followed were worth it, if they spared Greece what the people of Yugoslavia had to go through in the years of unmitigated terror after 1945.

That is a debate I would like to hear. But nobody around here is trying to start it. Instead, we get the Rambo rubbish of this 'Eleni' film, in which Reds almost do manage to eat babies. And that film is only the gutter version of our Establishment's insistence that the 'Democratic Army' were foreign-backed terrorists, while the royalist-nationalist side were noble democrats. The real Eleni did not deserve to be buried a second time under lies.   [1986

The Strange Death of the Peasantry

Not long ago, I heard the historian Eric Hobsbawm remark that Karl Marx had got his timing wrong. Two European institutions which he thought to be moribund had survived for a full century after his death: the peasantry and the Church. Only now, in the last decades of the twentieth century, were they going into their terminal decline.

I write this in a village half-way up an Italian mountainside. The one-track road from the valley below, winding up to the top village 2,000 ft above sea level, was only built some 20 years ago. Until then, the people of these settlements – more like tiny towns built of stone and huddled round a church – walked for two or three hours down forest paths, carrying goods by donkey or on their backs, to reach a market or a shop.

They lived off the chestnut forests which cover the mountain range, grinding the nuts into flour, tending vegetable and vine patches and cows stalled in cabins scattered around the hills. Their sons were periodically taken to fight in distant wars. Otherwise, the State ignored them. The priest in each village, ringing his tinny bells, was the only representative of a wider world.

The road changed everything. Nobody harvests the chestnuts now, and the outlying cabins are roofless, buried in long grass and bracken. The population drained away, until this village, which once held perhaps 200 people, has fewer than 50. The children work in factories in the valley or in the Tuscan cities, driving up at weekends to see elderly relations.

Some have gone further, to Australia, Germany, or – an old immigration from this region – to Scotland. Many houses are derelict; others, like this one, have been converted for the summer holidays of foreigners.

On the way here we visited my sister who married into a French family after the war in one of the most fertile districts of Provence. So much has changed that she has made a picture book to show incredulous grandchildren how life used to be.

The old peasantry is vanishing. Where every square foot was used to cultivate salad and spring vegetables, melons and herbs, one can now see the unimaginable: weeds. The mule-carts have vanished, like the hordes of scraggy sheep being driven in clouds of dust up to summer pastures in the foothills of the Alps. A whole agrarian society – scarcely changed since the French Revolution, with its smallholders, its ragged sharecroppers, its family vendettas over access to precious water – is dissolving.

With it, many tensions have also dissolved. Babies thrive without swaddling; women visit the café on their own without scandalising their families, and can take driving lessons without a chaperone. The small town where my nephews and niece grew up no longer lives in a state of frozen civil war where every child was born Red or White, where everyone knew whose house would be attacked if the revolution came. The anti-clerical faith in Science and Progress has gone, and so has the suffocating, reactionary piety it fought. The lay State schools and the Catholic *écoles libres*, once irreconcilable, are beginning to merge and – rather to my regret – no longer teach totally different versions of French history.

As the peasantry goes, the relationship between town and country changes. Instead of feeding the towns, the villagers are fed by them, repaying the debt with clean air and silence. Food comes from industrial farming and imports, the small fields grass over and melt into 'forest parks' or 'areas of natural beauty.' Children born into poverty among those fields can now afford to regain touch with their roots, plastering and plumbing at weekends to transform the farmhouse into a holiday home.

The Catholic Church retreats more slowly. In these two patches of Italy and France, the congregations diminish and the processions grow fewer. The bells still ring, sometimes on tape through loudspeakers; a friend near here is fighting lawsuits in her effort to run a birth-control clinic. But without an unchanging society to reinforce unchanging authority, the transformation of the Church into something at once more-and-less majestic – 'League for the Significance of the Individual' – will gather speed.

So it is over much of Western Europe. The people leave the hills; the little fields in the plain are merged into prairies owned by a capitalist farmer who works them with a few machines. Queer that one must go to a Communist country to see a Christian peasantry – the hundreds of multicoloured strips that make a Polish landscape, the families driving to Mass by cart drawn by blond-maned horses wearing almost as many ribbons as their owners.

What are we getting instead? Years ago, people used to talk and write darkly about the 'Americanisation' of Europe. If they no longer do, is it because we are already Americanised? Yes and no.

Part of my holiday reading has been an early novel by Malcolm Bradbury, 'Stepping Westward.' Written about a quarter of a century ago, this, too, recalled how much has changed – in Britain. A fattish, not very angry young writer goes to the States on a Fulbright. He leaves Nottingham by steam train, and crosses the Atlantic by liner complete with stewards handing round beef tea. He reaches an utterly strange continent: here are universities with cement towers and wooden hutments, students who go to lectures in their own towers, couples in ranch-style houses with patios, extractor fans which start when the bathroom door opens, dental floss, paper cups, supermarkets, hot showers in private bathrooms. Everyone is obsessed by sex, and everyone wants to be masterless.

So strange? It was then. Now it sounds like prosperous life in outer Richmond or outer Stirling – or Fontenay-les-Roses, or the new suburbs of Bonn. A gap has closed. The United States no longer seems marvellously unfamiliar. It impresses a European by its wealth and space, its Rocky Mountains and military power. But not its newness; we have the gadgets too, sometimes better ones, and gawky adaptations of the lifestyle. The grandson of a Methodist cobbler says to the girl in his Creative Writing class: 'Hi, gorgeous, wanna get laid?' The politics of the American cowboy Right which baffled Bradbury's hero, for whom 'conservatism was a defunct intellectual fashion,' have been the rhetoric of the British Government for the last seven years.

Western Europe has taken most of what it wanted from America. The first time I went to Warsaw, I was served Coca-Cola in a nightclub by a waiter who brought it in an ice bucket, poured a little into a champagne glass, and stepped back to let me taste it, while the other dancers crowded round to goggle. That seemed to me very comic, but I see now that it was only the carrying of British or French worship of Americans to a logical extreme. In the West, at least, we have satisfied these fantasies and begin to understand that an American type of society is only a station on our journey, not the terminus.

The generation which has left the land and often the Church has, after all, brought something with it. This is a particular dream of liberty. Once that meant owning a field. Now it means owning a small business and a house, a determination not to be lost in the proletarian mass. Peasant politics are tough and seldom liberal. In an overcrowded continent whose industry is declining, where urban socialism is running out of energy, the children of the peasants are planting the seeds of a new turbulence.   [*1986*

Apartheid in Europe

As South Africa burns, the world stands peering into the smoke and chanting abuse against apartheid. The very use of that Afrikaans word suggests something unique to South Africa, a localised disease. But the mechanism underlying apartheid is, in fact, world-wide.

Most outrage boils down to several statements. South Africa is a police state, where the forces of order kill, torture and arrest at will. South Africa maintains grotesque inequality based on skin colour. It is an undemocratic place in which a white minority holds a monopoly of political power. It segregates the races, who must live, play, travel and – until recently – love apart.

Although true, these statements suggest that apartheid is a stagnant condition, something like slavery in the Roman Empire. Americans often imagine South Africa as rather like the old South before the Civil Rights movement, a plantation where pouchy old men with shotguns invigilate black chain-gangs. All that's needed, they may conclude, is to give blacks equal rights and a vote.

But apartheid, at its core, is not so much a condition as an engine. Beneath the race laws lies a huge economic machine which, far more than whites-only bathing beaches, preserves white domination and prosperity and minimises their political cost. This engine, designed by Hendrik Verwoerd a generation ago, is a labour pump. It sucks in cheap black labour, pours it through the wheels of industry and agriculture, and then expels it to distant pools of unemployment until required again.

Its name is 'influx control.' First, blacks in the white regions of South Africa were declared to be 'migrants.' Even those resident for generations in white areas were redefined as citizens of black 'Homelands' and denied rights of settlement or citizenship in their place of work. Labour was to be recruited on

limited contracts from the Homelands (arid tribal areas established by the British as 'native reserves'), pumped in to work
and then, if and when it is no longer required, pumped out
again to be 'dumped' in one of the Homelands.

Migrant labour was nothing new in South Africa. But the
horrible brilliance of the apartheid system was to see how the
idea of the nation-state could be perverted to serve it.

In any capitalist economy subject to slumps and booms,
workers become costly and dangerous when they are unemployed. Deporting the unemployed back to their villages still
leaves the Government responsible for them. But what if the
workers can be transformed into foreigners?

So there was born the idea of constructing around 'white'
South Africa a periphery of 'independent' black states. Many
miners, especially, already came on contract from abroad, from
Mozambique or Lesotho. Dr Verwoerd and his successors now
began to convert the Homeland reserves into 'Bantustans,' into
statelets like Bophutatswana or Transkei whose independence
was basically fraudulent but which took over responsibility for
their so-called 'citizens.'

The influx-control engine pumped away, recruiting labour as
it was needed and deporting hundreds of thousands of
unwanted men and women back to the Bantustans. What
became of them there no longer concerned the Pretoria Government or their white employers. South Africa seemed to have
discovered the philosopher's stone of economic management:
how to export unemployment.

Human beings have paid a grim price for this discovery. The
price includes incessant police raids for illegal migrants and
blacks with no pass. It includes the brutal bulldozing of Cross-
roads and the other vast squatter camps near Cape Town. It
includes the misery of those dumped in camps in Homelands
they had often never seen, and the shocking rise of hunger,
disease and overcrowding there.

These are South African realities. But the South African
system of influx control is not isolated. There are other places
where nation-states have been used as the foundations of a
machine to exploit migrant labour.

One of these engines has been pumping away on our doorstep
for many years. The European Economic Community,

especially the old EEC of the Six, had a structural resemblance
to South Africa. The overt violence of the European machine
was far less, but the mechanism was the same.

Northern Europe, especially West Germany, came to rely on
migrant labour as its own internal labour reserves were absorbed
or became too expensive. In the boom years of the Sixties and
early Seventies, millions of short-term contract workers were
recruited from Spain and Portugal, then from Greece and
Yugoslavia, finally from Turkey. Sweden, Austria and Switzerland, though not EEC members, recruited too.

Here was another industrial heartland – the Witwatersrand
of Northern Europe – served by a periphery of small states
which were politically independent but economically dependent.
The heart's diastole drew in trainloads of dark, bewildered little
men clutching cardboard suitcases, guitars, parcels of mother's
cake. The heart's systole pumped them back again, richer by a
Grundig stereo or a second-hand Volkswagen, to dying hill
villages in Croatia or Anatolia. And West Germany's unemployment figures remained negligible. It was all exported.

Much the same goes on in the United States. Anyone who
saw 'El Norte,' the marvellous film by Greg Nava and Anna
Thomas about migrant workers in California, was watching yet
another influx-control pump drawing in cheap labour from
Mexico and Central America and sluicing it out again when it
was no longer required. Along the Rio Grande frontier, helicopters and jeeps hunt down the 'wetback' illegal immigrants. The
inlet valve must not open too widely.

But when migrants are allowed to settle in the heartland,
the pump can't work. Britain, in its casual, good-natured way,
brought in West Indians to correct the labour shortage of the
Fifties without any plan to export them again: it was supposed
that unemployment was as extinct as smallpox. Before Algerian
independence, Algerians flocked freely to France and settled in
dismal *bidonvilles* around the cities. By the time that Britain
passed immigration acts and France limited labour movement
from independent Algeria, it was too late to dislodge these 'new
Europeans.'

Even in Germany, the pump is breaking down. Recession
means that the demand for immigrant labour is slack, but over
a million Turks have managed to settle and acquire residence.

And now Portugal, Spain and Greece have entered the EEC, which means that their citizens have freedom of movement within the Community.

Foreign contract labour is an ugly thing. It is about cheerless barrack-hostels, about men without women bawled at by foremen of a 'superior' race. It is about homesickness for villages with no young men to break the earth, about the hostility of rich 'host' nations too mean to share their freedoms. It would be good to feel that its day is over, even in South Africa, where employers now want their workers to settle permanently and learn skills and become consumers.

But it is not yet over. As long as there are rich nations, poor nations and trade cycles, it will go on. The world is growing small; whole continents are bursting to discharge their surplus peasants into the international labour market. The rich want them as miners and houseboys, not as neighbours or fellow-citizens on the dole. The poor used to be always with us. Now they can only visit us if they have a return ticket.   [*1985*

Toads, Journalists, Cats and Policemen

Spring has reached Germany, and the *Frankfurter Allgemeine Zeitung* has published a truly majestic photograph of two toads copulating. The male is about half the size of the female, but both have eyes half-closed in amphibian bliss. A long, learned caption informs us that 'toad fences' (whatever they are) and special traffic warnings are being erected along the routes of their mating migration by the German League for Bird Protection.

Bird protection? Yes, because in the complex hierarchy of German nature-loving bureaucracy, the *Deutscher Bund für*

Vogelschutz (the bird people) has somehow attained a superior status which allows bird-lovers to boss around all kinds of other species – even certain mammals, which after all are supposed to incarnate a higher level of evolutionary progress than egg-laying lizards which grew wings.

I had bitter experience of this many years ago, when we lived in Berlin. We had at the time an elegant little marmalade cat. This we had obtained from the *Verein der Katzenfreunde* (cat-lovers), run at the time by a bony war veteran. Whatever he may have done to his own species, his humanity to cats was beyond question, and that in a city where – I don't know why – cats were not generally liked. They had done their bit, after all, fighting the rats which infested the city's ruins after the war. But I often saw old Berlin ladies taking a swipe at some unoffending pussy with umbrella or shopping-bag.

One day, our cat killed a sparrow in the small garden in front of the apartment block. Within hours, neighbours were hammering on our door and shrieking abuse through the keyhole. The police were telephoned, and next day an apologetic Berlin cop appeared on our doorstep. The neighbours, gloating, hung over their balconies, no doubt hoping that we would be dragged off to the Moabit prison.

Two grave offences had been committed, it turned out. First of all, the cat had entirely violated its civil status. It was a 'House Beast,' not a 'Garden Beast,' and possessed no licence to prowl out of doors in an irregular manner. Second, by attacking a sparrow the cat had shown an anarchic, revolutionary contempt for constituted order. In the hierarchy which broadens out beneath the general roof of the Union of German Animal Friends, the League of Cat Friends occupied a subordinate level to the German League for Bird Protection. If the sparrow had murdered and eaten our cat, only a minor breach of civil discipline would have been involved, excusable given the cat's crime in venturing out of doors. But the cat's assault on the sparrow was a deliberate blow against the legal structure.

We survived this, however. The policeman observed with a smile that spiteful (*gehässige*) neighbours were common in Berlin, and advised us to keep a closer eye on the cat. And the cat survived, too. His portrait was painted by Sara Haffner and exhibited in Warsaw, and when we left he took up residence with a Marxist woman professor in an altogether leafier, more tolerant quarter of the city.

I have great affection for Berlin, in spite of that sort of rubbish. The place is now celebrating its 750th anniversary. A part of my family came from there a century ago. When inspecting the hole in East Berlin where their house used to stand, a policeman shouted at me for stepping off the kerb in that perfectly empty street to get a better look. I had forgotten that a human being was a Pavement Beast (*Bürgersteigtier*). The Cold War and the labyrinth of Four-Power rights, looked at in one way, are only nit-picking Berlinish legalism raised to the universal.

At the time, I was chairman of the Foreign Press Association. The Wall was at its most impenetrable in those years, but somehow we managed to hang together: I think the only all-Berlin association to survive. The Soviet, Polish and Czechoslovak correspondents would cross over from the East to attend our meetings, and only a handful of Americans chose to break away rather than share press conferences with Commies. There were problems, like the day our Eastern members were seized in West Berlin by the police as they prepared to join an outing to Lower Saxony. But on the whole it worked.

Now, 750 years after the first Berliner picked up his quill to inform the second Berliner that he could have no residence permit without a work permit that could only be obtained by producing a residence permit, the Foreign Press Association is again tackling a problem which I failed to solve in my time. This is the bank balance left behind by the previous Association.

Right up to 1945, a foreign press corps survived in Berlin, Swiss, Finns, Japanese, Slovaks and so on, the journalists went to press conferences in the Propaganda Ministry or were taken on Goebbels press trips to what remained of the Front. When the city fell to the Soviet armies, they left their Association funds in the bank, in Reichsmarks.

Ever since, the new Association has been trying to lay its hands on the money, claiming to be the legal heir. Not so simple. The West Berlin authorities say they can't decide: the Federal government in Bonn is the legal successor to the Reich. But the Western Allies in Berlin dispute Bonn's rights, claiming that they and the Russians have sovereignty by right of conquest in Greater Berlin. Even if the British, Americans and French agreed to pay out the money, the Soviet authorities might well veto them on the grounds that the German Democratic Republic now has sovereign rights in their sector and is entitled to a say.

Prague, in such matters, is a contrast to Berlin. The Czech state bureaucracy is even more obsessive, pedantic and nasty than the German. The population, however, observes a sort of 'Germanity with a human face': where rules can be dodged and fiddled, they will be. This has been shown in the current struggle against the pigeons of Prague, who now number at least 140,000. They spoil the hats of Party members, block drainpipes, and are afflicted with mites and – so the papers say – gout.

Everything from a pair of falcons to ultra-sound has been tried in vain, in the effort to reduce them. Now the feeding of pigeons is punishable with a fine of up to £30. The police have shown zeal in jumping on citizens, almost all old-age pensioners, who are caught sharing their bread with pigeons in public parks. But elderly Czechs refuse to cooperate. 'I was in a concentration camp, and I know what hunger means,' protested one old lady. 'Have you no pity?' The police gave up and left her to her crumbs and birds. Then the falcons vanished. One, it turned out, flew into an attic belonging to a Czech 'League of Bird Friends' member, who took it to a forest and released it. The other collided with a chimney and broke its wing.

This tale of toads, journalists, pigeons and cats has a point. There is civil society – the web of private and independent associations – and there is the state bureaucracy. The latter has certainly some rights to regulate the former. But when the frontier between them is overthrown, then we have trouble.

When the police can be summoned because a cat kills a sparrow, then the social soil could grow a police state if the political weather were right. When the excellent Mr Karel Srp and his colleagues from the Jazz Section of the Czech Musicians' Union are sent to prison for running an independent and legal publishing house, the state's totalitarian claim over civil society is exposed. Toad-lovers, throw off the chains of the bird-lovers this spring! Reptile rights may be human rights as well.

[*1987*]

Frontiers

The first of this year's Christmas pantomimes opened the other day in Strasbourg. I refer to the British Euro MPs who began by singing carols and ended rolling about the floor and punching one another on the nose. This particular debate, if I remember it correctly, was about a most interesting point of principle: how much of the EEC food surplus should be sent to starving Africa or, to put it in a more refined way, whether some frontier should be set to the goodwill and charity of the Christian West.

Setting frontiers has taken up much Christian energy in the past, especially the setting up of frontiers in other people's countries. Writing this column in Warsaw, I have been reflecting on how many European nations have proclaimed themselves to be the 'eastward bastion of Christianity.' The Germans did so, as the Teutonic knights pushed along the Baltic coast and exterminated the aboriginal Prussians. The Poles still do so, who colonised the borderlands of the Ukraine and Byelorussia and Lithuania, and whose great king John Sobieski saved Vienna from the Turks. The Hungarians set their 'bastion' in Transylvania. The Serbs spent centuries resisting the Turkish occupiers. Even the Russians, who were eventually to add all northern Asia to their empire, still fancy themselves as the outpost of something which they no longer define as Western Christendom.

Britain, as usual, is rather an exception. For long centuries, these islands were a Christian bastion against nothing more menacing than marauding herring-gulls. But, for most Europeans, Christendom has been a place to keep others out of – pagan Mongols and Huns, and above all Turks.

And so it remains. For this coming year of 1986 will be, for Western Europe, another year of preparing for Turkish invasion. This is not a matter of hordes of horsebowmen and banners embroidered with the crescent of Islam. It is a matter of treaty.

More than 20 years ago, in 1964, the European Economic Community signed an agreement with Turkey which soon made its way to the oblivious back of the filing cabinets. It was, indeed, only recently that certain provisions of that agreement were remembered. The papers were fished out, dusted and inspected, and the faces of many a statesman and Brussels bureaucrat turned pale. For the 1964 agreement provided that, with effect from 1 December 1986, the Turks will enjoy the right of free movement into the EEC already assured to all the member states under article 12 of the Treaty of Rome.

Turkey admits officially to 3.5 million registered unemployed. How many more millions in that huge and impoverished peasant country have nothing profitable to do is mere speculation. But, unless something happens in the next 12 months, all of them will acquire the right to enter the EEC, still in deep recession, to search for work.

Above all, they will head for West Germany and West Berlin. West Germany in the boom years was by far the biggest employer of Turkish contract labour, and that was the destination of some 90 per cent of all Turkish emigrants. As 'guest workers,' they built the whole superstructure of the 'economic miracle' in the Sixties and Seventies. In spite of regulations designed to prevent settlement, 1.4 million Turks are already resident in West Germany.

And the Germans resent it. A recent poll showed that 80 per cent of the sample felt that there were already too many foreigners in West Germany, above all in the cities (a quarter of the population of Frankfurt is foreign-born now, and 18 per cent of the population of Stuttgart). A special buy-out scheme has encouraged over 300,000 Turks to return to their homeland in the past two years. But the inflow of foreigners from outside Europe goes on, helped by West Germany's liberal asylum laws. Not all of them are poor, either. Some arrive in Berlin by East German airlines, and hire a West Berlin taxi for nearly 200 marks to drive them straight to the West German frontier at Helmstedt, where they demand refugee status.

Faced with the December deadline, Chancellor Kohl is trying to persuade the Turkish government to restrain emigration in return for lavish West German aid – some industrial and some military. The Community has also tried to erect a dam against the coming flood, suggesting that Turkish freedom of entry and movement in the EEC is only 'inspired' by, not equivalent to, article 12 of the Rome Treaty. But Turkey still insists on 'totally free movement,' and has so far declined to be bought off.

In the end, it is all futile. Slowly but with a tremendous inevitability the frontiers and bastions of Europe are crumbling. All the Immigration Acts, all the shipments of tractors and jet fighters, all the arguments that 'there is no room at the inn' will not be able to hold back for ever the movement of Asia and Africa into Europe which is just beginning. The peasant masses of the world are becoming mobile, transport is becoming cheaper. They will come, and they will settle.

As this century runs to its end, other European countries will study Britain – or more properly England – to see what happens when Third World populations begin to settle in a small and overcrowded Western society. They won't find a model. The black and white British have not yet decided how to live with one another, or on what terms. But they will discover this much: that the old 'melting pot' theory is out. The idea that the newcomers – except for a marginal few – will assimilate into 'new Germans' or 'new Belgians' with a few pretty folk customs of their own is an illusion, and an illusion born of the remnants of European imperial arrogance.

Social workers in Hackney, for instance, talk now about a 'salad-bowl' society, made up of contrasting ingredients whose different flavours must each be sharpened. The West Germans, to judge by a government report last year, still think that 'there is only one alternative to voluntary repatriation and that is integration.' I don't say that integration of a sort does not take place, where cultural difference is not too wide or numbers are not too great. One Luxemburger out of 10 is now Portuguese, and these immigrant children speak the 'Letzeburgesch' tongue in the street. But the sheer scale of the population movements to come will make that type of assimilation impossible.

I can't say that this worries me. The ideal of cultural unity in one country – everyone studying the same history book under the portrait of the same President – belongs to the dying ideology of the modern nation-state.

There are other models, anyway. I look out of this Warsaw room at the snow and the statues, and remember the Polish commonwealth of many centuries ago, a region of Europe inhabited by Poles, Jews, Ukrainians, Germans, Lithuanians and Scots, held together only by consenting loyalty to a Crown. In 100 years, all Europe will be like that.

Let it come. Let the new Attila be a foreman in Ford's, Cologne, let the new Great Khan open a chain of nightclubs on the Riviera, let the new Sultan of Turkey take his seat in the House of Lords. Let us stop thinking, however subconsciously, of Christendom as a matter of frontiers to be held. It was, after all, a skilled migrant worker (Local Work Permit: none; Spouse/s: one, pregnant; In Temp. Accom. Unlicensed Agricultural Premises) who started all that.   [1985

IV

WALTZING WITH MOLOTOV
Eastern Europe

Gorbachov's Gift

Twice since the war, the Soviet Union has delivered to the West an enormous gift-wrapped parcel whose label read 'Utopia.' Twice, the leaders of the West have stood round the parcel, nervously fingering the ribbons and bows, wondering whether the act of cutting the string and opening the lid will fill the world with peace and harmony – or detonate a booby trap.

The first time was in March 1952, when Stalin produced a famous Note on the German question. In the Note, he offered the reunification of Germany in return for the withdrawal of all foreign troops and neutral status. That time, the West, and especially Chancellor Adenauer of West Germany, decided to send the parcel back unopened.

The second time is now. The Gorbachov proposal for a step-by-step abolition of all nuclear weapons is astonishing, universal in scale. It offers concessions which the Soviet Union has refused to make in the past: for example, Britain and France would retain their nuclear arsenals for a transition period, and Gorbachov would permit on-site inspection of Soviet missile bases.

There are some obscurities, some things missing. But if the idea worked out, our children in the twenty-first century would live in a world free of the nuclear threat, in which even the superpowers would have no nuclear weapons.

Should we open this parcel? It is the Americans who will decide. Gorbachov has set the condition that President Reagan's plans for an anti-missile shield in space – 'Star Wars,' or the Strategic Defence Initiative – must not be put into practice, although he does not ask for a ban on SDI research. But a flat American refusal to touch this offer might hand Gorbachov a propaganda triumph and drive European alarm over Reagan's policies to a new height.

The question in 1986 is really the same as it was in 1952. It is a double question. Does he mean it? And, even if he does, do we want it?

By coincidence, West Germany is arguing passionately over a new book about the Stalin Note of 1952. The historian Rolf Steininger, in his book 'A Missed Chance,' insists that Stalin was in earnest. If his offer had been accepted by the West, the East German state would have been liquidated. Out of an international agreement would have emerged 'a reunited Germany free of the military blocs.'

Two things are certain, whether we believe Steininger or not. One is that the rejection of the Note finally confirmed the destiny of West Germany as an integrated member of the Atlantic Alliance, and ended – may be for ever – the possibility of a united Germany between the Rhine and the Oder. The second is that opinion polls today show that over half the population of the Federal Republic would welcome something like Stalin's solution, an approval which ranges from the far Left, the peace movement and the Greens across to German nationalists of the far Right.

The second part of the double question is easier to answer than the first. Whether Stalin meant it or not, the West did not want reunification, even with free elections. Adenauer, a conservative Catholic, knew that a united Germany would sweep him from power; it would contain an invincible majority of Protestants and Social Democrats. The West had more funda-mental objections.

It comes down to what you think the Allies' war aims were. The answer may seem obvious: they fought to smash Hitler and the Nazis, so they could never revive. But it has always seemed to me that, as the war approached its end, the Allies became half-consciously possessed by another aim. The German Reich – the state which had existed since 1871 – had proved impossible to live with. Its size and power unbalanced the continent. Its aggressive wars had bled Europe white. Its position 'in the middle' had allowed it to play off Russia and the western democracies against one another and to make a European security system impossible.

The Allies meant to destroy not only Nazi fascism but the German Reich itself. And they did. Germany is divided, and divided it will remain until – or unless – a Europe can be constructed strong enough to contain it.

That, really, is why the West refused to open the 1952 parcel. Anthony Eden summed it up when he asked who would be able to keep a neutral Germany disarmed – and who would be able to keep a disarmed Germany neutral.

But the Germans, ever since, have been obsessed by the other question: did Stalin mean it, or was his offer just a final propaganda trick to stave off West Germany's entry into NATO? Some, like Steininger, talk of the 'missed chance.' Others talk sceptically about the 'legend of the missed chance.' Without the Soviet files, Rolf Steininger cannot prove that Stalin was in earnest. All he produces is an anecdote: Otto Grotewohl, the East German Premier, told an Italian politician some years later that in 1952 Stalin had wished to put the East German Communists in 'a new situation, and we did not know what would happen to us.'

It does not much matter whether the chance was real or mythical. The West did not care about Stalin's motives. It was the label on the parcel they did not like.

Now comes the Gorbachov offer. The West – above all West Germany – is plainly fascinated, and much more approachable than in 1952. Perhaps this is just a manoeuvre to delay Star Wars, and perhaps, if they achieve that much, the Russians will cheat on the rest of the package. But on the other hand, this may be the last and greatest chance to end the arms race, and our descendants will curse us for missing it as they die in a radioactive twilight.

Last week in southern Germany, I talked to Erhard Eppler, a leading Social Democrat whose voice is respected by the peace movement and by the Greens. 'It's very logical,' he said. 'Reagan says to Gorbachov: We will build Star Wars, then offer it to you, and then we can scrap the weapons. Gorbachov is retorting: Why go such a long way round? Why don't we just start scrapping the nuclear arsenal now?'

But, just as Stalin in 1952 smoked out those who did not want a reunified Germany, Gorbachov is beginning to smoke out those who actually do not want to see nuclear weapons abolished. The *New York Times* now writes openly that a world in which the superpowers did not have such weapons would be a worse world. 'No sane Soviet or American leader would give up weapons that simultaneously keep the peace and assure his nation's pre-eminence.'

So should we open the parcel, and agree to explore the Soviet plan? It is a matter of two Utopias which confront each other. For President Reagan, it is the 'dream of invulnerability' through defence in space; he reminds Erhard Eppler of the aggressive Siegfried who fancied that he was invulnerable because he had been dipped in dragon's blood. For Gorbachov, it is the Utopia of total nuclear disarmament, which does not tell us how these weapons would be taken away from China, or how their use by Libya or Israel would be prevented.

I believe that we should untie the string – but I do not believe that we will. The Americans will not give up Star Wars. That whole fantasy will probably pass into oblivion when President Reagan passes, but not before then. The Soviet negotiators, now busy touring Western Europe to explain their plan, almost certainly know that too. The best that we in Europe can hope for is to keep the parcel intact, on the table, until the climate in America has changed.   [*1986*]

Changing Partners

This week, the man who danced with Molotov tells all. I beg every student of history-as-absurd-theatre to read the current number of *Granta*. It contains extracts from a book called 'They,' in which those who ruled Poland in the time of Stalinist terror, now garrulous old pensioners, spill their beans to an interviewer.

One was Jakub Berman, for eight years responsible for the

secret police. Here he is describing a party in 1948 at Stalin's villa:

> 'Once, I think it was in 1948, I danced with Molotov.
> You mean with Mrs Molotov?
> No, she had been sent to a labour camp. I danced with Molotov
> – it must have been a waltz, or at any rate something simple. . . .
> As the woman?
> Molotov led; I wouldn't know how. He wasn't a bad dancer,
> actually, and I tried to keep in step with him. . . .
> What about Stalin, whom did he dance with?
> Oh, no, Stalin didn't dance. Stalin wound the gramophone: he
> treated that as his duty. He would put on records and watch.
> He watched you?
> He watched us dance.
> So you had a good time?
> Yes, it was pleasant, but with an inner tension.
> You didn't really have fun?
> Stalin really had fun. But for us those dancing sessions were
> good opportunities to say things to each other which we wouldn't
> have been able to say out loud.'

And so on. Yes, this is genuine; these things really happened. Policy was made that way. Molotov didn't ask Berman if he came here often but (one, two, three; one, two, three) murmured that Poland was being infiltrated by hostile organisations. No doubt Berman went home and arrested thousands more.

Another snatch of that forgotten music will be heard this week in Warsaw. They are holding a 'World Congress of Intellectuals in Defence of Peace,' a title which instantly recalls those ancient Stalinist times when fellow-travellers and innocents trooped about waving Picasso's dove and signing appeals for struggle against Wall Street Fascism. Indeed, the congress is presenting itself as a repeat of that famous Congress of Intellectuals at Wrocław in 1948, held among the ruins 'in times of enthusiasm and hope.'

This is a very weird scheme indeed. The world, thank God, has changed since 1948. The species 'fellow-traveller' is extinct, or seriously endangered. Everyone knows that most Polish intellectuals refuse to have anything to do with the congress, and it is not at all clear who will consent to come. Wildly-compiled invitation lists mention everyone from Graham Greene to Woody Allen, Vanessa Redgrave and Meryl Streep, Dr Runcie, Lord (Harold) Wilson, Kurt Waldheim and Marcel Marceau. How many of these worthies have actually been sent an invitation card is quite obscure.

The Polish authorities insist that this is a non-governmental affair. But 'we won't ask those who eagerly await a world war or have a colonialist attitude to the third world.'

What staggers me is that the Polish organisers apparently look back on the Wrocław congress as a great success. It certainly was historic. It was historic because Wrocław 1948 was for many Western intellectuals the moment of blinding light on the Damascus Road. It was there that the true nature of Stalinist power, its bullying, menacing and cheating, was revealed in a way that no open-minded 'progressive' could ignore.

The British delegation included Kingsley Martin, Julian Huxley, the novelist Richard Hughes, Edward Crankshaw of the *Observer*, J. B. S. Haldane, George Weidenfeld, Ronald Searle, the 'Red Dean' Hewlett Johnson and A. J. P. Taylor. The British Embassy noted nastily that 'a factor in the invitation which was undoubtedly strong in the case of some of the British was that the trip was in the nature of a free jaunt.' Cigarettes were free, but vodka was not.

On the first day, a group of Polish professors and linguists offered to act as guides to the delegates. On the second day, 12 of these guides were arrested for 'giving false information about Poland.' The congress began with a speech by Alexander Fadeyev, Stalin's head writer, who said that the Soviet Union had won the war unaided, that Western culture was trash, and that if monkeys could type, they would produce the poems of T. S. Eliot.

Rapturous applause from most of the hall, but the British were appalled. Huxley and Ritchie Calder suggested a walkout. Behind the scenes, Jakub Berman was also horrified and rang his dancing-partner in Moscow to get a muzzle put on the Soviet delegation. Molotov obliged, but it was too late.

A. J. P. Taylor hit back. He spoke, then as now, off the cuff, so nobody could censor his speech. It was 'not less violent in delivery and scarcely less aggressive in content than that of Fadeyev.' The embassy observer noted that this speech, 'represented in the Polish Press as a typical reactionary outpouring of a travelling salesman for American imperialism. . . . was at first greeted by the 500 delegates with gasps of astonishment; next there were some hisses and boos from the massed ranks of the Slavs. . . .'

Crankshaw drafted a resolution of protest at the way the congress was being manipulated. Some of the British party signed, but Kingsley Martin, editor of the *New Statesman*, withdrew his signature when Taylor suggested publishing the resolution in the *Manchester Guardian*. The American delegates, terrified, refused to touch it. The French crumpled it up and flung it in Crankshaw's face. The congress platform said they had lost the resolution and then, when a copy was produced, said that the British had withdrawn it – a lie. A message to the congress from Einstein, critical of State power, was read out in a heavily falsified version, and the congress broke up.

'One might even judge,' the embassy summed up, 'that the Polish authorities had the worst of the bargain, by putting themselves seriously out of pocket for something of no real gain but possible loss to themselves, since the Communists in the foreign delegations merely remained Communists, while the non-Communists went away warned, roused and enlightened by this personal demonstration of Communist intrigue.'

Berman himself recalls that 'we lost Huxley among others, who issued a protest and left for London, and we were never able to exploit him for the Communist movement again.' In the intellectuals' attitude to the Cold War, this was a turning-point.

Some righteous fellows will now rush into print and denounce any Westerner who goes to Warsaw as a traitor to freedom. Three valiant Poles in prison, Adam Michnik, Władysław Frasyniuk and Bogdan Lis, have warned the delegates that they are 'participating in a totalitarian farce' and 'legitimising those who sent tanks against a defenceless people.'

My own feeling is different. People should go and say what they think, as A. J. P. Taylor did, and see that their words are not suppressed. Among the working groups are two covering 'cultural values' and 'intellectual responsibility. Here are opportunities which should be loudly taken.

Someone has written on a Warsaw wall: 'A Fight for Peace

is like a Fuck . . . for Chastity.' I know what he means, but in
this case it is better to fight than to stay chaste.   [*1986*

The Polish Ghosts

Not long ago, a diplomat told me that 'relations between Poland
and France have hit bottom.' This is always an unwise sort of
announcement. The Polish aphorist Stanisław Jerzy Lec, once
wrote: 'I hit bottom – and then I heard someone tapping from
underneath.'

Never assume that things cannot get worse. And, sure
enough, they have. France now has only a chargé d'affaires in
Warsaw, but he was summoned to the Foreign Ministry the
other day and handed a furious protest about 'the anti-Polish
campaign developing in France.'

Genuine quarrels between European nations across the
dividing line, as opposed to dutiful variations on whatever abuse
the Soviet Union and the United States are exchanging, are
surprisingly rare. Czechoslovakia and Austria are conducting a
noisy feud, mostly about shootings on the border and Austrian
television programmes. But the Franco-Polish row, which has
been going on since General Jaruzelski's imposition of martial
law in 1981, has deeper roots.

Mr Jerzy Urban, the Polish spokesman, gave the game away
when he accused France of being 'painfully treacherous.' This
is a row about unrequited love.

Ever since Poland was partitioned in 1795, Poles have looked
to France as their true friend in the struggle to regain independence. In practice, the French did little to help. But sentiment
survived disillusion. In 1939, France left Poland in the lurch
by promising an offensive against the Germans which was never
carried out. And yet, when General de Gaulle visited Poland
in 1966, people wept in the streets for joy.

Incredible as it sounds, General Jaruzelski and his men were at first staggered and then outraged, when President Mitterrand's France condemned their December military putsch in 1981. They had imagined, on no rational grounds whatever, that a socialist France would be the first to be understanding and forgiving about what they had done. Instead, there was freezing official reproof from Paris, and the biggest upsurge of spontaneous public protest of any nation in Western Europe.

Since then, reproaching and abusing President Mitterrand has become almost a routine for Polish officials. The latest outbursts from Warsaw relate to two events. First of all, Laurent Fabius, the French Prime Minister, has invited Lech Wałęsa to take part in a conference in Paris on 'Human Rights and Liberties.' But worse, far worse, is a new film called 'Shoah.'

The film, by the French director Claude Lanzmann, purports to be an account of the murder of the Polish Jews during the Nazi occupation. But it is also an attempt to show that the Poles themselves shared responsibility for the Holocaust. Lanzmann states that Polish anti-semitism was one of the main reasons why the Nazis established the extermination camps on Polish soil: 'The Germans could expect the Polish people's silent approval. . . . They were indifferent witnesses to actions committed before their eyes. Those few Jews who escaped were then mostly denounced.'

Nothing is harder to discuss with Polish friends, I have long ago discovered, than anti-semitism. The terrible charge levelled by 'Shoah' is in no way new; it is widely accepted, for instance, by Jews in the United States. Novelists like Leon Uris and William Styron have spread it to their readers. Some – not all – Zionist leaders have insisted on this version of history, mostly because it justifies their campaign before the war to persuade the Jewish population of Poland to emigrate to Palestine.

And yet Lanzmann's accusation is a cruel distortion of the truth. The biggest concentration of European Jews settled in the lands of the ancient Polish Commonwealth because Polish kings invited them. Anti-semitism became strong only during the partitions, when some Polish nationalists accused the Jews of transferring their loyalty to Tsarist Russia and when the peasantry blamed its misery not only on Polish landlords but on the largely Jewish middle class.

When Poland became independent in 1918, most Jews proclaimed their loyalty to the new republic. But the small Communist Party, which at first opposed independence and preached fusion with Bolshevik Russia, was overwhelmingly Jewish in its leadership. This made it easier for right-wing parties to foment anti-semitism, with support from the Catholic hierarchy in many cases. By 1939, discrimination against Jews was government policy, although it was nothing like as brutal as the persecution of other minorities such as the Ukrainians and Byelorussians.

A few years ago, I picked up on a bookstall a novel by the pre-war writer Zofia Kossak-Szczuczka. 'Blaze' is one of the most viciously anti-semitic books I have ever read. But later I discovered that during the war the author joined 'Żegota,' the underground group devoted to saving Jews from the Nazis, and was herself sent to Auschwitz. It was a warning to me of the complexity, the intimate mix of tragedy and heroism, which was the relationship between Catholic Poles and Jews. Even between the wars, most political parties saw anti-Jewish demagogy as an evil irrelevance.

Just over six million Polish citizens, a fifth of the population, were killed or murdered during the Nazi occupation; 2.9 million of those victims were Polish Jews. There were cases in which Polish resistance units shot Jewish fugitives, where Poles made a profession of spotting disguised Jews and denouncing them, where peasants sold Jewish children. But there were also Poles like those who hid a friend of mine smuggled out of the Ghetto as a little girl, or like the Catholic peasants who brought up the Jewish boy who was to become Roman Polanski. The penalty for this was death, and thousands paid that penalty. Claude Lanzmann's generalisation about a whole people is a lie.

In Poland today, where almost no Jews remain, anti-semitism survives as an outrageous ghost, kept walking by political manipulation. For this, the régime itself has been responsible; in at least three times of crisis since the war, a party faction has tried to blame Poland's failures on 'Zionists' and 'cosmopolitans.' The worst occasion was 1967–68, when a hysterical campaign led by the security police drove thousands of Poles 'of Jewish extraction' into exile. The damage done to Poland's good name in the world has never been healed.

Who can calculate whether the Poles took a quarter, a half or most of their pathetically slight opportunities to save the Jews? The historian Norman Davies has called this 'one of the meanest of modern historical controversies.'

And yet it is still being fought by politicians. On May Day, General Jaruzelski referred to 'Shoah' as 'a hideous libel against our nation designed to cover up the shameful chapters of (the French) past.' In other words, the French – even French Jews – have no right to criticise Poland, because the Vichy Government enthusiastically helped the Nazis to send Jews to the gas chambers.

While insults like this fly, the Poles will go on being denied the full, merciless, honest confrontation with their own past which they so deeply desire. And yet there are signs of hope. Last year at Oxford, a conference of international historians met to discuss the topic of Poles and Jews. Most delegates were one or the other – or both.

There were tense moments. But, by the end, the scholars from Poland and a new generation of young historians from Israel were drawing together. They saw that this was a single history, common to all of them. They put aside bitterness and – at last – began to put together the truth.   [*1985*

Piłsudski, or How to Ignore Defeat

A columnist is a sort of unlicensed dentist. One pokes about in the national subconscious, and sometimes the patient yelps or twists his feet. All the same, I was surprised when some readers wrote crossly the other day about the Polish-Soviet war of 1920. They said I had been too kind to the 'Fascist dictator of Poland, Piłsudski.'

One of those buried British folk-memories lies here. It goes a bit like this: 'Churchill, the old warmonger, wanted to smash the Russian Revolution. He got Piłsudski, dictator of Poland, to invade Russia. But the British working class said "Hands off Russia!" and refused to load arms onto that ship bound for Poland called – yes, I've got it – the "Jolly George." That settled Piłsudski's hash.'

It's 50 years since Piłsudski died. It's exactly 65 years ago last week that, with a dazzling counter-stroke, he checked and utterly routed the Bolshevik invasion of Poland at the Battle of Warsaw, as the Red Cavalry headed for Berlin. This seems a fair moment to talk about that choleric but gifted man, and to dispel a few of the myths.

I remember how, when President de Gaulle visited Poland in 1966, he acutely embarrassed his Communist hosts by stopping at a plain stone slab in the Wawel cathedral at Cracow. He looked down at the engraved word 'Piłsudski' and grunted, to no one in particular, '*J'ai connu cet homme.*'

He had indeed. The young de Gaulle had served on the French military mission in Warsaw in 1920. Older people could remember his stork-like figure, advancing down Nowy Swiat with a small packet of cakes from Blikle's dangling from one gloved finger. Piłsudski ignored French advice and won the war his own way, but de Gaulle learned a lot from Piłsudski's lofty, irascible style of leadership and his emphasis on patriotic unity. His own long exile at Colombey-les-deux-Eglises was a parallel to Piłsudski's disgusted retirement to his country house at Sulejowek in 1923, waiting for the call to return and save the nation which came three years later.

And there are unexpected parallels, too, between the lives of Józef Piłsudski and Lenin. Both were born to families of the minor aristocracy of the Russian empire. Both were caught up in the 1887 plot to murder the Tsar; Lenin's brother Alexander was hanged for it, while Piłsudski's brother Bronisław received a prison sentence of 15 years. Both spent periods of political exile in Siberia, and both split their parties and led a minority to victory.

To summarise the tangles of Polish history, Piłsudski was born when the nation was still partitioned between Germany, Russia and Austria. He was a founder of the Polish Socialist

Party, but a socialist who set the goal of independence before international revolution. In 1905, he broke with the party majority to lead an armed-struggle faction which fought the Tsarist authorities with bombs, pistols and robbery.

For him, Russia was the great enemy. In the First World War, he raised Polish legions to fight alongside the Austrians and Germans against Russia, bargaining for the independence of Poland. In 1918, with all three empires dead or dying, he returned to Warsaw as the leader of a free nation.

He dreamed of a grand federation with the Ukraine, Byelo-russia and Lithuania. Piłsuldski's march into the Ukraine, which provoked the Bolshevik invasion of Poland in 1920, was an attempt to build this federation. But the Treaty of Riga was a disastrous half measure. No federation emerged, but the new Poland acquired huge and resentful non-Polish minorities and earned the hatred of both Germany and the Soviet Union, a hatred which led to the destruction of Poland by Hitler and Stalin in 1939, four years after Piłsudski's death.

After a century of suppression, Polish democracy emerged brawling and unstable. Piłsudski, a highly intelligent man with a very short fuse, never learned to live with Parliament, an 'assembly of whores' whose speeches, he once told the chamber, made the flies fall dead with boredom. In 1926, he led a military coup. Parliament survived, but opposition leaders were imprisoned and, as he grew old, Poland degenerated into an authoritarian state run by uninspired veterans of his legions.

Why, then, is Piłsudski's legend so potent in his country today? In so much, he failed. The Tsardom survived his terrorism. Poland was not freed by his legions but by the simul-taneous collapse of three empires. His hopes of dismembering Russia failed, like his dream of an eastern federation. His army proved hopelessly under-equipped in 1939, and his policy of balancing Germany against Russia died in the same disaster.

I think it is because he was the man who said: 'To be defeated, and not to give in, is victory.' It is also because he saw Russia as Poland's historic enemy, and because his nationalism was not Fascist but – badly as things went after 1918 – included a vision of social justice and tolerance. But the main thing, for young Poles today, is Piłsudski's faith that the struggle is worthwhile, that even through defeats, like the fall of Solidarity in 1981, the nation grows steadily wiser, better equipped to take and use freedom when it comes.

The Piłsudski cult is about the conspirator, not so much about the ageing Marshal on his war-horse, 'Kasztanka.' His pre-1914 world is simply the world of many Poles today. When he writes (and he was a brilliant essayist), about how he produced the clandestine socialist paper *Robotnik* in the 1890s – problems of noisy machines, of paper, of setting up chains of devoted boys and girls to distribute it – this is just 1985 for hundreds doing the same job now.

When he writes about smuggling forbidden literature – women were best, and one managed to transport 75 copies of August Bebel's tome on 'Woman' under her dress, each weighing a pound – these are still the brave comedies of beating the censor. When he recalls the stress of hiding – the pacing, chain-smoking, the glasses of tea – he is writing for the underground Solidarity committee today.

Piłsudski wrote a textbook, still used, on standing up to imprisonment. To him, it was part of being a Pole. But he asked himself whether 'all those prison experiences of Poland with all their sacrifices and terror, with all the beauty of the human soul tormented in abnormal conditions, garrotted, beaten, tired out and yet prompt to rebel, whether this beauty is not one of the traits peculiar to our generation.' He foresaw a free Poland whose young people would not understand this. 'May they forget us . . . may they advance to a new life where the charm of prisons will not bring a smile to the lips nor poison to the heart.'

Poland has certainly changed. As a society, it is more at peace with itself (though not with its Government), more confident about its ability to manage itself in times of liberty, than it was in Józef Piłsudski's time.

But not long ago I received a handsome card announcing a wedding. An invitation was not possible. Two young people were getting married in Warsaw, but in the prison on Rakowiecka Street. The bridegroom was Janusz Onyszkiewicz, once the spokesman for Solidarity. And the bride, tasting for herself the 'charm of prisons' – she was Józef Piłsudski's granddaughter.

[*1985*

1956: How Poland Got Away With It

Thirty years ago this month . . . I had half made a resolution not to be captured by anniversaries, those meaningless indicator-boards in decimals which command us to exhume feelings. But the three words 'nineteen fifty-six' break through all common-sense, like a tank – British, Polish, Hungarian, Israeli, Soviet – lurching through one of the flimsy barricades of that year.

I was far from all that, a reporter in Manchester. But I remember the first trainload of Hungarian refugees, many still wearing crusted bandages, sitting down to supper at the Styal Homes. A silly Red Cross woman went to the piano and suddenly struck up the Hungarian national anthem. When she had finished, she turned round with a proud smile which vanished instantly. All over the hall, men and women had flung down their spoons and – faces in their hands or even on the bleak wood of the table – were weeping as I have never seen people weep.

In the Suez demonstration in Whitehall, after Aneurin Bevan spoke, I was next to a friend of mine who had been badly wounded as an officer in Korea. A mounted policeman hit a woman with a baton. My friend beside himself, shouted: 'You can't do that – I saw you, I've got your number!' The policeman heard him, turned his horse and rode him down. There went a fragment of the enormous innocence that a young British generation lost in those weeks.

It is right to remember all this with horror and contrition: the tragedies and the crimes which – as one of their side effects – left Britain rather less of an island. But images of Budapest and of Egypt encourage us to overlook what happened in Poland, that October. There, too, a 'captive nation' broke with

Stalinist tyranny and sent the Russian controllers home. Poland, however, got away with it.

That should be qualified, of course. Nearly 80 people were killed in the riots at Poznań on 28 June, the event which pushed the Polish crisis into top gear. Although a reforming party leadership replaced the Stalinists that October, some Soviet troops remained in Poland, and the Soviet Union retained a general control – indirect, rather than direct – over policy. The new Communists, although a much more engaging bunch than the gang they threw out, still kept a monopoly of political power, and eventually misused it so grossly that a far bigger workers' rising took place 14 years later.

All the same, Poland by the skin of its teeth avoided a bloodbath and war with the Soviet Union. It was a better, freer, cleaner place after 1956 than before, and for a few years infinitely better and freer. The Hungarians were only trying to imitate the Polish success when, on 23 October, the students marched to the statue of Jozef Bem, the Polish general who had led Hungarian insurgents in 1848. Why did they fail, and the Poles – relatively speaking – succeed?

On 10 June 1956, the *Observer* published what it called 'its oddest issue'; the entire text of Nikita Khrushchev's secret speech to the twentieth Party Congress, in which he revealed and denounced the crimes of the idol Stalin. We carried it as a single news story 26,000 words long, covering eight of the paper's 14 pages. We got it, indirectly, from Stefan Staszewski, chief of the Warsaw party organisation, who grabbed one of the few numbered texts to reach Poland, ran off another 15,000 copies and gave three to French and American correspondents in Warsaw.

The point of this tale is that it shows how early and how rapidly Stalinist authority in Poland began to fall apart, and how effectively the party there managed to keep one jump ahead of public opinion. The aim of the reformers was to bring back to power Władysław Gomułka, who had tried to keep Soviet interference to a minimum while party leader between 1944 and 1948.

The climax came on 19 October, when the party's 'Eighth Plenum' met in Warsaw, its majority determined to restore

Gomułka to the leadership. Khrushchev had demanded an invitation. The Poles told him he wasn't welcome.

Khrushchev appeared all the same, shouting and screaming on the airfield at 7 a.m. about a sell-out to 'Americans and Zionists.' With him came a colossal delegation of Politburo members, generals, secretaries and even cooks bringing special food. Meanwhile, Soviet armoured units moved out of their camps and began to encircle Warsaw. The Polish Communists, who had anticipated something of the sort, had already stored arms for the Warsaw factory workers and now prepared to hand them out.

The rest, as they say, is history. Khrushchev eventually simmered down. Gomułka stood up to him, insisting that the thousands of Soviet officials lodged in every level of government, security and the armed forces must go home; Poland would stay in the Soviet alliance but must be allowed to run its own affairs. Khrushchev decided that this insolent jailbird was, after all, a loyal Communist in his fashion and flew home.

Gomułka was elected First Secretary. He told an ecstatic nation on the radio that there would be democracy and no more lies, independence along a Polish road to socialism and no more illegality. Two days later, in Budapest, the Hungarians marched to Bem's statue. The secret police fired on them; the people found weapons and fired back, and the city exploded into insurrection.

Why was the outcome so different? The passions of ordinary Poles and Hungarians were much the same: intense patriotic hatred of Soviet tyranny; pent-up rage against the misery of police terror, starvation wages and censorship; the hunger for justice, free speech and political democracy. It is true that Stalinism in Hungary had been more vicious than in Poland. But by October 1956, the mood of the Polish nation was as explosive as it was in Hungary.

The difference, frankly, was that Communist Party manipulation of the crisis in Poland was much more astute. Except for one day in Poznan, the Polish masses never got the bit between their teeth. The Polish Communists were divided, but in comparison the Hungarian Communists entered the crisis in utter confusion and panic. When Imre Nagy declared a multi-party system and then, on 1 November, Hungarian neutrality, he was being blown along by the hurricane of events. The fate of Hungary on 4 November, when the Soviet tanks re-entered Budapest, sobered the Poles and helped Gomułka to retain control.

I admit to one doubt about this theory. If the Polish security police had slaughtered demonstrators in the capital Warsaw, rather than in Poznan, a full-scale insurrection might have followed. But as it was, the regime survived, playing the patriotic card and granting concessions from press freedom to the disbanding of most of the secret police.

Most of these liberties were revoked in the next few years. But what remained was decisive: the restoration of the private peasantry, the collective farms dissolved, the return to influence of the Catholic Church, the party's enduring fear of the people's anger.

Hungary today is a comparatively prosperous place, run with tolerance and craft by Mr János Kádár. Poland, three years beyond martial law, is restless and crippled by debt and economic failure. And yet there remains an openness about Poland, a bad-tempered but lively jostling of social forces, which makes it in the end a healthier place. The room for real change is wider, and the air is somehow fresher. That is the legacy of the 'Polish October.'   [*1986*

Requiem for an Old Piano Banger

Last month, in writing a column which suggested that a song might be a better memorial than a stone, I seem to have hit on one of those topics which you, the readers, enjoy. Many interesting letters arrived. A happy New Year to you all, and what better way to start it than to continue this discussion of death, the tomb, and the meaning of memorials?

One of you described to me the Japanese monument to the

war dead – of all nations – at Kyoto. Another wrote about the memorial to the Italian dead in the Isonzo battles during the First World War, inscribed with hundreds of thousands of names. Martin Green sent me his poem 'Gandesa,' which – not unlike Dunbar's 'Lament for the Makaris' – celebrates by name every single British soldier who fell in the XV International Brigade during the Spanish Civil War.

Some liked the idea of remembering the dead through music. Others did not, like the reader whose wife died last year. He wanted no stone for her, but instead arranged for some trees to be planted by the Woodland Trust. He is a man who fought in North Africa and Italy, and he ended his letter: 'Let us have trees as memorials, not songs. There is too much music already!'

I can't agree with that last sentence. I am waiting impatiently for one of the most spectacular commemorations-by-music to be staged in London for years. This is the concert to celebrate the one-hundredth anniversary of the birth of Artur Rubinstein, the mighty pianist who died in 1982 at the age of 95, which will be held in the Festival Hall on Sunday 25 January.

The music is the first British performance of Penderecki's 'Polish Requiem,' conducted by the composer. All kinds of rich complexities arise. The concert honours one of the most glorious sons of Polish Jewry, but the music is a form of Catholic liturgy and commemorates the death of Polish workers, a Catholic saint and a Cardinal, as well as the Jewish martyrs of the 1943 Warsaw Ghetto rising.

Krzystof Penderecki, now in his fifties, belongs to the generation of Polish composers who astonished the world some 20 years ago with their avant-garde music. Since then, after a prolonged love affair with nineteenth-century Romantic compositions, Penderecki has been producing work which is more directly emotive and accessible than his early music. In some ways, he has become a 'composer of occasion,' who creates in response to public events which move him.

The Requiem is partly new and partly a building-together of separate works from recent years. It includes a 1981 'Agnus Dei' which Penderecki wrote on the night after the death of Cardinal Stefan Wyszynski, the 'Recordare' inspired by the canonisation of St Maximilian Kolbe and the 'Dies Irae' done in 1983 on the fortieth anniversary of the Ghetto Rising. And there is also his 'Lacrimosa,' composed at the request of Solidarity for the ceremony at Gdańsk in December 1980, at which the monument to the dead shipyard workers of the 1970 riots was dedicated.

The Requiem itself is also a reaction to a moment in history. Penderecki was moved to construct it in December 1981, when martial law was imposed on his country. As he told an American interviewer, 'in Poland, liturgical music is not only an expression of religion. It's a way for composers to show which side they are on.'

The only bit of the Requiem I have heard is the 'Lacrimosa.' I was lucky enough to be in Gdańsk that bitter night in 1980. Tens of thousands of people gathered outside the shipyard gate, under the soaring triple cross of steel raised by the workers to their comrades who perished 10 years before. Leaders of the State, the Church, the Communist Party and of the new free trade union stood around the plinth. Ships and factories blew their sirens. The names of the dead were called into the wind and darkness. Then, with a monstrous, droning chord, the 'Lacrimosa' began.

In that context, the 'Lacrimosa' was about reconciliation as well as grief, about the hope – background to the whole ceremony – that Solidarity and the Communist State would be able to work together in a cleaner, freer Poland. That hope proved vain. But the Requiem, in the context of this Rubinstein centenary, is about reconciliation as well as about an individual genius who adored life so much that his death still seems like a mistake. It is about Poles and Jews coming to terms about their mutual history.

The names on the concert committee are intriguing. Here on one list are Polish princes and counts from the emigration alongside famous Jewish intellectuals and business tycoons, as well as a local British marquess and duke. There were times when leaders of the Jewish community might have felt uneasy in such company, given the anti-Semitism common in the Polish upper crust in the old days. But times, finally, are changing.

Not without a few splutters, mostly from younger members of the Jewish diaspora brought up to believe that there was little to choose between Nazi Germany and Catholic Poland. There were some mutterings about the idea of honouring Rubinstein with a Catholic requiem. A *Jewish Chronicle* reviewer though the choice of Penderecki was a 'false note': he particularly resented the tribute to Maximilian Kolbe, the priest who gave his life to save another prisoner in Auschwitz, because Kolbe – before the war – supervised a distinctly anti-Jewish Catholic newspaper.

I'm told that the reviewer has had second thoughts about this. But as often happens, opinion in Israel has developed more rapidly than in the Diaspora, and the 'Polish Requiem' was received with delight by Israeli music critics. *Maariv* wrote that it was 'one of the outstanding and impressive creations of the century'; *Haaretz* said that the Requiem was 'not just another Christian religious work' but 'a cry of pain and a prayer for better days.'

For many centuries, most of the world's Jews lived in Poland. The relations between Catholic and Jewish Poles were never easy and became worse in the course of the last century, but they were intimate in a way now difficult to explain. Neither commmunity could quite imagine life without the other, until two political forces brought the symbiosis to an end: Zionism, which offered Jews the vision of a nation-state of their own, and then the catastrophe which Zionism came too late to avoid: Hitler's systematic murder of Poland's Jews.

Behind this concert is a new mood in which Poles and Jews are gradually understanding what they owe to one another. From the Jews, through the Bible, the Poles took the idea of a nation whose claim to survive and commandment to remember were holy. The Jews learned from Polish struggles for independence the theory and practice of modern politics – and of modern nationalism.

And yet, amid all this solemnity and significance, among Penderecki's mourning for victims and martyrs, there is some danger of losing Rubinstein himself. He lived with a rare joy in life, defying melancholy.

When he was 75, he said: 'Eat a lobster, eat a pound of caviar – live!' When he was 90, he said: 'Mozart died at 36, Schubert at 32, and I stick around like a mad old piano banger. Why me? I don't know. But I thank God.' On Sunday week, we will thank Rubinstein.   [*1987*

Invisible Men

As the Invisible Man began to die, so he began to become visible. Readers of H. G. Wells will remember the episode, as the bystanders saw appearing in the thin air at their feet the gossamer outlines of veins and sinews, then the thickening blur of limbs and skin, until a naked young man lay dead before them.

Censors are Invisible Men. And, in the same way, they gradually become visible as the life and authority ebb out of them. Contemporary Poland is a case in point. For years, some publications which are officially licensed but oppositional in their views – much of the independent Catholic Press, for instance – have been marking the place at which the censors have excised material.

I have on the desk a copy of *Res Publica*, an intellectual periodical which used to appear as illegal 'samizdat' but which has now been licensed. In an article about the politics of Bertolt Brecht, there appears suddenly the following: ' (——) (Law of 31.7.81 on the control of publications and spectacles, article 2, section 3; Official Gazette No. 20, item 99; 1983, Official Gazette No. 44, item 204).

The article then continues to say what it was saying when it was so rudely interrupted. The reader is made aware that the censor has cut out a passage, and the context usually lets him or her guess roughly what the missing passage was about. I have seen articles which consisted only of an exciting headline, the formula quoted above, and nothing else: the whole piece has been forbidden. The authorities do not like the insertion of the formula. But they tolerate it, with occasional protests. Censorship has become visible – and weaker.

The regime's own Press, especially publications sponsored by the Communist Party or the Government directly, has naturally played safer. Cuts are not shown, although such papers suffer from pre-censorship too, and although they, like the independent Press, frequently use the appeals procedure against censorship which survives in a mutilated form from the Solidarity period. But even here, the first gauzy traces of the Invisible Man are beginning to appear.

The weekly *Polytika*, published by the Central Committee of the Party, has just brought out a long article on one of the great taboos of history: the Nazi-Soviet Pact. The pact of 23 August 1939 included a secret protocol allowing for the partition of the Polish State between the 'spheres of influence' of Germany and the USSR.

The secret protocol and the detailed agreement on partition which followed it have been the taboo within the taboo for almost 50 years. But the author of the article, Professor Duraczynski, decided to tackle it in the least provocative way that he could think of.

This is what happened. 'According to German sources, a strictly secret protocol was appended to the Pact providing for the demarcation of "spheres of influence" of both powers in Eastern Europe. The authenticity of this document has not been confirmed by the Soviet side (. . .).'

This information will hardly startle the Poles, who have known all about the secret protocol since it was published in the West in 1948. Two things matter here. The first, of course, is (. . .). A Party publication is marking for its readers the interference of censorship, rendering it visible.

The second point is what the censors allowed the Professor to write before they hit him with a (. . .). Mr Gorbachov has told the Poles that there should be no 'white spaces' in the history of Soviet–Polish relations. *Polityka* is beginning to fill in some of these spaces. The latest number, for instance, has an account of how Polish troops fought the Red Army when – as an outcome of the Pact – it invaded Poland on 17 September 1939 and met the Nazis advancing from the West.

Again, this is only a symbolic revelation. All Poles know these things: because they or their fathers were there, or through Western publications and broadcasts. When the Professor says that 'according to German sources' there was a secret protocol, he is playing games: there was, full stop. When he warns that the Soviet side hasn't confirmed it, he is playing again: he knows and we know that it hasn't confirmed it precisely because it is true and puts the USSR in a bad light.

But *glasnost* is not less important because it largely consists of stating in public what everyone knows already. Silence and lies form a pillar of tyranny, national or international. Telling more of the truth about history makes a better foreign policy at least possible, which is why the Poles – in a historians' committee – have now given the Soviet Union a long list of 'white spaces': the massacre of Polish Communists, the Katyn atrocity, the fate of Polish deportees after 1939, Soviet behaviour during the Warsaw Rising, the kidnap and 'trial' of Polish resistance leaders after the war, and so on. The Nazi–Soviet Pact is on the list, too.

The Polish official spokesman complained the other day that some people were merely filling the white spaces with dirty smears. How black will be the space where that Pact should be, when and if it is filled in?

I have been reading the manuscript of a forthcoming and fascinating book by Geoff Roberts, provisionally titled 'Soviet Russia's Pact with Nazi Germany.' He has rejected the old excuse that 'we will never know until Moscow opens its archives,' and done his best with what is available.

One of the mysteries is when Stalin decided to seek an understanding with Nazi Germany. When the Pact was signed, an Anglo–French delegation was still in Moscow discussing military co-operation to contain Hitler. Was all that a sham on the Soviet side, the 'option for Hitler' having already been secretly adopted? Or – as the Soviet side prefers – was there a sincere wish for a 'triple pact' with Britain and France, destroyed by evidence that the Western powers hoped that Hitler would fight Stalin and would do nothing to help the USSR in that event?

Much depends on what one makes of a meeting in Berlin on 17 April – four months before the Pact. Merekalov, the Soviet ambassador, said there was no reason why Nazi–Soviet relations should not become normal and then better than normal. Was this the first sign of a new policy unimaginable to the rest of the world?

If Merekalov was really hinting at a non-aggression pact, then the present Soviet account is false. Oddly enough, Professor

Duraczynski is more inclined to that view than Geoff Roberts. The Roberts conclusion is that Merekalov was really talking about *trade* relations. Stalin did not make his final choice until August, when he and Molotov concluded (a) that European war following a German attack on Poland was now inevitable, and (b) that France and Britain would leave the USSR in the lurch in that war.

It remains a space still more white than otherwise. We are still uncertain why, when or how the great reversal was decided. In the end, the Soviet armies were to crush Hitler and save us all. But it can't even be said for certain that the Pact made that possible, that the USSR was better prepared to fight Hitler in 1941 than in 1939.

So much for problems of fact. Moral judgments are rather easier. The surrender of Britain and France to Hitler at Munich made the Nazi-Soviet Pact thinkable, if not inevitable. The alliance with Hitlerism to abolish Poland, and the fate of Poles under Soviet occupation, are great crimes. From that point of view, what begins to appear in the space as censorship weakens is still only darkness.   [*1987*

The Berlin Wall as Holy Monster

Many years ago, in the British embassy in Bonn, there was a small, impassioned, well-loved man named Dr Kohn. A lawyer who had been a refugee from Hitler, one of his duties was to instruct successive British ambassadors on the tortuous complexities of divided Berlin. Dr Kohn knew every precedent over this rusted railway line, that grass-grown bridge or ruin, when staff-car windows should be wound down or kept shut at checkpoints – the whole, gigantic, dog-eared encylopaedia which might one day stop a world war.

He had a set speech for ambassadors, which began like this.

'Remember, please remember, the words of the great jurist Puffendorf about the Holy Roman Empire: *monstro simile*, like unto a monster: with Berlin as with the Empire, seek not to understand, only to preserve!'

When I went to live in Berlin, the place was a nature reserve of monsters, dozing about the place but occasionally emitting puffs of fire as they snored. There was Gross–Berlin, under Four-Power control. There was Berlin-Capital-of-the-German-Democratic-Republic, and West Berlin. There were islets of West in East, like the enclave of Staaken, and promontories of East in West, like the ruins of the Potsdam Station inhabited by ghouls, crooks and maniacs evading the jurisdiction of the West Berlin police.

But the greatest monster of them all was the Wall, writhing across the middle of the city in grey and white concrete or breeze-block, becoming a broad, sandy stripe of wire-fences and watch-towers as it encircled the outer suburbs and forests of West Berlin. That Wall is 25 years old this week. It has eaten nearly a hundred lives, though its diet of blood is very sparse these days. It continues to horrify millions, who come to see it and to peer across. They 'seek to understand,' and fail. On the other side, they 'seek to preserve,' and I regret to say that the Wall – apart from graffiti and the odd bomb from the West – is in excellent health.

The Berliners have grown used to it. Over a quarter-century, family ties which caused such agony when they were sundered in August 1961 have naturally diminished. West Berliners can visit the East, and elderly East Berliners can usually return the visit if they have relations on the Western side.

But the monstrosity of the barrier, the sense of inhumanity and crime, remain. Living in Berlin is like inhabiting the map of ancient cartographers: not only 'here be dragons,' but the feeling that if you stray too far, you come to the edge of the world: the blank white face of concrete across the street, the rails sawn off suddenly as they enter a purposeful curve.

And yet it was even stranger to visit Berlin before the Wall. It was already two cities. But you could wander at will and freely between two universes, climbing into the train among the oranges and advertisements of the Zoo station and getting out at Marx-Engels-Platz among the shabby crowds, the huge red banners stirring in the Siberian wind against half-ruined buildings. The Wall came as a shock, hardly as a surprise.

For the anniversary, the East German authorities have expanded their exhibition which shows how, in August 1961, they 'saved peace in the heart of Europe.' The claim isn't entirely untrue. For many years, the generals of NATO had agreed (when their West German colleagues were not listening) that the main threat of war in Europe was the possible collapse of the German Democratic Republic, by insurrection or economic disaster; it would be hard and perhaps impossible to stop the West Germans piling in to rescue 'the brothers and sisters in the Soviet Zone,' and then Soviet intervention and Western counter-intervention would become inevitable.

By the summer of 1961, Khrushchev's efforts to force the Western Allies out of Berlin by threats were flagging, after three years of crisis. But the outrush of East Germans through the open Berlin border rose rapidly; by August, some 1,500 refugees were arriving daily in West Berlin. Closing the border on 13 August ensured that the German Democratic Republic would not bleed demographically to death. In its brutal way, it stabilised not only Berlin but all Europe.

The Western Allies did nothing beyond protesting. There was relief mixed with their outrage. In fact, the pass had already been sold by President Kennedy on 25 July when, in a television speech, he insisted on the freedoms of West Berlin and the rights there of the Western Allies but – deliberately – implied that the East Germans and the Soviet Union could do much as they pleased in their part of the city.

Only two months before, at Vienna, Khrushchev had warned Kennedy that any status quo was dynamic, that no Power could bring historical changes to a halt. Now Khrushchev had tried to achieve exactly that. Two years later, Kennedy came to West Berlin and proclaimed that he was 'ein Berliner.' But his words in July 1961 had been the first guarantee in the Cold War that the West would not try to overthrow the East German State – or any other State in the Soviet part of Europe. The tragedies of Czechoslovakia seven years later and of Poland in 1981 suffocated authentic social changes, while the West stood by and wailed.

There are walls to keep people out, like the Great Wall of

China or Hadrian's. There are walls to keep people apart, like those the British have built along the 'Peace Line' in Belfast. Walls to keep people in are less common. Here the Germans have more practice than most, having bricked millions of Jews into ghettos during the occupation of Poland.

And yet, just as the point of minefields in war is to force an enemy into the gaps between them, so walls are also for letting people through. This reminds me of a conference about political bridge-building years ago in Prague: the German said bridges meant unity, the Czech observed that bridges were the first things to be blown up and the Russian (this is a true story) said the point of bridges was that you could control who was crossing them.

The Berlin Wall has been used exactly like that. Sometimes for political concessions, sometimes for money, sometimes just to make trouble, the East Germans have made energetic use of their power to unlock it. At the moment, the problem of the West Berlin border is that the authorities of the German Democratic Republic are letting through a torrent of 'refugees' – Iranians, Tamils, Pakistanis – who are claiming asylum in West Berlin and West Germany, swamping all efforts to cope with them. Some 50,000 have come in since January. If the Bonn Government recognises the Wall as an 'international frontier,' then East Germany might consent to shut the gates again.

A monster of irony. But then, to keep sane, I imagine my great-great-uncle, a Berlin botany professor famous for rambles with his students through these forests now split between worlds. There they go, girls with sketchpads and boys in knickerbockers, behind a happy, bearded old man in a straw hat. I see them float from the pines and across the 'Death Strip,' through the barbed wire, over the mines and electronic sensors and into the shade of the trees the other side, engrossed in Latin names and a new sub-species of vetch, ghosts of a place without zones or sectors, where walls were for wallflowers.

[1986

Why Burning People is Always Wrong

'Rehabilitation' of the dead: this is a ritual peculiar to the times we live in. This is something which could happen only in the century of Orwell.

A troop of dignitaries, trembling with the sense of their own generosity, advances to some dishonoured grave and says: 'Sorry we executed you! It was all a misunderstanding. We see now that you were in some ways right. We forgive you. Indeed, we forgive ourselves. Have these flowers. Have this street named after you. You were a dead unperson; now you are a dead person. Congratulations!'

Communist parties, or at least those in power, are famous for rehabilitating. Khrushchev did it for some – only some – of Stalin's victims among the old Bolsheviks. The Czechoslovak Communist Party did it for the dead and the living dead of the Slánský trials. In Hungary, they forgave the ashes of Lázslo Rajk. In China, after the Cultural Revolution and the fall of the Gang of Four, the dead were rehabilitated by the thousand.

I am not talking about what happens after a revolution, when men and women exhume and honour their martyred comrades in the struggle. I am interested in the moments when the murderers or their heirs pay respects to those whom they murdered. There are, of course, certain rules to this game. The dead sign a declaration of loyalty to the living. It always turns out that they stood for precisely the principles that the present regime is applying. But they stood for them at the wrong moment – as the Czechs say, 'in complex, exceptional situations . . .'

A system which rehabilitates in this way has to be a closed system, a corporation which is always fundamentally correct in the past, present and future but whose individual members or ruling figures may 'depart from the norms' at times. The late Arthur Koestler used to say that there were three closed systems, each of which was capable of explaining away criticism in its own terms: Communism, Freudianism and the Catholic Church.

Communism has been mentioned. The Freudians, to the best of my knowledge, have never sent their dissidents to camps or burned them alive. There remains the Catholic Church.

All these reflections rushed to my mind the other day when there appeared in the sky, small but a great deal more noticeable than Halley's Comet, a trial balloon. It was launched in the old city of Cracow in Poland. It was a front-page article in a Catholic weekly noted for its intimacy with the present Pope, who was for long years the Cardinal of that city, and it demanded – in passionate and impatient terms – the rehabilitation of Jan Hus.

Jan Hus, the greatest of pre-Reformation reformers, was a Czech. Born in about 1372, he spent most of his life as an academic at the Prague university. It was a time when the Czechs were already crying out both against the corruption of the Church in Bohemia and against the encroachment of Germans in economic and intellectual life. Hus was at once a scholar, who invigorated the Czech language and gave it a new spelling, and a patriot and social reformer who toured and inspired his nation.

But he was, above all, a preacher. Borrowing some ideas from John Wycliffe, in England, Hus came to argue that the Church was not just a hierarchy but 'God's People,' the totality of all born to be saved. Christ was the Head of the Church, and the Pope only his representative. Hus took a traditional view of sacraments, but said that they could not be administered by a priest in a state of mortal sin. He called for a return to Scripture, for a Church which abandoned worldly wealth and became a Church of all the people – and of the poor. He believed that Jesus had ordained the Eucharist 'in both kinds' – not only the bread to the congregation but also the wine of Christ's blood.

He was to be the victim of a show trial as vicious as any in the Soviet Union under Stalin. Hus was called to explain himself at the Council of Constance, under a safe conduct which was torn up on the grounds that 'pacts with heretics are not binding.' He was arrested, charged with a list of heresies he had never uttered and, when he refused to retract beliefs he had never held, burned to death on 6 July 1415. Two years later, his friend Jerome of Prague went to the stake for refusing to sign a statement that the condemnation of Hus had been just.

Most Catholics now agree that the trial of Jan Hus was a disgrace and an atrocity. But – writing in the weekly *Tygodnik Powszechny* – the historian Stefan Swieżawski goes further. He asks the Pope to annul the Constance trial. But he also demands the rehabilitation of Hus as a Christian thinker, 'the cleansing of this great martyr-figure from the unjust accusations against him.' Jan Hus, he asserts, was not a heretic at all. Quite the opposite. All he did was to express the ideas of the Second Vatican Council (1962–65), some 500 years before that huge conclave brought the spirit, life and practice of the Church up to date with the modern world.

It's a classic rehabilitation plea. What interests Mr Swieżawski is the idea that the 'correct line' of the Church as a whole is unbroken, immaculate; it simply takes a curve through Jan Hus and isolates his killers as 'deviationists' who happened to lead the Church at a certain moment in history.

Could Hus be rehabilitated, and his trial for heresy annulled, as the trial of Joan of Arc had to be annulled before she could become a saint in 1925? That depends on whose hand is holding the string of this balloon. Just possibly, it is the broad hand of Karol Wojtyla, Pope John Paul II.

It would be in his style, and to his purposes. He is sometimes accused of lacking enthusiasm for things ecumenical, for over-coming the divisions between faiths. Here he could begin to do so in the region which interests him most: Eastern Europe. And it would embarrass the Czechoslovak regime, which exerts crushing pressure on the Catholic Church and constantly argues that while Hus and the Hussites were a 'progressive,' patriotic Czech movement, Catholicism in Bohemia has historically been pro-German, pro-Habsburg and hostile to Czech independence. If the Vatican took Hus to its bosom, this argument would collapse, Jan Hus remains beloved by the Czechs, and a fusion of his tradition with Catholicism would move the Catholic Church in Bohemia toward the status of a patriotic 'Church of the nation' – more like the Church in Poland.

Good politics, perhaps. But not good history. Master Jan Hus was a brave, witty but above all independent man; must he now be reduced to a mere pioneer of modern Catholic orthodoxy? As someone in the Vatican remarked to me: 'Vindicate the truth about him, yes – but you can't put a fifteenth-century man into a twentieth-century context.' In Eastern Europe, however, history has always been melted down to cast modern ammunition, and this Pope, as a Pole, is not immune to the temptation.

I do not want to be mean to the learned and well-meaning Mr Swiezawski of Cracow. But perhaps he overlooks the real point. The mighty preacher of the Bethlehem Chapel in Prague needs nobody's forgiveness (and he forgave his judges before he died). It is not so important to admit that Hus was 'right.' It is infinitely more important to say that it is always, everywhere, wrong to kill people for their opinions – even if they are mistaken.   [*1986*

'You Lose Freedom by Fighting for It'

Killing off an old doctrine is a task which pains any statesman of feeling. A faithful family pet, grown smelly and pathetic and no longer able to frighten mice or burglars, has to be discreetly put down. One does not make a drama out of it, and so it was the other day when President Reagan took the Kirkpatrick Doctrine on its last journey to the vet.

The principle associated with Jeane Kirkpatrick – she certainly publicised it, even if she did not exactly invent it – was a distinction between 'authoritarian' regimes and 'totalitarian' regimes. With the first – Latin American dictatorships, for example – the United States could live in a relationship that was morally justifiable. With the second, meaning essentially regimes classified as Communist or Marxist, no relationship founded on any form of approval was possible. Now, President Reagan simply states that America will 'oppose tyranny in whatever form, whether of the Left or the Right.'

The politics of the change are obvious enough. The Administration wants to have its hands free to disentangle itself from failing 'authoritarian' regimes in Chile and South Africa, and to claim some retrospective credit from the fall of Marcos in the Philippines and Duvalier in Haiti. The Kirkpatrick line also embarrassed the developing relationship between the United States and China. All this is just opportunism. But was there anything of intellectual substance in the doctrine itself?

I consulted Roger Scruton's 'Dictionary of Political Thought,' a lucid and original guide by a man who is himself a strict authoritarian. He defines totalitarianism as the rule of a State which 'permits no autonomous institutions,' in which 'freedom of association cannot be permitted.' He adds that 'complete state control of communication is also essential, together with an ideology . . . for the sole origin of all legitimation is the State itself.'

Authoritarianism, on the other hand, is 'the advocacy of government based on an established system of authority rather than on explicit or tacit consent.' Scruton notes the belief that 'people need authority,' without which no consent should arise, and adds that more radical authoritarians see ' a need to ensure stability against the advance of sceptical reflections' – in other words, the repression of new ideas.

These definitions create severe problems for the Kirkpatrick Doctrine. To start with, they exclude a number of Communist or semi-Communist States from the totalitarian camp. It would be absurd to say that Poland or Nicaragua, to say nothing of Hungary, 'permit no autonomous institutions.' Look at the status of the Church, for a start. These may be governments whose ideology aspires to a totalitarian condition. But China, for example, is far closer to what Scruton is talking about.

In fact, the doctrine was about something else. As philosophy, its definitions were pretentious humbug. As description, however, they said something very important. Forget the 'totalitarian' and 'authoritarian' labels, which don't stick properly. The real distinction is between Communist and non-Communist autocracies.

Tyrannies in Latin America or Asia may be terrible, Jeane Kirkpatrick said. But they can be overthrown. Communist tyrannies, on the other hand, seem to be permanent. They are a bourne from which no traveller returns, a fish-trap with an entrance but no exit. They are like that American device for killing cockroaches: 'The Roach Motel – They Check In, But They Don't Check Out!'

The Czech novelist Milan Kundera wrote: 'In a Fascist dictatorial State, everyone knows that it will end one day. Everyone looks to the end of the tunnel. In the empire to the East, the tunnel is without end, at least from the point of view of a human life.'

This is the argument that counts. It is passionately embraced by opposition groups and dissidents throughout Eastern Europe. It is the root for their disconcerting affection for the New Right in the West. 'Don't talk to us about the poor Chileans,' they say, 'and don't tell us how wicked Reagan is over Nicaragua. Pinochet can be removed. But Sandinista Marxism will be for ever. Sure, right-wing dictators kill far more people. But even that is better than sealing a whole nation in the tomb, however peaceful that tomb may be.'

I often hear this. I have heard it from a man translating Irving Kristol for samizdat, from a woman crouched over a spluttering radio to listen to Roger Scruton – no other – explaining why universal free education is an evil. I still think it's a feeble explanation of the world.

It is true that Communism is more efficient at suppressing internal challenge than Fascism – always prone to praetorian struggles – and much more efficient than the murderous oligarchies of Latin America. But the frozen, unalterable face of Communist regimes owes most to the Cold War in general and Soviet policy in particular. Without Soviet tanks, used to preserve a Soviet version of Marxist orthodoxy, Eastern Europe would have changed out of recognition. Without the danger that sudden change would lead to a world crisis, Vietnam and Cuba would find it harder to be so rigid.

And beyond this war of distinctions between Pinochet and

Jaruzelski – this grisly attempt to work out how many murdered Honduran peasants and starving babies in KwaZulu weigh as much in the moral scales as one hopeless and wasted life in Prague – there is a huge collapse of human nerve. For the argument about 'totalitarian' and 'authoritarian' regimes reveals that we in the West have not merely lost faith in the idea of the State. We have forgotten why anyone ever wished to erect one.

The wretched millions who live beyond the political margins, kept out by poverty and frequently by government terror, dream of a mighty State of all the people which will arise to enforce equality and justice. In the West, however, we have come to think of State power in terms of Auschwitz or the Gulag, as the totalitarian monster into which the State can (but need not) develop.

The poet Czesław Miłosz, a dignified pessimist, believes this development can't be avoided. 'The egalitarian tendency . . . favours the installation of the totalitarian State, as does the riddance of hunger and misery for those who have nothing to lose except their chains.'

And here, finally, the whole flesh-creeping argument vanishes up its own backside. To fight for freedom and equality is to ensure that you will lose them for ever. We have arrived at the central nonsense of the Kirkpatrick Doctrine. It is 'authoritarian' indeed, for it accepts and sanctions that 'need to ensure stability against the advance of sceptical reflections.'

It's good that President Reagan has dropped it. It would be better if one did not suspect that he still subscribes to it in his heart.   [1986

Suffering Writing

In Budapest, the Europeans have been talking about European culture. And for one unforgettable week they talked in counterpoint: officially in one place, unofficially in another. There was a Festival, but a Fringe as well.

In the new conference centre at the foot of the Eagle Hill, the diplomats and bureaucrats of 35 nations made their opening statements. This was the first phase of the European Cultural Forum, part of the 'Helsinki Process' of the conferences on European security and cooperation which have been plodding on for over 10 years now. And sitting packed like sardines on the floor of a loft-flat on the Gellert Hill, writers from Europe and America discussed freely for two days the problems of censorship, of exile, of how to define a 'European spirit' in the literature of a divided continent.

In the first of these columns, I proposed that it was no longer useful to talk about 'European civilisation,' that Europe is a vigorous, dangerous, barbarous place. So I found it tedious at the Cultural Forum to listen to one highly-educated bureaucrat after another fluting on (the Western ones especially) about the nobility of the European heritage, about cathedrals and the international baroque, about the values of individual creative liberty that we are supposed to have treasured so tenderly, about the legacy of Christendom from the Atlantic to the Urals.

How pretty, if European history had really been like that! How simple to talk as if an immemorial European unity had been suddenly partitioned by the wicked Communists and their barbed wire! Europe was never united, and those who came nearest to uniting it were Napoleon and Hitler. But the Communist speeches were no better, mostly recitations of publishing statistics and totals of students in higher education, coupled with pious outcries about the vileness of Western pornography.

But it is unfair to judge the Forum by its vapid start. Something can be achieved here. The West has managed to secure an agenda which includes 'creation, dissemination and cooperation.' The Soviet Union wanted only to discuss the safe topic of 'cultural cooperation,' but – as an unspoken condition for getting some progress in the Stockholm talks on military 'confidence building measures,' which the Russians care about – must now put up with five weeks of detailed accusations about censorship, the denial of visas to artists, the 'blacking' of artists and the jamming of radio programmes.

With luck, there will be agreement about the exchange of cultural centres, about more travelling theatres and exhibitions, even about translations from smaller languages. The Russian classics are almost as familiar to us in the West as our own. But most Hungarian writing, and the tremendous literature of nineteenth-century Poland, remain unknown to us. If the Forum gave us Słowacki, Mickiewicz, Norwid, Petöfi, Ady and Attila Jozsef, our children would understand their world in a way that we cannot.

So the dead would cross frontiers and cast new spells. The living, however, have no such hope. The Forum cannot play Leonora in 'Fidelio' and lead into free daylight the prisoners of cultural dictatorship in the Soviet Union, Czechoslovakia, Romania, Poland. Czechoslovakia, for example, will continue to censor and blacklist thousands of its best writers, scholars, artists and actors.

This was what the writers gathered in the flat on the Gellert Hill were talking about. But they did not moan about their condition. They did not lavish praise on the West; indeed, one Hungarian spoke of the West as a 'masturbating culture' which had lost the energy to plan the future or take initiatives. Instead, they talked self-critically about the illusions of writers, about the occupational diseases of literature under dictatorship.

Danilo Kis, a Yugoslav of Hungarian nationality, described self-censorship, the lonely struggle which 'compromises the most moral individuals whom external censorship has failed to break.' Even those who won the struggle found their writing marked by it, in the form of a 'dominance of metaphors.' For a very few, there would ultimately be a 'violent collapse of years of prudence: metaphors collapse and there remains only the raw language of action.'

The Czech novelist Jiři Gruša, who now lives in exile, mocked the whole 'prophetic' tradition of literature in Central Europe. Writers could hardly complain that the state took such a suffo-cating interest in them, when – in the struggles for national independence – they had 'glorified the modern state, first as godhead, then as universal provider.' Now the ex-prophets were sorry for themselves. But 'if we want to talk about our "right to history," we should remember that our patriotic odes are found in all the schoolbooks of Europe and contributed substan-tially to the disaster of this continent.'

In the air hung an unspoken apology, the guilt of Western writers about their own freedom. This guilt produces some silliness. There is a tendency to exaggerate the difficulty of achieving literature in the lands east of the dividing line. And there is an opposite tendency to suppose that the struggle against censor and policeman can actually generate writing of a splendour which the West cannot attain.

This second line has been taken by the critic George Steiner. But he was attacked by Philip Roth, in a recent interview, who went to the other extreme and argued that the repression of writers in Czechoslovakia was so severe that it had practically destroyed literature. 'That system doesn't make masterpieces, it makes coronaries, ulcers and asthma, it makes alcoholics, it makes depressives. . . . Nine-tenths of the best (writers) will never do their best work, just because of the system.'

Milan Kundera, the great Czech novelist who lives in Paris, also fears that Czech culture itself may be dying: 'Finis Bohemiae.' But those who have stayed in Bohemia don't share that pessimism. In a book called 'A Besieged Culture: Czechos-lovakia Ten Years After Helsinki,' published in Sweden to coincide with the Forum, the writer Ivan Klimá counter-attacks from Prague.

He retorts, in effect, that good writing can and does go on. Oppression doesn't debase it, even though it often cannot be published. 'Good literature and good art do get created in places where, according to a simplified outlook, you would expect to find nothing but "ulcers, asthma, depression and insanity".' Klimá argues that 'to say that no genuinely great work of art (but for one or two exceptions) can come out of this entire huge part of the world seems to me no more justified than to say that it cannot be created in conditions of freedom because writers who are free lack suffering . . .'.

And all these passionate disputes among writers have – it seems to me – a message for the delegates at the Budapest Cultural Forum. Not a long one, either. It could be put into a telegram. It would read something like this:

'You do not own us. You did not create us. Actually, we created you – a mistake we are working on. You cannot make us write well, and you cannot stop us writing either. Kindly clear up the mess you have made in Europe, as it is difficult to devise characters when history is petrified. Meanwhile, please supply the following: paper, typewriters, passports, the foreign books we need for our work, and publishers in our own countries. Yours, without much affection, the writers of Europe.'

[*1985*

The Unsung Heroes of Chernobyl

'The Soviet news coverage of Chernobyl was late, meagre but not untrue. The Western coverage was fast, massive and misleading.'

The speaker was Dr Hans Blix, director of the International Atomic Energy Agency. The audience was the International Press Institute, a body composed mostly of editors from the non-Communist world, and Dr Blix – just back from Moscow, Kiev and Chernobyl itself – was addressing the IPI assembly in Vienna last week.

I thought there would be an insurrection in the hall. Not a bit of it. The assembled editors and managers were for the most part meek, almost penitent. This may have had something to do with the fact that about half the enormous American contingent had been too frightened of terrorism to turn up. Be that as it may, Chernobyl thrust its way into almost every session of the meeting, and there was an unmistakable feeling that the Western media had wildly overdone their reporting.

Dr Blix, a peremptory, even authoritarian figure, has his own corner to defend. He is the world's senior spokesman for the nuclear industry, in its peaceful aspect. He is concerned to keep the Soviet Union cooperating with the IAEA, rather than to pillory Soviet failings over Chernobyl, and has secured a Soviet commitment to come to Vienna in about a month's time and lay a full, detailed analysis of the disaster and its causes before the Agency.

Understanding all that, I still felt Dr Blix was far too kind to the Soviet media. Nobody would excuse a fire brigade that was 'late and meagre,' but which poured a trickle of genuine water rather than petrol on the embers when it finally turned up. For a population showered with deadly radiation, instant information is a matter of life or death. No 'right to know' can be more desperate, or more immune to the argument of 'let's wait till we have the full picture.' It is also undeniable that some of the first Tass information, in good faith or bad, was indeed untrue.

The crass, defensive silence in Moscow, however, allowed full resonance to the terrific scream of jubilation that burst from the Western media – the Anglo-Saxon, above all. The Murdoch Press, for example, gave inimitable tongue, from the *New York Post's* reports of over 20,000 dead through the *Sun's* 'Red Nuke Disaster' – '2,000 Dead Riddle' down to the merely absurd *Sunday Times* picture of a 'radiation cloud' over Kiev.

Television in Britain, on one memorable night, was able to assure the nation that a full-scale core melt-down was actually taking place at that moment, with 180 tons of molten uranium descending through the Chernobyl foundations to reach the water table. It was the same night that 'experts' debated the economic prospects of the Soviet Union, robbed of the entire grain province of the Ukraine.

Sucked along in the updraught of all this hot air, whole governments began to leave the ground. In Washington, officials blithely speculated about a Ukrainian apocalypse until their own agonised nuclear industry pointed out the damage they were doing at home. The European Community imposed a quite unnecessary total ban on East European produce. Utter confusion reigned in West Germany, where the State Government of Hesse – with a Green Minister – declared a radioactivity threshold for milk eight times lower than that of the Federal Government. Austria told parents not to let children sit on the grass. Sainsbury's in Muswell Hill, London, ran out of bottled water and Long Life milk. Never in history have so many people said so much about something they understood so little.

None of this tale of exaggeration, however, is meant to underestimate what happened. As the invisible plume waved slowly across Europe, something said by a few people for a long time became – I think permanently – recognised as wisdom. The release of radioactive material into the environment is a crime against humanity. Those responsible for the release – negligent planners, corrupt contractors, bungling engineers, servile managers – are criminals against humanity. Some would say that those who accept any use of nuclear energy are criminals too. I don't agree. But this disaster is universal, and to say: 'Red nukes are bad; ours are good' is more dangerous than any melt-down.

So Chernobyl has been not just a catastrophe but a missed chance – missed so far, at least. Its effect has not been to make manifest a common interest in the survival of life. Instead, it has sharply intensified the mutually hostile images of East and West: what Germans called the *Feindbild*.

It did not have to be like that. Arrant nationalism dances on the frontiers of technology, and yet there is still a feeling among ordinary people that physical discovery, with all its risks and its unknowns, should unite rather than divide. When Challenger exploded and its seven men and women perished, there was – so friends in Moscow tell me – a spontaneous wave of horror and sympathy in the Soviet public.

Why has there been almost nothing like that in the West over Chernobyl? In part, it's a matter of presentation. The fearsome film of Challenger's disintegration was given to all the world to see, more powerful than hours of ideological footnote. The long, long silence of the Soviet Government over Chernobyl changed fear abroad into wrath and came to seem like a hostile act – which in effect it was, as Mr Gorbachov now seems tardily to grasp. The propagandists of the West were presented with the issue of the decade, and they used it.

We know now that, in the horror of Chernobyl, scientists at the other reactors on the site stayed at their posts. It also came out that technicians from all over the Soviet Union have been entering the intense radiation of the stricken Chernobyl IV to fight the fire and secure the controls. They go for brief spells, in relays. A casual answer to a journalist's question revealed that they are volunteers.

A few Western newspapers and broadcasts speculated on the awful courage of these men (and possibly women), and on what could be happening to their bodies. But for the most part, a combination of official Soviet dislike of 'personalisation' and Western indifference have kept them on the margin of the picture. It was not until last Wednesday that Mr Gorbachov called them 'heroic' – still without details.

But they were, and are, heroes. And I don't think that I am misreading the mood in this country, at least, to say that many people would have been glad to have honoured them, to have read or heard far more about them, and to have had confirmed their feeling that beyond the curtain of political hostility there still live individuals as brave, generous and reckless as Russians always have been.

Blame Soviet paranoia and secrecy, blame Cold War opportunism in the West: for both reasons, the chance that their acts might make Chernobyl something to unite rather than divide was lost. All the same, the invisible thing they fight, as it comes out of the reactor, is the mortal enemy of us all, not just of the Soviet Union. So was that other enemy, in 1941. And – then as now – if they lose, we lose.   [1986

Russian Mist

A few days ago, they unveiled a statue of Raoul Wallenberg in Budapest. Wallenberg, it will be remembered, was the Swedish diplomat who rescued thousands of Jews from death in Nazi-occupied Hungary, and vanished in 1945. The World Jewish Congress, meeting in Budapest last week, also paid reverence to his memory.

The statue is by Imre Várga who, in my view, is Europe's master of the unfashionable art of 'public sculpture.' Next to the Parliament building, looking out over the Danube, stands Varga's statue of Count Károlyi. He is a slight figure, framed in a broken Gothic arch. He is the loneliest man in the world, upright Károlyi who tried and failed to save his country from defeat, mutilation, economic ruin, revolution and Fascist terror, who died in exile. But you don't need to know any of that, not even his name, to understand from the statue that this was a good person abandoned by history and his friends.

So Wallenberg is lucky, at least, in his sculptor. It isn't the first monument. The guests assembled in Budapest to unveil the original one in 1948, but soon observed that – under the tarpaulin – there was nothing left to unveil. The statue had been removed in the night and, like its subject, vanished into the mists of time and rumour.

Wallenberg remains in those mists, but the original statue does not. A few years ago it was found, shorn of identifying inscriptions and standing outside a factory on an industrial estate at Debrecen. As it is a highly symbolic work rather than a portrait, showing a male figure wrestling with a snake, the workers had supposed that it was Peace Triumphing over Warmongers or something equally banal.

A visitor to Budapest today will soon notice, if he has Hungarian friends, that this is the last Central European capital with a large, lively Jewish population. Two men made this possible.

One was the Regent Miklos Horthy, who saw that the war was lost and managed to halt the deportations to Auschwitz in the summer of 1944, when Eichmann had taken the Jews from the provinces but had not completed the 'clearing' of Budapest. The other was Raoul Wallenberg. As an emissary of the Swedish Government, he distributed Swedish passports, set up refuges and saved the lives of perhaps 100,000 human beings.

In January 1945, Wallenberg and his driver set off to make contact with the headquarters of the approaching Soviet Army. They never returned. Wallenberg apparently reached the command post of Marshal Malinovsky at Debrecen. Then . . . nothing. For years, the Swedes demanded news about him, and were told that he was not in the Soviet Union. In 1957, however, Andrei Gromyko, Deputy Foreign Minister, informed Sweden that Wallenberg had died in the Lubyanka prison in Moscow on 17 July 1947.

Even *glasnost* has not induced the Soviet authorities to change this version – or add to it. But the Swedish Government, unconvinced, has never ceased to demand his release, or to suggest that he may still be alive (he would now be 74). Meanwhile, the Wallenberg family continues to take seriously an apparently endless trickle of 'sightings,' some from Gulag survivors claiming to have met Wallenberg, others from somebody who met somebody in the camps who knew him or his driver, others again just Gulag folk-lore about 'a Swedish diplomat' in a camp in Norilsk or Mordvinia.

A couple of years ago, I met two Swedes with a very different story. Hans Ehrenstrale and Lillan Broman – they were not married then – were Swedish aid workers in Poland just after the war. Civil war was still raging, as remnants of the old Home Army partisans loyal to the exile government in London and Ukrainian guerrillas in the south-east fought the Communist authorities. Lillan – a startling historical detail – was secretly passing money from the American Embassy to partisan units in the southern hills who used it to buy weapons across the border in Slovakia.

In October 1947, Lillan's American contact 'Jimmy' told her that a Soviet military train had been ambushed, and that several badly-injured foreign prisoners had fallen into Polish partisan hands. The Poles reported that one was a Swedish diplomat from Hungary. 'Jimmy' asked Lillan to go and find this man, whom he believed to be Wallenberg, and to ask him if he had certain documents still with him.

Hans and Lillan set out, and after various adventures she was taken to a forest camp near Tarnow. Here she found an unconscious and dying man. Lillan had met Wallenberg twice before the war, on a sailing party and at a ball when they danced together. She says now that she is almost totally certain that the dying man was Wallenberg, but 'I could not prove it beyond doubt.' The partisans were nervous, anxious to move on: Lillan took the man's empty knapsack and pressed his fingers against it to leave fingerprints. Back in Warsaw, she gave the bag to 'Jimmy'; it was returned to her later, but if the prints survived, she was not told.

And that is almost all. Later she helped the local village priest to emigrate to the United States. He told her that he had buried the man up against the wall of a church near Pilzno, south of Debnica, under an old tomb-slab.

It would be worth a visit to Pilzno. The train was heading West, towards Prague, and the prisoners may have been due for release there. At all events, I found the Ehrenstrales highly respectable and sober witnesses; Hans later had a distinguished career as a UN civil servant. But in Sweden, this story has provoked every sort of ridicule and irritation. Believing Wallenberg is still alive has become, it seems, something of a loyalty test.

I think that he is long dead. But what, exactly, is the queer appeal of this idea that somewhere far, far away, behind the dim perimeter lights of some forgotten labour camp in a forest, Raoul Wallenberg lies toothless on a wooden bunk and dreams of the fresh breeze, the diamond spray of the islands around Stockholm? It is, I suspect, that we require Russia (or the Soviet Union) to be an infinity.

Once it was 'the Amazon jungles' or 'darkest Central Africa'; before that, it was endless and undiscovered America. Now Amazonia is a rapacious lumber camp, Africa is bright with flashbulbs and World Bank inventories. But in great Russia, you can still get lost, be forgotten, stumble on a mammoth's ginger head poking from the ice, or enjoy the masochistic thrill of countlessness. Only in this land, slothful and secretive, can a world hero like Wallenberg sink away as Colonel Fawcett sank away into the Amazon forest, in the 1920s, leaving only ambiguous bubbles to reach the surface.

Such is the Western fantasy. In a way, Russians share it. The sense of infinite resources is ingrained in Russian attitudes – and is one of the worst problems that Mr Gorbachov has to face. 'we have so many diamonds, so much gold, oil for a thousand years, a continent of trees, a world of soil.' Scarcity, mother of invention in the West, is there understood as a mere distributive problem, a bungle which obliges the people of the richest nation on earth to queue before empty shops.

The late Nikita Khrushchev was vexed and puzzled by the Swedes' obsession with Wallenberg's fate. 'We have hundreds of millions of people,' he might have said. 'Take your pick, but why this one?' Perhaps because Wallenberg was, after all, a little like Count Károlyi, a lonely and just man who waded by himself against history's tide of blood until it swept him away.

[*1987*

Dream of Escape

Not long ago – last autumn, in fact – a small, uncanny thing happened to me in Prague. I was in a museum of ancient musical instruments, housed in a baroque palace down by the river, and paused to lean on the window-sill and stare out of the window.

It was a brilliant, blue afternoon. The trees outside were losing their leaves, which fell as I watched and formed a glittering, golden scatter on the cobbled square below.

Something came into my mind, a story I had been told of the terrible days in the autumn of 1938 when Britain and France – through the Munich Agreement – betrayed Czechoslovakia to Hitler. Thousands of Czech veterans who had fought in

France during the First World War had gone to the French embassy and had flung down their medals until the stones of the square outside were covered with gleaming silver and gold. It must have looked just like this, I thought. And, later that day, I discovered that it was the very same square.

In those weeks, almost 50 years ago, there began the tearing apart of Europe's living body. The Yalta Conference completed it, cauterising the wounds with pious words. The last, finishing slashes of connecting nerves and sinews were done when Communism took power in Prague in 1948, and when the Berlin Wall appeared in 1961.

The fashion remains to blame Western cowardice and cynicism for the division of Europe. This is blind. The future outlines of Europe's partition were decided in June 1941, when Nazi Germany attacked the Soviet Union and brought about the conjunction which statesmen had managed to avoid for over a century: the flooding of Russian power into the European heartlands. We live in the Europe which Hitler created.

But wounds can heal and lesions may at least skin over again. The partition of Europe is no longer absolute, and in many places there is a tentative rejoining: a physical one of travel and trade, a mental one of nations either side of the line reviving a sense of common culture. In this atmosphere, people have begun to write and speak again about 'Central Europe.'

Richard Bassett has just published a 'Guide to Central Europe' (Viking), a clever, useful, comic invitation to treat as a single region the lands from Lower Austria to Transylvania, from north Bohemia through Hungary and Slovenia to Trieste and its 'Austrian Riviera.' This takes in two Warsaw Pact states, one NATO member, one capitalist neutral and a non-aligned socialist republic. But Bassett writes of 'a unique culture,' a shared mental background which is still flourishing.

If Bassett's 'Central Europe' is really the southern part of the old Habsburg Empire, others draw the term more widely. The German writer Karl Schlögel writes of 'roughly the geographical area between Germany and Russia, between the Baltic and the Adriatic' – which takes in Poland and perhaps the Ukraine and the Baltic states as well. Tim Garton Ash, in a long and imaginative piece in the *New York Review of Books* last year, dissects the way that opposition writers in Czechoslovakia,

Poland and Hungary use the term and suggests, disarmingly, that while they all live in 'Eastern Europe' – the predicament of the Soviet empire – they would all wish to live in a 'Central Europe', a place of free, truthful societies outside all imperial systems.

Eastern Europe is what exists, according to Garton Ash, while Central Europe remains only an idea. But it is a powerful idea, just because it is generated by the reality of Eastern Europe and finds its values in all that Eastern Europe is not. It is a political and moral programme as much as a place: 'its territory is the space between the State and the individual, between the power and the powerless.'

This approach has the advantage of not presenting Central Europe as something past which could be revived. That is good because revival is impossible. The supranational Habsburg Empire is fit only for nostalgia, as long as its stupid, oppressive aspects are ignored. The Jews, whose sceptical, liberal, rationalist genius was the real catalyst of a common culture in those lands between Germany and Russia, can never be brought back.

Professor Seton-Watson wrote recently of the paradox that 'it is among the weakest nations of Europe . . . that the strongest European consciousness exists.' And yet two wars which wrecked the continent began in those 'lands in-between.' The conflicts which principally caused the outbreak of 1914 resulted, as Professor Seton-Watson puts it, from 'the penetration of economic forces and social ideas from the West into societies unprepared for them.' Garton Ash remarks that although this intellectual generation stakes out Central Europe as a zone for tolerance and humanism, its fathers made it the breeding-ground for the most fanatical and ruthless ideologies.

And yet Central Europe is more than just a dream Canaan for opposition intellectuals in the smaller nations of the Warsaw Pact. Others are sharply interested. And among those others are many Germans.

They, after all, invented the term *Mitteleuropa*. And it began as an imperial term. Squeezed between Russia to the east and the great colonial powers of France and Britain to the west, Germany was to establish a 'third bloc', a Central Europe including the Balkans dominated by German military and industrial power. For some Germans, like the great Friedrich

Naumann writing during the First World War, it was to be a fatherly, paternal dominion over lesser races. In Hitler's demonic version, it was a Great-German empire founded on genocide and slavery.

To leave modern Germany out of talk about Central Europe is a dangerous mistake. The new West German generation is not interested in domination. But it has adopted the idea that the strip of Europe between Baltic and Adriatic is a place where German policies can be made with more sovereign freedom than within the constraints of the Western Alliance and the Common Market. As the writer François Bondy puts it, 'when Central Europe is discussed in West Germany, a certain separation from the West is usually meant . . .'

The vision here is of a great band of neutral or semi-neutral states in the middle of Europe, without foreign armies of occupation and their nuclear weapons. Britain and France would cease to count much. They might well stay tied to the United States, but Germany – reunited or a federation of two states – would find its destiny in a new *Mitteleuropa* balanced between the West and a pacified Soviet Union that had withdrawn behind its own frontiers.

We may already be in the very first stages of this process. If so, it will end with a Central Europe rather unlike the vision of Czechs like Vaclav Havel or Hungarians like György Konrad, for it will be a region completely overshadowed by the wealth, industrial energy and sheer numbers of the Germans.

It is, of course, a far better thing to be swamped by Quelle mail-order catalogues, German porno movies and BMW salesmen than by censorship, Trabant cars, which fall to bits even if you live long enough to afford them, and the secret police. But it will be swamping, all the same. Beyond the Elbe, the idea of Central Europe is about decency, truth, sceptical lucidity. I hope those values survive when, and if, the idea becomes reality.   [*1987*

Bad Dreams

How do we see 'The Threat' – the possibility of attack by the other side on the Cold War? Last weekend, I was in Budapest at a conference organised by the Alerdinck Foundation to discuss 'mutual perceptions of threat.' A powerful Soviet delegation attended. When asked to muse on The Threat, Mr Vladimir Lomeiko, now an 'ambassador at large,' told a story.

A woman in New York has a dream. She is walking home at night (do New Yorkers still do that?) when she hears heavy footsteps close behind her. She walks faster, then runs. The footsteps come pounding after her, until she reaches her flat, slams and locks the door and falls on her bed in breathless relief. And then she hears the footsteps advancing through the hall and entering the bedroom. 'What do you want of me?' she screams. A voice replies: 'What do you want of *me*? After all, this is *your* dream!'

I liked that story. The night before, I had been reading an article entitled 'The Soviet Rubber Fleet Sails the Pacific,' from the bulletin of a New York organisation called the Centre for War, Peace and the News Media. The centre specialises in reviewing and mordantly criticising the performance of those who write or broadcast about military matters.

The article, by Betsy D. Treitler, examined what the *Washington Times* called 'the extraordinary growth of the Soviet Navy in the Pacific.' That is an understatement. The *New York Times* gave data revealing the mightiest Stakhanovite feat of instant shipbuilding in history. On 10 August 1986, the paper referred to 410 ships and submarines, but a week later it had grown to 530, and by September 'across the Western Pacific, the Russians have amassed 830 ships.' The *Washington Times* spoke that summer of 840 vessels.

But then, all unreported, there arose a sea-serpent or typhoon which smote that fleet and devoured it. In November 1986 *Time* magazine wrote of a mere 166 warships. In March this year the *New York Times* managed to raise part of the fleet from the ocean-floor, referring to the 500 warships of the Soviet Pacific Navy. Where all this news of the expansive-contractile fleet came from, Ms Treitler was unable to say, for no sources were quoted. But 'Soviet Military Power,' published by the Pentagon, wrote in its 1986 edition that the Soviet Union had only 175 'principal combatants' and submarines in the Pacific theatre.

Our conference in Budapest was not about the Pacific, but about the military confrontation in Europe. At the centre of argument was the security of Western Europe, in the case that intermediate and short-range nuclear weapons were removed from the Continent and the forces facing one another were conventional. Given the superiority of the Warsaw Pact in conventional armaments, would the threat increase?

All agree that the Warsaw Pact has more men and tanks than NATO. But how many more? Back in London, I took out the Fleet Street newspaper cuttings on the subject. They made a curious read.

In June 1986, *The Times* reported that NATO had 5 million men and the Warsaw Pact 6.4 million. Two days later, the *Daily Telegraph* wrote of 2.29 million NATO soldiers and 2.8 million Warsaw Pact soldiers. In March this year, the *Independent* gave figures of respectively 5 million and 6.2 million. As for tanks, the *Independent* gave the figures as 20,300 in the West and about 46,000 in the East. On the same day, however, the *Daily Telegraph* stated that NATO had 9,000 tanks and the Pact 22,000, although almost a month later it gave the figures as 20,314 and 46,610.

In all that, too, there are elements of Lomeiko's dream. A horrible hairy bear, constantly changing size but always irresistible, is tramping into the bedroom of *Daily Telegraph* readers. In numbers of men, tanks and tactical aircraft, the Warsaw Pact is stronger. But it seemed to me, listening to the debate in Budapest, that this was not a very threatening superiority, all the same. We are living in a military period rather like that of 1914–18, when defensive conventional weaponry has the edge over attacking equipment, and unlike that of 1940 when the opposite was true. NATO is obviously in no condition to attack the Warsaw Pact, but the Pact's superiority in tanks, for example, is nothing like enough to assure victory.

The Eastern side at Budapest would not define a threat to itself, beyond the proposition that any arms race could end in accidental catastrophe. But for the Westerners, there seemed to be three varieties of menace. The first, to me almost negligible, was the risk of direct attack. The second was the use of military force against a single nation by its own allies, which we have seen in Hungary in 1956, and in Czechoslovakia in 1968. The third was that, in a Europe stripped of nuclear weapons, the Soviet Union would be able to dominate the West by political leverage deriving from its own military strength – 'nuclear blackmail,' or just 'tank blackmail'.

Some of those fears are legitimate. But they didn't quite explain the startling contradiction between the hopefulness of public events and the wariness at that Alerdinck meeting.

Outside, the great Rubicon of a treaty reducing nuclear weapons is slowly being crossed, leading probably to further reductions in strategic and chemical weapons. Two Warsaw Pact states, Hungary and Poland, are opening socialist economies to market forces and offering more democracy in political life at the same time. In the Soviet Union, Mikhail Gorbachov is attempting the biggest transformation of his land since 1917. And yet the Western guests in Budapest could not, with odd exceptions, find words of optimism.

I remembered the utterly different climate of such East-West meetings 10 or 15 years ago, when we would talk merrily of the coming dissolution of the military pacts and of how Western trade and money would help to bring about pluralism in Eastern Europe. Why this change now, which puzzled the Eastern side?

We live in the aftermath of Afghanistan and of Jaruzelski's coup, in the reigns of Reagan and Thatcher. During that 'little Cold War' which began in 1979, after the détente years, a grimly mistrustful climate was fostered in the West. To disperse it again, when East-West relations have so suddenly turned back to negotiation and movement, will take time.

That new awareness of threat has its sense as well as its rubber-fleet nonsense. Women dream of being followed because women are followed – and raped, and murdered. Visitors from Moscow ask rhetorically what more they can possibly do to convince the West of their good intentions. But there is an answer to that.

During the conference, I went to a small meeting to commemorate what began in Budapest just 31 years ago that day. The lights were cut off, and candles were lit among Hungarian flags with a hole cut out of their centre. Men now old talked to the young of what was hoped and done in 1956. One said: 'It was love – joy without guilt, for the first time.'

So far, we do not know what *glasnost* and *perestroika* in the Soviet Union will mean for Eastern Europe. So far this movement has begun to transform the USSR itself and East-West relations, but not yet East-East relations. One waits to see if these changes will lead to a liberating and peaceful revolution in the relationship of Soviet power to Hungary, Czechoslovakia, Poland and the others.

If that were to change, the West too would begin to escape its nightmares. And all things would become possible.   [*1987*

V

CONSOLATIONS
AND
DISCONTENTS

Picts

Three years ago, at the time of the Falklands war, there was a television chat show which featured Mr Enoch Powell and Mr Roy Hattersley. I have forgotten everything about it except for two sentences.

Mr Powell was chuntering on about the imperial mission. Mr Hattersley, growing impatient, interrupted: 'Oh, come on, Enoch, we aren't living in the nineteenth century!' Mr Powell turned slowly towards him and said, with frightful emphasis: 'But we *are* living in the nineteenth century!'

His words came back to me the other day in an improbable place. Readers in the south of England may have missed the 1,300th anniversary of the battle of Nechtansmere, when King Brudei of the Picts overwhelmed the Anglian host led by Ecgfrith of Northumbria. But the Society of Antiquaries of Scotland did not miss that day. We assembled at Dunnichen, near Forfar, to inspect the battlefield and witness the unveiling of a monument. We had brought sandwiches, and some of us wore green wellies and tweed fore-and-aft hats. The minister of Dunnichen church was there, and the Provost of Forfar with his chain, and the pipe band of the local British Legion, and several dozen inhabitants with expectant looks on their faces.

It soon became clear that another element was also present. From the back of a van, leaflets and stickers were being distributed. The speakers proclaimed a Pictish free state. The leaflets announced that 'Dunnichen Day' was a new holiday. 'Up to now it has been celebrated almost privately by dedicated Pictophiles and folk who happen to be sitting near them. . . . The Pictish Cultural Society ask you to be courteous to the folk living in the neighbourhood and give them no cause for complaint.'

The Pictish Cultural Society! Here was the nineteenth

century indeed, for nothing was more characteristic of that century in Europe than the revival of buried nations and the emergence of new ones. That was the time when cultural societies dug up and redecorated the identity of the Czechs and the Irish, the Flemings and the Germans and the Italians, the Serbs and the Scots, the Croats and the Welsh. Here at Dunnichen was a latecomer to that great movement. It turned out that several hundred people had attended Pictish ceilidhs and discos over the past few evenings.

The Pictish revival can be safely wished good luck. Its brand of nationalism is hardly aggressive: 'The New Picts should be an example of gentle nobility,' says a leaflet. And luck is what it needs, for the Picts are the lost tribe of the British Isles. They inhabited the whole of what is now Scotland 2,000 years ago, but vanished almost without trace in the ninth century after their conquest by Scottish invaders from the west.

One version speaks of genocidal slaughter. More probably, Pictish culture – already weakened by Viking raids – was dissolved by the Scots who imposed their own Gaelic language and the religious forms of their Columban Church.

All that remains of the Picts that can be identified is their mysterious sculpture in stone, decorated with symbols that still defy the historian, with Celtic interlacing and sometimes with the figures of men and creatures. The Romans, who fought them, said that the Picts either painted or tattooed themselves. A Norwegian chronicle, written not long after the battle of Nechtansmere, says: 'They little exceed pigmies in stature: they did marvels in the morning and in the evening in building walled towns, but at midday they entirely lost all their strength and lurked through fear in little underground houses.'

What I like about Pictish studies is that they have made so little headway. Here is a large, artistically gifted nation that was famous in Europe for 800 years, and yet we know less about it than eighteenth-century cockneys knew about Central Africa. The historian Isobel Henderson confesses that 'the Pictish personality is utterly lost to us.' In spite of the mass of classical and Dark Age references, archaeologists have failed to identify a single settlement or fort as beyond question Pictish.

No complete sentence in the Pictish language has survived. They left a number of inscriptions, elegantly described as 'perfectly legible yet ... utterly unintelligible.' One of them reads as follows: ETTOCUHETTS AHEHHTTANN HCCVVEVU NEHHTONS. The last word may be the name of King Nechtan, who gave his name to the battlefield. The other words suggest that there is some mistake here, surely, and make archaeologists cry.

So relating to the Picts is going to be hard. On the battlefield, the minister of Dunnichen did his best. He called solemnly for forgiveness and reconciliation, for respect to the memory of the dead and their widows and orphans, citing the ceremonies for the fortieth anniversary of victory in the last world war. I thought he was wrong about the moral débâcle which was the VE Day commemoration, and probably wrong about the Picts as well. Their Christianity, when they acquired it, did not put much emphasis on the bits about brotherly love.

A few miles away from Dunnichen stand the Pictish sculptured stones of Aberlemno. One of them bears what seems to be a scene from the battle of Nechtansmere, in which a bird can be seen devouring the face of an Anglian prince in a helmet. The carving has been shown to illustrate a text from Revelations: 'And I saw an angel standing in the sun, and he cried with a loud voice, saying to all the fowls that fly in the midst of Heaven: Come and gather yourself unto the supper of the great God, that ye may eat the flesh of kings and the flesh of captains.' Gentle nobility?

I am always fascinated when people talk about 'the forging of a nation.' Most nations are forgeries, perpetrated in the last century or so. Some nationalism relied on literal forgery: the epics of Ossian in Scotland, the phoney 'Libuse' manuscripts supposed to date from the Czech past, the ancient Welsh literature which was actually written by Iolo Morganwg in the King Lud pub at the bottom of Fleet Street. 'Great Britain' itself is an arrant forgery, invented by John Dee to flatter Queen Elizabeth with the notion that the Welsh Tudors were heirs to the pre-Saxon empire of King Arthur.

But millions of Saxons, and a fair number of Scots and Welsh, now happily consider themselves British. Fakes last longer than antiques, and are more versatile. If a Pictish delegate ever rises to address the United Nations, it won't be because he has proved himself to be the successor of King Brudei.

And the historic Picts, I suspect, will soon become more visible. No nation vanishes as completely as that; we are staring at their relics without recognising them. Ruins, tombs, jewellery, now attributed to others, will turn out to be theirs. The glorious Lindisfarne Gospels, it's being whispered, may not be Northumbrian at all, but the masterpiece of an unknown monastery in Pictland. And the people of Forfar district, today a stronghold of the Scottish National Party, are in reality the descendants of the Vacomagi, one of the great tribes of the Pictish federation.

Meanwhile, anyone interested in nationalism, still the most powerful source of political magic on earth, will watch this small test case of the Pictish renaissance. And those who feel they belong can apply to the Pictish High Commission, at 53 St Leonard's Street, Edinburgh. Tel. 031 667 4222, open Mondays to Saturdays.   [*1985*

Brothers

I was in Italy when the English crowd brought about the death of 31 Italians at a football game in Brussels. In the cities, there were attacks on British cars; they wrote on walls: 'Inglesi, Assassini, Bastardi!' But in the village where I was, although everyone had watched the horror on television, they tried to be consoling. 'There are mad people who want war in every nation.'

The villagers were trying to find something universal in what, we now recognise, has become a British speciality of savagery. Edward Vulliamy, describing the Brussels scene in the *New Statesman*, threw out such generous 'rotten apple' excuses. He wrote that the Italians 'did not understand that the red and yellow crowds to their left harboured a lunatic code of self-esteem; that it was a matter for their drunken, bloodthirsty and racist English 'honour' that the terraces be cleared of "spiks" . . .'

He saw there the blatant influence of the Falklands War; English fans now attack any Latin foreigner as an 'Argie.' But Vulliamy added: 'It is hypocritical to belabour them for besmirching British values when in so many other areas of national life violence is made heroic, narrow chauvinism is appealed to.'

As I brooded on this, two propositions came to my mind. The first: football, especially in this country, remains over-whelmingly a working-class game. The second: for over a century, it has been an article of faith on the Left that inter-nationalism is the special destiny of the working class.

Was the massacre in the Heysel Stadium a sign – one among many – that the whole theory of 'socialist internationalism' is a fraud? Is it true that, instead, the workers have turned out to be the class in which old-fashioned chauvinism is most deeply rooted?

It isn't that bad. If the sense of common humanity across state frontiers had perished, the human race would now be dead as well. But 'internationalism' as an *idea* has been almost suffocated by those who have wrapped it up in political dogma, who have debased it into an illusion.

The Marxist phrase 'proletarian internationalism' was once a useful piece of theory. But today, after 60 years of misuse by Lenin and Stalin, all it means for their heirs is the alacrity with which a Communist Party obeys the Moscow line.

This emerges from a fascinating, painful post-mortem which the British Communists held recently on their own behaviour in 1939. When the war began, they declared that it was a 'war on two fronts,' against Fascism abroad and the Tory Govern-ment at home. But Stalin and the Comintern, loyal to the new Nazi-Soviet Pact, swiftly stamped on the British comrades. A month later, the British Party performed a U-turn: the war between Britain and Hitler was now merely a clash between 'two imperialisms,' and all good progressives should demand an immediate peace.

Eagerly supporting the new line, the fellow-traveller D. N. Pritt dashed into print. 'Is it not clear,' he asked, 'that Hitler and the ruling class of Germany would be unable to persuade their workers to carry on the war against a British Government which ... was offering an immediate and just peace?' If a peace-loving People's Government were formed in Britain, he predicted, the workers of Germany would rise and throw off their oppressors.

Blindness on that scale about Nazi Germany and its grip on the German people was not uncommon on the Left. Many remembered how, a few years before, workers from all over the world had gone to join the International Brigades in Spain – German exiles among them.

That was no illusion. But neither was the fact that when revolutionary Russia invaded Poland in 1920, the Polish workers marched in their hundreds of thousands to throw the Russians out again. In our own time, there was no illusion about Mr Arthur Scargill's scathing contempt for the workers' movement called Solidarity. And no illusion about the reluctance of Polish coal miners to do anything for Mr Scargill's men four years later, when his own strike was being weakened by coal imports from Poland.

Nobody is saying that modern workers have lost the sense of international brotherhood entirely. Workers at the Ford plants in Europe, to take one example, often refuse to take work from a striking Ford factory in another country. But the dogma that 'class-conscious proletarians' will always put class solidarity above nation contains a massive fallacy.

At its crudest, this dogma says that internationalism is the normal, healthy condition of working people, while nationalism is an aberration. To be equally crude, this is history inside out. Nationality is the force which dominates our world. Internationalism is still the noble exception.

Tom Nairn, that shrewd political judge, put it like this: 'The overwhelmingly dominant political by-product of modern internationality is nationalism. Not the logically prescribed commonsense of internationalism, but the non-logical, untidy, refractory, disintegrative, particularistic truth of nation-states. Not swelling "higher unity" but "Balkanisation," a world of spiky exceptions to what should have been the rule.'

Where did the muddle begin? Partly in confusion over what Marx meant when he wrote that 'the working men have no country,' and that the industrial proletariat was a 'universal class.' Partly in the frightful trauma of 1914, when almost all the 'internationalist' socialist parties of Europe voted for war.

After that, 'internationalism' was twisted into grotesque shapes. Worst of all, it came to be used as a mask to make greedy nationalism look 'progressive.' The Nazis claimed that they were transcending petty national divisions by creating a 'New European Order.' For Communists, internationalism became a disguise for the defence of the Soviet Union's national interests. 'Nationalism equals Fascism' was the instinct of many English members of the Labour Left – who could never imagine themselves as English nationalists – when faced with the question of Welsh and Scottish devolution.

And yet, if internationalism based on class is in a bad way, the idea of social and political justice '*sans frontières*' is stronger than it has ever been. The world is smaller; its survival is threatened by nuclear weapons and effluent.

The millions who fork out for famines, earthquakes and cyclones now do so out of solidarity as much as charity. In Europe, dissidents of East and West try to agree on an 'anti-politics' through which nations can evade and resist the grip of their own governments. The 'higher unity' of multinational corporations and military power blocs strikes people increasingly as false fraternity, and encourages them to look for a brother-and-sisterhood of the human race which is based on human beings rather than on contracts and treaties.

But the first condition for this journey towards fraternity is that we stop trying to argue the nation away before its time. Internationalism means helping other societies to survive physically, but also to develop in their own way and defend their diversity – which implies their freedom. Somewhere in the future, the nation-state will perish. But to assume that it has already perished can lead only to delusion, then to impotence, then to disaster.

'There are mad people who want war in every nation.' But especially in nations which remember war as victories rather than miseries, which fancy they are still islands. An Italian villager can imagine another nation as a liberator. An English football crowd, it seems, sees nations as game-cocks – bred only to fight. [*1985*

Nations on Parade

Perhaps the French know something we do not. Last week's Fourteenth of July parade was the biggest rumble-past of military hardware seen in Paris since the war.

'Stone, bronze, stone, steel, stone, oak-leaves, horses' heels Over the paving.' I think of *Le Monde* as a loosely leftish paper, forgetting – as the British usually do – that no contradiction between socialism and militarism is seen in France. But its report of the parade reminded me of Eliot's lines: 'Apart from the detachments of the higher military academies and the *sapeur-pompiers* of Paris, of the Foreign Legion and state security and the national gendarmerie, the march included 636 vehicles of which 382 were armour of every model from the 3rd Army Corps at Lille . . .'

And so on, with the crew of a French nuclear submarine, and the fly-past of '64 aircraft including Mirage IV nuclear bombers and Mirage 2000 attack planes, and 20 helicopters.' Insatiable for more tramping and clanking, President Mitterrand then flew to Verdun and reviewed the march-past of the 4th Aeromobile Division complete with its anti-tank helicopters.

Why does the Fifth Republic find it still necessary to celebrate the identity of France by a display of force? I have no doubt that if Dominique Prieur and Alain Mafart had not been serving their last days in a New Zealand jail before transfer to a desert island, they too would have strutted past the stand, probably towing a replica of the Rainbow Warrior.

The nasty answer is to recall that the Fifth Republic itself was born by the forceps of military violence: in the terrifying army mutiny of May 1958 when the forces in Algeria rebelled, seized Corsica and were preparing to install a semi-Fascist régime in Paris when de Gaulle stepped in. Though true, this is unfair. It is modern France itself, through the Great Revolution, that was born through war, and the Jacobin tradition which associated the Republic, 'united and indivisible,' with the 'nation in arms.'

The victory parade, as old as Rome, is understandable. I would like to have seen General Maczek march his Poles through liberated Breda, or the British going through the streets of Brussels in tanks smothered with flowers and girls ('Your old woman would give you Vive la Belgique if she could see you,' says one Tommy in the Giles cartoon to another). The point of Mrs Thatcher's victory parade after the Falklands War – the bombers passing the windows of this office in one dark thunderclap after another – was undeniable, even if one felt like denying it. But what about countries which hold victory parades every single year, in peacetime?

The Soviet Union famously does it every November, with military attachés peering under their fur hats at the huge sausages of the missiles on their trailer. The East Germans love to do it, goose-stepping along in their jackboots with an unselfconscious zeal that brings a tic of irony even to the faces of Warsaw Pact diplomats. France apart, the West Europeans are sparing with this sort of show.

Most British public parades have the aspect of a pageant, like Trooping the Colour. They suggests a toy-soldiers' view of soldiering, and in that are related to the growing passion of otherwise sane human beings for getting into chainmail, topboots or Peninsular War shakos to re-enact battles of the past.

All that is pretty harmless. Afterwards, gasping and purple-faced men get their helmets off and reach for the beer, and have at least a dim idea of the hellish exhaustion of a real battle. The march-pasts of professional soldiers with modern weapons, in contrast, usually happen in the privacy of barracks or sandy training-grounds closed to outsiders. I can testify to the hellish exhaustion of those occasions, for which I once bought from a comrade a pair of boots burnished like obsidian but three sizes too small.

I wonder, though, whether even the long-suffering British officer caste sometimes looks across the Channel in envy. As Alfred de Vigny reflected, the peacetime officer must be a stoic indeed to bear the public's lack of interest in, even mild disdain for its defenders when they are not defending. The Royal

Tournament is hardly enough, and anyway the show is always stolen by the glamour boys of the SAS or the paras. Why not just one day in the year when the tanks roll and the line regiments tramp down Whitehall in the full view of the nation?

Many civilians would prefer something more educational. A parade in which every marcher would represent a hundred of the dead in the two world wars, for example. Better still, a huge annual armoured drive-past, but one which would display all the weaponry taken out of service that year under international disarmament agreements, and tow it proudly past the reviewing dais on its way to the scrap-heap. Mrs Thatcher could take the salute, and even shout 'Rejoice!' at intervals into the loudspeakers.

These are nice but sentimental ideas. National parades are about much more than war. They are about power *within* a society, and can be divided into two types.

There are parades when They show themselves to Us. On the Fourteenth of July, the full coercive might of the State, political and military, shows itself to the French people and says: Applaud us! – which they invariably do. So it is in Moscow each November. But there is another sort of parade in which We show ourselves to Them.

Those We-to-Them parades are, I admit, pretty rare. Protest demonstrations don't count, as They are more likely to be tucked up behind lines of police than on the stand. In fact, I can only think of one or two. There were some occasions like that in Allende's Chile. And, best of all, there was the First of May in Prague in 1968, when the people went out in the street with their families and posters they had made themselves because they wanted to say to Alexander Dubček: 'We are with you – Be with us!'

That was a good day. The Czech We inspected a rather bashful Them, still incredulous at finding themselves genuinely popular, and gave approval. That day outshines all the other May Day parades I have seen, in which the thousands marshalled by the Party from factories and offices, with banners about Peace thrust into their hands and balloons tethered to indifferent fingers, shuffle past their rulers and greet them with a fishy stare.

I wouldn't say that those occasions are utterly joyless. They celebrate Labour by giving people a chance to stop work, breathe some fresh air, and unload a great deal of gossip and chatter until they are shushed as they approach the podium where the Vanguard of the Proletariat stands with tight grins. There are even unplanned moments, as when Lech Wałęsa slipped into one May Day parade and gave the astonished General Jaruzelski a two-finger salute – the Solidarity greeting, that is.

With rare exceptions, though, the parade is a one-way transmission, a form of party political broadcast. The Rhineland carnivals, with their cartoonish floats of politicians, try to reverse the flow. But in Britain all official pageantry is about rulers displaying power and plumage to the ruled. Whit Walks and Miners' Galas, two exceptions, take place at a long, safe distance from Westminster. A cat can look at a king, but kings still feel degraded by an invitation to look at cats.   [*1986*

F3080

The first time I visited Auschwitz, they said: 'Go for a little walk. Pull up the turf, and see what you find.' I found a whiteish soil, white with the ash of calcined human bone. The poplars planted at SS orders to mask the gas chambers were small and scrawny.

The last time I went there, the earth had become brown again, like the soil of any field. And the poplars – tyrants love poplars, which offer rapid, orderly, spectacular results – had become huge, graceful trees, waving their tips innocently in the morning breeze.

Time has begun to purify even the worst place in the world. I thought of those trees and that earth – images of how our view of history changes insensibly but, in the end, almost out of recognition – when I watched a preview of a film to be shown on Granada television late tonight.

'A Painful Reminder' – strangely innocuous title – is about what the Allies found when they liberated the concentration camps. It contains the most sustained and terrible images of death and degradation ever shown on a screen. But, more importantly, it is about the first efforts by normal people to cope morally with suffering and brutality on a scale entirely outside their assumptions about the nature of 'civilised' human beings.

It is a film within a film. The core of it is a 50-minute documentary, made in 1945 on official initiative. It was directed by Sidney Bernstein, and Alfred Hitchcock was brought over from Hollywood to assist him. Richard Crossman and Colin Wills, of the *News Chronicle*, wrote the script. It was to be shown to the German population with the object, as defined by Bernstein, of proving beyond any possible challenge that these crimes did take place and that the German people, not only the Nazi Party or the SS, bore the responsibility for them. Around the original film (the last reel has been lost but reconstituted), the producer Steve Morrison has assembled interviews with camp survivors and with the men who entered Belsen and shot the documentary.

But the film was never shown. As soon as the Allied forces began to occupy Germany, conflict began between the political aims of the occupation – the purging and re-education of German society, and the punishment of Nazi criminals – and the military authorities. All order had collapsed: the economy and currency had died, and the population, exhausted and in many places starving, was being swelled by million after million of desperate refugees from the East.

For local military governors, often relying on ex-Nazis to reconstruct a semblance of administration, the priority was to rally Germans out of their apathy to save themselves. Purges, punishments and efforts to instil the notion of collective guilt into the population seemed, to the soldier's mind, designed only to increase the chaos and demoralisation.

Bernstein got a first whiff of changing attitudes as early as August 1945. An official in the Political Intelligence Department of the Foreign Office warned him that 'there are people around the C-in-C who will say "No atrocity film." I would say that the atrocity film, if really good and well documented, would be shown willingly and successfully in nine months' time when the difficulties of the winter have been tackled.'

There was no ban. But time passed, and the right moment for the film never seemed to have arrived. It was shelved, and in time passed to the Imperial War Museum where, under the cryptic title 'F3080,' it has reposed ever since.

It was a victim of the great change in Anglo-American policy towards Germany. The motive for not alienating the population gradually changed from the need to mobilise society against starvation to the need to establish a new West German State as part of an anti-Communist alliance. Wartime declarations that Germany would be 'de-nazified' and all Nazi criminals punished were left only half-fulfilled.

Should the film have been shown? In 1945, the Germans were so blinded by disaster that the film's accusations might well have rolled off them. The novelist Günter Grass, as a young prisoner, was marched by the Americans to see Dachau, but still did not believe what he was told until he heard it from German radio journalists reporting the Nuremberg trial a year later.

But in the years of recovery, when Germans could reflect again, the Allies preferred to leave it to the Germans to settle their own accounts. It was over 30 years before a syrupy American soap-opera called 'Holocaust' brought home a version of the truth to millions of German viewers.

The word 'Holocaust' raises an even more startling point about the Bernstein-Hitchcock film. This was a documentary about mass murder in the concentration camps. Yet the original script uses the word 'Jew' only three times – and then quite tangentially to the main theme.

A passage about Buchenwald lists no fewer than 31 categories of dead, starting with 'African negroes.' The Jews are not mentioned. On Auschwitz, the script states that 'transports of prisoners from all over Europe were sent for extermination.' There is no hint that the main purpose of the gas chambers was to murder the Jewish population of Europe.

Today, this omission seems utterly incredible. A pendulum has swung, and the planned murder of six million Jews towers so high over our notion of history that the five million non-

Jewish victims of the camps (eight, if the Soviet prisoners systematically starved to death are included) are often overlooked. But there it is: this film, made by passionate anti-Fascists, does not mention the Holocaust.

Why not? Bernstein was Jewish; Crossman an expert on Germany who had worked in psychological warfare and later became an ardent supporter of Zionism. The explanation seems to lie partly in propaganda tactics, partly in the very idealism of the group which made the film.

A key principle of war propaganda was to make its targets identify with Hitler's victims. A dreadfully revealing Ministry of Information guideline, sent out in 1941, warned propagandists that to make the Nazi evil credible, they must always deal with 'the treatment of indisputably innocent people, not with violent political opponents and not with Jews.' This was for the British public. Crossman, trained on such principles, must have feared that they were infinitely truer for the Germans. If the film presented victims as Jews rather than 'innocent people' it might not pierce the indifference built up by 12 years of official racialism.

So the film spoke only of men, women and children 'from every European nationality', defined the victims by their humanity and innocence, not by their faith or race. The film-makers had not, in fact, had time to grasp the horror within the horror. The scale of the 'Final Solution of the Jewish Problem' had scarcely dawned on them, and it was to be many years before the word 'Auschwitz' (implying the gassing of millions), replaced 'Belsen' in Britain as the ultimate metaphor of evil.

But they also felt that to single out 'the Jews,' even as victims, was somehow to play the Nazis' game. This had been a war for humanity, for the 'common people' of the world, a liberation from the iron compartments imposed by Fascism. In the long years while 'F3080' lay forgotten on its shelf, that big-hearted vision of human unity gathered dust too, until today few can remember what it was like. And that is our loss.   [1985

Exiles

I had never seen a president of a republic inaugurated. So the other day I put on a respectful tie and went along to Eaton Square in London. Here, in the presence of several hundred witnesses, Count Edward Raczynski laid down the office of President of the Polish Republic in Exile and Mr Kazimierz Sabbat took the oath as his successor.

It was a ghostly, fantastic moment. Skeletons emerged from cupboards and put the *Sunday Express* into a nervous fury: 'Pathetic, isn't it, that more than 40 years after the end of the war there should still be the meaningless façade of a Polish Government-in-exile?'

But it is that beefy, numbskull comment which is pathetic. Meaningless? The ceremony at Eaton Square, like the exile government itself, does not have a literal meaning, but there are other kinds of meaning. When Mr Sabbat, promoted from the office of Prime Minister of his small Cabinet, took the presidential oath by 'Almighty God and the Holy Trinity' to 'apply the law of the Constitution [of 1935]' and to 'defend the state against evil and danger,' none of his hearers and not even – I think – he himself supposed that he would ever sign decrees in Warsaw.

And few men are less 'pathetic' than Count Raczynski, now in his nineties. His dignity and irony are inviolable. He was ambassador to the Court of St James in 1939, when Britain offered him its sword to defend Poland. He was ambassador in 1945, when Britain informed him that she was withdrawing recognition from his Government and leaving Poland in the lurch. He received the slap, as he had received the sword, with the bow of a grand diplomat.

Governments in exile are a way of saying No. They do not deny unwelcome reality. They consciously defy it, which is different. Absurdity is their business, for they are saying that the world as it exists is absurd. They are aware, as the Spanish Republic in exile was aware, that it will probably be unknown people far off in Warsaw or Madrid who will eventually regain freedom, and that those unknown people will not invite them to resume authority.

Gradually losing touch with the homeland is an inevitable process. The Russian writer Alexander Herzen, looking at the political exiles of nineteenth-century London, observed: 'They are like the court clock at Versailles, which pointed to one hour, the hour at which the king died . . . meeting the same men, the same groups; in five or six months, in two or three years, one becomes frightened: the same arguments are still going on, the same personalities and recriminations: only the furrows drawn by poverty and privation are deeper; jackets and overcoats are shabbier; there are more grey hairs, and they are all older together and bonier and more gloomy. . . .'

Exile as a condition has a whole scale of descending misery. There is the expatriate or emigrant, who lives abroad by choice. There is the *émigré*, whose choice is determined by politics. Then comes the exile who cannot safely return, the refugee who has fled from pursuers, the deportee who has been expelled from his own home, and finally – at the bottom of the heap – the slave labourer driven away to work the mines and factories of a foreign conqueror. At Eaton Square, I saw men and women who have known each of these fates. They looked composed. Perhaps they recall the Polish aphorism: 'I hit bottom – and then I heard someone tapping from underneath.'

All exiles, and especially politically active exiles, know the occupational diseases of the condition. Squabbling and faction-fighting are one. In Chile, up to General Pinochet's coup in 1973, there was a revolutionary Catholic party called Mapu. A Chilean informs me that abroad it split into three, the third fragment comprising those who didn't want a split. He added that two of the fragments were being led by the same man using different names. At home, a politician's insistence upon being in the right is kept under control by events, which are unpredictable. In exile, where there are no events but only highly predictable fellow-exiles, political arrogance and dogmatism can grow as tall as giant groundsel in the Ruwenzori Mountains.

Belligerent cultural assertion is another disease. It afflicts the expatriate, above all, who feels he must justify his choice of life abroad. California is infested with braying Englishmen with yellow moustaches, insistent on telling one the Test score.

But a proper exile – an involuntary one – does not need to prove a loyalty. The Expellee Leagues in West Germany are led by aggressive windbags. But their rank and file at those enormous rallies, wearing the costumes and eating the sausage and potato cakes of a lost '*Heimat*,' are not really aggressive at all. They belong to a very special exile plight: that of people whose homeland has actually ceased to exist, like a sunken Atlantis. Where German Pomerania was, there is a Polish province: their villages have different names. After 40 years, their cities have foreign histories of their own. We will not see a loss so total until survivors gather after a nuclear war.

Political exiles who decide to defy reality, or even those who merely hope to overthrow it, still have to settle somewhere. For some, it is important to raise the standard in a positively sympathetic country, offering political support and perhaps even money or weapons. France before 1848 gave the Polish *émigré* leaders pensions corresponding to their rank and comforted them with liberal rhetoric. The Cuban exiles are assured that the United States will never abandon their cause; the Palestinians find effusive but unreliable welcome in various parts of the Arab world.

Other exiles have learnt that those who defy reality have no true friends. Every 'sympathetic' host will try to use an emigration for its own purposes, dividing it, distorting its aims, in the end betraying it.

Perhaps it is better to live in an indifferent country, which does not pretend to care, to be a free carp in a huge and turbid pond rather than a goldfish exhibited to admiring guests – and cats.

London was and is a pond. The Metropolitan police are more inquisitive than they used to be. The population is not. I remember the German revolutionary Rudi Dutschke living in northern London, his face on the cover of every Continental magazine. His neighbours had no idea who he was, and would not have cared if they had known.

Even today, individuals who will raise or destroy nations are quite certainly serving in kebab shops at night, reading philosophy in launderettes, wheeling corpses around London hospitals. Indifference, to them and to their queer foreign leaflets, is what they prefer.

In the end, exile is about the loss of Eden, or about the waters of Babylon. It is about the refusal to forget or to despair in the face of temptation, usually dressed up as bracing 'realism.' How tiresome of the old people at Eaton Square, who insist on remembering what cannot be restored! But (they might reply) to accept that which is unjust as if the passage of time rendered it just – that would be to replace history itself by a 'meaningless façade.'

[*1986*

Terrorists

In the museum at Naples, there is a statue of two terrorists. Harmodius and Aristogeiton stand naked, brandishing their daggers, their empty eyes bulging and exalted.

They have just killed Hipparchus, brother of the Athenian tyrant Hippias. They think the crowd is about to surge towards them with cheers and flowers. They are wrong, for Harmodius was instantly cut down by the bodyguard while Aristogeiton was arrested and tortured to death. And the tyrant ruled on.

They had meant to kill Hippias too, but failed. They struck for liberty, but also because Hipparchus was the unfaithful lover of Aristogeiton. While Hippias lived, they were called degenerate assassins. When he died, they became 'The Liberators'; statues were made of them, and their relations were granted the right of free meals for ever in the official dining room.

All these events in the sixth century BC have a bearing on modern terrorism. They illustrate its genius for political miscalculation, its tendency to kill the wrong person, its capacity for making bad worse, its steamy mixture of motives, and its gift for making history behave like a whore.

These seem to me points worth following up in the context of the Hezbollah, the Provisionals and all the rest. None of them occurred in the speech on terrorism made, before his operation, by President Reagan, which strikes me as one of the most hypocritical and dangerous bags of wind ever inflated by a modern Western leader.

It is dangerous, not because (I think) it presages violent action but because it nudges already nervous millions towards paranoia. It is hypocritical, because the Reagan list of 'terror states' – Iran, Libya, North Korea, Cuba and Nicaragua – has omitted Syria, always previously high on the American list but now owed something for helping to release the TWA hostages. And because, less surprisingly, neither South Africa nor Israel figure. Neither of those countries use terror against the United States, of course.

President Reagan spoke of a new 'Murder Inc.,' a co-ordinated international conspiracy directed against his country by governments 'united by one simple criminal phenomenon – their fanatical hatred of the United States.'

To hate America may be misguided and deplorable, but until now it has not been a crime. Embarrassed diplomats tell us privately that this was a speech only for domestic consumption . . . probably written by Patrick Buchanan . . . not meant to be taken seriously abroad, and so forth. One gets tired of this sort of explanation. A loud enough bark amounts to a bite, in politics.

To define terrorism is almost as hard as to suppress it. The late Senator 'Scoop' Jackson tried valiantly to dispel the fog of moral relativism when he said; 'the idea that one person's "terrorist" is another's "freedom fighter" cannot be sanctioned. Freedom fighters or revolutionaries don't blow up buses containing non-combatants; terrorist murderers do. . . . Freedom fighters don't assassinate innocent men, women and children; terrorist murderers do. It is a disgrace that democracies would allow the treasured word "freedom" to be associated with acts of terrorists.'

That is a quotation constantly used by Secretary of State George Shultz, who added the other day that 'We know the difference between terrorists and freedom fighters, and as we look around the world, we have no trouble telling one from the other.'

Mr Shultz may have no trouble as he looks around the world because he is not, in fact, using Jackson's definition of terrorism by methods but a much cruder definition by intentions. Those who use guerrilla and urban guerrilla war against the United States and its friends are terrorists. The others – Mr Savimbi's men or the Afghan resistance – are freedom fighters. This is a useless distinction, but Senator Jackson's is not much better.

Put hindsight away for a moment. In 1940, the legal government of France signed a peace with Germany. But a handful of 'irresponsible' people put the lives of Frenchmen and even the survival of the State at risk by conducting a terrorist struggle against the German occupiers and the collaborators of the Vichy government. Many innocent people died. Four years later, the terrorists were marching down the Champs-Elysées as the saviours of the nation. This is the whoreishness of history, manifested also in the freedom struggle of Israel through terrorism to statehood, in the transformation of Kenyatta from the leader of blood-smeared Mau Mau to the father of modern Kenya, in Zimbabwe's way from merciless guerrilla war to independence.

So method is not the measure of the terrorist. Almost all freedom fighters, whether we like their sort of 'freedom' or not, use terror at some time and to some degree. Nicaragua supports guerrilla rebels in Salvador, but the Contras, publicly sponsored by the United States, use terror much more directly. And there is also government terrorism. Noam Chomsky distinguished the 'retail terror' of rebels from what he called 'wholesale terror,' referring to 'the numbers tormented and killed by official violence.'

It is a lot easier to say what we mean by 'terrorist acts.' Here Senator Jackson's examples will stand, and even Mr Shultz's certainties. I have watched blood pouring down the gutter from the skulls of innocent men, and the tatters of what had been a bus queue enlaced in the twigs of a tree. The deliberate murder of uninvolved civilians for the end of intimidation is always abominable and always wrong.

But there are two disagreeable – morally queasy – riders to that. One is that terror sometimes 'works.' I am pretty certain

that if the IRA were able to mount a far more terrible and
sustained bombing campaign on the British mainland, public
opinion would force a British withdrawal from Northern
Ireland. The second rider is that the use of terrorism does not
always or automatically vitiate the cause in which it is used.

President Reagan is deliberately creating confusion between
guerrilla movements which include terrorism in their armoury,
and groups – like the left-wing bands in Western Europe which
he mentions and the right-wing bands which he does not –
committed to terrorism and nothing else. To equate the Red
Army Faction in West Germany with the Salvador guerrillas,
and then to portray the Soviet Union as the controlling spider
at the centre of the web of world terrorism, is not only fatuous
but makes the question of how to respond to events like Shia
air piracy far more difficult.

Retaliation? A hundred years ago, 'punitive expeditions'
burned villages in the bush. Violating another State's sovereignty by air strike or commando raid is much more complicated. To its credit, the United States has always been reluctant
to do this, even to combine a hostage rescue with a satisfying
thunderclap of vengeance like the Israelis at Entebbe or the
French at Kolwezi. President Carter's failed rescue of the Iran
hostages in 1980 allowed for heavy losses among raiders and
hostages, but not for a 'retaliatory' slaughter of Iranians.

But this reluctance may be weakening. With actual terrorists
hard to find, 'terror states' become an inviting target. Libya
exported some 25 acts of terror last year; Iran about 60. And
a first step to retaliation is to bring the target into sharp focus,
to remove the shadings of motive and method and responsibility
which are inherent in the ambiguous nature of terrorism. This
initial focusing is what President Reagan's speech has done.
But so far he has not moved his finger to the trigger.   [1985

Alive and Well

The Nazi-hunting season is upon us again. Mengele is finally dead, it is a year or two since anyone found Martin Bormann, and hot tips on Nazi gold in lakes and mine-shafts have become rare. But President Waldheim sits alone in Vienna, contemplating the well-deserved contempt of the world which landed on him last year. And Tom Bower, in 'The Paperclip Conspiracy,' has reminded us that Britain as well as America welcomed Nazi scientists after the war. Now the Home Office is anxiously checking out the charge that at least 17 war criminals have been living in this country.

Yes, Nazi murderers should be pursued for their crimes as long as they live. And yes – the hypocrisy of those who for reasons of state and expediency helped to conceal their crimes should be exposed. And yet the competitive zeal to ferret out and name guilty old men sometimes make me uneasy.

So we gave shelter to 17 men who are now accused of atrocities. Let me remind readers of an episode which has been not so much concealed as simply and totally forgotten. Just 40 years ago, the British authorities brought to this country some 8,000 men who were the survivors of a Waffen-SS division. And many of them still live here.

Put like that, it sounds like an inconceivable, unpardonable scandal. But it was not. The decision to bring these men to Britain in May 1947, and eventually to permit them to settle and acquire British citizenship, was a strange compound of casualness, British self-interest and – above all – of a merciful generosity rare in those years.

I am talking about the formation which began its life as the XIV Waffen-SS Infantry Division (*Galizien*). It was composed of Ukrainians and led by German SS officers. Established rather late in the war, in 1943, the division fought against the Red Army on the eastern front and was then transferred to

Slovakia, to the Jugoslav frontier regions and finally to Austria.
In the last days of the war, the unit got rid of its German
officers, renamed itself the First Ukrainian Infantry Division of
the Ukrainian National Army, and on 8 May 1945, surrendered
to the British near Graz in Austria.

This isn't the place to explain the miseries of Ukrainian
nationalist politics. But the Ukrainians are the largest European
people who never managed to establish and maintain a State of
their own. Everyone manipulated them against everyone else.
During the last war, many Ukrainians felt that while they
disliked the German invaders, they hated the Russians infinitely
more. Tens of thousands of them were induced to put on SS
uniforms and fight their arch-enemy – on the understanding
that they would not be asked to fight against the British and
Americans.

Among their leaders were some fanatical pro-German
Fascists, whose predecessors had been subsidised for years by
German military intelligence. Anti-semitism was rife, and – as
the Demjanjuk trial in Israel shows – Ukrainian police and
militia units under German command carried out some of the
most revolting mass slaughters of the war. But the *Galizien*
division after a bloody defeat by the Red Army at the battle of
Brody in 1944, became increasingly composed of Ukrainians
either conscripted against their will or anxious to join the retreat
away from the vengeful Soviet advance.

So, at the end of the war, they threw themselves on the mercy
of the British. They were disarmed and transferreed to a huge
camp near Rimini in Italy. The Soviet authorities visited them
and informed the British that, under the terms of the Yalta
conference, they wished all renegade Soviet citizens to be
repatriated.

And here something remarkable happened. We all now know
that, at the same time, the British were forcibly repatriating the
Cossacks and Russians who had belonged to German units,
and that by doing so we consigned thousands of human beings
to their deaths. Nobody remembers that we refused to give up
the Ukrainians.

The key was a legalism. Many of the Rimini men came from
the western Ukraine, from areas which until 1939 had belonged
not to the Soviet Union but to Poland. The Soviet authorities

claimed that they were now 'retrospectively' Soviet citizens –
and traitors. But the British decided to treat them as 'Poles':
citizens of an Allied nation. Those who in fact came from
beyond the 1939 border now lied about their places of birth.
The British pretended not to notice.

In February 1947, a British commission carried out a sample
screening at Rimini. It concluded that the Ukrainians had given
'aid and comfort' to the enemy for understandable reasons
which were 'incidental and not fundamental': patriotism, ignorance, fear and 'to have a smack at the Russians, whom they
always refer to as "Bolsheviks." ' The commission backed up
the argument that most of them were *de jure* Polish citizens,
and recommended 'most strongly' that they all be defined as
Displaced Persons.

In May that year, they were moved to Britain, where they
worked as farm labourers with 'prisoner of war' status in the
English Midlands. In September 1948, they were released and
registered with the police as Displaced Persons. In 1950, the
Home Office began to screen them all individually in order to
'formalise their stay.' Some went to Canada. Many remained
in Britain, where the Ukrainian community now numbers something over 30,000.

But did we 'turn a blind eye to murder'? What did the SS
Galizien division really do? German veterans of the Waffen-SS
claim that they were merely soldiers, but in fact some Waffen-
SS divisions committed barbarous crimes. Survivors of *Galizien*
to whom I have spoken say that there were no massacres, only
straightforward fighting or garrison duty in occupied regions.

Soviet sources, rather naturally, say the opposite. They attack
Britain for 'illegally listing Ukrainians as refugees,' and denying
them 'the possibility of liberating themselves from capitalist
slavery' by 'forcing' them to stay in the West. But they also
allege atrocities.

Some are nonsense. The division did not take part in the
massacre of civilians after the Warsaw Rising: that was a
different Ukrainian outfit. A few allegations, however, sound
more solid. The division is said to have murdered the population
of Huta Pieniacka, a Polish village. And the divisional chronicle
– unless it is a Soviet forgery – records that the third battalion

of the fourth regiment, at Tarnopol on 6 March 1944, drove 'all the Poles into a cathedral and exterminated them.'

It's hard to know. My guess is that evil deeds were done. A unit in SS uniform commanded by German Nazis and operating in hostile territory against partisans has about as much chance of emerging with clean hands as a snowflake has to survive in hell. But for what it is worth, the SS *Galizien* seems to have behaved less horribly than some other Ukrainian formations.

I would guess that there are a few old Ukrainians in this country with plenty to hide. Neither their compatriots nor the British have bothered to find out what, and that is culpable. On balance, though, most of these men were ignorant victims of oppression and war. The decision to open Britain's doors to them was – also on balance – something to be proud of. But if this country had opened its doors as widely to Jews fleeing from Hitler a few years earlier, I would be prouder still.   *[1987*

Spies

The little exchange of populations between Britain and the Soviet Union has stopped. It has cost us our Moscow correspondent, Mark Frankland, a shrewd but not unaffectionate watcher of the Russian scene. It has devastated Anglo-Soviet relations, damaged the careers of some quite blameless individuals, and brought joy only to transcontinental furniture-movers.

The British, though shocked by the force of the Soviet response, are not as outraged by the activities of the KGB in London as they affect to be. An open political system invites spying, among other prices which are not too high to pay. But Whitehall sees a decent limit to everything, and Soviet intelligence has become indecently greedy. The Foreign Office view is that the KGB should show some table manners when faced with this luscious buffet of easy information, and should not push their luck too hard.

It is a stoic way of looking at what has happened. It also reveals how generations of Cold War have taught the West to live with the fact of espionage, or at least to think in terms of a 'reasonable' level of spying. Many years ago, when the use of spies in international relations was considered as disgraceful as the use of poison gas in war, moral categories were firmer. Later, 'our' spies were secret heroes, while 'their' spies were monsters. Today, there are those who regard foreign intelligence as no more than a shady section of the mass media.

Writing in the *Spectator*, Tim Garton Ash has attacked such moral indifference: those who ask whether the new flock of West German spies can really be described as 'traitors' forget that the democracy and tolerance of the Federal Republic deserve the patriotism and loyalty of its civil servants – and secretaries. But this fair comment also asks us to go on treating the Cold War as a real war – as an emergency in which a good end justifies the means used by the secret agent, while an evil end does not.

This is what people in the West find increasingly hard to accept. They do not wish to be ruled by the KGB; they don't seriously deny the need for secret intelligence work. But – encouraged by John le Carré and a tribe of other novelists – they have become fascinated by the nature of the spy, by the traits which make him resemble his 'colleague' in the opposite camp rather than by the contrast between the systems which divide them. What are they like, these special people who carry a card dispensing them from the first rules a child is taught – not to lie, not to cheat, not to steal and, in certain cases, not to kill?

And there's a new, sharp resentment of secrecy. Once – almost out of memory – the man with secrets aroused only respect. He was patriarchal, he was priest-like. His great locked brief-case made lesser mortals feel safer. In Imperial Germany, a senior official was a *Geheimrat* – a secret counsellor. But in the 1960s, Ray Hawkey designed a memorable book-cover for a Len Deighton spy novel. The crested leather briefcase gaped open – and inside there was only a toothbrush, loose pistol cartridges, a packet of condoms, a girlie magazine.

Secret authority, the paternal power, is exposed and its mystery ridiculed. This is an adolescent democracy in which we demand the right to know, but in which the secrecy of the State is actually spreading as rapidly as respect for the habit of official secrecy is crumbling away. The Official Secrets Act still survives; the BBC journalists whose job is to inform and to dispel ignorance now know that they only hold their posts by permission of the Security Service. This is a contradiction which is going to explode.

In childish revenge against secrecy ('No, you can't come in, you haven't got the password!'), it's put about that there's nothing interesting in the brief-case, that spies are drab little bureaucrats anyway. Like most foreign correspondents, I have run into a good many spies – no doubt, into many I still don't know were spies – but they were certainly not drab.

I used to carry Kim Philby's typewriter for him around this office, because he seemed so frail, and he was good company. George Blake was aggressive, because the girl he was courting was a childhood friend of mine. There was the boastful, boozy gang who tried to recruit me as a student into M16 (that mercifully ended almost before it had begun, when one of them made a homosexual pounce on me). There was the melancholy double agent in Berlin, no more than a black-marketeer in information (a good definition of most inter-German spying). There was the nasty little Pole who handed me a choking glass of Passover slivovitz and said: 'Mr Ascherson, I have you on my hook!' He hadn't, and I found a way to settle his hash.

All this taught me that intelligence work spells death for journalism. Whatever you do, the other side is sure to know about it. This may not matter much to a professional spook, but a mere hack is dispensable – for the hard men in either service.

But it also gave me a sense of the strain, the ill-fittingness, of those who lead secret lives. All of them seemed oppressed, even to emit a silent appeal for sympathy. All but one, that is. He was the Czech journalist in the next office in Bonn. Every evening, he would give me a wink and patter off down the street dressed to kill, shoes twinkling, silver-grey blow-wave tossing. He turned out to be a 'Romeo,' one of the agents who seduce secretaries in Bonn ministries, but he was back in Prague before they could arrest him.

All decent people fear and despise informers. Yet I have known some who were more than narks, people who so much longed to talk to a Westerner that they were willing to pay the price of having to pass on a version of the talk to the police. This isn't far from the position of the censor who admires the writer he mutilates, who feels he understands him better than any normal reader. I have no doubt that there have been KGB officers in London who told themselves that their intelligence reports might help to make the Soviet Union a more liberal and 'British' place.

There are romantic twilights here. And, I admit to finding something essentially romantic about the whole profession, after all. By that I mean the feigning, the cover names and cover jobs, the playing of parts in street, office and bed, which amount to the old romantic game – what Karl Miller, in his book 'Doubles,' calls 'the dynamic metaphor of the second self.'

The Cold War itself offers an escape from self, into the other half of a dual world. There is a sort of rebirth, in a quiet dacha among the birch forests or in a country house smelling of floor-polish and roast lamb (Gordievsky's second birthplace). No less of a romantic escape, though an inward one, is performed by the spy and specially by the double agent or mole, who realises our buried longings to release and confront our second self.

The girl I knew married George Blake, in the end. When they arrested him, she wrote in a newspaper that she had never been married because her husband had turned out to be somebody else quite unknown to her. I sympathised with her, but felt that she had overlooked the terrifying capacity in all of us to be more than one person. In that, spies are more like us than we are.   [1985

Traitors

The other day, I found myself in a taxi queue with Anthony Blunt. He looked frayed but fervently cheerful, much as if he had just been dug out of the ruins of his own bombed house. Never mind the furniture, the books and the glass: the ceiling had come down, but the dear old family dining-table had taken the strain. Nobody is going to try him, nobody is going to bump him off. The worst that can happen now is abuse by newspapers, and that will only hasten the process of reconciliation with his friends. Newspapers are 'they' and we, after all, are 'we'. As Andrew Boyle relates, it turned out that a great many old acquaintances of Burgess and Maclean were much more horri-fied – felt, indeed, much more betrayed – by the fact that the late Goronwy Rees gave a version of their flight to the *People* than by the flight itself. When Stephen Spender showed the *Daily Express* a friend's letter about Burgess, he was held to have disgraced himself.

The book is a great feat. Andrew Boyle went through archives and memoirs in two continents, but above all persuaded people to talk – people in the know, who had given out little or no information before. So much has been written about the Two and then the Three and now the Baker's Dozen, as far as one can see, that it hardly seemed possible that Boyle could do more than rehash old evidence or bomb the rubble. How wrong! It wasn't so much that he flushed out Professor Blunt: smart fellows about Cambridge and St James's seem to have known all about Blunt for years. It was – first – that Boyle opened out the whole American dimension of the affair, through the FBI/CIA files and the secret chronicles of James Jesus Angleton – that rather Jamesian secret agent, an American from an English public school, who began by admiring the style of SIS and ended by discovering how many of them were traitors or bunglers. And secondly, it was that so many British spooks, retired or still in the trade, decided that Andrew Boyle was the man to whom they would finally spill their lapfuls of wizened beans.

There must be a connection here. The British intelligence services don't divulge the sort of stuff they gave Boyle out of the kindness of their hearts. Most 'authoritative' books about them have rather the status of Palace memoirs by governesses and grooms: as a brass watch for long service, a few veterans of relatively menial status are allowed to publish mendacious and exaggerated books (some of the books about Ultra, for instance) which grossly overstate either the importance of some operation or the credit due to SIS, or both. But 'The Climate of Treason' is not one of these hagiograms. They really talked: David Footman, Nicholas Elliot, Sir Robert Mackenzie, George Carey-Foster, Sir Frederick Warner, agents and diplomats on the security side, and a large anonymous group of Intelligence men from both branches of the service, retired and active.

The reason can be guessed at. Boyle's American break-through depended upon the Freedom of Information Act, which brought him baskets of US Intelligence material on matters still secret in Britain, but also upon anonymous CIA sources who were anxious to enlighten him on – especially – the Philby and Maclean affairs. What he discovered suggested that the business was even more humiliating for SIS than had been supposed by the public, and that the injury it dealt to Anglo-American Intelligence co-operation was correspondingly graver than had been understood. At the British end, one can assume, news of what Boyle had got his hands on led to a decision for a *Flucht nach vorn* – a controlled but corrective release of more British material about the Cambridge spies.

Boyle's discovery, essentially, was that the Americans had identified Maclean and Philby as Soviet spies by 1948. They did not pass on their information to the British, partly because they no longer trusted them, and partly because the CIA agent in charge of the case, Angleton, was the sort of counter-intelligence cat so fascinated by mice that he would almost prefer to let them escape with the cheese than to pounce. Angleton was tipped off by Israeli Intelligence to the effect that a British physicist working on nuclear weapons development in the States was a Soviet spy. This was the man Boyle calls 'Basil', or 'the fifth man'. He was easily turned round by the Americans, after he had confessed that he was helping Maclean to collect and assess for the Russians information about nuclear weapons cooperation (Donald Maclean was at this time in the British Embassy in Washington). When Kim Philby arrived in Washington in 1949, as the SIS liaison man with American Intelligence, the double-agent 'Basil' was able to confirm the suspicions of James Jesus Angleton that Philby was working for the other side. None of these discoveries were shared with the British. In a paroxysm of informational avarice, Angleton decided that the Brits could find out the hard way. They already knew, through the chance error of a Soviet cipher clerk, that there had been a diplomatic leak in their Washington embassy, and years of cryptographic detective work would eventually lead them to Maclean. So why should Angleton share his best sources with the British, in whose barrel, no doubt, other rotten apples nested? Although 'Basil' was a British citizen, it does not appear that SIS were told anything about his espionage, let alone his 'turning', until after Burgess and Maclean had fled in 1951.

Boyle's careful account of these later years, when the Cambridge spies were coming to the end of their free run, shows how astonishingly ineffective security was in their case – even allowing for the presence of Philby at the top of the MI6 counter-espionage department. Mosaic-work, the logical assembling of a pattern of guilt, played only a minor part in their detection. It was mostly luck, and almost all the luck came from a series of defecting Soviet agents, starting with Krivitsky in 1937 (who had already warned that the USSR had spies in the British diplomatic service) and ending with Golitsin in 1961, the man who finally gave SIS the proof that Kim Philby had been a Soviet agent for the whole of his working life. Meanwhile evidence that the British loyalty of the Cambridge spies was wobbly lay scattered across the land. Nobody cared to pick it up. They could have stood in Piccadilly Circus and screamed that they were Communists, to no effect. In fact, they more or less did so: the old Gargoyle, where Maclean howled drunkenly at Goronwy Rees that 'you were one of US, but you ratted!', wasn't far away. Nor were all the flats and pubs where Guy Burgess and Donald Maclean had told people exactly what they were, and at the top of their voices. But the reaction was always much the same, always the nanny's pursed lip: 'Overtired again! Don't look at Master Guy or Master Donald, it only encourages them . . .' The British reaction, that is. James Jesus Angleton was different. When Kim Philby, after being decorated at Buckingham Palace, said that what Britain needed was a good stiff dose of socialism, James Jesus wondered if he might not be a Communist.

In all the new details he adds to the story, Andrew Boyle doesn't clear up a point which must be of central importance in the history of the Cambridge spies. We have been offered a series of books about the Ultra triumph, about the breaking of the Enigma codes and the work at Bletchley Park, about the constellation of Cambridge genius which was assembled there. What we don't know, and it's a very relevant question, is how much the Russians were told. The Americans were informed, indeed participated. But did the Russians get Ultra after the Nazi invasion of June 1941 transformed them into allies?

Boyle is ambiguous. At one point he observes that 'Stalin and his underlings were . . . being told nearly everything they required to know at first hand,' rendering information from their agents within British Intelligence unnecessary. But later on he quotes Muggeridge's account of a 1944 row, in which Victor Rothschild and Kim Philby protested that Ultra intercept material was being withheld from the Russians. Boyle goes on to say that it was 'standard practice' to withhold Ultra from the Soviet Union, but that it was reaching Moscow anyway through 'Lucy', the Soviet espionage centre in Switzerland. This is additionally puzzling, because 'Lucy' has been described as a personal German source, not a code-break. But in any case, the significance for Boyle's main story is obvious. If in the years 1941–3, when the Russians were carrying almost the whole burden of the war against Germany, substantial numbers of Russian soldiers were dying because they were denied the war's most important source of secret information, the actions of the Cambridge spies at that time must appear in a better light. What justification could the British advance for withholding the information – the military radio traffic of the enemy – from their own ally? Only one: that Britain's best interest was to stand aside and watch Nazi Germany and Soviet Russia slaughter each other to the last man. Nearly 40 years later, we have drifted so far to the right that many young people of liberal mind can accept that as a good policy. Why choose between Hitler and Stalin? One dictatorship was as bad as the other. But the 'climate' then was very different. The appeasers who hoped that Hitler and Stalin could be set at each others' throats, and thought that a Nazi victory in that particular contest might even be preferable, had lost a political battle. Churchill ruled instead, ready to make a favourable reference to Hell in the House of Commons if the Devil were prepared to join the anti-Nazi coalition. To accept that Ultra could be shared with the Americans but not with the Russians would have seemed, then, like an admission that, after all, the Cliveden Set still ruled from the back seat. This is a point of historical fact which ought to be settled.

Boyle is a bit of a prig. Nobody gets away with anything. Political hindsight dominates. Communists, Tories, imperialists, idealists all get the back of his hand: there are no heroes. He certainly makes the case that treachery doesn't pay in personal terms (although we know little about Blunt's inner torments, if any). Burgess, Maclean and Philby all took to drink in the most satisfactorily Victorian way, Maclean driven to the verge of madness by Presbyterian guilt. As for Marx, he was 'inhuman' and wrote 'turgid tomes'; even Donald Maclean's book 'British Foreign Policy after Suez', written after his flight, has to be dismissed as 'somewhat ponderous'. (Unfair: it's penetrating and very readable.) But Boyle's study of the three main personalities is more impressive. Guy Burgess turns out to have been a much more forceful figure than the 'Etonian mudlark and sick toast of a sick society' version. Maclean, for all his convulsions of conscience and drunken violence, clung more persistently than the others to the hope that he was not just a spy and a traitor but the representative of a serious alternative for Britain. Kim Philby, in contrast, is diminished: he had skill and sang-froid, but little of political originality or inner conflict to hold attention.

British Intelligence, in Boyle's chronicle, remains as weird a community as ever, in spite of all the author's new information and captures of confidence. Amateurism, class prejudice and what Boyle calls 'the sad pleasures of sodomy' composed its peculiar flavour. The circumstances of my own unhappy brush with the service only confirm it. My background was 'right', and I was duly recommended as a likely lad by a Cambridge don (Boyle rids us of the myth that Cambridge tutors recruited assiduously for Russia, but does not add that they recruit assiduously for the home side). There followed a lunch at the Reform Club, where this 23-year-old ass received the proposal that he should go to the new Communist state of Betelgeuse in order to write a biography of its ferocious leader. An argument about where Betelgeuse was had to be settled by a visit to the *Times* Atlas, dated 1910, in the Club library. My real assignment, they said, was to approach leading Betelgeusians and 'get them round to our point of view'. Uneasy, I objected that I knew nothing of the place or its language. 'Old D. will put you in the picture,' they chortled, returning to their port. A few days later, I was summoned to meet D. in his home. After a silent but delicious dinner, D. asked me to sit next to him on the sofa. I supposed that I was at last to be put in the picture, but D. merely grasped me tightly and wordlessly by the penis. I extracted myself and ran away, and after some days of great confusion, wrote to say that perhaps I was not mature enough for this service.

An outfit like that – and these events took place years after the 'flight of the diplomats' – deserves everything it gets. I suppose there was a wild brilliance about the Betelgeuse project, which would almost certainly have cost me my head. But what most impresses me, in retrospect, is their sublime confidence that after that lunch and dinner I would still be their loyal man and true. This was a service which, even then, still assumed that people of our sort didn't let us down. It is not surprising that SIS were so incredulous, in the face of plain evidence of internal treachery, at the suggestion that somebody one had been at Cambridge with or whose father one had known could be a 'mole'.

And these assumptions about class loyalty, it seems to me after reading Boyle, also relate to the final question: why did the Cambridge spies spy? It would be silly to argue that Communism had little to do with it, but the Communist Party of Great Britain was clearly not the point, nor the source of inspiration. Even if their Soviet recruiters and controllers had wished it, none of these three (or indeed four) had the stamina to become active CP members, to sell the *Daily Worker* anywhere but on King's Parade, to throw themselves into the problems of who should be elected to the Executive Committee or the Political Committee. They didn't have the *partinost*, or 'party spirit', of friends like James Klugman of John Cornford. To put it crudely, the CP in Britain was beneath them. They were unwilling in the end to leave the Establishment, and became prominent figures in the BBC, the Foreign Office, Intelligence and so forth – just as they were destined to. Except that they also spied.

They all leave one with the odd impression, even Philby in his early years, that they became Soviet agents *faute de mieux*. What they needed was something else: a British movement of total opposition to the regime which was both respectable and formidable. They needed a *divided* Establishment, an alternative regime-in-waiting which they could join. Continental republics know this dualism. In France or Italy, Maclean would probably have been a prominent Communist with a bourgeois lifestyle, and quite possibly a good desk in the Foreign Ministry whose contents he would not have felt moved to microphotograph each night. In Britain, still an *ancien régime* in this respect, Labour did not offer such an alternative, while the price of CPGB activity would obviously be impotence and ostracism. The spies didn't see why they should be impotent and ostracised.

The Thirties were a decade of rapid social change and improvement in popular living standards, as well as a time of poverty and misery for many. But Britain remained governed, financed, exploited and largely represented by the upper class. There was no alternative ruling group, waiting in the wings with its own governors, financiers, civil servants, generals and even spooks. Labour was a party which, as far as the student leftist could see, would deferentially leave the old élite in place. The Cambridge spies wanted something else for Britain, something which now sounds absurd: a socialist revolution which would both smash the patrician hegemony to which the spies were such guilty heirs, and restore British greatness and independence. Objectively, we can now see them as Stalin's pawns. They don't seem to have taken that view, even with a thrill of masochism. The future spies sought a centre of full-blooded, total opposition to the status quo in Britain. They could find such a centre only abroad, in Moscow.

They really were traitors. Swedish colonels, West German

bureaucrats who betray secrets to the East, are not in their league. They usually do it for money, or because they are under pressure or because they have some personal grievance. Nor are their fellow citizens as fascinated by their treachery as the British public are by the tale of the upper-crust spies. Philby, Burgess, Maclean and Blunt were doing something more fundamental: they betrayed what their country was doing but by the same act destroyed the way their country did things. After them, the delicate muscle-tissue of the executive, uncritical trust moving in sheaths of class loyalty and schoolmate confidence, never worked so well again. This isn't to say that state servants do not still use it. They do, but with misgivings and with much greater difficulty. The damage done by the spies here was irreparable in the long run, but if one considers that the old-boy system was overdue for replacement, one could argue that the Cambridge spies betrayed their friends, in this instance, but not necessarily their country.

At the edge of the story, other elements of motive – even stranger – can be sensed. A certain crude psychologism fits, the spies savaging their Patria as substitute for an absent or unconvincing father. But there is another approach. Birth, the accident of birth in the privileged upper tenth of a caste society, imprisoned these men in a cell with the gnawing rat of guilt. Nothing they could do in life would efface the original sin of that unfair birth – except rebirth. Not just the Communist faith but the actual existence of the Soviet Union – isolated, hated, mysterious – glowed to them across Europe as a second chance for themselves as well as for humanity. Cross that snowy frontier, die for the old world, awake purified in a new one clutching 'a white stone with a new name writ thereon . . .'

In the end, there is Protestantism, English and Scottish, in these men. Boyle leaves us with the picture of an ageing Burgess in Moscow, slowly picking out on the piano hymn tunes from his schooldays:

> My soul, there is a country
> Far beyond the stars,
> Where stands a wingèd sentry
> All skilful in the wars . . .

If thou canst get but thither,
There grows the flower of peace,
The Rose that cannot wither,
Thy fortress and thy ease.

[*1980*

A review of 'The Climate of Treason' by Andrew Boyle (Hutchinson, London, 1979).

Witness

On the wall of my office, some years ago, I pinned up the postcard reproduction of a portrait. It is the picture of a man in the black robe of a Jesuit, a dark-haired, bearded man a little past his youth whose features are curiously worn. There is something strange, too, about his eyes, a look at once hurt and defiant.

This man is Friedrich Spee von Langenfeld, who died of the plague at Trier, in western Germany in 1635. I try to avoid anniversaries, and this is not his – though it happens that I am writing on the day of his death. But some fuss is being made in 1987 because it is just 500 years since the publication of one of the most evil of books: the *Malleus Maleficarum* (The Hammer of Witches), which was to become a manual for the great witch-hunt of the sixteenth and seventeenth centuries. It was Spee's fate to become part of that hunt.

He was a Rhinelander and a scholar. In Trier there still stands the old Jesuit college which became the city's most famous school, now the Friedrich-Wilhelm Gymnasium. This school, always a centre of liberal Catholicism, had two well-known pupils whom many citizens would prefer to forget: Karl Marx and Klaus Barbie. Friedrich Spee, in his own times, was a teacher there.

In 1627, when Spee was 36 years old, the Bishop of Würzburg asked the Jesuits to send him a confessor for condemned witches. They chose Spee. In the next two years, he accompanied nearly 200 human beings to the stake, and tried to comfort them. Not all were women. There were also town councillors and priests. There was a blind girl, and there were two children only nine years old. We do not know whether Spee was also present at their interrogations by torture, but it is pretty clear from what he wrote afterwards that he sometimes was.

Spee said that out of all those victims, there was 'not one whom I could have asserted to be guilty, after comprehensive and sane reflection.' It is reported that his hair turned grey, although the portrait does not show this. He never described directly what he saw, heard and smelled at the pyres, saying only that 'it is not good to tell all that I experienced there.'

The nearest that he came to that was by quoting Ecclesiastes. 'I saw the tears of the oppressed, and I saw that there was no one to comfort them. Strength was on the side of their oppressors, and there was no one to avenge them. I counted the dead happy because they were dead, happier than the living who are still in life. More fortunate than either I reckoned the man yet unborn, who had not witnessed all the wicked deeds done here under the sun.'

In the end, Spee could take no more. The bishop's men and the city fathers were preventing him from hearing confessions, fearing that Spee would take the victims' protestations of innocence to higher authorities. He went away, and wrote a book which seems to me an enduring monument to human courage, intelligence and decency, and which helped in some measure to bring the great atrocity to an end in Germany.

The book, which caused a huge sensation when it appeared in 1631, was entitled *Cautio Criminalis*, or 'An Essay on the Trials of Witches, Addressed to the Magistrates of Germany.' Written in Latin, it is made up of 51 'Doubts,' subdivided into 'Reasons,' a work whose anger and misery is tightly controlled in philosophical form. In the 'Cautio,' Spee systematically demolished every aspect of the trials, revealing all the private vengeances and financial corruption behind them, and denouncing what remains the fundamental contradiction of torture: 'The accused either confesses on the rack, in which case she is guilty, or she doesn't confess, in which case she is also guilty because to have withstood such terrible torture she must have been in league with the Devil.'

Although witch-hunting raged on in Germany until the end of the century, Spee's book was rapidly reprinted and circulated, and in several regions the trials were banned. But the scars on Friedrich Spee were indelible. He returned to teaching and preaching, and became a poet. The 'Nightingale's Rival' gave to Germany a new form of Christian pastoral poetry. They are delicate songs of sunlight and countryside, and yet, ever and again, there recur the images of consuming flame, of darkness and abandonment.

Spee went back to Trier, at the height of the Thirty Years' War. He looked after the wounded, when the Imperialists stormed the city, and nursed the sick in the plague epidemic which followed. He caught the disease, died and was buried in the Jesuit church by the school where he taught.

It makes me angry that although the *Malleus Maleficarum* has been translated into English – by an English vicar who seems to take a horrid delight in that discharge of woman-hate and cruelty – the *Cautio* seems never to have been thought worthy of attention in this country. Yet it is Friedrich Spee who should belong to us, not the two bloodthirsty Dominicans who wrote the *Malleus*.

For this Spee, who redeemed himself, is also guilty, in a very twentieth-century way. How would it go with him if he were charged with crimes against humanity, as Klaus Barbie was? It would be no defence that he acted under Jesuit orders. He took part in the crime, just as certain SS officers at Auschwitz took part not by killing but by soothing and deceiving the victims about their fate.

His case would resemble that of some Auschwitz doctors, who refused to select victims on the ramp but whose work to improve camp conditions – sometimes sincere – only had the effect of making the death machinery run more smoothly. His subsequent rebellion would count in his favour. But no court could encompass the real moral paradox here: that Spee would not have acquired the knowledge and motive required to denounce this crime without participating in it to some extent.

I think Spee knew this, and was strong enough to comfort and carry his own guilt. He never whined, or tried to pose as a hero. Only his choice from Ecclesiastes suggests that, after Würzburg, he wished that he had never been born.

There is a second modernity. Spee fought as a lonely intellectual against a mass madness led by intellect. Professor Norman Cohn, in his 'Europe's Inner Demons,' shows that the witch-hunt only took its pandemic form when educated men connected 'sophisticated' fantasies about Devil-worshipping covens of flying witches to old peasant beliefs in *maleficium* – harm done by spells. Then the holocausts began, as bishops and princes mobilised ignorant millions behind a new ideology: the purge of a Satanic fifth column within the gates.

We have seen other purges and holocausts led by ideology. And there have been others like Spee: the handful of men and women who first obeyed Hitler and then defied him, hoping not for life or honour or even personal redemption, but only that, for the sake of a few just men, their city would be spared from brimstone. This forgotten Jesuit, whose portrait – now I look at it again – is illuminated by a red and flickering glow, belongs in a small but good company.   [*1987*

Critics

Some literary critics aim to wound; few aim to kill. They carry small-arms: a shotgun to sting, a rifle to drill holes in the fleshy part of a chapter. Inflicting pain on their thin-skinned quarry is part of the fun, bombing them out would end the sport.

But the other day I came across the rudest review I have ever read. Rude? It was annihilating. It was a megaton warhead, plunging out of the intellectual ionosphere on its victim, intended to leave – when the roar of detonation and the clatter of falling limbs was over – a silent hole in the ground.

This was a review in the *Frankfurter Allgemeine Zeitung* entitled – simply and horribly – 'A Catastrophic Book.' Its target was

the latest novel by Günter Grass, 'The She-Rat.' Its author
was Marcel Reich-Ranicki, the most awe-inspiring critic in
Germany. After wading through his gamma-radiating words, I
see why.

He does not just say that he dislikes the novel. The agony
would be over far too soon. Reich-Ranicki opens his performance with a heart-breaking elegy for the lost powers of a great
writer, once a master of prose. Then he raises the curtain on
a tableau of Grass at work, sitting down every morning at his
typewriter to struggle with the ghastly certainty that his talent
has fled and he has no more to say. 'Nothing emerges. Ah, how
he must have suffered!'

Grass is more to be pitied than his readers, gloats Reich-
Ranicki; they will not even throw the book away in disgust but
will drop it unread after a few pages. 'The She-Rat' could
even discredit all modern German literature, the critic sighs:
'Reading new books is no unmixed pleasure, but the state of
contemporary writing is really nowhere near as dire as that of
the writer Grass. . . .'

The idea of the novel was worth no more than a newspaper
article, perhaps a medium-length lecture. 'Instead, he strives to
transform his lamentably banal views and warnings into an epic.'
Grass is worn out, his creative gift is used up, his attempts at
fantasy are yawn-inducing, his readers are treated as idiots, his
satire is 'shamingly cheap,' his political imagery is absurd ('Does
such rubbish deserve comment?'), his prose is 'lifeless and
uninspired,' his novel has no structure because its component
parts are 'rotten and brittle.'

Enough? Not quite enough for Reich-Ranicki. At the end,
thousands of words on, Reich-Ranicki leans solicitously over
what was once Günter Grass and sheds a final, scalding tear
for his departed greatness. ' "The She-Rat" is just an empty
space, concealed by withered laurels and painstakingly tarted-
up with long-faded garlands.' Thank you, and good night.

Fortunately for literature, Günter Grass is a tough, truculent
soul who can look after himself. He may be irritable, but fragile
he is not: he will survive Reich-Ranicki. I haven't read the
novel, but I now certainly will. There are some duds on the
Grass bookshelf, but nothing suggests that the man has finally
lost his enormous fertility of fable and narrative. A less resilient

writer, though, might have been silenced by such reviewing for ever.

Oddly enough, Reich-Ranicki has since given a lecture in which he deplored the German critical practice of declaring – every few years – that 'German literature is dead.' The worth-less, scribbling midgets of the day, as Thomas Mann or Brecht were called in their time, turn out to have staying-power. And yet there are always mighty critics who – in the mood of Germaine Greer preferring no sex to bad sex – declare that the time has come for less literature rather than more.

This reminds me of the London family publishing firm in Anthony Powell's 'Afternoon Men': two elderly brothers whose aim was to find sound reasons for not publishing anything offered to them. I feel for them at moments. Watching the endless procession of new books arriving daily in their Jiffybags for review is as intolerable as watching the endless stream of arriving human beings at a Heathrow terminal. How about . . . well . . . putting the whole machine into reverse?

Heinrich Heine warned that where books are burned, they will shortly be burning people. Rosa Luxembourg repeated it. Not all of her prophecies and theories have stood the test of time and misunderstanding (why the current Margarethe von Trotta film presents her as a premature CND pacifist I can't imagine). Those words, however, came more than 10 years before the Nazi book-bonfires, and more than 15 years before the SS lit the crematoria at Auschwitz. Rosa Luxembourg never said a truer sentence – but I am talking not about book-genocide so much as book-contraception. Something is being swamped under all these hyped-up bricks of printed paper. One can call this process the triumph of universal education. One could also see it as another example of machine getting the upper hand of master.

Karl Kraus, the prince of all central European critics, wrote in 1908: 'Of the terrible devastation being wrought by the printing press, it is still not possible today to have any concep-tion. The airship is invented, and the imagination crawls along like a stage-coach. Automobile, telephone and the mass dissemi-nation of stupidity – who can say what the brains of the gener-ation after next will be like?'

This thought also occurred to an acquaintance of mine called

– let's say – Szmit, a writer in the People's Republic of Slobodnia. He was awarded a literary prize, and then invited to go on state television to add his voice – as a decorated man of letters – to the national campaign for the eradication of illiteracy.

Szmit, whose view of the Republic was sardonic, passed the hours before the programme in the company of several bottles of plum brandy. On camera at last, he replied to the TV presenter as follows: 'Comrade, I utterly agree that literacy is the curse of our nation. Literacy hinders the unfolding of the full human personality. Literacy keeps the masses in ignorance, helpless and credulous before unscrupulous demagogues and exploiters. Yes, comrades, let us tour our land with teams of antiliteracy volunteers to stamp out this scourge, this blot, this . . .'

At this point, they pulled the plug on him. Later, they withdrew the literary prize from Szmit. Not wishing to be outdone, the provincial authorities then fired the headmaster of the school whose hall had been used for the presentation. Unwilling to be found lacking in zeal, the municipality demolished the nice nineteenth-century house in which Szmit had passed the night before accepting the prize. Szmit, although still recovering from typhoid, induced by eating too much of the perch in aspic at the prize banquet, continued to laugh at them all, and is laughing to this day.

I remember discussing with Szmit the old French financial Press before the war. The aim of these *Bourse* papers was to publish as *few* copies as possible. They would run off a proof, full of horrible revelation and gossip, and then invite members of the stock exchange to pay to have the print run reduced. On a middling day, one put out a hundred or so copies. On a good day, one published none at all.

And here, in a metaphor, is the answer to the questions raised by Reich-Ranicki's treatment of Günter Grass. Yes, any thinking person should be frightened by the amount of junk that's published. But reducing it means corruption, and then censorship, and then tyranny. Writing is not improved by contraception or genocide or even by selective critical murder. It does respond to education, through good criticism. Writers are sometimes worth stinging, never worth bombing.   [*1986*

Diaries

Men everywhere supposed (as A. J. P. Taylor tends to begin sentences) that he would join in the general execration of Lord Dacre over the Hitler diaries. A lot of men, indeed, were looking forward to this: historians wrestling in mud is a common spectacle that never loses its power to give pleasure – like dissent between taxi-drivers. They were disappointed. Taylor stayed out of the mud. More accurately, he wrote in these pages that he found the whole affair boring – 'cold mutton', as he said about the Anthony Blunt affair. Perhaps he did. Historians are queer. Still, boredom is ruder than execration. I have nearly finished imitating A. J. P. Taylor's rhythms now. Let me add this. I once wrote a whole book in what I conceived to be his style – short, choppy sentences bouncing the reader rapidly up and down so that he does not fall asleep. The book received a kind notice from Taylor, and sold almost no copies at all. Men thought it too expensive. I only paid the indexing bill years later. This was not because I was cross or indigent, but because I was mean.

This diary salutes a diarist who has often filled this page: it celebrates the publication of A. J. P. Taylor's memoirs, 'A Personal History',* which would, as he points out in the preface, have been a great deal longer but for the laws of libel, or at least for publishers' nervousness about the laws of libel.

There is one way out. If the person allegedly libelled is dead, all is well. How eagerly I have gone through the obituaries killing off not only my enemies, not that I have any, but my best friends. If the aggrieved person is still alive, there is only one remedy: strike out the entire passage. Any friend or acquaintance who turns to the index and does not find his name there can console

* Hamish Hamilton, London, 1983.

himself that he was originally the subject of a passage which the lawyer condemned.

However, matters have not become as dull as this implies, as references to Professor Hugh Trevor-Roper, now Lord Dacre (or Lord Dakar, as the Argentinian papers call him), demonstrate. Taylor is actually quite forgiving about the fact that Trevor-Roper and not he was awarded the Regius Professorship after Suez: he asserts that J. C. Masterman, Vice-Chancellor of Oxford at the time, and Taylor's own friend Namier were responsible. Taylor writes that he never wanted the Chair anyway and would have refused to accept it 'from hands still stained with blood' – a reference to Harold Macmillan, then Prime Minister. However, it was the end of his lifelong friendship with Namier. 'I put down the telephone and never spoke to him again . . . Namier was dead so far as I was concerned.' All he says about the victorious candidate at this point is that 'he tried to repeat my success on television, not however successfully, and also made some fruitless attempts to break into popular journalism.'

Later on, however, Taylor is more mordant about Trevor-Roper's objections to 'The Origins of the Second World War'. The question was, of course, whether Hitler had planned the Second World War years before or whether, as Taylor maintained, he took a gamble which seemed promising at the time. 'Hugh Trevor-Roper was . . . claiming that he had deduced Hitler's every move from the moment he read *Mein Kampf*. If so, he was cleverer than Hitler himself, who dismissed *Mein Kampf* as "fantasies from behind bars" ' He goes on: 'Trevor-Roper thought he had taken out a patent in Hitler and made a great cry.'

And now another great cry. The patent in Hitler seems to have ended in tears. But the affair of Lord Dacre and the fake Hitler diaries is too awful for gloating, and it should be said that Dacre came out of it all less shamefully than most of the other principals. He committed one dreadful error – whether out of over-excitement, vanity or a combination of both is hard to say – but showed a good deal of courage in then wrecking the party in Hamburg by owning up to doubts and finally by changing his mind. It all shows that historians pushed into snap judgments are as silly as the rest of us, and should never let themselves be so pushed.

Taylor is more of an exception in this respect than he admits, thinking fast on his feet and never letting himself be bounced into rash or half-baked judgments by others. He would probably confess to a fair quota of rash and half-baked judgments of his own, but would claim full paternity. All the same, the Hitler diaries affair will have given comfort to Taylor's crustier opponents, who – as he records with irritation – insisted over the years that historians who get involved with Fleet Street and decorate television chat-shows run the danger of making fools not only of themselves but of their profession. The diaries fiasco shows how easily this can happen, and Taylor was only the exception who proved the rule when, as he immodestly points out, he became the most extraordinary television performer this country has ever known: 'I was a one-man University of the Air.'

The guilty men, apart from the forgers themselves, are the press barons and their editors: Henry Nannen, Rupert Murdoch, Frank Giles and Charles Douglas-Home. That Trevor-Roper should have 'taken the *bona fides* of the editor' – of *Stern* – 'as a *datum*' passes belief. Probably he has never read the magazine. However, journalists, excluding proprietors, generally have a better nose for phonies than historians. The misery of the *Sunday Times* reporters, pumping away at their investigative talents to keep this leaky fabrication afloat, was wretched to behold. When it finally sank, they cheered and went out for a drink. A few days before, they had given their editor a memorandum recalling the frightful precedent of the false 'Mussolini diaries', which he refused even to discuss with them. Now I hear that a sensational document from an anonymous 'top Chinese source', purporting to give the full inside story of the Lin Biao affair, has been paid for somewhere in Gray's Inn Road. Cash first, verification later.

If the British have found the whole Hitler diary business funny, the West Germans have not. It has been taken as a national '*Blamage*' – a good word, meaning sudden and total public humiliation. The reaction has been to snuff a conspiracy against West German democracy, the '*freiheitlich-demokratische Verfassung*', by sinister forces beyond the frontiers. The East

Germans confected the diaries – or else a network of old and new Nazis based in South America and intent on restoring the *Führer*'s reputation. This is all scapegoatery. The perfect territory for a fabricator of historical documents is an open society rich in assorted stationery and inks, blessed with good libraries and with press barons at once gullible and magnificently extravagant: in other words, a place like the Federal Republic. Why should the West Germans be so reluctant to admit this? After all, their own state is a kind of forgery, knocked together by Allied typists and then given a spurious attribution to men like Konrad Adenauer and Carlo Schmidt, and it has worked out quite respectably.

I have always liked the old phrase about 'the forging of a nation'. Most young nations carry false birth certificates, either some teleologically-twisted brand of history which proves that Slobodnian independence was the inevitable outcome of the dialectics of progress, or else – and not infrequently – literal forgeries. Look at the Libuše manuscripts, forged by a nineteenth-century Prague archivist to prove that a glittering, advanced Czech civilisation existed in the Dark Ages when the Germans were still licking rye porridge off their fingers. (They were denounced by Thomas Masaryk, another example of how journalists and politicians are more sensitive to the smell of fraud than academics. At the time, Czech patriots rewarded Masaryk's exposures by calling him a Hun-loving traitor – probably Jewish, too. A generation later, he led them to independence, and in 1968 people were selling his portrait on the Prague street-stalls by the thousand.) Look at Ossian. Look at the Welsh, who have a Dark Age epic poetry of their own, but felt it necessary to cook up a little more, the cooking being apparently done by Iolo Morganwg in the back room of the King Lud pub at the end of Fleet Street. Look, finally, at the Bible, guarantee and user's manual for 'Western Christian Civilisation'. Much of the Old Testament purports to be the table-talk of Jehovah, brought to us by pseudonymous but highly-placed Israelite sources. Much of it could reasonably be termed forgery. Yet the protests would be relatively mild if Nannen and Murdoch acquired some scrolls from a cave and sold world rights to a fresh 'eye-witness' account of the Flood, even if it were proved to have been composed five centuries after the event.

The thought of romantic nationalism and its necessary frauds reminds me of the least attractive side of A. J. P. Taylor's memoirs, which is his ruthlessness about the post-war settlement in Europe. About Hungary, 1956: 'Better a Communist régime supported by Soviet Russia, I thought, than an anti-Communist régime led by Cardinal Mindszenty. Hence my conscience was not troubled by the Soviet intervention.' About the '*coup de Prague*' in 1948: 'I came to see that those friends of mine had brought it on themselves by trying to achieve a Czech government in which the Communists would have no part.' Taylor's approval of the Soviet occupation and then annexation of Poland's eastern teritories in 1939 and 1944 is equally unsentimental: most of the inhabitants were non-Poles, and Stalin needed an extra stretch of *glacis* between him and Hitler. None of these views is entirely without foundation, of course. It is the boorish reductionism of it all which is so ugly. Taylor wants a disarmed Europe and an end to the Cold War, like everyone else. But he seems to think that this requires of East Europeans that they should pipe down – Poles especially – and make the best of the 'socialism' they have been presented with, instead of milling around and imperilling the balance of power.

This is the 'Little Englander' in Taylor coming out, a super-annuated cast of mind he shares with his close friend Michael Foot. It is English history that one writes, the Scots, Irish and Welsh constituting 'the lesser breeds [who] were allowed in when they made a difference in English affairs, as they often did.' It is also a lingering sense that Britain is still a world power, heir even now to the status of a 'Victor Power' of the Second World War. At one point, Taylor admits this. Discussing his long commitment to CND, he confesses: 'We made one great mistake, which ultimately doomed CND to futility. We thought that Great Britain was still a great power whose example would affect the rest of the world. Ironically, we were the last Imperialists.' All that is left of that sort of Imperialism today in the Labour movement is a grumpy isolationism: if England cannot guide the lesser breeds, Slav or Celtic, then she will retreat indoors, switch off the lights and turn the key. If there is one prospect in our politics that frightens me more than another spell with Mrs Thatcher, it is the idea of being locked in a dark nursery cupboard playing sardines with aged Tribunites: out of the European Community, out of our alliances, out of touch with the world economy, out of our collective minds.

Unfortunately, this isolationism is the ink in which the Labour Manifesto seems to be written. As a boy, I received instruction in political principles from an old Forestry Commission gamekeeper in Argyll. 'At election time,' he used to say, 'a man should take himself alone to the hills and seek to listen to the voice of his own heart.' If he were alive today – and if he could hack his way up through the Forestry's prickly Christmas trees now covering the hills – the voice of his heart would tell him to come straight down again and book a Mediterranean holiday over the week of 9 June. Nothing good seems likely to come out of this campaign or its results. Everybody is fighting to impose his or her own vision of the past, dolled up as the future. Once it looked as if Labour might go into the fight genuinely committed to a 'fundamental and irreversible shift in the balance of power in favour of working people and their families' (FISHBOPWIFWAF), something worth fighting for, which in its way recognised the basic truth about British failure. The old English dogma – that there is nothing essentially wrong with British political institutions, which function badly only because the economy is decayed – is precisely wrong. Our political institutions are in terminal decay, and until they are knocked down and modernised neither capitalism, socialism nor any mixture of the two can flourish. However, FISHBOP-WIFWAF has declined with the sinking star of Tony Benn, and Labour is left with an uninspiring programme deriving from Keynes, Churchill and Pitt the Younger. The Alliance proclaim the need for institutional reform, which is to their credit, but their motives still seem conservative – restoring assumptions smashed by Mrs Thatcher. This wish to get back to a comfortable. Jenkinsite way of running things cannot square with revolutionary proposals like a new electoral system and devolution all round. If you set out to break the mould of British politics, you have to realise that it is only mould that holds British politics together.

So, at the moment of writing, it does not seem that there is much to stop Mrs Thatcher proceeding with her mission of turning Britain into a version of West Germany, a society nervous, expensive, insecure and docile. She has made certain discoveries about British political behaviour today which cannot be covered over again, and there is no way back from them. Monetarism is not such a discovery but a fraud which we will hear little about in this campaign: any fool knows that inflation can be reduced by strangling productive forces and creating mass unemployment. What nobody knew, but nobody can now forget, is that the British will tolerate four million unemployed without a revolution. It is not simply that those in work have lost almost all sense of solidarity with those who are out of work, but that a substantial number of those unemployed seem to feel guilty about it. They sit gloomily at home, having run out of decorating jobs to do about the house, contemplating the idea that this is their punishment for producing commodities that nobody really wanted to buy, or for having clung too long to closed shops and excessive manning levels. This self-lacerating mood contributes to Mrs Thatcher's other discovery, which is that in hard times the Trade Union movement knuckles under. No wonder that a poll the other day disclosed that public anxiety about militancy or radicalism in union leaderships was rapidly declining. There is bluster from the leaders, but not much action.

[*1983*

Media Heroes

In spite of Wapping, journalists are figuring as heroes this winter. Not real journalists (though *The Times* man who lost his job by refusing to go to Wapping on his first morning in his new house, on the day the first mortgage payment was due, deserves a decoration for 'complete disregard of personal safety').

I mean journalists as the heroes of films and television plays. A whole spate of them, of which the film 'Defence of the Realm' is the most stylish and distinguished, offer us brave reporters risking their lives to challenge the British State machine by exposing noxious secrets. All assume – a sinister sign of the times – that our security establishment would not hesitate to cripple or murder an inquisitive hack. That is as new as the treatment of the investigative journalist, suddenly promoted from drunken anti-hero to the natural champion of justice and democracy.

Whether the Press deserves this glory is another matter. Clearly there is a mood which at least wishes that it did. So it is an odd coincidence that another film now in our cinemas proceeds to debunk one of the genuine anti-establishment scoops of the century.

This is 'Colonel Redl,' the latest work of the great Hungarian director Istvan Szabo. It is a fictional version of a true story. In 1913, Colonel Alfred Redl, a brilliant Austro-Hungarian officer of lowly birth who had become the chief of counter-intelligence, was discovered to have passed military secrets to the Russians. Redl was a homosexual who had fallen victim to Russian blackmail. He was presented with a pistol, in the old style, and shot himself in the bedroom of a Vienna hotel.

The film is, in itself, moving and magnificent. Inspired by John Osborne's play 'A Patriot for Me,' it warns the audience at the outset that liberties are being taken with history. But at the end, it is suggested that the mighty newspaper scoop which exposed the Redl scandal to the world and rocked the Empire was itself a phoney. It was planted on a journalist to conceal the true story, and to suit the devious purposes of Archduke Franz Ferdinand, the heir to the throne who was shot a year later at Sarajevo.

In this version, Colonel Redl was framed by the Archduke. The heir required a shattering public scandal which would rouse the Empire to an awareness of the inner and outer danger which was threatening its survival. In the film, the Archduke and his cronies are shown deciding to let their fraudulent leak take place in Prague, once Redl is dead, and discussing which gullible but prominent journalist would suit their purpose.

Now, fiction or 'faction,' this is a dire slander on one of the most outrageous and brilliant journalists who ever dribbled cigarette-ash into his typewriter. Egon Erwin Kisch, who died just after the last war, was born in Prague in a Jewish shop-keeping family. His native language was German, and he made his name as a crime reporter. After 1918, he became the best-known journalist in central Europe, fled into exile in Mexico in 1940 and returned to Prague only at the end of the war.

Kisch, like many journalists today, was a keen Sunday foot-baller. On 25 May 1913, his team, all Prague Germans, had its big game against its Czech rivals in the amateur league. Promotion hung on the result, but Kisch's best player, a lock-smith called Wagner, failed to turn up. The Czechs won 7 – 5 (3 – 3 at half-time).

Next day, the wretched Wagner sidled into the office of the *Bohemia* newspaper to apologise. A bunch of army brasshats from Vienna had hauled him away from home on Sunday morning, he explained; they had ordered him to get into an empty house and open all the desks and cupboards to find some papers. The papers were in Russian, and there were photographs of military plans. One of the officers kept shaking his head and moaning: 'Who would have thought it?'

At first, the enraged Kisch shouted Wagner down; he would hear no excuses. Then he began to listen. He knew the house. It belonged to a Colonel Alfred Redl, chief of staff to the army headquarters and head of intelligence. And that very Monday, an official bulletin from Vienna had announced the 'tragic death' of Redl, praising to the skies the virtues of this rising officer who was expected to become Minister of War, perhaps even Commander-in-Chief one day.

The incredible truth burst on Kisch. Redl must have been a spy, and the bulletin about his death was a cover-up for some-thing horrific. The problem was how to publish it without getting the paper instantly confiscated. Kisch fell back on the trick which still keeps *Private Eye* alive. *Bohemia* ran on its front page a grand *démenti*, in which 'high sources' denied outrageous reports that Redl had been a Russian spy and stated that the military commission which had ransacked his house on Sunday and broken open all the drawers and safes had not been looking for stolen plans at all, but for 'material of another nature. . . .'

Nobody, of course, was fooled. The story blazed across the world Press. Within a day and a half of Redl's forced suicide, the political world in Vienna was in convulsions, and the Archduke Franz Ferdinand – contrary to Szabo's version – was firing generals right and left for having tried to keep him in the dark.

Kisch could embroider. He was almost engagingly candid about it, like the reporter who burst into the old Europa Hotel in Belfast when I was eating breakfast, shouting: 'I've got a terrific story, and it's trueish!' But his account of the Redl scoop does stand up. It is a pity that almost nobody in this country knows his books, and it would be another pity if those who do read Kisch thought that he had been swindled over Colonel Redl.

It is not very comfortable to compare Egon Erwin Kisch to the image of the investigative journalist which comes at us now off the small and large screen. Kisch was a happy warrior. He was a left-wing Socialist, who later gave his heart to the Russian Revolution; he sympathised with Czech nationalism, and he regarded the Habsburg Empire as a ludicrous old heap of repressive superstition, falling into the hands of militarist maniacs who had to be brought down before they deluged Europe in blood. He knew what he wanted, professionally and politically, and the Austrian police and censorship apparatus was far too mild and cumbrous to stop him doing it.

Contrast him with the gloomy protagonists of these current reporter-versus-MI5 dramas. They are defensive, always expecting the worst. They go about their digging with a curious fixed stare, professional news-getting automata with no ideals and no politics. If they show any optimism at all, it is in the belief – childish, in practice – that if they can evade the spooks and get their story rolling off the presses, their enemies will scatter and dissolve like snow before the fiery sun of public knowledge.

It is too easy just to say that journalists are not really like that. One can see the reasons why script-writers have turned to pressmen: the old thriller tradition of setting good policemen against bad crooks grew unconvincing, and Punch-and-Judy contests between tough British security men and evil Commie spies wore thin in their turn. The public is always basically decent in thrillers, but who is now protecting the public against whom? It has come to this: that the State is the villain and the only knightly Order defying the State's intention to crush society with the big stick and the big lie is ... the mass media.

Kisch at least believed that politics could change things. Have we lost all our weapons except the printed or broadcast word? We have not, and we should reject these invitations to frighten ourselves to death.

[*1986*

Tempers

The Spanish referendum on NATO is over, and Europe – as I see the result – is the poorer by one potentially neutral state. Felipe Gonzalez, the Prime Minister, is covered with glory. His main opponent, the conservative leader Manuel Fraga Iribarne, is covered with egg, if nothing worse.

I do not like Fraga's politics. In a surreal contest, rather like a football match in which each team tries to score as many own-goals as possible, he persuaded his *Alianza Popular* to campaign against NATO membership because he was in favour of it. He is an authoritarian and a bully, and he has deserved the mess he is now in.

And yet, I have to confess, there is something endearing about the man. Small, balding and Napoleonic in appearance, he is an original. The first time I met him, he was Franco's Minister for Information and Tourism. At the end of a brilliant interview, which included a minor scoop, he declared that he would like to give me a souvenir. Rummaging in a cupboard, he staggered back to me bearing an object the size of a small tombstone. It proved to be a book entitled 'Death in Spanish Painting.'

Its weight produced a dangerous list in the taxi back to my

hotel. Unwilling to pay a fortune in excess baggage, I left it in the flat of a protesting British friend in Madrid. I accepted this gift in the spirit in which it was offered, but I have wondered ever since what that spirit was.

But the most appealing thing about Fraga is his combination of high intelligence with a fatal, explosive, uncontrollably bad temper. He has the lowest boiling point, the shortest fuse, of any politician I have met. This makes for delicious comedy. In 1977, at an election meeting in his home territory of Galicia, Fraga broke off a grandiose speech to fly through the air, like a tubby little rocket, and land on the throat of a heckler. One never knows when he is going to go off bang. Neither does he.

My favourite Fraga memory is of his eve-of-poll party political broadcast in 1977 – Spain's first, chaotic exercise in free elections for 40 years. He started imposingly, scowling at the nation and rushing through his speech at a great pace. Then, quite suddenly and for no apparent reason, Fraga lost his temper with himself. His own oratory no doubt overheated him; spontaneous combustion took place. He began to scream and bellow. He waved his arms imprudently, and all his notes escaped and flew about the studio. Scrabbling for them, his rage only grew worse. Next day, he got even fewer votes than the Communists.

Genuine bad temper and politics seem unlikely consorts. In fact, though, they combine quite often – and even in democracies. I say 'genuine' deliberately. For this definition, rage has to be uncontrollable, something which can undo a politician's own purposes. This excludes what one might call the '*furia fascista*,' the calculated outburst of screeching and raving which Hitler and Mussolini taught themselves to switch on and off at will.

It also excludes those who govern by tongue-lashing. Old Konrad Adenauer did that; I still remember how Bundestag members used to squirm on their heavy hunkers as his sarcasms cracked over their heads. Fraga once gave a lunch at which he proclaimed: 'There are only three real men in Europe. Me, Franz-Josef Strauss and Maggie Thatcher!' Here we have two genuinely filthy tempers and one mere tongue-lasher, in that order.

Strauss, however, certainly qualifies. In that Manichean

figure, intellect and base nature are perpetually at war. Nobody in West Germany has a more lucid and penetrating under-standing of how democracy should work. Nobody in that country has such a fatal capacity to grasp the cup of democracy when it is handed to him and then – in a convulsive tantrum – to smash it against the wall.

Let it not be thought that bad temper is an affliction only of the Right. I think of the late Władysław Gomułka, of Poland. Aware of his weakness, he was given to clutching the table-edge at politburo meetings, in order to stop himself shooting to his feet and bellowing. In this and some other ways, he resembled another Polish leader: Marshal Piłsudski, in many ways an extremely intelligent and cultured man, also suffered from volcanic impatience with those who questioned his judg-ment – with the result that they questioned it even more.

The most frightening bad temper was that of Nikita Sergeye-vich Khrushchev – frightening, because the man wielded absolute power not only over his subjects but over nuclear weapons. Men were known to suffer heart attacks when he exploded. The Russians, rightly, did not consider this funny, and in the end it was largely fear of his unpredictable temper and moods which led to his deposition in 1964.

Even our own Labour Party has had its Roman candles – now mostly extinguished. The late George Brown undid himself as much by his bullying rages as by the drink which helped to provoke them. Dick Crossman, another short fuse, once knocked him down in a Committee Room corridor. George Brown, in turn, once punched Eric Heffer. (But Heffer, though trained in unarmed combat in his youth, is said merely to have complained to the Chief Whip.)

The paranoiac fears the secret persecutor. The authoritarian (and all choleric politicians are authoritarians) is never free from a morbid suspicion that somebody is contradicting him – or even suppressing a contradicting thought. As the mercury rises, a mere snigger, even an inanimate object which shows signs of mutiny, may be enough to touch off the blast. Once when Fraga (to mention him for the last time) was briefing journalists, the telephone kept interrupting him until he snatched a pair of scissors from his desk and severed the cable.

In this absurd scene, there is a hidden significance. A politician who cuts his own telephone cord is performing an act of self-mutilation, wrecking his own central purpose of communicating. Those who lose their tempers in public alienate that public, which will never take them quite seriously again. We are looking at a sort of primitive fail-safe system, a fuse but this time an electrical safety-fuse which time and again operates to bring a truly arrogant figure to a halt and limit his influence.

Modern political training, the choice and maintenance of an image, eliminates people like that. The politician who can be ignited by a television interviewer's impertinent question is scarcely to be seen now. The performance is cool, bland, patronising, polished until the joints in the armour can no longer be found.

I fear politicians of that kind. They never put a foot wrong because their foot is already firmly planted on our chest. We can love them or hate them, but they never drop their guard or their fixed smile.

Mustafa Kemal Ataturk, the founder of modern Turkey, was often seized by rages against his own subjects. At night, temper inflamed by drink, he would sometimes write orders for artillery to demolish some recalcitrant village. But all orders had to be shown to him again in the morning – and he usually tore them up. I do not ask for unpredictability on that scale. But I do ask the image-makers to leave us a few politicians – just a few – who are their own worst enemies.   [1986

Sex

As the past week's news has been largely – and rightly – devoted to terrorism and the flight of families from nuclear fall-out, I thought I would change the subject and write about love. Perhaps I really mean sex; perhaps the conclusions will be equally depressing. Anyway, last week produced one of the saddest and weirdest love stories ever told.

This was the story of the French diplomat Bernard Boursicot and the Chinese dancer Shi Peipu, sentenced in Paris last week to six years in prison for betraying secret diplomatic intelligence. They met in Peking in 1964, when Bernard was 20. Shi Peipu was a male opera dancer and, as the French police have established to their satisfaction, is biologically a man. However, he told his new French friend that he was really a woman in disguise. Not only did Bernard believe him, but he continued to believe him throughout a passionate and loving sexual relationship which lasted, with interruptions, for 20 years.

So much, one might say, for French sophistication in these matters. It was not until 1983 that Bernard, 'shattered,' yielded to the evidence of the police doctors. He explained that Shi Peipu had always been 'modest' about undressing. The French papers talk knowingly about *'une certaine gymnastique'* and *'apparences trompeuses.'* Anyway, Bernard objected, they had a baby son, the little Shi Du Du, who even looked like him. Here again, poor Bernard has bowed to the verdict of tests which prove that, whoever the father of Shi Du Du may have been, it was not Bernard Boursicot and Shi Peipu was certainly not his mother.

The spying was the least interesting part of the tale. A shadowy Mr Kang soon appeared, demanding from Bernard the inevitable quid for the quo of letting the affair continue. From the French embassy in Peking and later from Ulan Bator, Bernard provided various banal scraps of paper; for example, the notes of his ambassador on a Mongolian journey ('we passed gigantic herds of yaks' and 'the horse is to the Mongols what the automobile is to the Americans'). But it was not until 1983, when Shi Peipu and Shi Du Du appeared in Paris and moved into Bernard's flat in the Boulevard Raspail, that French counter-intelligence pounced.

Pleas by Bernard's lawyer that this was a 'crime of passion,' or alternatively that Mr Kang could not be proved to represent a foreign State, were ignored by the court. The sentence could have been worse; the maximum penalty is 20 years. But in the circumstances, the imposition of six years' 'criminal detention' is no less than an unfeeling atrocity.

The damage done was trivial. And whatever went on between Bernard Boursicot and Shi Peipu was love – a faithful, exemplary love maintained for many years through frightening circumstances and in spite of huge separations. As Stendhal wrote in the first sentence of his *De l'Amour*, 'I seek to comprehend this passion whose every sincere development has a character of beauty.'

Grotesque in detail, this is an old-fashioned story told in a time when relationships between the sexes, and inside the sexes, are provoking a lot of morose reflections. Some of this gloom arises from the AIDS plague. A lot of people – women in particular – are thinking about the 'bath house' phenomenon which AIDS illuminated, the interest of male gays in wild, indiscriminate orgy as an essential component of a way of life. And they do not like what they think.

One approach, which isn't anything like an explanation, is to assert that hectic promiscuity is somehow a built-in element of male homosexuality, a tendency which may not always show itself but which is simply a part of the gay syndrome. I doubt this, not least because it is one more way of treating homosexuality as if it were a sickness, with symptoms like rashes or warts.

But some gay men provide a very different answer. They say: 'If you think that a taste for promiscuous, orgiastic sex is to do with homosexuality, you are on the wrong track entirely. We are male. The lust for orgy is a basic male characteristic, whether a man is gay or straight. The difference is that we, without the restraint imposed by relationships with women, are able to face this need in ourselves and to indulge it.'

Shocking! There rises in reply a chorus of male voices insisting – sincerely – that they do not recognise this element in themselves, that sex means for them a 'caring one-to-one partnership,' and so on. But I wonder.

Moderate feminists of the 1968 generation hoped that enlightenment and the liberation of women would coax out of the chauvinist pig a sensitive, sexually considerate and loyal partner. The 'separatist' and lesbian wing of feminism does not share that optimism. The bath-house theory of male sex suggests that men who adapt their sexuality to that of women, let alone to conventional morality, do so by repression.

Orgy is an antique fantasy, usually a heterosexual one.

Professor Norman Cohn has demonstrated that almost all societies have accused their dissidents – religious, especially – of indiscriminate group sex, starting with Roman slanders against Christians. But even where sexual orgies really went on, they were evidently male games played by male rules. A few acquaintances who have tried out this sort of thing report the female team as unenthusiastic, getting through on alcohol or the thought of a cheque afterwards. This was decidedly not their scene.

But the fact that men-women orgies are one-sided, indeed close to gang rape, doesn't reduce the ominous persistence of this male hankering. A want which has survived so long against such violent disapproval from churches, women and nice people in general has a right to be taken seriously, if only as a threat.

We may think of the male-female relationship in the West as still one of male domination, but there's a hint here that without our particular social pressures it might be far worse. I have come across a small African tribe in which men and women regarded each other with open fear and hatred, and reproduction was inflicted by violent rape. In his book 'Mafia Business,' Pino Arlacchi writes: 'Virility and sexual shame (in Sicily) were linked to a clear opposition between the sexes . . . the *uomo di rispetto* (man worthy of respect) had the task of demonstrating his virility at every opportunity, even if this meant committing violence against women or seizing them by force.'

These dark thoughts from the bath-house also leave a lot of psychological theory in disarray. Repression was supposed to be a bad thing, wasn't it? It seemed fine when Herbert Marcuse wrote that 'the unsublimated, unrationalised release of sexual relations means the most emphatic release of pleasure as such and the total devaluation of work for work's sake . . . the hopelessness and injustice of working conditions would penetrate the consciousness of individuals and render impossible their peaceful regimentation. . . .'

In those days, the German revolutionaries threw copies of Reich's 'The Function of the Orgasm' at the police. Now they throw grenades. The release of sexuality no longer sounds like an escape into peace and love. Those who worry about the male nature have learned something from experience. Those who smashed the eccentric little refuge built by Bernard Boursicot and Shi Peipu and sent them to prison have learned nothing.

[*1986*

Precision

In his book 'The Russian Album,' a study of his father's family, Michael Ignatieff provides a reflection on the family photograph. 'In a secular culture, they are the only household icons, the only objects that perform the religious function of connecting the living to the dead and of locating the identity of the living in time.'

We live in an individualist society, a place of lonely nuclear families isolated both horizontally from other human beings and vertically – in time – from the past. Ignatieff says: 'I never feel I know my friends until either I meet their parents or see their photographs, and since this rarely happens, I often wonder whether I know anybody very well.'

A hundred years ago, not just in Russia, a person's identity was a larger, vaguer thing, composed not just of data about a self but also about mothers, fathers, grandfathers and grandmothers, many of them firmly encamped in the same household. It was not just Mr Ignatieff, but Michael Georgevitch, son of George. Now most Westerners sit alone with wife, children and photograph album.

But the photograph does not replace ancestors and family. In a way, it removes them even further. The picture stares from the album page, stating: 'This is how we were. This is us.' It's a spurious claim. They were a million things which were not the frozen impression of a second of light. But the statement is convincing, because we are addicted to precision. Even a grandmother has to have an instant, accurate definition.

Preciseness is the keystone of Western material culture. A

world in which distances might vary, or time sag in and out like a concertina, seems a nightmare. In this sense, we are still Victorians, largely untouched by the idea of relativity.

On a tour of China, watching the way in which some of my companions compulsively photographed whatever and whoever passed before them, I saw that the camera was being used as a weapon of self-defence. By snapping people, the Western tourists were killing them, robbing them of their power to unsettle or puzzle by turning them into motionless contact prints. Late in the tour, as it dawned on even its densest members that the poor Chinese crowding about the bus actually despised them as big-nosed primitives with some interesting gadgetry, the clicking of shutters grew desperate.

Some 20 years ago, the West Germans built a steel mill at Rourkela in India. There were endless misunderstandings. One arose from the insistence of German foremen that the slots on screws had to be parallel when they were tightened up. The Indian workers did not see the point of this: if a screw was firmly home, it was home wherever the slot lay. One German writer, in the self-flagellating mode of the day, suggested that his compatriots were revealing their innate fascism: 'Death is a German craftsman,' as the saying goes. But all the foremen were doing was revealing that precision is not only a necessity of Western 'civilisation' but a fetish.

It is a precise prison that we have built for ourselves. Budgets totalling millions of pounds are costed to the last penny; pistons are milled to a tolerance of a thousandth of an inch. The Slobodnian frontier runs exactly here, but a millimetre further you enter the fearsome jurisdiction of the Zachvatchik Republic. There's no room for argument. A penny out and it isn't a budget; an infinitely tiny inaccuracy and it isn't a piston; a state with non-delineated frontiers isn't a state.

In the precision world, there is only one correct version. The man who happily signed himself Shakspere or Sheakspire, or whatever the quill felt like at the moment, would today be a man hunted on suspicion of cheque fraud, while his history plays would be taken off by the Royal Court after demonstrations by Plantagenets, Danes, Scots and Venetians concerned for 'historical accuracy.' If I say 'tomayto' and you say 'tomarto,' one of us is wrong. Or, more accurately, one of us would be wrong if we were both citizens of the same country. In matters of language, the monopoly of one version is still limited by frontiers. The Poles remain entitled to study the plays of Szekspir.

Linguistic conformity is very much part of the history of modern States. In his brilliant little book 'Imagined Communities' Benedict Anderson points to the way that the arrival of printed books gave spoken tongues a new fixity. 'For three centuries now, these stabilised print-languages have been gathering a darkening varnish: the words of our seventeenth-century forbears are accessible to us in a way that his twelfth-century ancestors were not to Villon.'

The print revolution did not only flood Europe with millions of precisely similar self-contained artefacts, perhaps 20 million books by the year 1500. It standardised one dialect out of dozens in each country. It gave millions of people who would never meet a sense of cultural membership in an abstract whole: an 'imagined community,' which was to develop into the modern State. The magical language of Latin has bound together the ruling castes of the Christian West. Now High German was to become the official language in Germany. Other dialects, like North-West German, Northern English or Provençal, were condemned to become or remain just speech.

The State is all about this sort of con-trick. 'The national language' may well be spoken by a minority of the population. The claim to impose a monopoly version of spelling and grammar and vocabulary goes with the claim to a monopoly of power over life and death. Industry and bureaucracy between them added the tyranny of clocked time, of simultaneous behaviour throughout a nation. It's night in Lerwick and morning in Littlehampton, but the post office opens at the same moment. Weights and measures, too. Not for nothing was it called an imperial pint.

Against this, I would like to honour all that's imprecise, all that has vague outlines, all that sort-of-works although in theory it should not. The true memorial of a grandfather should not be a flat photograph but a bungling, ambling, fiddling, mumbling, twiddling, three-dimensional smudge. I agree that this would be hard to fix in an album. But the human race survives not by norms but by hazard and improvisation. If Lech Walesa had been a microchip assembler rather than the acknowledged wizard of Gdansk at making clapped-out cars run on cannibalised parts, he would never have been able to keep Solidarity going for 15 months.

In the end, the cult of precision is deeply conservative. It teaches that there is only one way of doing things correctly, which has to be repeated again and again. This is not craftsmanship, which consists in endless, subtle variations to suit new materials or even worn tools. A deadening formalism has swept over the conduct of British politics: innovating Thatcherite policies contrast strangely with electoral and party practices which are repetitive as any industrial process.

I hope to see a more erratic public life, and a social architecture in which straight lines and right angles give way to rambling borderless shapes like those of Antonio Gaudi's buildings in Barcelona. There is a rumour that once, in nineteenth-century Europe, the surveyors drawing frontiers went askew. Just where Belgium is supposed to join France and Luxembourg, near the railway line at Petange, I have heard it said that there is an Imprecision: a patch of grass and trees (some say a meadow) which is officially nowhere. There, in the space between definitions, one might make a fresh start.   [*1987*

Pity, Love and the Accident of Birth

'We are a form of infinitely variable robot.' Wilfred Beckerman of Oxford wrote that in *The Times* the other day. Dr Beckerman is a determinist. All that we are and do, for him, proceeds from a mixture of 'the genetic base of personality' and the impact of upbringing, events, the individual's environment in general. Free will is an illusion, and actions – he was talking about Myra

Hindley – cannot be called morally bad but only 'bad' in that they inflict suffering on others.

This is a deeply unpopular thing to say in England, and especially around Christmas. At this season, there is supposed to be a moment of reflection on birth, babies and their destinies. The English – and this is one of the reasons why they remain a kind people, in spite of growing discouragement – do believe in free will.

A nineteenth-century German would have regarded a human being as a self-realising subject, crowned with fire. The English philosophy takes a lump of this Hegelianism and dissolves it in a comforting cup of Anglican weak tea. There are absolute moral laws, and people can shape their own actions and character, for which they are ultimately responsible. When evil is done, poverty, terror or passion are only extenuating circumstances.

This has never convinced me. A certain revelation, not easy to put into words, came to me the first time I saw a baby born. There emerged into loving hands a form apparently of clay, just that blue-grey colour of the volcanic clay which is the bed of the sea in Argyll, where I was a child. It was exactly the shape of a human baby, and then it moved and cried.

I knew – in a split second – that this was both clay and baby, that there exists no real difference between man and nature, life and inanimate un-life, and that the appearance from the womb of a piece of the earth which has in every detail the form and powers of a human being is an accident – an accident even though it is repeated thousands of times every day all over the world. So, for me, the contradictions of predestination and free will, of determinism and chance, solved themselves in a flash of understanding gone before it was fully grasped.

This has been a 'Calvin Year,' in which many divines and scholars from different continents have gathered in Geneva and talked about John Calvin, the sixteenth-century Reformer, and his doctrines. I am an unbeliever, but of all Christian faiths. Presbyterianism has the strongest pull on me. The effects of primitive Calvinism on human beings have often been cruel and disastrous. One source of Scotland's weakness, for example, has been the split between the national religion and the intellec-

tuals, who have through all the modern age nursed hatred of
the Kirk's 'lovelessness.' But there is another side.

The Presbyterian faith is an incomparable metaphor for the
unity of creation, for the inner conflict between our sense of
freedom and our scientific understanding that, in another way,
we control nothing that happens. The metaphor says that the
human being on his or her own is a component of 'corrupt'
nature, incapable of achieving salvation. Those who are good
are so because the Holy Spirit has entered them, an invasion
of grace from outside whose choice of individuals is not explic-
able and was predestined before the Creation.

Many people regard this as an 'immoral' faith. On the one
hand, there is an insufferable company of the 'elect,' all too
certain – in the manner of Burn's 'Holy Willie' – that all that
they do is justified before Heaven. On the other, there is the
mass of what used to be called the 'reprobate,' those who have
received no signal of grace and who may well conclude that, if
no decent action they choose to perform will make any difference to their rejection by God, they might as well be as wicked
and selfish as they please. As Luther said, 'Sin powerfully!'

But, human beings having the needs they have, matters do
not work out so neatly. The 'elect' in practice wrestle with
doubts about the quality of their assurance of salvation, while
the rest – apart from a minority who do decide that if God
hates them, they will hate Him – seldom give up the hope of
grace. All behave infinitely better than – in logic – they should.
Awareness of predestination or determinism in no way makes
them resemble Beckerman's 'variable robots.'

We live in a society which is becoming not so much individu-
alistic as atomised. The Chinese fanatically pursue the individual profit motive, but their sense of community and
conformity remains so strong that it would stifle most of us.
Here, however, we are beginning to lose the fundamental
confidence that we know each other's minds and motives, even
in a rough, handy sort of way.

As other people become closed houses, behind whose shutters anything might be going on, the cult of free will decays
into a vague respect for all behaviour which does not actually
harm others. This is not toleration – Queen Elizabeth saying
that she did not wish to make windows into men's souls. It is

a defeated agreement that if we cannot judge actions by motives, grown impenetrable, we should not judge them at all. This is the place for whatever turns you on: stamp collecting, party politics, gay love, tin soldiers, novel writing, breeding lizards. This is the place of small, mutually indifferent ghettos.

Two things seem to be wrong about this. One is the abandoning of hope that we can see the universe as a whole, the world of rock, stars, things alive and things inanimate, as something coherent even though we can neither fully control nor comprehend it. The other is a horrible arrogance.

Hegel's ethic has run mad. The 'do your own thing' society assumes that everyone has a nice, personal destiny which he or she can develop and fulfil – that marshal's baton in every soldier's knapsack. I would answer that with a fable, told once among Podolian Jews. At the instant of birth, for a split second, an angel appears and unfolds enormous wings. If it can spread them fully, the child will be happy. If the room is too small, so will the child's soul be cramped. But the first person I told that fable to replied: 'I was born when my mother was in a Gestapo cell.'

In that sense, most of us are still born in cells. Christian religion, I think, asks us to recognise that, and therefore asks for the most unfashionable of all virtues: mercy and pity. The Presbyterian faith is one of those that understand that we are simulacra of clay, made living by incomprehensible accident. Those who forget this when they rule, who pretend that all our angels spread their pinions without hindrance, are pitiless and merciless.

Many readers, I hope, will remember the end of Tolstoy's 'Resurrection.' Nekhlyudov, the young noble who has tried to redeem himself and the peasant girl he seduced, sits alone reading the parable of the lord and the servant who was forgiven his debt but then cast into prison another servant who owed him money. 'Shouldest thou not also have had compassion on thy fellow servant, even as I had compassion on thee?'

' "And can that be the whole answer?" Nekhlyudov suddenly exclaimed aloud. And the inner voice of his whole being said, "Yes, that is all." '

He sees then that 'society and order generally existed, not thanks to those legalised criminals who judge and punish other men, but because in spite of their depraving influence, people still pity and love one another.' I am not sure that Britain's governors deserve a Christmas card. But that is what should be written upon it.   [*1986*

The Good Soldier Schimek

In the village cemetery of Machowa, in southern Poland, the grave of a Nazi soldier is covered with flowers. The grass around it has been trodden by pilgrims, by Catholic bishops, by journalists from several European countries and – most recently – by the boots of ill-tempered policemen. A touching cult of symbolic reconciliation has been kicked apart, leaving a scatter of recriminations.

Private Otto Schimek, an Austrian conscript in the Wehrmacht, was only 19 in November 1944 when he faced a firing squad. He left behind him a letter to his brothers and sisters: '. . . my heart is calm. Have we anything to lose except this miserable life? And they can't kill the soul . . .' After the war, his family, from a poor district of Vienna, managed to have his body exhumed and transferred to consecrated ground in the Machowa churchyard.

Gradually the rumour spread that Otto Schimek had been executed because he had refused to obey an order to shoot Polish civilian hostages, mostly women and children. It was a story very moving to many, in Poland and Austria. And it was highly convenient to some.

For the Polish Catholic Church, Schimek's sacrifice was a symbol of the reconciliation between Poles and their wartime oppressors which the Church had begun to preach from the mid-1960s, in the teeth of outraged abuse from the Communist régime. He was given a lavish gravestone, complete with photograph and an inscription commemorating his deed. And the cult became popular. One young friend of mine remembers the priest in his parish church at Gdansk, far away on the Baltic, leading prayers for the canonisation of Schimek as a saint.

Catholic Austria, too, was delighted. Here, at last, was public proof that at least one Austrian who was not a Communist or Socialist had resisted Hitler's dictatorship at the price of his life. Cardinal König travelled from Vienna to pray at the grave. Austrian Catholic journalists wrote respectful articles, noting that Schimek's grave was drawing not only pilgrimages but votary offerings imploring Schimek's intervention in heaven to cure sickness or loss. The Polish authorities, deciding to make the best of it, published some of these articles in the official Press.

But then, last year, some left-wing and anti-clerical Austrian journalists began to check the Wehrmacht archives and court-martial record. Nowhere did they find any evidence that Schimek had refused to take part in executions. Instead, he had run away from his unit apparently out of general dislike of military service, and after trying to hide among civilian Poles for a few weeks, had been tried and shot for desertion.

There was consternation in the Church, glee in the Polish Government – and not only there. In West Germany, the social-democrat *Frankfurter Rundschau* published a disagreeable article remarking that 'Austria had boasted of its own hero, a victim of National Socialism whose rarity made him precious, while Polish Catholics . . . venerated Schimek as an example of resistance to political authority, a symbol of Solidarity's resistance to the regime. . . .' The article was reprinted in a Polish government newspaper, while an official went on Warsaw television to jeer at Schimek as a mere deserter too cowardly to join the Polish partisans.

A 'mere deserter'? This was too much. The respected writer Edmund Osmańczyk retorted with an article beginning: 'I was a deserter from the Hitlerite armies. And I have never hidden the fact.' Living in Germany at the outbreak of war, he had been conscripted into the Wehrmacht but had escaped to join the Polish resistance, partly with the help of anti-Nazi Austrian soldiers. He could have added that deserting from the armies of foreign occupiers has been a mark of Polish patriotism through the ages.

And things have come to a pretty disgraceful pass when a European government – even one as erratic as Poland's – suggests that a soldier who deserted from Hitler's armies deserved his fate. As the famous Cracow columnist Kisiel asked last week: 'A 19-year-old soldier from a poor Viennese family who escapes from the army and manages to hide among Poles for a few weeks – is that a small thing, in those times of arch-savagery and arch-barbarity?'

I will watch with interest to see whether the Catholic Church, faced with the truth about poor little Otto Schimek, will decide that this is a failed martyr and quietly snuff out his cult. I hope not. Young Poles will not give him up, anyway. As a deserter rather than as a man who refused to commit an atrocity, he is still the patron of the 'Freedom and Peace' movement, a small Green-ish opposition group which recently tried to demonstrate at his grave but was dispersed by police.

The meagre data about Schimek which remains, mostly letters to his family, show that he hated being a soldier and in particular disliked the duty to kill. He had been called up at the age of only 17. To his mother, he wrote: 'I will aim away so as not to hit anyone. After all, they want to go home just like I do.' For these views, he was bullied and mistreated until, finally and pathetically, he ran away in enemy territory.

It's worth thinking about the pressures upon Schimek to conform. Fear, to begin with, of course: the ruthless punishment awaiting any soldier in the German army who disobeyed. But Schimek also stood up to the seductive thrust of Nazi ideology, inviting him to numb himself against the human identity of others classified not only as enemies of the Reich but as inferior subhumans, with no claim to arouse normal instincts of compassion or fraternity.

Finally, this boy without any resources of education or privilege resisted the temptation to 'double' himself. By this, I mean the practice of dividing the moral world into two: that of 'home' in which one remains guided by the conventional moral standards of one's family, and the 'soldiering world' in which a new, second self acts in accordance with utterly different standards without any real sense of contradiction. This division was too much for Schimek. Whenever he aimed his rifle, he wondered first what his mother and sisters would say.

For his army companions, Schimek probably seemed a despicable weakling. With battalions of Schimeks, nobody wins a war. But it is also true that this boy remained a whole personality which the entire weight of Hitlerite tyranny and ideology could not split.

And perhaps the disappearance of the 'martyr against atrocity' element makes Otto Schimek more universal rather than less. Kisiel calls his desertion 'a European gesture.' He didn't run away because he was Austrian, or because he admired Poland, or even – as far as one can see – because he was anti-Nazi, although he probably was.

He deserted because mass obedience and moral self-mutilation in the name of the State made no sense to him. It is the Greens rather than the Church who have a claim to Schimek.

To shoot, you have to close one eye. Schimek couldn't do this: both eyes stayed open. He said naïvely: 'I'm not interested in war.' I suspect that now, and only now, he will become a real hero of our time.   [*1987*

Remember Them in Song

It's more than 41 years ago that an American sergeant blew the Kaiser's head off. His battery had arrived on the outskirts of Koblenz, already so comprehensively mashed to bits that there was almost nothing vertical left to aim at. The exception was the gigantic monument to Emperor Wilhelm I, on the spit of land where the Moselle runs into the Rhine.

It was well over a hundred feet high, counting the equestrian statue of the Emperor on top. A few minutes later, it was considerably shorter. The head flew off (it now rests with a cross expression in the garden of a museum), and was followed by the body and the horse. All that remains is the pedestal, itself about the size of the British Museum, decorated with scowling eagles and stylised pythons in the neo-heathen manner that was popular in Germany at the end of last century.

I read the other day that the town of Koblenz is thinking of putting the Kaiser back. It would put the burghers back some £3 million to cast and erect a new statue. There are many Germans who have moral and aesthetic doubts, as well as worries about the cost. The plinth is ugly as it is, and would be uglier still with the statue on it. Politically, it stands for an age of noisy self-assertion and hubris which Germans prefer to forget.

I am grateful for that preference. All the same, the colossi of that period which survive are fascinating to me. They are actually so big that their ridiculous and sinister elements may seem to matter less. There is Hermann, conqueror of the Roman legions, glaring from his column over the treetops of the Teutoburger Forest. There is Kaiser Wilhelm I (again), towering above the road to Berlin at the Porta Westfalica, near Minden. There is the wreck of the Tannenberg Monument, now in Poland, where – so I'm told – the 10-ton heads of Prussian heroes lie with their broken noses pressed into the grass. And, best or – depending how you see it – worst of all, there is the memorial to the 1813 Battle of the Nations at Leipzig, the *Völkerschlachtdenkmal*.

From the outside, the thing looks as if a stone Zeppelin had half-buried itself in the earth. Inside, the eye slowly gets used to the darkness of the great vault until one makes out the masks of barbarian warriors brooding far overhead. It is very cold, but that's not why the hair begins to prickle on the spine. Two lines return, from Brecht: ' . . . the womb is fertile yet – From whence THAT crept.'

Why so big? Partly it's a deliberate violating of 'civilised' scale, another aspect of the taste which insisted on pagan motifs – Aztec, Nordic, anything as long as it was huge, cruel and non-Christian. But partly, of course, it's bluff. These are the expressions of a 'late nation' not quite confident that it is as tough as it pretends to be. Almost all these monsters, including the ziggurat-pedestal at Koblenz, belong to the period between German unification as an Empire in 1871 and the outbreak of war in 1914.

The further away you get from the reality of war, the bigger the monuments get. The Soviet Union shows this wonderfully. Its war memorials were never small. But in recent years, as the Great Patriotic War dwindles into the past, there has been a mad inflation of scale. There is 'Motherland,' the statue on the Mamaev Hill at Volgograd, whose visitors are proportionately the size of ladybirds. It would take a fire-ladder even to reach the 'Motherland' small toe. Or there is the plan – now I believe under criticism – to remove a whole hill on the outskirts of Moscow to build a war monument which would make the Arc de Triomphe look like a keyhole.

The Great Patriotic War is now an official cult of a rather late-Roman kind, the temples of Jupiter growing taller as personal feeling or faith grows slighter. These are monuments to State power rather than to the individual dead. They resemble the mausoleum which still glowers over the Romanian steppe at Adamclisi, built after Trajan's victory over the Dacians to remind the conquered of the strength of Rome.

Infinitely more touching are local war memorials. In their classic period, between about 1870 and the 1920s, they not only convey real grief but often tell a great deal about popular culture. In France, naked women can be seen pressing the weary *poilu* to their breasts. In Britain, absolutely literal soldiers of stone or bronze display every piling-swivel, pouch-buckle and puttee-eyelace of weapons and equipment, as if the loss of one detail would begin the slow betrayal of forgetting those who died.

In Germany, the memorials of the First World War are often highly stylised, almost Expressionist: patterns of helmeted heads and shouldered rifles in relief. Here grief is made communal. 'Eternal Fatherland, for love of Thee not one too many fell. . . .'

I hate those words. But there is genuine sorrow in them, as well as blind nationalism. I hate them less, anyway, than the revolting half-jest inscribed on the back of the Machine-Gun Corps memorial in London at Hyde Park Corner, now on a traffic island which – perhaps fortunately – is hard to reach. It is a text: I Samuel 18.7. It reads: 'Saul hath slain his thousands, but David his ten thousands.'

The Russians, I suppose, will carry on their competition of gigantism until they have built a monument which is actually visible to the naked eye from the moon. (Incidentally, the Great

Wall of China is not: that was a piece of Cultural Revolution hype.) But in the West, this sort of thing is out of fashion. Victory columns, triumphal arches, even statues have come to seem 'inappropriate' – that primmest of words. Instead, there is the discretion of the Vietnam memorial in Washington, where the names of the American dead float in dark reflections of sky and trees. Grown uncertain of one another's private thoughts, we hesitate to inflict one symbolised 'view' on the public.

There is a puzzle here. Print and television now obsessively mark every public or personal anniversary. Yet the gravestone is vanishing: I would guess that most of those who die in Britain this year will have no solid memorial. People, I am sure, still wish to remember. But between old ways of keeping memory and new ones not yet chosen, there is a gap.

Music remains. Old soldiers in Germany gather and sing: 'Ich hat' einen Kameraden . . .,' which some democrats suspect as militaristic but which I find deeply touching – no politics, no nonsense, just mourning for dead friends.

And it's not just a soldier's song, anyway. German miners sing it too, when they meet in their black uniforms and black-plumed shakos to commemorate workmates who have perished. Most miners would rather be remembered in a song. A monument marking a colliery disaster which essayed any rhetoric about sacrifice would be obscene.

Of all memorials, I would choose the lament for Donald Ban MacCrimmon. Nobody is sure who composed it. For this sort of pipe music, it is unusually long and highly abstract. Its infinity of variations and grace-notes slowly develop their interlace until it seems that every hour in the life of this man – not an important person, killed in an almost accidental scuffle at Moy Hall after the battle of Culloden – is caught and recorded in one of these minute sparkles and sprays of sound. Not in basalt or bronze, but invisibly, impassively, in the air itself, the days alive of Donald Ban MacCrimmon are preserved for ever.　　[1987

Sources

The following pieces first appeared in the *Observer*, whose permission to reproduce we gratefully acknowledge:

Chords of Identity in a Minor Key; The Nostalgia Game; 'Tell the Children . . .'; The Lost World of Small-Town England; Dead Houses; Settlers and Natives; Caring Colonists; Intelligentsia Wanted; The Spreading Slime; Dracula in Britain; Greater Privilege Hath No Man . . .; The English Riot; Enforcing 'Culture'; Stonehenge and its Power Struggles; The Means of Grace, the Hope of Glory; Secret Passions of the British; A Spectator Sport; Policing the Market-Place; Druids; Mr Gladstone the Land Raider; Gladstone's Defeat and Our Loss; Telling Sid; The Case for a Bill of Rights; The No-Go Area; A Dumb-Bell World; Thatcher's Dream; The Great Cash-In; Capital; The Land and the People; A Scottish Temple; Coals in the Bath, Sun on the Brain; Journalists Behind the Wire; Tiring the Romans; Axel's Castles; The Cost of Bitburg; The Shadows Over France's Feast; Greek Civil War – Rambo-Style; The Strange Death of the Peasantry; Apartheid in Europe; Toads, Journalists, Cats and Policemen; Frontiers; Gorbachov's Gift; Changing Partners; The Polish Ghosts; Piłsudski, or How to Ignore Defeat; 1956 How Poland Got Away With It; Requiem for an Old Piano Banger; Invisible Men; The Berlin Wall as Holy Monster; Why Burning People Is Always Wrong; 'You Lose Freedom by Fighting for It'; Suffering Writing; The Unsung Heroes of Chernobyl; Russian Mist; Dream of Escape. Bad Dreams; Picts; Brothers; Nations on Parade; F3080; Exiles; Terrorists; Alive and Well; Spies; Witness; Critics; Media Heroes; Tempers; Sex; Precision; Pity, Love and the Accident of Birth; The Good Soldier Schimek; Remember Them in Song Not Stone.

The English Bourgeoisie first appeared in *Bananas*, 1976.

'Don't Be Afraid – and Don't Steal!' was an Inaugural Lecture at the SNP Annual National Conference, Dunoon, September 1986, and is reproduced courtesy of SNP Publications Department.

Scottish Contradictions was a lecture at the Dunblane Consultation of the Church of Scotland 1976.

Last Leader, *Traitors* and *Diaries* first appeared in the *London Review of Books*.

Ancient Britons and the Republican Dream first appeared in *The Political Quarterly*, Vol. 57 no. 3, whose kind permission to reprint the essay is gratefully acknowledged.

The 'Bildung' of Barbie and *The Death Doctors* first appeared in *The New York Review of Books*, and are reproduced here courtesy of the *New York Review*.